The TUDORS

G. J. Meyer is a former Woodrow Wilson and Harvard University Fellow with an M.A. in English literature. His other books include *The Tudors: The Complete Story of England's Most Notorious Dynasty*, *Lady Jane Grey to Elizabeth I* and *A World Undone: The Story of the Great War* ('Magnificent... researched to the last possible dot' *The Washington Times*, 'Masterful... has an instructive value than can scarcely be measured' *Los Angeles Times*, 'A worthy counterpoint to Hew Strachan's magisterial three-volume scholarly project' *Publishers Weekly*). He lives in Goring-on-Thames.

The TUDORS

Henry VII to Henry VIII

G. J. MEYER

AMBERLEY

For Rosie

This edition published by arrangement with Delacorte Press, an imprint of the Ramdon House Publishing Group, a division of Random House, Inc.

Amberley Publishing Plc
Cirencester Road, Chalford,
Stroud, Gloucestershire, GL6 8PE

www.amberleybooks.com

British Library Cataloguing in Publication Data.
A catalogue record for this book is available from the British Library.

ISBN 978 1 4456 0143 4

Typesetting and Origination by Amberley Publishing.
Printed in Great Britain.

Contents

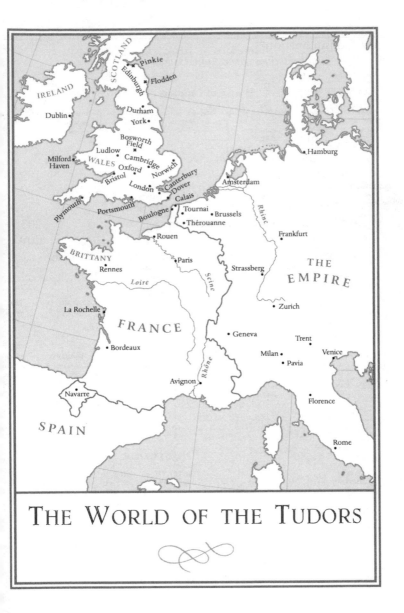

THE WORLD OF THE TUDORS

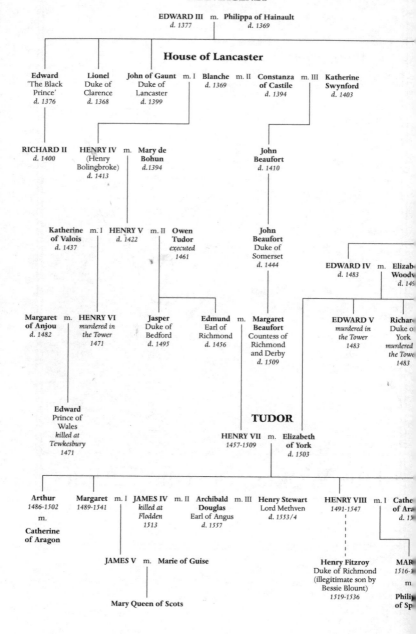

PLANTAGENET

EDWARD III m. **Philippa of Hainault**
d. 1377   *d. 1369*

House of Lancaster

Edward 'The Black Prince' *d. 1376*

Lionel Duke of Clarence *d. 1368*

John of Gaunt Duke of Lancaster *d. 1399* m. I **Blanche** *d. 1369* m. II **Constanza of Castile** *d. 1394* m. III **Katherine Swynford** *d. 1403*

RICHARD II *d. 1400*

HENRY IV (Henry Bolingbroke) *d. 1413* m. **Mary de Bohun** *d. 1394*

John Beaufort *d. 1410*

Katherine of Valois *d. 1437* m. I **HENRY V** *d. 1422* m. II **Owen Tudor** *executed 1461*

John Beaufort Duke of Somerset *d. 1444*

EDWARD IV *d. 1483* m. **Elizab** **Woodv** *d. 149*

Margaret of Anjou *d. 1482* m. **HENRY VI** *murdered in the Tower 1471*

Jasper Duke of Bedford *d. 1495*

Edmund Earl of Richmond m. **Margaret Beaufort** Countess of Richmond and Derby *d. 1509*

EDWARD V *murdered in the Tower 1483*

Richar Duke o York *murdered the Towe 1483*

Edward Prince of Wales *killed at Tewkesbury 1471*

TUDOR

HENRY VII *1457-1509* m. **Elizabeth of York** *d. 1503*

Arthur *1486-1502* m. **Catherine of Aragon**

Margaret *1489-1541* m. I **JAMES IV** *killed at Flodden 1513* m. II **Archibald Douglas** Earl of Angus *d. 1557* m. III **Henry Stewart** Lord Methven *d. 1553/4*

HENRY VIII *1491-1547* m. I **Cathe** **of Ara** *d. 15*

JAMES V m. **Marie of Guise**

Mary Queen of Scots

Henry Fitzroy Duke of Richmond (illegitimate son by Bessie Blount) *1519-1536*

MAR *1516-* m. **Phili** **of Sp**

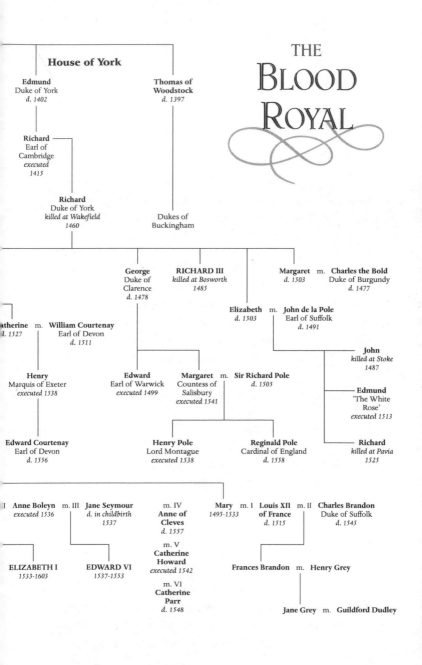

THE BLOOD ROYAL

House of York

Edmund
Duke of York
d. 1402

Thomas of Woodstock
d. 1397

Richard
Earl of Cambridge
executed 1415

Richard
Duke of York
killed at Wakefield 1460

Dukes of Buckingham

George
Duke of Clarence
d. 1478

RICHARD III
killed at Bosworth 1485

Margaret m. **Charles the Bold**
d. 1503   Duke of Burgundy
             d. 1477

Elizabeth m. **John de la Pole**
d. 1503   Earl of Suffolk
             d. 1491

...**atherine** m. **William Courtenay**
d. 1527   Earl of Devon
              d. 1511

Henry
Marquis of Exeter
executed 1538

Edward
Earl of Warwick
executed 1499

Margaret m. **Sir Richard Pole**
Countess of   *d. 1505*
Salisbury
executed 1541

John
killed at Stoke 1487

Edmund
'The White Rose'
executed 1513

Edward Courtenay
Earl of Devon
d. 1556

Henry Pole
Lord Montague
executed 1538

Reginald Pole
Cardinal of England
d. 1558

Richard
killed at Pavia 1525

...I **Anne Boleyn** m. III **Jane Seymour**
executed 1536   *d. in childbirth 1537*

m. IV
Anne of Cleves
d. 1557

Mary m. I **Louis XII** m. II **Charles Brandon**
1495-1533 of France   Duke of Suffolk
             d. 1515   *d. 1545*

m. V
Catherine Howard
executed 1542

ELIZABETH I
1533-1603

EDWARD VI
1537-1553

Frances Brandon m. **Henry Grey**

m. VI
Catherine Parr
d. 1548

Jane Grey m. **Guildford Dudley**

A Tudor Timeline

1457	January 28	Henry Tudor is born to Lady Margaret Beaufort, thirteen-year-old widow of Edmund Tudor, Earl of Richmond
1485	August 22	Tudor is crowned Henry VII of England after defeating Richard III in the Battle of Bosworth Field
	December 15	Catherine of Aragon is born in Spain
1486	January 18	Marriage of Henry VII to Elizabeth of York
	September 19	Birth of Arthur, Prince of Wales
1491	June 28	Birth of future King Henry VIII
1494	September 12	Birth of future King Francis I of France
1495	April 27	Birth of Suleiman I, Sultan of the Ottoman Empire
1500	February 24	Birth of Charles of Hapsburg, future Emperor Charles V
1501	November 14	Catherine of Aragon is married to Arthur, Prince of Wales
1502	April 2	Death of Arthur, Prince of Wales
1503	February 11	Death of Elizabeth of York, Henry VIII's mother
1509	April 22	Death of Henry VII
	June 11	Henry VIII is married to Catherine of Aragon
1513	June 30	Henry crosses the Channel to take command of the campaign against France
	September 9	Scots army is destroyed by the Earl of Surrey's English force at the Battle of Flodden
1515	December 24	Thomas Wolsey becomes chancellor of England
1516	February 18	Future Queen Mary I is born to Catherine of Aragon
1519	June 15	Birth of Henry VIII's illegitimate son Henry Fitzroy

1527	*May 21*	Birth of Philip of Hapsburg, future King of Spain and husband of Mary I
1529	*September 22*	Thomas Wolsey is stripped of chancellorship, replaced by Thomas More
1532	*March 30*	Thomas Cranmer is consecrated as archbishop of Canterbury
	May 16	More is allowed to resign after the submission of the clergy
1533	*January 25*	Henry VIII is quietly married to Anne Boleyn
	April 13	Anne is proclaimed queen
	May 28	Cranmer's court declares Henry's marriage to Anne to be valid
	June 8	Parliament extinguishes papal authority in England
	September 7	Birth of future Queen Elizabeth I
1534	*April 20*	Execution of Elizabeth Barton, "Nun of Kent"
	April	Thomas Cromwell is confirmed as Henry VIII's principal secretary
	November	The Act of Supremacy establishes Henry VIII as head of the church in England
1535	*June 22*	Execution of John Fisher
	July 6	Execution of Thomas More
1536	*January 7*	Death of Catherine of Aragon
	March	Dissolution of monasteries begins
	May 19	Execution of Anne Boleyn
	May 30	Marriage of Henry VIII to Jane Seymour
	July 1	Mary and Elizabeth are declared illegitimate
	July	Ten Articles assert reformist religious doctrines
	July 22	Death of Henry VIII's illegitimate son Henry Fitzroy, Duke of Richmond
	October 8	Start of Pilgrimage of Grace in Yorkshire
1537	*October 12*	Birth of future King Edward VI
	October 24	Death of Jane Seymour
1539	*June*	Act of Six Articles returns the church to a more conservative position
1540	*January 6*	Henry VIII is married to Anne of Cleves

1540	July 9	Cleves marriage is dissolved
	July 28	Henry VIII is married to Catherine Howard; Thomas Cromwell is executed the same day
1541	May 27	Execution of Margaret Pole, Countess of Salisbury
1542	February 13	Execution of Catherine Howard
	December 8	Birth of Mary Stuart, future Queen of Scots
	December 13	Death of James V of Scotland
1543	July 12	Marriage of Henry VIII to Catherine Parr
1544	July 14	Henry crosses the Channel to make war on France
1547	January 28	Death of Henry VIII

Introduction

The Tudors ruled England for only three generations, an almost pathetically brief span of time in comparison with other dynasties before and since. During the 118 years of Tudor rule, England was a less weighty factor in European politics than it had been earlier, and nothing like the world power it would later become. Of the five Tudors who occupied the throne—three kings, followed by the first two women ever to be queens of England by right of inheritance rather than marriage—one was an epically tragic figure in the fullest Aristotelian sense, two reigned only briefly and came to miserable ends, and the last and longest-lived devoted her life and her reign and the resources of her kingdom to no loftier objective than her own survival. Theirs was, by most measures, a melancholy story. It is impossible not to suspect that even the founder of the dynasty, the only Tudor whose reign was both long and mostly peaceful and did not divide the people of England against themselves (all of which helps to explain why he is forgotten today), would have been appalled to see where his descendants took his kingdom and how their story ended.

And yet, more than four centuries after the Tudors became extinct, one of them is the most famous king and another the most famous queen in the history not only of England but of Europe and probably the world. They have become not merely famous but posthumous stars in the twenty-first-century firmament of celebrity: on the big and little screens and in popular fiction their names have become synonymous with greatness, with *glory*. This is not the fate one might have expected for a pair whose characters were dominated by cold and ruthless egotism, whose careers were studded with acts of atrocious cruelty and false dealing, and who were never more than stonily indifferent to the well-being of the people they ruled. It takes some explaining.

At least as remarkable as the endlessly growing celebrity of the Tudors is the extent to which, after so many centuries, they remain controversial among scholars. Here, too, the reasons are many and complex. They begin with the fact that the dynasty's pivotal figure, Henry VIII, really did change history to an extent rivaled by few other monarchs, and that appraisals of his reign were long entangled in questions of religious belief. It matters also that both Henry and his daughter Elizabeth were not just rulers but consummate *performers*, masters of political propaganda and political theater. They created, and spent their lives hiding inside, fictional versions of themselves that never bore more than a severely limited relation to reality but were nevertheless successfully imprinted on the collective imagination of their own time. These invented personas have endured into the modern world not only because of their inherent appeal—it is hard to resist the image of bluff King Hal, of Gloriana the Virgin Queen—but even more because of their political usefulness across the generations.

Henry, in the process of forcing upon England a revolution-from-above that few of its people welcomed, created a new elite that his radical redistribution of the national wealth made so rich and powerful so quickly that within a few generations it would prove capable of overthrowing the Crown itself. No longer needing or willing to tolerate a monarchy as overbearing as the Tudors had been at their zenith, that new elite nevertheless continued to need the *idea* of the Tudors, of the wonders of the Tudor revolution, in order to justify its own privileged position. It needed to make the mass of English men and women see the Tudor century as the supreme forward leap in England's history, a sweeping away of the dark legacy of the Middle Ages. (This whole "Whig" view of history requires a smug certainty that the medieval world was a cesspit of superstition and repression.) It demanded agreement that the Tudors had put England on the high road to greatness, and that to say otherwise was to be not only extravagantly foolish or dishonest but actually unfit for participation in public life. Centuries of relentless indoctrination and denial ensued, with the result that England turned into a rather curious phenomenon: a great nation actively contemptuous of much of its own history. One still sees the evidence almost whenever British television attempts to deal with pre-Tudor and Tudor history.

It was not until the second half of the twentieth century, really, that historians of some eminence in England and the United States began, often slowly and grudgingly, to acknowledge that the established view of the Tudor era was essentially mythological and could never be reconciled with a dispassionate examination of the facts. Not until even more recently was the old propaganda pretty much abandoned as indefensible. Tudor history remains controversial because, quite extraordinarily for a subject now half a millennium old, its meaning is still being settled. The truth is still being cleared of centuries of systematic denial.

With the academy still bringing sixteenth-century England into focus, we should not be surprised that much of the reading public and virtually the entire entertainment industry remain in the thrall of Tudors who never existed. Whether this will ever change—whether the cartoon versions of Henry VIII and Elizabeth I that now shine in the celebrity heavens alongside James Dean and the Incredible Hulk will ever give way to something with a better connection to reality—is anybody's guess. Perhaps such a change is no longer possible. It is certainly not going to happen as a consequence of this book. I do entertain the more modest hope, however, that a single volume aimed at introducing the entire dynasty to a general readership might prove useful in two ways: by helping to show that the true story of the Tudors is much richer and more fascinating than the fantasy version, and by showing also that the whole story is vastly greater than the sum of its parts. That it contains depths and dimensions that cannot be brought to light by focusing exclusively on Henry VIII, Elizabeth I, or any other single member of the family. That if it is as deeply tragic as I believe it to be—as I hope I have shown it to be—the extent of the tragedy can become clear only when the five reigns are joined together in a narrative arc that begins with Henry VII building a great legacy out of almost nothing, moves on to his son's extravagant abuse of a magnificent inheritance, and follows the son's three children as, one after another and in their joltingly different ways, they attempt to cope with what their father had wrought. If a writer should have an excuse for adding to the endless stream of Tudor literature, I therefore offer these: that not enough has been done to deal with the Tudor dynasty as a continuum, a unity, and that popular perceptions of the family have fallen so far behind scholarly understanding that it is necessary to try, at least, to narrow the gap.

I disavow any claim to competing with, never mind replacing, the many splendid biographies of the Tudor monarchs and their spouses, agents, and victims that have appeared over the last half-century or so. To the contrary, I have drawn heavily on many such works in assembling the facts with which to weave my story, and I am not merely in their debt but could scarcely have even begun without them. And I am mindful that my approach carries a price: dealing with five reigns obviously makes it impossible to provide the depth of detail available in (to cite just one distinguished example) J. J. Scarisbrick's magisterial *Henry VIII*. But it seems fair to question whether so much detail is necessary or even desirable in a work aimed at a general readership, and in any case forgoing it brings a gain too. The story of the whole dynasty is not only bigger in obvious ways than any biography—encompassing more personalities, more drama, more astoundingly grand and ugly events—but also, if paradoxically, *deeper* in one not-insignificant sense. The story of any one Tudor becomes fully rounded only when set in the context of what had come before and what followed, with causes and effects sketched in.

Not being a work of scholarship in anything like a strict and academic sense—not the fruit of deep tunneling into original source materials—this book is not intended for professional Tudor scholars. I can only express my gratitude to the members of that community, most of whom will be familiar with my facts and my arguments and some of whom (any still attached to the old conception of the Tudors as "builders of England's glory," certainly) are likely to reject my conclusions. In any case those conclusions, based on years of reading and reflection, are my responsibility entirely and not to be blamed on anyone else.

I am indebted to my editor, John Flicker, whose suggestions unfailingly prove to be perceptive and helpful (even and perhaps especially the ones I don't welcome at first), to my agent, Judith Riven, for her unflagging support and encouragement, and above all to my partner, Sandra Rose, who cheerfully shared and endured the whole years-long, life-devouring process.

G. J. Meyer
Goring-on-Thames, England
June 2009

Prologue

It is an astonishing fact, and a measure of how much the world has changed in five hundred years, that of the thousands of men who were present at what would come to be called the Battle of Bosworth Field, not one left us a description of it. By any reckoning it was one of the great events of English history—even a glorious event, assuming that your idea of glory is broad enough to embrace the firing of arrows into the bodies of living men and the breaking open of their skulls with axes. It was the blazing sundown of the Middle Ages: men in armor, gleaming blades, banners waving in the summer breeze. It would bring the last charge by mounted knights ever seen on English soil, the last death of a king of England in battle.

But because we have no eyewitness accounts, nor even any accounts written while memories of the battle were still fresh, we know far less about it than historians have traditionally pretended.

We know of course that King Richard III was on the scene—a tough little man with reddish-gold hair, only five foot four but a seasoned warrior, awesomely courageous, the hardened veteran of many bloody fights. We know with certainty that he was there, because he was within minutes of his famously nasty death. We can be sure that he wore a sword, the familiar tool of his trade, and that he carried it as easily as a carpenter carries his hammer. His armor would have been covered with a tunic, made of silk, probably, bearing the colorful symbols of his Plantagenet ancestry. We are told that his horse was white. Being the king's, no doubt it was a majestic horse; feel free to picture it snorting and prancing. That Richard wore a lightweight crown, a coronet, over his iron helmet also is plausible, as his purpose that day was to defend his possession of the crown. With him was his standard-bearer, his old comrade-in-arms Sir Percival Thirlwall, holding aloft a staff from which streamed a long standard displaying Richard's emblem, the blue boar.

And of course Henry Tudor was there—a good distance from Richard, necessarily, but not quite so far away as to be out of sight. As it happens, he too was astride a white horse, one he had been given at some point in the previous two weeks as he and his ragged little army of French and Breton mercenaries and English runaways made their long trek across Wales. No doubt people would have been surprised to learn that, at twenty-seven, Henry was only four years younger than Richard; he was so unknown, had so much less experience and apparent *substance*, as to seem a boy by comparison. So far as we know, he had never been in a fight of any kind. He had never commanded soldiers or ruled anything. Until that month he had not set foot in Wales in almost fourteen years, and the time he had spent in England could be measured in days.

Richard could trace his descent in the male line back through three hundred years of royalty—he was a shoot of the same family tree that had produced Richard the Lion-Hearted and any number of other legendary heroes. Beyond that his ancestry reached to William I's granddaughter and so finally to the Conqueror himself. By contrast, Henry Tudor was the grandson of a Welsh commoner who had had his head chopped off in a town square, and this at a time when most Englishmen regarded the Welsh as a scarily alien race. And yet here he was, presuming to call himself the Earl of Richmond, come to the gentle green hills of the English Midlands for the declared purpose of making himself king.

That he might ever be able to launch even a semicredible effort to take the throne would have seemed impossible just thirty months before. Until 1483 he had been living an idle, pointless life at the court of Duke Francis of Brittany, whose guest and political pawn he had been for nearly half his life. He had been adopted, by then, as the focus if not necessarily the real leader of England's Lancastrian faction—as the man who would be king if somehow the House of York could be overthrown, though increasingly that seemed an empty honor. The leader of the Yorkists, Edward IV, was a strong king in secure possession of the throne, the picture of boisterous good health at age forty, if soft and overweight after almost a decade and a half of peace. He also had a large brood of daughters and sons, the eldest of them just entering adulthood. There was every reason to expect that he and his descendants would rule for generations—and that there would be no place in England for the likes of Henry Tudor.

But then in March 1483 King Edward suffered something like a stroke and within a few weeks was dead. His heir, another Edward, was only twelve and therefore not possibly ready to rule, but that should not have been a problem because the boy had uncles—men of proven loyalty and talent—to govern on his behalf and guide him to maturity. On the paternal side was the dead king's youngest and last surviving brother, Richard, Duke of Gloucester, still barely thirty but deeply experienced in the arts of war and governance. Opposite him was Anthony Woodville, Earl Rivers, eldest of the numerous ambitious brothers of Edward IV's widow, Queen Elizabeth. There *was* a problem, however: bad blood between Richard (who was supported by many of the old noble families) and the upstart Woodvilles, who were resented bitterly because of the wealth and power that had come to them for no better reason than the fact that King Edward, while still a very young man, had impulsively married the obscure if powerfully attractive widow Elizabeth Woodville Grey.

Duke Richard, it is clear, saw the situation as fraught with danger for himself. Earl Rivers had a close relationship with their nephew, whereas Richard, who for years had been far from court governing the north as his brother's representative, scarcely knew the boy. The duke need not have been paranoid to fear that if the Woodvilles could maintain custody of young Edward V—hardly an improbable development, considering that the child's mother was the most prominent Woodville of them all—they could also control the government and destroy their rivals. Whatever his motives, whether he was driven by ambition, hatred, or fear, Richard struck first, setting in motion a series of atrocities that would not end until eight of the last ten legitimate Plantagenet males, five of them boys too young to marry, had died violently. He came down from the north and ordered Rivers to bring their nephew to him. When Rivers did so, both he and the boy were taken into custody. In short order Rivers was executed along with young Richard Grey, Queen Elizabeth's son by her first marriage. Edward V and his ten-year-old brother were sent to the Tower, and Duke Richard had himself crowned.

Convulsion followed convulsion, and with each new upheaval the existence of Henry Tudor became both more significant and more precarious. The princes in the Tower were heard of no more—it was impossible to doubt that they had been murdered—and many of the men who had figured importantly in Edward IV's regime left England rather than support the new King Richard III. Ineptly and for reasons that remain obscure, the Duke of Buckingham, probably the richest noble in England and a man whose royal blood gave him a claim to the throne, raised a rebellion not in his own name but in Henry Tudor's. Francis of Brittany gave Henry a tiny fleet and army with which to invade England, but it was scattered by storms. By the time the ship carrying Henry hauled alone into Plymouth harbor, Buckingham had been defeated and executed and the rebellion was over. Richard's agents met an advance party sent ashore by Henry and, by reporting that the rebellion had already succeeded, tried to lure him ashore. He learned the truth in time, however, and made his escape. Fresh storms then drove him into port in France, and with great difficulty he managed to make his way overland back to Brittany. When on Christmas Day the English exiles who had gathered in Brittany assembled at Rennes Cathedral and pledged to support Henry, their oaths must have seemed nearly meaningless. Equally empty was Henry's promise, made that same day, to marry Edward IV's eldest daughter, Elizabeth of York, then in sanctuary at Westminster Abbey with her mother and four sisters.

Worse soon followed. An exiled bishop with sources of information at the English court sent word that the Duke of Brittany was negotiating an agreement by which he would be richly rewarded for delivering Henry to King Richard. Henry opened communications with the French court and, upon establishing that he would be welcome there, laid plans to get himself and his followers across the Breton-French border. This ended in high drama: Duke Francis's soldiers were hard on Henry's heels as he galloped to France and safety. From that point, however, all his luck was good. The French king, Charles VIII, was a boy in early adolescence. His older sister, Anne of Beaujeu, headed the government as regent and badly needed to make trouble for Richard III, who was attempting to encircle France by allying himself with the two autonomous duchies of Brittany and Burgundy. (It is worth noting, in this connection, that Charles and Anne would have regarded young Tudor not only as a useful political tool but as a near kinsman. Henry's grandmother Catherine of Valois had been their grandfather's sister.) They added to the money coming to Henry from England to provide him with the means to again assemble some ships and hire a mercenary army. The resulting invasion force sailed out of Honfleur in Normandy on August 1, had good weather all the way this time, and made landfall at Milford Haven in the southwestern corner of Wales just six days later. It is said that Henry had to set one of his ships afire to prevent some of his more fainthearted troops from returning to France.

Richard, meanwhile, was experiencing much misery. His son and heir had died early in his reign, and when his wife died not long afterward, it was widely rumored that he had had her poisoned in order to free himself to marry his niece Elizabeth of York. The rumors became so damaging that he was obliged to take the humiliating step of denying them publicly. His subjects, evidently, were prepared to believe anything of him so long as it was sufficiently horrific. He made efforts to shore up his base of support—raising John Howard to Duke of Norfolk, for example, and giving offices and lands to the Stanley family—but the estimated number of his troops, when they came face-to-face with Henry Tudor's on August 22, suggests that he should have done more along that line, done it sooner, and been more careful in selecting the beneficiaries.

We don't know the size of the armies that faced each other that day. Henry must have had about five thousand men: several hundred displaced Englishmen who had made him the centerpiece of their quest for revenge, a few thousand thuggish soldiers-for-hire contributed by the regent of France, and a disappointingly small number—no more than a thousand or two, surely—who had joined him after he came ashore in southwestern Wales. Richard may have had twelve thousand, possibly ten, possibly fewer than that; the estimates vary, and there is no way of choosing among them. Whatever Richard's total, it would have been cause for concern. It was pathetic compared to the thirty-five thousand or more troops that his late brother Edward IV had taken into the Battle of Towton on Palm Sunday in 1461, or the army of fifty thousand Lancastrians that Edward's men had shattered that day. Richard had known months in advance that an invasion was being prepared. He had learned on August 11 that the invaders had landed four days earlier, and he had sent out summonses for the nobles of England and Wales, all of whom had been put on alert weeks before, to muster their soldiery and join him at Leicester. No more than one in every five had done so. It was unsettling evidence of how little support Richard had, and of how badly the old feudal system had decayed.

Strangely, ominously, there was a third army on the field; it might even be accurate to say that there were four. These were the forces of the Stanley clan, raised to the nobility less than twenty years before but already a major power, the greatest landowners in the northwest and de facto rulers of the Isle of Man. The Stanleys had remained loyal to Richard in 1483, when he seized the throne after his brother's sudden death and the Duke of Buckingham raised a rebellion against him, and they had been richly rewarded for doing so. The head of the clan, Thomas Lord Stanley, had been made constable of England and steward of the royal household. His brother Sir William was chamberlain—governor, in effect—of Chester and North Wales. Upon receiving word that Henry Tudor was ashore, Richard had ordered the Stanleys to join him with their liegemen. They had done so, but more slowly than Richard could have wished, and their behavior had become increasingly suspect. Much earlier than Richard himself, they were in a position to intercept the invaders as they emerged from Wales. Instead of doing so they had continually fallen back, allowing the advance to continue. Now, with the showdown clearly at hand, they had some five thousand men with them, separated into two groups, each commanded by one of the brothers. Nobody knew whose side they were on; apparently they were pretending to be on both sides while not yet knowing themselves what they were going to do. Their first loyalty had always been to themselves, and they had long ago demonstrated that they would betray even kings when doing so was more or less certain to be to their advantage. Richard, aware of their history and fearful of their power, was holding Lord Stanley's son hostage. It is said that he threatened to have the son executed if the Stanleys failed to join their forces with his, and was told by way of response that his lordship had other sons. It is said also that when Henry Tudor asked Stanley to join *him* on the morning of August 22, he was told to mind his own business.

One of the more bizarre aspects of this story is that Stanley was

Henry Tudor's stepfather, the third husband (or fourth, if one counts a childhood marriage that ended in annulment) of his mother, Margaret Beaufort. It was a purely political marriage—the contract stipulated that the bride's chastity was not to be compromised. Though it is almost certain that Henry had long been in secret communication with the Stanleys and was counting on their support, he could not have been confident of getting it. The brothers were hanging back, Sir William with his men in one place and Lord Thomas with his in another, watching the situation unfold. If they could be counted upon to do anything, it was to wait until someone was winning and then strike at the loser in order to be in on the spoils.

The detailed descriptions in countless books notwithstanding, we have no way of knowing how the various forces were arranged. We don't even know where they were, except somewhere within a circle with a diameter of several miles. When the earliest account finally was written, presumably drawing on the testimony of participants, its author was an Italian retainer at the English court who had good reason to want to please his Tudor masters. He tells wonderful stories: That Richard was uneasy all through the night before the battle, and that the little sleep he managed to get was punctuated with horrible dreams. That he rose while it was still dark (which means that he must have been up by four A.M.), inspected his lines, and ran his sword through a sentry who was sleeping on duty. That he wanted to hear mass, but the only available priest was unable to find the necessities. That when he called for breakfast, it too proved to be impossible. And that the most powerful and dependable of his henchmen, long-faced old John Howard, Duke of Norfolk, awoke to find a handwritten verse fastened to the entrance of the house where he had slept:

> *Jack of Norfolk, be not too bold,*
> *For Dickon, thy master, is bought and sold.*

"Dickon" would be Richard. For "bought and sold" we would today say "sold out." We are told that Richard's army was melting away like snow in springtime, some of the deserters joining the rebels, others running for home.

These stories have come down to us at second or third hand, selected by a writer who was a propagandist at least as much as a historian, and any or all of them could be inventions. We can't even be certain that the Battle of Bosworth Field was fought at the place called Bosworth Field, which is now a popular attraction with walking tours and a visitor center and all the paraphernalia of the tourist trade. Richard is supposed to have positioned his forces there, atop a high point called Ambien Hill, from which he could look out and see his enemies approaching in the distance. Henry Tudor would have been accompanied by his standard-bearer William Brandon, who hoisted a banner on which was displayed the red dragon of Wales. They would have been surrounded by a life-guard of pike-wielding foot soldiers and mounted knights.

Supposedly the battle began when the main body of Tudor troops, commanded by the dashing Earl of Oxford, recently escaped after ten years as Richard's prisoner, started up Ambien Hill. Perhaps it happened that way, but students of the battle now living claim that the two sides collided not at Ambien Hill but on flatter ground some distance away. The evidence they offer is complicated but not easily dismissed. The author of the present work can attest, after visiting Bosworth and walking its length and breadth, that the landscape as it exists today does not make the traditional version of the story particularly convincing.

This we do know: at some point after the first clash of troops under the command of Oxford on one side and Norfolk on the other, with the situation stalemated and the Stanleys still hovering like vultures on the sidelines, Richard made a decision that would lead to one of the most dramatic climaxes in the history of warfare. He decided to forget about defeating the invader army with his army and instead settle things personally, in something very close to single combat, himself against Henry Tudor. In the absence of sources, it is permissible to imagine him summoning his lifeguard of perhaps a hundred knights to gather round, unsheathing his sword and pointing with it in the direction of the red dragon, and shouting for his men to follow while spurring his charger into a headlong gallop. Something like that has to have happened.

Why it happened we can never know. Possibly Richard acted out of desperation: apparently Norfolk had been killed by this point (taken by an arrow in the throat by one account, executed on the spot after surrendering to Oxford by another), and if indeed his troops had failed in an initial assault despite their superior numbers, this must have been deeply unsettling. Or perhaps Richard saw a target that was simply too tempting to ignore: the tiny far-off figure of Henry Tudor, as passive as the king in a game of chess, remote from the action and not that strongly protected. If Henry's guard could be penetrated—and why not, if Richard himself brought a phalanx of heavy cavalry down on it like the blow of a mace—killing him would become a simple matter. It would no longer matter what the Stanleys or anyone else did. The Tudor cause would be decapitated, the whole invasion rendered pointless.

What ensued was a poetically fitting end to three centuries of rule by Plantagenet warrior-kings. The last link in that long royal chain, sword in hand and blue boar unfurled above his head, thundered across the battlefield with his knights just behind, the hooves of their chargers throwing up fat clods of earth. Richard crashed headlong into the first defenders to come out to meet him, laying about him with his sword, bringing down the banner of the red dragon by instantly killing William Brandon, and sending the biggest of Henry's knights crashing to the ground with a clang of armor plate. His horsemen hit like a wave of flesh and iron, driving into the melee with lances lowered, hacking away with clubs and blades. Whether any of them got close enough to engage Henry personally is not known, but the onslaught had to be terrifying. It is to Henry's credit that, despite never having experienced anything like this, he did not turn and run. Nearby, perhaps steadying him, was his uncle Jasper, as tough and fearless an old campaigner as anyone on the field that day.

For a long moment things hung in the balance. In one recent treatise on the battle, the writer claims to have found evidence that Richard's assault was foiled by a tactic he had not encountered before: French pikemen, forming up in a square around Henry and planting the butts of their weapons in the earth to create a wall of iron points that no cavalry could penetrate.

To return to what we know: suddenly, from the side or rear, scores and then hundreds and finally thousands of men in red tunics came pouring in, swamping Richard and his band. These were William Stanley's men, wearing the Stanley livery. In the moment of crisis—perhaps as soon as it became clear that Henry was not going to die—Stanley had seen his opportunity and gone in for the kill.

Richard was swept back and unhorsed. Shakespeare, more than a century later, would have him crying out for a fresh mount: "My kingdom for a horse!" Older accounts say something very different: that one of Richard's companions urged him to flee, offering him a horse. If that happened, the king refused. Again we can only guess at his thinking. He could have had little hope of assembling another army if he managed to escape, and perhaps he could accept nothing but victory or death. He fought on as, one after another, his men were cut down around him. The faithful Thirlwall held the blue boar aloft until his legs were chopped from under him. Finally it was Richard's turn: men he could not get at with his sword, Welsh troopers, jabbed at him from all directions with their long-handled points and hooks. He screamed defiance, cursing them as traitors. It must have been even more like butchery than most battlefield deaths in the Middle Ages, the pikemen probing for the seams in the king's armor. Without question it was a brave death; even those who depict Richard as a monster have always acknowledged that. When it was over his body was stripped naked, thrown over the back of a horse like a sack of grain, and hauled off for public display. Those of his men who were not dead or captured ran for their lives. Lord Stanley's son was still alive. In the confusion no one had remembered, or bothered, to kill him.

The whole thing must have seemed a dream or a nightmare, depending on which side one was on. In seconds Richard had been reduced from a king at the head of an army of thousands to a mangled lump of dead flesh. Henry had been vaulted from adventurer to conqueror. Survivors must have stumbled about the field, trying to absorb what had happened.

It fell to the ever-resourceful Lord Stanley, who had played no part in the battle even after his brother went in, to focus the moment. Someone retrieved the crown that Richard had lost in the moment before his death. The legends say it was found in a hawthorn bush. Sober historians have dismissed this as a romantic fabrication but fail to explain why, not many years after the battle, a crown in a thornbush became a royal emblem. In any case, Stanley arrived on the scene while everything was still in confusion and took possession of the crown. Putting himself at the center of a great occasion that he had done nothing to bring about, he placed the crown on his stepson's head and led the assembled company in a hearty round of cheers.

At which moment, in a turn of fate as improbable as any in history, Henry Tudor became King Henry VII of England.

PART ONE

An Excess of Good Fortune

1485–1532

1

The Luck of Henry Tudor

None of the events that have made the second Henry Tudor the most famous king in history happened in 1534. Henry VIII divorced no one that year, married no one, killed no eminent person. But the year was a milestone all the same, arguably *the* great turning point in his stunningly eventful career. When it began he had deteriorated only enough to be the sort of person you would hate to be seated next to at a dinner party: arrogant, opinionated, a bully inclined to self-pity, invincibly confident of his own charm, and certain that he knew best about everything that mattered. Before the year ended he had become what he would remain for the rest of his life: a full-fledged tyrant in the strictest sense of the word, a homicidal monster, absurd, pathetic, mortally dangerous.

A person in Henry's predicament, a man whose pride has walled him up in such impregnable isolation, becomes incapable of an emotion as healthy as gratitude. Certainly he cannot see himself as merely lucky. His fate, he thinks, is coterminous with divine will. Everything good that befalls him does so in fulfillment of God's great plan for the universe. Every disappointment can be traced neither to God nor to some failure on his own part (that is impossible; he could never commit a serious error) but to something outside himself that is cosmically out of joint. Nonetheless, lucky is what Henry was—one of the luckiest human beings who ever lived.

Much of his good fortune he owed to his father. In the quarter-century between his victory at Bosworth and his death in 1509, Henry VII had made the English Crown more secure and powerful than it had been in generations. He had filled the royal treasury with gold and accustomed his subjects to the benefits of peace. He is today a remote and elusive figure, a king about whom most people know almost nothing, and he appears to have been much the same in his own time. Though his life before Bosworth had been studded with moments of high drama and hairsbreadth escapes, little of the excitement had been of his choosing. Mainly his early years had been spent waiting. Even what we know of his part in the fight that won him the crown suggests that it could have been played by a deaf mute, a mannequin. Henry was attacked, Henry was defended, Henry was crowned—every episode finds him in a passive role.

And yet something tremendous was achieved, and the achievement *was* Henry's. None of it would have been possible if, even in his youth, there had not been something about him—something not quite explainable at a distance of five centuries—that won the support and even the affection of the Duke of Brittany, the ruling family of France, and one after another of the older, more experienced men who had fled England after Richard III became king. Nor could he have succeeded if, whenever enemies appeared to be closing in on him, he had not had the courage and resourcefulness to outwit them. However colorless he may seem to us, however much the contemporary chronicles fail to make him a fully three-dimensional figure, the one thing that always comes through is his unfailing *competence*. In temperament he appears to have been more like a modern corporate executive of remarkably high caliber—coolly savvy, demanding but amiable enough, a good judge of risk and reward—than some swashbuckling medieval warrior-king. He always had himself firmly under control, and he seems always to have been somewhat inscrutable.

He took the one great chance that fate offered him, pulled it off, and devoted the rest of his life to the careful consolidation of his winnings. He was disdainful of military glory, and though he sought and won the respect of the continent's ruling families, he displayed no wish to cut a particularly great figure among them. If he left almost no mark on the world's imagination (biographers have taken little interest in him, perhaps in part because they could never be confident of understanding him), his reign is important all the same. It built the stage upon which his son and then his granddaughter would be able to show themselves off for almost the whole of the century that followed his death.

The most impressive thing Henry did after reaching the throne was to establish himself securely on it. This was no small achievement: to grasp its magnitude it is necessary to remember the hundred years before Bosworth, with their tragic succession of Plantagenet kings and claimants clashing and killing and being killed. Henry, his dollop of royal blood inherited from a bastard line that even when legitimized had been excluded by law from succession to the crown, could not have been given good chances of lasting long when he became king. But step by slow step, in his methodical and undramatic way, he made it clear to England and the world that he was a real king and a strong one and not to be taken lightly. He did so carefully, confiding in only his oldest friends, never moving so fast as to provoke reaction, watching for opportunities to eliminate rivals and seizing those opportunities as they arose.

The death of Richard III had left only one legitimate male Plantagenet still alive: the boy Edward, Earl of Warwick, the orphan son of Richard's suicidally troublesome elder brother George, Duke of Clarence. Immediately after Bosworth, Henry sent a lieutenant to find the child and lock him in the Tower, out of reach of anyone who might hope to make him king. He then fortified his own claim to the loyalty of the Yorkist party by fulfilling his pledge, made when he was still in exile in Brittany, to marry Edward IV's eldest child, the twenty-year-old Princess Elizabeth. The marriage made it impossible for anyone to oppose Henry on grounds that the crown rightfully belonged to Edward IV's descendants. Significantly, however, Henry delayed the wedding until months after his coronation. In this way he underscored his claim to be king in his own right, by right of conquest as well as descent, rather than thanks to his wife. He was as shrewd about chronology as about most things, dating his reign from the day *before* Bosworth so as to make everyone who opposed him there guilty of treason.

From Rome Henry procured a papal declaration not only that he was the rightful king of England but that anyone who refused to acknowledge him would be subject to excommunication. This was no mere formality: it meant that the kingdom's bishops, with all their wealth and influence, could find no basis for opposing him. As his counselors and ministers he chose trusted cohorts, men who had shared his dangerous years on the continent and fought for him at Bosworth. The Earl of Oxford, his ancestral lands restored, became admiral of England (land and sea warfare not yet being distinct disciplines). John Morton, who had been bishop of Ely under Edward IV and an exile during Richard's reign (it was he who had warned Henry that the Duke of Brittany and Richard were plotting against him), was not merely restored to his see but elevated to lord chancellor, archbishop of Canterbury, and cardinal. Morton and two other former exiles, Bishop Richard Fox and the layman Reginald Bray, would remain the king's chief administrators for nearly twenty years. Their services helped Henry to limit his dependence on, and need to share power with, the nobility.

His apparent vulnerability during the early years of his reign—the inability of some subjects to accept the emergence of such a nobody as king—gave rise to two of the most ludicrous rebellions in English history. Just two years after Bosworth a youth of lowly and obscure birth named Lambert Simnel (he may have been a carpenter's son and may have been from Oxford, but little about his origins is certain) was put forward as Edward, Earl of Warwick, and therefore as the boy who should be king. Simnel was the tool of John de la Pole, Earl of Lincoln, the royal nephew whom Richard III had named as his heir after the death of his own son and who had been with Richard at Bosworth. Lincoln, like Warwick, had been imprisoned after the battle, but Henry soon freed him and restored part of his patrimony. Disgruntled and ungrateful, the earl left the country, found support in Europe and Ireland (where Simnel was crowned King Edward VI), and invaded England in the pretender's name. Met by Henry's troops at Stoke in Nottinghamshire, he was defeated and killed. The dupe Simnel was captured but not punished. In perhaps the most attractive act of his life, King Henry gave the youth a job in the royal kitchens. Later he would be promoted to falconer.

In the early 1490s another false Plantagenet appeared: a young Frenchman called Perkin Warbeck, the handsome servant of silk merchants, chosen by disaffected Yorkists to impersonate Edward IV's son Richard, Duke of York, the younger of the two princes who had disappeared in the Tower. The threat this time was more serious, and it simmered for years. Warbeck, like Simnel, found much support in Ireland, always a hotbed of Yorkist sedition. He was recognized as king by James IV of Scotland (who gave him a young woman of high birth as his bride), by Charles VIII of France (now Henry Tudor's rival rather than his boyish admirer), by Maximilian the Hapsburg "king of Rome" (a title borne by sons and heirs of Holy Roman emperors), and even by the dead princes' aunt Margaret, the embittered sister of Edward IV and widow of the Duke of Burgundy. Things threatened to get out of hand when taxes levied by Henry to provide money for military operations in the north sparked an uprising in Cornwall. The insurgents, marching on London, declared their support for the pretender. They were defeated at Blackheath less than a day's march from Westminster, and after further misadventures Warbeck was captured and hanged. At the same time charges of conspiracy were concocted against the Earl of Warwick, who was twenty-four years old by this time and had been a prisoner more than half his life. Though guilty of nothing and apparently mentally impaired (whether congenitally or because of the miserable conditions of his upbringing cannot be known), he too was put to death. Thus did the first judicial murder of the Tudor era extinguish the last Plantagenet. It was the darkest act of Henry VII's life.

Along the way—this was perhaps the greatest of his gifts to his heir—Henry VII brought the nobles to heel. His whole reign was a prolonged exercise in stripping away their autonomy. First he marginalized them, making room on his council for those he did not actively distrust but excluding them from offices of highest importance. The few nobles who dared to oppose Henry, especially but not only if they had royal blood, were destroyed. The death of John de la Pole at Stoke was followed in 1506 by the return of his brother Edmund to England, in chains, by the Hapsburgs. He was promptly locked away. With the passage of time Henry found it possible to move against more and more of the nobles, even the strongest of them. Sir William Stanley, who had saved him at Bosworth, was put to death after being implicated in the Perkin Warbeck affair. His possessions, including enough land to generate the stupendous sum of £1,000 annually, went to the Crown. Other members of the Stanley family, including the king's stepfather, the Earl of Derby (the former Thomas Lord Stanley, promoted after Bosworth), were required to pay heavy bonds as a guarantee of good behavior. Bonds and recognizances of this kind proved an effective way of neutering mighty subjects and were levied against more than half of England's nobles during Henry's reign. Half-forgotten laws—statutes, mainly, that the nobles had found it convenient to ignore when the Crown was weak—were dusted off and used to cripple great families financially. Henry was so unwilling to create new peers that their number shrank from fifty-five at the start of his rule to forty-two at the end. A substantial number of the 138 persons that he had attainted were nobles, and the resulting confiscations of land played a major part in making him richer than any previous English king. That he was able to do all these things without provoking the nobles to rise against him testifies not only to his political skill but to just how much the peerage had been reduced in power—how negligible a factor it would prove to be when his son's reign entered its revolutionary phase.

Henry milked the church too. As much as at any time in the history of the kingdom, more than at most times, bishoprics became a reward for service to the Crown. Thus the ecclesiastical hierarchy came to be dominated by administrators and politicians accustomed to serving the king and aware of owing their positions to him; this would have momentous consequences when, a generation after Henry VII's death, the bishops found themselves having to choose between submitting to the Crown or defending their church. Henry regularly transferred bishops from one see to another for no better reason than his own financial advantage: each new appointment required the payment of substantial fees to the Crown, and the revenues of vacant bishoprics went to the king as well.

Henry avoided war in spite of the fact that the nobility, generally not understanding that the kings of France were no longer as weak as they had been a few generations before, were eager to loot and pillage on the continent as their grandfathers had done and perhaps even recover their families' lost possessions there. He took an army across the Channel only once, in the early 1490s, and then mainly to demonstrate his objection to France's absorption of Brittany. He was pleased to return home after little more than a month, as soon as Charles VIII agreed to pay him handsomely for doing so and promised to stop encouraging Perkin Warbeck. War, as Henry knew well, was risky. Even worse from his perspective, war was expensive. He was satisfied to do nothing about the time-honored but now meaningless claim that kings of England were also rightfully kings of France. By the end of his life only the oldest people living had any memory of the bloody conflicts of the past, or of their costs. As for the continental powers, they could see no profit in meddling in the affairs of a distant island kingdom that was no longer meddling in theirs.

Sadly, it is probably his reputation for greed, for being willing to bend the law in every feasible way to relieve his wealthiest subjects of as much of their property as possible, that stands today as the most vividly remembered part of Henry VII's legacy. This reputation is not entirely deserved. Henry was not *merely* a miser, certainly—he cheerfully gambled away substantial sums, and spent lavishly to impress subjects and foreigners alike—and a full treasury was undoubtedly the best form of security at a time when the Crown still had no standing army and the old practice of depending on the nobility for fighting men in times of need was in an advanced state of decay. Still, the lengths to which Henry went to increase his revenues, and the glum and solitary figure that he became after the deaths of his queen and several of their children, made him so unloved that his death, when it came, was received with more gratitude than grief. By then he had accumulated so much wealth in gold plate and jewels—certainly no less than a quarter of a million pounds, possibly twice or even four times that amount—that his heir was free to spend as much as he wished without giving a thought to the consequences.

Henry's unpopularity in the last years of his reign was his last great gift to his son. By the end, in a kind of foreshadowing, he appears to have become not only a miser but something very like a tyrant, the joyless ruler of a joylessly submissive realm. In his final illness he is said to have repented—to have vowed that if he recovered, his subjects would find him a changed man. There was no recovery. He was barely fifty-two when he died but seemed very old. England did see a new man, but it was not Henry VII restored to health. It was his son and namesake and heir, the dazzling boy who ascended to the throne like the dawning of a new day. The seventeen-year-old Henry VIII arrived on the crest of England's first uncontested transfer of power in almost ninety years—a transfer that itself testified to how much the dead king had achieved. He was greeted with shouts of joy and was filled with joy himself.

There had never been so good a time to be king. The emergence of artillery was rendering the dark and cold stone fortresses of the Middle Ages, long essential for defense, vulnerable and therefore obsolete. At the same time the new big guns, though primitive in their technology and as difficult to move as they were treacherous to use, were giving central governments an unprecedented advantage over anyone inclined to rebel: rebels might have swords and lances and even handguns, but they were unlikely to be able to buy or build many cannons. Old castles were rebuilt or abandoned in favor of a new kind of royal habitation, a kind intended less for defense than for ostentation and pleasure, rich in windows and therefore in light and designed to provide the ruling families of Europe with a degree of luxury that would have been unimaginable just a few generations before. In all of Europe there were few more impressive examples than Henry VII's huge and sumptuous Richmond Palace—so named because he and his father had both been earls of Richmond—which now of course passed to his son. The new royal lifestyle was apparent even in Richmond's tennis courts.

Henry VIII was blessed with more than a secure throne and the wealth that came with it. Nature had endowed him with a fine intelligence, a six-foot-two-inch frame that was as strong as it was handsomely proportioned (broad shoulders tapered down to a waist that in his young manhood measured only thirty-two inches), robust good looks (though his eyes were small and he had a puckered little rosebud of a mouth), and even better health. He was the third of the four children of King Henry VII to survive childhood; his sole elder brother, Arthur, Prince of Wales, appears to have been a frail runt and died, in all likelihood without achieving sexual maturity, at age fifteen. Henry's parents and his imperious paternal grandmother, Margaret Beaufort, had seen to it that he was splendidly educated—able at an early age to converse easily in Latin as well as French—and taught to be a faithful son to Holy Mother Church. No one ever overburdened him with duties and responsibilities. Through the first decade of his life, as a younger son, he was free of the pressures and expectations commonly brought to bear on heirs being prepared for rule. Thereafter, in the seven years between his brother's death and his father's, he was the king's sole surviving son and therefore too precious to be exposed to risk. He was kept in almost monkish seclusion, rigorously protected not only from the many fatal diseases of the time but even from the stresses that might have accompanied a serious apprenticeship in governance. His mother died when he was eleven, and by all accounts his contacts with his father were neither frequent nor notably pleasant.

Such a cheerless and constrained life must have been intensely frustrating for a youth of Prince Henry's vitality and capacity for enjoyment. When he entered upon his own reign, suddenly not only free but ruler of the whole kingdom, he was without preparation or experience. He was also less interested in ruling than in having the best possible time. He liberated himself from celibacy by marrying almost immediately, even before he was crowned. Such speed was possible because he had close at hand a young woman who was not only pretty and accomplished but unquestionably suitable: his late brother's widow Catherine, daughter of the mighty King Ferdinand of Spain. Henry and Catherine were quietly married at the church of the Franciscan friars in Greenwich on June 11, just fifty days after the old king's death. Thirteen days after that, bedecked with diamonds and other precious stones, the two were anointed king and queen of England in a lavish ceremony at Westminster Abbey. By then the royal court, a dark, dour place during the last years of Henry VII, was being transformed into a scene of music and dance, games and laughter.

At the court's center were the royal couple, both of them all but swooning with happiness. The young king was besotted with his wife, who was at least his equal in intelligence and education and, with vastly more experience of how hard even royal life could be, much more mature. For Catherine even more than for Henry, this new life was a deliverance, a rescue that could hardly have been more unexpected or welcome. And she more than most women was equipped to make the best of it. Her late mother, the formidable warrior-queen Isabella of Castile, had schooled her almost from the cradle to become a worthy consort, capable, supportive, and submissive, to some king as great as her father, Ferdinand. Upon being sent to England, however, she had found only marriage to a boy who could not or in any case did not consummate their union, early widowhood followed by illness, and years of mistreatment at the hands of her increasingly mean-spirited father-in-law. All this had ended, to general astonishment, with the sudden decision of the new king, who was six years her junior, to fulfill the old king's half-forgotten pledge by making her his wife. As Henry VIII gathered around himself an entourage of high-spirited and fun-seeking courtiers, Catherine assumed a role even bigger than that of bedmate and partner. She appears to have become a kind of indulgent and approving mother figure, one in whose eyes he could find confirmation of everything he wanted to believe about himself and loving acceptance of his every self-indulgence.

There was, however, a kingdom to be ruled and a government to be run, and during the two and a half decades of Henry VII's rule England had become accustomed to a very personal style of management, one in which the king's household directly controlled everything of real importance and nothing significant was undertaken without the king's knowledge. Such a system was scarcely workable under a new king who had no intention of submitting to the tedium of daily administration. Except when dealing with matters that engaged his interest in some personal way, Henry was willing to talk business only during morning mass—evidently he was not an attentive worshipper—and just before retiring at night. He disliked having to read official documents, generally insisting that they be read aloud to him, preferably in abridged form. And he regarded it as a nuisance to be asked to put his signature to things, so that such orders and approvals as he issued were often done by word of mouth. It was a recipe for disorder, but again Henry was lucky. From the start of his reign he was served by the same loyal and capable men—prelates of the church, mainly, headed by William Warham in his dual capacities of archbishop of Canterbury and lord chancellor—who had been the government's senior ministers during Henry VII's last years. They looked after whatever required attention, freeing their new master to pursue interests that ranged from hunting to music and dance (he was a talented instrumentalist and composer of songs), from jousting and gambling to tennis and the collection and improvement of palaces. (Eventually he would have fifty royal residences, more than any English monarch before or since.) The people, meanwhile, knew nothing of Henry's work habits and could not have cared less. After years of dreariness they were delighted by what they could see of the eager and energetic youth who now wore the crown. A new day seemed to have dawned for all of England.

The previous reign still cast its shadow, however. One of Henry VII's most detested innovations, the so-called "Council Learned in the Law," had become an all-too-effective way of compelling the wealthy to disgorge land and gold for the benefit of the Crown. The functioning of this council was the responsibility of two of the late king's most trusted lawyers, Edmund Dudley and Richard Empson, who had amassed considerable personal fortunes in the course of doing their work and thus made themselves the most hated men in England. Dudley was president of the King's Council, the first layman to hold that exalted post, Empson was chairman of the Council Learned in the Law, and both must have expected to play major roles during the transition to the new reign and thereafter. Instead, as a way for Henry VIII and other councilors to show that a new and better day really had dawned, the two were arrested even before Henry VII was in his grave. After sixteen months, when it became clear that resentment against them was not abating, they were attainted of treason (which meant they were stripped of everything they owned) and put to death. Their execution was a cynical act of judicial murder, done purely for political and propaganda purposes: ruthless and grasping Dudley and Empson certainly had been, but they had done nothing without the approval of the king and are likely to have been following his instructions. It is impossible to know whether it was young Henry or his council or both who wanted them dead. Whatever the case, the episode added an ominous background note to the jubilation that accompanied the accession of the new king. Henry himself learned a memorable double lesson, one that he would find ample opportunities to apply. He had been shown how easy it was to deflect blame for unpopular policies onto servants of the Crown—and how the anger of his subjects could be dissipated through the extermination of those same servants.

The ministers inherited from the previous reign satisfied Henry's needs for only a few years at best, and their dominance lasted no more than five years. Although they relieved the king of the mundane routines of governance, as a group they were unable to share his enthusiasm for adventures on the international stage. Even before the end of his adolescence, Henry displayed an almost desperate hunger for glory. He wanted to become a hero-king, a conqueror, a great romantic figure in the pattern of Richard the Lion-Hearted and his own great-grandmother's first husband, Henry V, the victor of Agincourt. And so he turned his attention to the place where his most honored predecessors had most often won their fame. He wanted to fight in France—not only to fight there, but to turn the long-standing English claim to the French crown into a reality. But the old men of the council could not be persuaded. They were bishops, many of them, churchmen not generally disposed to embrace war. And they had learned statecraft under Henry VII, who taught them to regard involvement in Europe's wars as a fool's errand, risky and wasteful. They exasperated their young master by raising such tiresome questions as the cost in gold and silver—never mind the likely cost in lives—of taking an army across the Channel. Henry had no patience with such quibbles. Like many people who are wealthy from birth, he regarded his riches not as a stroke of good fortune but as part of the natural state of affairs, what he was entitled to. He saw in himself the potential to become not only one of the major figures of his time, the equal and perhaps the leader of the greatest continental monarchs, but one of the giants of history. It could have made no sense to him to draw back from such a destiny because a gaggle of quibbling old celibates didn't want him to spend *his* money.

What Henry needed was new management, and again he was fabulously lucky. As if on cue, there stepped out of deep obscurity one of the last and most remarkable products of the medieval English church's meritocracy, an Oxford-educated butcher's son named Thomas Wolsey, a tightly packed bundle of talent and drive with a sharp eye for the main chance. A priest from age twenty-five, Wolsey had escaped the schoolmaster's life for which he seemed destined by securing appointment as one of several chaplains in the household of the archbishop of Canterbury. From there he moved on to become chaplain to the governor of Calais, England's last foothold on the coast of France, and then somehow at the court of Henry VII himself. Thus he was in royal service when Henry VIII took the throne in 1509, and that was all the advantage he needed. The new king first made him almoner, dispenser of charity, and then in 1511 appointed him to the council, the circle of royal advisers.

When in the fourth year of his reign Henry wanted to invade France—his opportunity to do so came in the form of an invitation from Pope Julius II to join a so-called Holy League against King Louis XII—he got no encouragement from the two dominant members of his council,

Archbishop Warham and Bishop Fox. This was Wolsey's cue to rise and meet his fate. Almost forty years old now, he offered the twenty-two-year-old king not only approval but a willingness to take responsibility for the logistics of the entire French campaign—a tremendously challenging assignment. Again Henry was freed, first to pursue his dreams of military greatness without actually having to do very much, and then, after he had landed in France, to indulge in jousting and festivities rather than subjecting himself to actual combat or, worse, the hard toil of keeping an army in good order on foreign soil. As a precautionary measure, before leaving England Henry saw to the execution of his cousin Edmund de la Pole, who by then had been a prisoner in the Tower for seven years. In strict legalistic terms the killing was justified: de la Pole, younger brother of the John de la Pole who had masterminded the Lambert Simnel affair, had committed treason by claiming the crown for himself. By the time of his execution, however, he had become an impotent and even pathetic figure. In practical terms the execution was simply another Tudor murder.

This was Henry's first war, and like all his European campaigns it turned out to be sterile militarily, financially, and diplomatically. The old-timers on the council had been entirely right in attempting to discourage him. The king's partners in the Holy League made a fool of him. His father-in-law Ferdinand of Spain betrayed him not once but three times, the Holy Roman emperor Maximilian and the Swiss mercenary army whose services Henry had purchased at immense expense once each. The bill, including both direct costs and the subsidies that Henry had naïvely paid his faithless allies, was nearly £1 million. This wiped out everything inherited from Henry VII and plunged the Crown into financial difficulties from which it would emerge only intermittently over the next century and more. But Henry returned home convinced he had achieved great things. Together his troops and those of Emperor Maximilian had captured the towns of Thérouanne and Tournai, successes of some value to Maximilian but none to England. At one of the few points of real drama English horsemen had put the French cavalry to flight in what was jokingly named the Battle of the Spurs, a skirmish of no consequence in which Henry played no part. In fact, though he loved to play at jousting and was big and strong and well equipped enough to be successful at it, Henry would never in his life face an enemy in battle. But he heaped upon his fellow campaigners rewards that might have been excessive even if something of consequence had been accomplished. Many were knighted, and Henry's boon companion Charles Brandon, son of the William Brandon who had carried Henry VII's banner at Bosworth and been cut down by Richard III, became Duke of Suffolk. More fittingly Thomas Howard, Earl of Surrey, who had fought on Richard's side at Bosworth, was restored to the title that his father had lost there along with his life: Duke of Norfolk. To his chagrin Howard had been left behind when Henry crossed over to France, but therefore had been on hand to take an army north when James IV of Scotland tried to take advantage of Henry's absence by launching an invasion. The victory that he achieved at Flodden, killing not only the king of the Scots but much of the Scottish nobility, overshadowed everything that happened on the continent.

Badly as things had gone in France, military operations were not Wolsey's responsibility, and what he was responsible for had been managed exquisitely well. When the fighting was finished, he took on the job of negotiating a settlement, thereby launching his eventful career in international diplomacy. He managed to put the best possible face on a miserable situation by working out a treaty in which Henry would receive a "pension" in return for staying out of France and was allowed, mainly for face-saving purposes, to retain Tournai as his trophy. The only lasting effect of the entire episode, Henry's emptying of his treasury aside, was the discovery in Wolsey's person of an ideal royal instrument: an able, intelligent, inexhaustibly hardworking minister who was prepared to take upon himself the whole burden of running the government but was always careful to understand what his king wanted and focus relentlessly on giving it to him.

The rewards were dazzling. In 1514 Wolsey was made bishop of Lincoln, then archbishop of York. In 1515 he replaced Warham as lord chancellor and, at the king's request, was given the red hat of a cardinal by a pope made desperate for friends by the failure and disintegration of his league. Somewhat less willingly, Pope Julius agreed also to make Wolsey his legate or representative in England. This last honor contributed to making the new cardinal's stature within the English church greater even than that of the official primate, Archbishop Warham.

As Wolsey gathered more and more reins into his own strong hands, the council declined in importance, Henry remained free to hunt and gamble and otherwise keep himself amused, and nevertheless the government operated at least as effectively as in the past. But the international political landscape began to change dramatically as the warrior-pope Julius II died and was replaced by one of the Medici of Florence, Ferdinand of Spain died and was succeeded by his (and Emperor Maximilian's) grandson Charles, Louis XII died after just weeks of marriage to Henry's beautiful sister Mary and the French throne passed to the vigorous and ambitious young Francis I, and James IV's death at Flodden left Scotland in the hands of his widow, Henry's elder sister Margaret. It fell to Wolsey to deal with all these changes, and he did so with his customary energy. Onlookers marveled at his ability to stay at his desk hour after hour, turning his attention from subject to subject without pausing even to relieve himself. He shared Henry's zest for international power games, for winning for England (and Henry, and of course himself) a place in those games that the kingdom's size and economy did not really justify. Being a player, however, involved him in an unending struggle to extract from a small, simple economy the money needed for a seat at the table. In taking all this upon himself, he made many enemies. He rarely disappointed his royal master, however, or gave him cause for complaint.

Even in the most intimate dimensions of life, Henry VIII could have found little to complain of. His wife Catherine had through two decades of matrimony remained an exemplary consort: capable, virtuous, admired by the people, and unfailingly loyal. If the years and numerous pregnancies ending in dead babies gradually drained away the queen's beauty and youth, Henry was free to divert himself with mistresses. And in his and Catherine's one living child, their daughter Mary, he had a bright, attractive heir who naturally adored her formidable father. By virtue of her position, Mary was growing up with the most brilliant marriage prospects in Europe. She seemed fated not only to wear the English crown but to become, like her mother and her grandmother Isabella of Castile, the wife and partner of some great prince. Her children, Henry's grandchildren, were likely to rule more than England only.

On top of all his other blessings, Henry had the inestimable advantage—one that fit beautifully with his increasingly grandiose conception of his own place in the world—of happening to rule at a time when the curious idea of the divine right of kings was becoming fashionable across much of Europe. The emergence of this notion was understandable as a reaction to the bloody instability of recent generations, and as an expression of the widespread hunger for law and order and therefore for strong central government. But it gave crowned heads a justification for turning themselves into despots with no obligations to anyone. It fed Henry VIII's inclination to think of himself as a quasi-divine being whom heaven intended to be all-powerful and had endowed with the wisdom to decide all questions. He did not have to look far, in the first decades of the sixteenth century, to find scholars eager to assure him that it lay within his authority to overthrow centuries of law, tradition, and precedent.

The effects of so much good fortune were, perhaps inevitably, tragic. Henry remained lord and master of everyone around him for so long, and became so accustomed not only to doing whatever he wished but to making everyone else do as he wished and being applauded for doing it, that he lost contact with the commonplace realities of human experience. Power corrupts, as Acton famously said, and a generation into Henry's reign there was beginning to hang over him the stench of corruption, of something like spiritual death. He was slipping into the special realm of fantasy reserved for those deprived too long of the simple truth even—or especially—about themselves. In ancient Greece or Rome he might have declared himself a god. Living in Christian England on the threshold of the modern world, he had to settle for being treated like a god.

Throughout the first half of his reign, from the 1513 war in France onward, the Crown's worst problems had been financial. To some extent this was a function of the times: revenues were inadequate to needs in all but the most prudently managed kingdoms, and as a rule Henry was little worse off than the kings of France, his wife's father in Spain, or even the imperial Hapsburgs. In any case his blithe assumption that the whole wealth of England was his to dispose of as he wished, that somehow money would always be available for whatever he wanted to do, meant that in practical terms the state of the treasury was not his problem but Wolsey's. Time after time the cardinal had to search out new ways of keeping Henry and his wars, his diplomatic intrigues, and his many amusements afloat. When the seemingly endless demands for new taxes reached intolerable levels, popular anger was always directed at Wolsey, never at the king.

But as the twentieth anniversary of his coronation approached, Henry found himself up against a problem that had nothing to do with money and that he could not possibly ignore because it was entirely of his choosing. It would become the defining challenge of his life and his reign—would come to be known, with good reason, as "the king's great matter." There were two elements to it, and there is no way for us to know which came first. One was the sad fact that Queen Catherine had become a rather dumpy little middle-aged woman whose childbearing years were clearly behind her. The other was Henry's passionate infatuation, obvious to the entire court as early as the spring of 1526, with the dark-eyed, swan-necked young Anne Boleyn, whose years as a lady-in-waiting at the court of the French king had given her an elegance and self-assurance that not even the grandest noble ladies of England could rival. Soon Henry was confiding to certain intimates, and then to anyone who might prove helpful, that his conscience—his regal and therefore exquisitely sensitive conscience—was suffering painful doubts about whether Catherine was actually his wife. Perhaps these doubts first entered his head because he wanted Anne and she, having seen her own sister become the king's mistress only to be discarded, would not give herself to him. But it is not impossible that Henry's doubts came first, and that they were not in fact doubts at all but a growing conviction that he had no queen and therefore was free to choose one. At which point he would have looked around until his attention settled on his former mistress's sister, now lady-in-waiting to his wife and as bright a jewel as his court had ever contained.

However it began, Henry's struggle with his conscience soon ended in what was, by his reckoning, a victory for truth and justice. What settled his mind was what Leviticus said in the Old Testament: "If a man shall take his brother's wife, it is an impurity: he hath uncovered his brother's nakedness: they shall be childless." That seemed conclusive: Henry's marriage to Catherine had violated the law of God, and ever since the two of them had been paying the price. If not precisely childless, they were certainly sonless. God was displeased not because of any wrong that Henry had consciously committed but because in the innocence of childhood (he had been thirteen when his father arranged his betrothal to Catherine) he had been made the victim of others' mistakes. It was not his right but his duty to put Catherine away. She could remain a member of the royal family as Dowager Princess of Wales, honored and comfortable and freed from the horrors of incest with her loving brother Henry. If their daughter became thereby a bastard ineligible to inherit the throne and possibly unmarriageable—well, such an unfortunate situation was bound to have regrettable consequences. The important thing was that he had uncovered the truth while there was still time to put things right.

Certain formalities had to be attended to first. Henry's marriage to Catherine had been made possible by a dispensation issued by Julius II. Everything would be resolved if the current pope, Clement VII, declared the marriage null. There seemed no reason to expect difficulties; relations between the English and the papal courts had long been excellent, and annulments of royal marriages were, if not exactly common, far from unheard of. Wolsey, when he turned his attention to the situation, focused on the prospect of marrying his master to a French princess—on the part that such a union could play in achieving the great pan-European peace that had long been the overriding objective of his diplomacy. On a more personal level, Wolsey had reason to want to be rid of Queen Catherine. She had long criticized his grandiose style of living—palaces more immense than those of the royal family, platoons of uniformed retainers, pomp and ceremony everywhere he went—as so inappropriate to his clerical state as to constitute scandal.

Inevitably, and for all we know to his complete satisfaction, Wolsey set about to make it happen.

THE ORIGIN OF THE TUDORS

WHY HAD HENRY VIII FOUND IT ADVISABLE, BEFORE GOING off to make war in France, to pull his cousin Edmund de la Pole out of prison and have his head cut off?

Because de la Pole had royal blood, obviously. And because his claim to the throne was quite good enough to rival Henry's. (He was the grandson of the Elizabeth of York who had been Edward IV's sister, whereas Henry was the son of Edward's daughter of the same name.) But could Henry, with his mountainous self-assurance, really have been *that* insecure about his hold on the throne? Could his bluster have been a mask behind which a very ordinary and frightened man was keeping himself hidden?

If it is perhaps a little too easy to say so, it is also not impossible. Especially if Henry knew the story of the strange path by which his father had come to the throne, as he certainly must have.

One of the threads out of which that story is woven goes back to 1422 and the premature death, of natural causes, of one of the most brilliantly successful of all the Plantagenet kings, Henry V. He was the second king in the so-called Lancastrian branch of the Plantagenet dynasty—his father, Henry IV, had overthrown their cousin Richard II—and in nine years on the throne he had risen to the heights of achievement and prestige. The most famous of his triumphs, the one that put him among England's immortals, came at Agincourt, where his outnumbered invasion force defeated the armies of France so conclusively that the French king acknowledged him as his heir and gave him his daughter, Catherine of Valois, in marriage. All this became the seedbed for decades of tragedy when, at age thirty-four, Henry suddenly died, leaving a beautiful widow with all the normal appetites of a healthy twenty-one-year-old woman and a son who, at the age of nine months, became King Henry VI.

This is where Wales becomes part of the story and the Tudors enter

English history. Wales was, at this time, less an integral part of the kingdom than a conquered territory—a remote, alien, somewhat mysterious, and definitely distrusted province. Only those few Welshmen whom the English occupiers deemed to be sufficiently loyal were allowed to hold office, carry weapons, or even live in towns. In the years before his father's death, while holding the title of Prince of Wales and spending time there, the future Henry V had seen that this state of affairs could not continue. He began to take selected Welshmen into the royal service. Among those so favored, we know not why, was the young squire Owain ap Meredudd ap Tudur—Owen son of Meredith son of Tudor. The word *squire* indicates that he was regarded as being of gentle origin, which in fact he was, his family having been important in North Wales until its participation in a failed rebellion brought it to ruin. Almost nothing is known of the early manhood of this Owain, who might have been expected to take the anglicized surname Meredith but somehow became Owen Tudor instead. It is possible though not proved that he served with Henry V in France and even fought in Greece. After the king's death he was kept on as a member of Queen Catherine's household staff, and what happened from that point forward makes clear that his was an adventuresome spirit.

The paternal uncles of the infant Henry VI, governing in his name, decided that allowing the nubile dowager queen to remarry was out of the question. If she took a husband of inferior rank, the dignity of the House of Lancaster would be compromised. Any bridegroom from the higher nobility, on the other hand, might become dangerously powerful simply by virtue of being Catherine's husband and therefore stepfather to the king. And so they decreed that any man who dared to marry Catherine before her son was old enough to give informed consent would be deprived of his lands. This removed from contention all those members of the nobility who might have been pleased to take the queen to their beds, but not at such a price. The field was left open to contenders as obscure as Owen Tudor, who owned no land and therefore had nothing to lose. By the late 1420s he was a member of the queen's inner circle, holding the suggestive title of keeper of the wardrobe. His position must have made him a familiar, if unimportant, face at court.

No one knows how it happened, but at some point around 1430, when both were about thirty years old, Owen and Catherine married.

Their union was kept secret, at least from the powerful men who dominated the boy-king's Council, until Catherine's death in 1437. (The cause of death was described in Catherine's will as a "long grievous malady, in the which I have been long, and yet am, troubled and vexed by the visitation of God." One cannot but wonder if this mysterious affliction, so ambiguously but intriguingly described, may have been the mental illness that had figured importantly in the life of her father, King Charles VI of France, and would recur in her son Henry VI). By the time of Catherine's death, she and Tudor had had four children. One was a daughter who died young, her name unknown to history. Another was a boy who bore his father's name, entered the church at an early age, and would live and die in deep obscurity as a member of Westminster Abbey's community of Benedictine monks. The two other sons, the eldest, were named Edmund and Jasper.

The widowed Owen had to flee when he was discovered to have broken the law by marrying the queen. He was captured and incarcerated in Windsor Castle, but after a year he was released and a comfortable place was found for him at court. Obviously there were no hard feelings on the part of his stepson the king.

Rather astonishingly, Henry VI's uncles now had in their care two boys who on their father's side were Welsh commoners, on their mother's were related to the royal family of France, and were also, and more important, half-brothers of England's king. The pair had no inheritance, no place in the world in spite of their lofty connections, and the council must have had some difficulty deciding what to do with them. For five years after their mother's death they were raised in a convent whose abbess was a member of the de la Pole family. Then, at about the time when they must have been entering adolescence, they were brought to court, where they continued to receive the kind of training and education appropriate to the elite. What happened next pivoted on the fact that Henry VI, himself a young adult now, was a remarkably sweet-natured individual (a saint in the opinion of some) who had grown up without siblings or a father and throughout childhood had seen little of his mother. He embraced the Tudors as brothers and made himself their patron. Eventually he did more than that. In 1552, as they were coming of age, Edmund and Jasper became the first Welshmen to be raised to noble rank in England. The former became Earl of Richmond, the latter Earl of Pembroke. Extensive holdings of land and castles came to them with their titles.

King Henry's next gift to his brothers would prove to be even more momentous. He gave them—and that is not putting the matter too bluntly—the girl Margaret Beaufort, still a child, an orphan of royal blood and the richest heiress in the kingdom. Like her cousin the king, the little Lady Margaret was a great-grandchild of that John of Gaunt who had been one of the numerous sons of King Edward III, bore the title Duke of Lancaster, and became the progenitor of the Lancastrian Plantagenets when his son usurped the throne and became Henry IV. In addition to a succession of wives, John of Gaunt had a mistress, Catherine Swynford, with whom he produced a litter of bastards called the Beauforts after the castle in which the first of them had been born. After being widowed, Gaunt married Catherine. Their children were legitimized by King Richard II, whom Henry IV would one day dispossess, imprison, and probably murder (most likely by starving him to death). The Beauforts, though specifically barred by Richard from ever inheriting the throne, made good use of their lofty antecedents: the only daughter became the wife of an earl, one of the sons became a cardinal of the church and for a time the most powerful man in the kingdom, and the offspring of another son would include a queen of Scotland, the dukes of Somerset, and (the only child of one of those dukes) Lady Margaret Beaufort.

Among the brutish aspects of life among the English nobility in the Middle Ages was the practice, hallowed by custom, according to which the minor heirs of deceased nobles became wards of the Crown. In theory this was a way of protecting orphaned children and preserving their inheritance until they came of age. In practice it was an opportunity for plunder. Kings could keep all the income from their wards' estates, which almost inevitably, the kings being chronically short of money, led them to maximize short-term revenues and do nothing to maintain the value of the property in question. Alternatively, kings could sell or give wardships to third parties, who would likewise be motivated to squeeze as much money out of them as quickly as possible. Worst of all, wardship brought with it the right to give—which often meant to sell—an heir or heiress in marriage.

Her enormous inherited wealth made an extremely valuable commercial asset of Lady Margaret, who was not quite one year old when her father died, a probable suicide. When only a few years old she was "married" to John de la Pole, the almost equally young son of the powerful Marquess of Suffolk. Suffolk was later accused of plotting to put his son and Margaret on the throne—striking evidence of just how potent and dangerous a possession the child could be. He was murdered in consequence of this, and the marriage was annulled when Margaret was nine. Some two years later the king made her the ward of Edmund and Jasper Tudor jointly. Rather than merely looting her estate or selling her off to the highest bidder, the brothers quickly made maximum use of this opportunity, and of the king's friendship. Margaret became Edmund's wife. (Her onetime fiancé de la Pole went on to marry a daughter of the House of York, with tragic consequences for his descendants.) The wedding took place no later than 1455, the year of Margaret's twelfth birthday. Rather horribly, she was pregnant by the middle of 1456.

Because Henry VI was not only weak, passive, and inept but at times deep in the grip of psychosis (for months at a time he would speak to no one and have to be carried from place to place), the young Tudor earls had little opportunity to enjoy their good fortune. The king had a Plantagenet cousin, Richard, Duke of York, the descendant of yet another son of Edward III, who was the richest and most powerful magnate in the country, ambitious, aggressive, suspicious, and easily offended. This cousin clashed not with the king (it appears to have been nearly impossible to rouse Henry out of his serene indifference even during his periods of sanity) but with Henry's French queen, Margaret of Anjou, a tigress every bit as ferocious as York himself. They fought not for the crown, which York never claimed for himself until the final weeks of his life, but for custody of the king's person and therefore control of policy. Their struggle sparked the long conflict that Walter Scott would, centuries later, name the Wars of the Roses (the red rose being a symbol of the House of Lancaster, the white rose representing York). By the standards of history it was not a terrible conflict. Towns were not destroyed and only rarely pillaged, the countryside was not ravaged or the economy greatly disrupted, and most of the population was left entirely undisturbed. Though the fighting went on for decades it was only intermittent, with far more days of peace than of war, and though there were savagely bloody battles they were usually limited in scope. But it was a time when barons and dukes and even kings were still expected to lead men into battle, to kill and be killed. All the branches of the royal family were inexorably drawn in, along with the nobility, and the toll on their numbers was cumulatively painful. Ultimately the great Plantagenet dynasty would annihilate itself in a long orgy of fratricide.

The Tudors were involved from the start, and prominently so. By 1455, long-standing conflicts for dominance in Wales had become part of the national struggle. Edmund Tudor, the Earl of Richmond and husband of Margaret Beaufort, was dispatched to Wales to take control on King Henry's behalf. He was almost immediately engaged in fighting, capturing Carmarthen Castle, being taken prisoner in the autumn of 1456, and dying suddenly (possibly of wounds, possibly of disease) shortly after his release. Three months later, at Jasper Tudor's big stronghold of Pembroke Castle at the southwestern corner of Wales, Margaret gave birth to a boy who was given his uncle the king's name and inherited his late father's title of Earl of Richmond. The birth was not only difficult but damaging to the young mother, leaving her incapable of bearing additional children. She was all of thirteen years old.

The next quarter-century was turbulent, and the two earls—first Jasper, but then his nephew Henry while still a child—were involved in the turmoil. Within a few years of Edmund's death, Jasper helped to arrange his sister-in-law's marriage to Henry Stafford, second son of the Duke of Buckingham. Somehow it came to pass that Lady Margaret left her son at Pembroke Castle when she went off to her latest husband. Jasper by this time was established as what he would remain as long as his half-brother lived: the king's and queen's most resourceful, energetic, and passionately faithful supporter in a conflict with the House of York that grew ever more savage as the cost in lives mounted. From start to finish it was a seesaw affair, and immensely complicated. The Duke of York was driven out of England in 1459, taking refuge among his partisans in Ireland. The following year he returned at the head of an army at the same time that his young son Edward, Earl of March, was leading an invasion of his own from France. King Henry was captured by the Yorkists in 1460, Margaret of Anjou fleeing first to Wales and then to Scotland, but on December 30 of that year York lost his life in a skirmish. His head, mockingly adorned with a paper crown, was put on public display.

This might have been fatal to the Yorkist cause if not for the fact that the duke's eldest son and heir, Edward, not yet twenty years old, was already a bold and determined military leader with no hesitation about carrying on the fight. On February 3, 1461, at Mortimer's Cross in the Welsh borderlands, this new Edward, Duke of York, thoroughly whipped an army, part of which was led by Jasper Tudor. Among those fighting on the Lancastrian side was Jasper's father, Owen, still soldiering in spite of being sixty years old or more. He was captured and taken to the town of Hereford, where, upon learning that York had ordered his execution, he was heard to say that "that head shall lie on the stock that was wont to lie on Queen Catherine's lap." After his death a madwoman placed his head at the top of a set of stairs in the market square, washed off the blood, combed its hair, and surrounded it with more than a hundred lit candles. Jasper, having escaped, made his way back to Wales. Early in March the Duke of York took possession of London and was proclaimed King Edward IV. Immediately thereafter he set off for the north, gathering as many men as he could along the way. At Towton, just south of York, nearly a hundred thousand men fought one of the most terrible battles of the late Middle Ages. Defeated, King Henry and the queen fled with their small son Edward to exile in Scotland. All of England and Wales thus fell into the hands of a new Yorkist king who was still only nineteen years old.

Jasper, already in exile, was soon attainted as well, meaning that he was deprived of his title and all his properties. Many of his Welsh possessions were given to the Yorkist Sir William Herbert, and along with them came custody of the fatherless, essentially motherless four-year-old Henry Tudor. The child was taken into the Herbert household, where he would spend the next nine years. The Herberts raised him as a member of their family, eventually making plans to marry him to one of Sir William's daughters. He was in fact a prisoner, however, and his estates had been given to King Edward's greedy and unstable younger brother George, the Duke of Clarence.

Jasper spent the 1460s trying without success to organize invasions of England, staging guerrilla-style raids into Wales where his family history and outsize personality made it easy for him to muster support, and conducting a kind of shuttle diplomacy on behalf of Margaret of Anjou and her hapless husband King Henry. Jasper's stature as brother of the exiled king of England and grandson and nephew of French kings assured him of a respectful reception in the courts of Brittany, France, and Scotland. His tirelessness and willingness to take risks—he would come ashore in secret, muster enough men to capture and burn a Yorkist outpost, and then disappear before the authorities could respond—made him the kind of folk hero about whom ballads were sung. Nearly a decade of this, however, accomplished nothing. All the leading Lancastrians remained exiles, dependent upon the willingness of foreigners to support them in a cause that seemed increasingly hopeless.

Then, with astonishing abruptness, everything changed and changed again. In 1469 the mighty Earl of Warwick, the head of northern England's powerful Neville family and known to posterity as "the kingmaker," broke with Edward IV. He and the king's chronically dissatisfied brother Clarence defected to France, where they won King Louis XI's support for an invasion that in 1470 caught Edward badly off balance and forced him to flee to the continent. Henry VI was freed from the Tower of London, where he had been in confinement since being captured four years earlier, and restored to the throne. Almost overnight Jasper Tudor was again Earl of Pembroke and a rich and powerful personage. He retrieved his thirteen-year-old nephew from Wales and is believed to have taken him to Westminster for introduction to his namesake the king and the mother he is unlikely to have seen since he was a small child.

But the high chief of the Lancastrian cause, Margaret of Anjou, was inexplicably slow to return to England and consolidate the victory, and she still had an implacable and able enemy in the exiled King Edward. In March 1471 Edward launched an invasion from Burgundy, where his sister was the wife of Duke Charles the Bold. He landed in the far north and, after a month on the march, met near London an army commanded by his onetime ally Warwick, whom he defeated and killed. Edward's frontline troops had been commanded by his youngest brother, Richard, Duke of Gloucester, then eighteen years old. Immediately the brothers set off in pursuit of Queen Margaret, who was trying to assemble a new army while simultaneously moving westward to rendezvous with Jasper Tudor and the men he was hurrying to muster. They caught up with her at Tewkesbury, achieving a smashing victory with young Duke Richard again leading the Yorkist van. King Henry's son and heir, the eighteen-year-old Edward, Prince of Wales, was taken prisoner. When questioned, he spoke defiantly and was beheaded on the spot. King Edward and Richard returned to London to reassert Yorkist control there, and within hours of their arrival the helpless and harmless King Henry, a prisoner once again, was murdered. Margaret of Anjou, her fires extinguished by the killing of her son, would spend four years in the Tower and then be returned to France, where she eventually died in poverty.

Jasper fled back to Wales with the Yorkists on his trail, taking his fourteen-year-old nephew with him and trying to make a stand first at Pembroke Castle and then in a smaller stronghold at Tenby. There was no way to avoid capture except by running. The Tudors set out in a small ship for France, but storms forced them into a fishing port in Brittany, at that time an autonomous duchy coveted, and therefore threatened, by the kings of France. Brittany's ruler, Duke Francis II, had had to spend his life in an endless struggle to find counterweights to the pressure exerted by Paris, trying to maintain alliances with England, with the Duchy of Burgundy on France's eastern border, and indeed with any potential source of help. It was established English policy to help Brittany remain independent of France because its north coast was directly across the Channel. Not surprisingly, Duke Francis received the Tudors with every courtesy and display of hospitality: two very useful bargaining chips had fallen into his hands as if out of the sky. King Edward of England wanted Jasper and Henry. Therefore Louis XI of France, a man so devious he was called "the universal spider," wanted them also. The duke saw immediately that, as long as he retained custody of his unexpected visitors, he would have leverage both in England and in France.

The military convulsions of 1470 and 1471, and the battlefield deaths and murders to which those convulsions gave rise, drastically changed Henry Tudor's place in the political firmament. With the killing of King Henry and his son, the House of Lancaster was extinct in the male line. So was the Beaufort branch; Henry's mother had been its last surviving member since her uncle Edmund was killed in the Battle of St. Albans in 1455, her cousin Henry was executed after an unsuccessful raid out of Scotland in 1464, and Henry's brother Edmund was among those executed after finding themselves on the losing side at Tewkesbury. (This litany of bloodshed is typical of what happened to more than a few noble families during this period.)

As Lady Margaret's son, Henry was now the only living adult male who could point to his ancestry in claiming leadership of the Lancastrian party. It was a thin claim all the same, one that for a long time appeared to mean almost nothing. Not even the Tudors themselves—not Margaret, not Jasper, certainly not the boy Henry—could possibly have imagined that in another decade and a half *they* would be England's royal family. Their highest political aspiration could only have been to somehow recover the titles and property that King Henry had bestowed upon them. Until the unexpected death of Edward IV, there would have seemed little chance of even that ever happening.

2

The King's Great Matter

In setting out to end his long marriage, Henry VIII enmeshed himself in an impenetrable tangle of political, diplomatic, religious, historical, and even philosophical complexities. In trying to cut his way through that tangle, he found himself in conflict with what must have seemed almost the whole world: a pope willing to do nearly but not quite anything to avoid offending him, his nephew-by-marriage the Holy Roman emperor Charles V, a thousand years of English tradition, a great many of his best-known and most respected subjects, and indeed a very large part of his kingdom's population. It was by plowing forward in the face of this opposition, by gambling that no one could stop him and responding to every setback by raising the stakes, that Henry had such an extraordinary impact on the world.

For the king himself, the question of his marital status was not difficult at all. The facts of the case were certainly simple enough in his eyes. When Henry was still a mere boy, his father, wanting to preserve an alliance with the royal house of Spain, had arranged his betrothal to his dead brother Arthur's young widow, Catherine of Aragon. Everyone recognized that such an arrangement raised questions—under canon law, sexual intercourse created a blood relationship and marriage to a sister-in-law was tantamount to incest—but these questions had been settled with a papal dispensation, a decree to the effect that in this case the prohibition could be set aside. But Henry had decided, no later than

1527, that the law against marriages like his to Catherine was not man-made but divine, God's own law, set down in the Bible for all to see. It was entirely consistent with Catholic belief for him to assert that not even popes could nullify the explicitly stated will of God. Therefore he and Catherine were not married and never had been.

Only to Henry and the most loyal of his supporters, however, was the situation that simple. Everyone else saw questions, complications—problems. First and most fundamental was the mystery of whether Catherine had actually *been* Prince Arthur's wife. There had been a wedding ceremony, of course, but that alone was not enough, under canon law, to constitute marriage. Physical consummation was required, and the question of whether the union of Arthur and Catherine had in fact been consummated was shrouded in uncertainty. After the wedding festivities the two young people had with great ceremony been put to bed together at Baynard's Castle, an old royal residence in London. Soon thereafter they were sent off to live as man and wife at Ludlow Castle in Shropshire, where Arthur was to prepare to become king of England by participating in the government of Wales, and where he died. From her earliest widowhood until the end of her life, Catherine not merely said but swore under oath—no small thing for a person of her character and strong religious convictions—that she and Arthur had never had intercourse. Not even Henry's most ardent champions ever attempted to deny that Catherine at all times and under the most trying circumstances showed herself to be a person of high integrity, and her credibility is reinforced by the little that is known about her young bridegroom. Arthur is a faint figure in history—the very fact that his contemporaries had so little to say about him raises the possibility that his appearance may have been a delicate subject—but he is reported to have been on his wedding day half a head shorter than Catherine, herself well below average in height. A question inevitably arises as to whether Arthur, who was born at least a month prematurely and appears to have developed slowly thereafter, had reached puberty by the time of his death. On balance it is improbable at best that he ever "knew" Catherine physically.

There were problems, moreover, with the biblical passage to which King Henry attached so much importance: "If a man takes his brother's wife . . . they shall be childless." One of the mentors of Henry's youth, the learned and revered John Fisher, bishop of Rochester, pointed out that nothing in these words indicates that they refer to a *dead* brother's wife. On the contrary, a reader's natural inclination might be to assume the opposite. As for the warning about childlessness, nothing could be more obvious than that Henry and Catherine had a living child, Princess Mary. Henry, clutching at straws, suggested that a mistake had been made when Leviticus was translated from Greek into Latin, so that the word *liberis* ("children") had been incorrectly substituted for *filiis* ("sons"). In an age when all educated people shared a knowledge of Latin and no one could have claimed to be a theologian without mastering it, this argument got him nowhere, having no basis in fact. Leviticus was in any case a peculiar foundation upon which to construct arguments about how Englishmen were supposed to conduct themselves in the sixteenth century. It included many rules, some of them intended for Hebrew priests, to which no one paid the least attention: instruction in the proper way of killing chickens, for example, along with prohibitions against the eating of rabbits and the incorrect trimming of hair and beards. The church had long taken it as settled that the relevance of Leviticus did not reach far beyond the time, place, and people for which it had been written.

Even worse for Henry's case, Leviticus was directly contradicted by another Old Testament passage, one from a book written later and therefore arguably preemptive. Deuteronomy 25:5–7 declared it to be not only permissible but *obligatory* for a man to marry the childless widow of his dead brother: "He shall go in unto her, and take her to him to wife." Failure to do this would mean that the dead brother was "put out of Israel," a deplorable fate, and therefore severe punishment was prescribed for those who did not comply. The straw that Henry clutched this time was the notion that the kind of marriage prescribed by Deuteronomy had been a mere ceremonial matter, and that in any case the Jews themselves had abandoned such practices many centuries before. About this, too, he was proved wrong.

No one saw more problems, or had better reason to see them, than the pope, Clement VII. He is too easily thought of as a kind of immovable and impersonal force against which Henry VIII threw himself uselessly—a sort of oriental potentate on a high golden throne, hurling anathemas down on all who displeased him, too insulated from reality and immersed in his own arrogance to respond understandingly to the needs of mere kings. In fact he was nothing of the kind, and undoubtedly would have been amused to see himself depicted in any such way. Almost fifty when word first reached him of the English king's marital difficulties, the former Giulio de' Medici had been pope for four years and had spent those years sinking steadily deeper into an ocean of troubles the likes of which Henry had never experienced—troubles that must have made him regret ever having been elected. A member of Florence's fabled ruling family, son of a father who had been stabbed to death in his home city's domed cathedral months before his birth, he had been raised by his uncle Lorenzo the Magnificent and grew up to become not only an intelligent and conscientious cleric but, at least by the standards of the Renaissance papacy, a model of responsible behavior. As cardinal-archbishop of Florence he had made himself a force for reform, during the reign of his incompetent cousin Leo X he had been a constructive influence on the papal court, and he then became a supporter of the virtuous Dutchman Adrian VI after losing to him in the election of 1522.

Elected following Adrian's death in 1523, just as the Treaty of London with which Wolsey had hoped to establish peace across Europe was falling apart, Clement was immediately caught up in a war between the emperor Charles and Francis I of France for control of northern Italy. (Not even the best-intentioned popes could keep out of such contests, because as rulers of the so-called Papal States they were themselves among the leading players.) Schooled in the Byzantine politics of Renaissance Italy but not nearly as shrewd or decisive as he needed to be, Clement made the mistake of allying himself with France and therefore shared in the disaster that followed Charles's great victory at Pavia in 1525. The consequences included the most savage sack of Rome in the Eternal City's long and bloody history, the humiliation of the papacy, a rearrangement of alliances, and finally the resumption of war. Until Henry VIII sent his request for a judgment on the validity of his marriage, England had not been a problem for Clement at all. Even after Henry filed his suit, it must have seemed an almost minor matter compared to the multiple nightmares that now faced the papacy: disorder almost to the point of chaos in Italy, the Ottoman Turks' conquest of Hungary and threat to Christian central Europe, and the upheavals resulting from the successes of Martin Luther and other radical reformers.

The Vatican was in desperate need of friends, England had been among its best friends as long as anyone living could remember, and Clement had no reason to want the relationship to change.

King Henry, even as his doubts about his marriage hardened into a determination to be rid of Catherine, tried to conceal from her his plans for securing a divorce. (Henceforth we will follow convention in using the word "divorce" although, strictly speaking, that was not what the king sought. He was asking not for the termination of his marriage but for an annulment, a finding that he and the queen had never been married. Canon law contained no provision for divorce: marriage was forever. But annulments—findings to the effect that a couple had never entered into a valid union—were not at all rare.) The secret, inevitably, was soon out, and when the queen learned of it she was angrier than she had ever been in all the years of her marriage—angrier, even, than when her husband had raised his illegitimate son Fitzroy to the highest rank of nobility, possibly positioning him to inherit the throne. Court and clergy began to pull apart into two camps, one supporting the dignified little woman who after a quarter of a century in England could be faulted for nothing except her failure to produce a living son, the other rallying to the king. The dispute, at this point, was about the marriage only. It had not yet metastasized into an epic struggle over bigger issues.

Henry, characteristically, thought himself entitled to everyone's support because right was so obviously on his side. Cardinal Wolsey, as chancellor, was with the king from the start—from the point, at least, at which it became clear that Henry was not going to relent. Catherine blamed Wolsey for everything, believing that the idea of a divorce had originated with him rather than with the king, and that his motive was revenge for her criticism of his lavish way of life. About this she may very well have been wrong; in years to come Henry and Wolsey would both state publicly that it was the former who had first raised questions about the Spanish marriage. Though both would have had reasons to lie (Henry to assert his independence, Wolsey to show that he was never more than the king's good servant), it seems unlikely, all things considered, that they did so. Henry was neither a habitual liar nor a very good one, appearing rather to believe his own most outlandish untruths, and his years in royal service had shown Wolsey that he had little to fear from the queen's disfavor. He would have needed no better reason to go along with the king than simple self-interest—his expectation that a divorce could be obtained without great difficulty and would please his master. It is entirely plausible that he simply saw an opportunity to turn the king's latest brainstorm to political advantage. He would be stunned to learn that Henry had already decided on a second wife, and that his choice was a member of Queen Catherine's entourage.

Behind all these intrigues stood the slender figure, still fascinating and more than a little mysterious after four and a half centuries, of Anne Boleyn. It is of course impossible to say, especially at such a remove in time, just why the king had fixed his attention on her of all the women available to him both in England and abroad, but her allure is entirely understandable. Though less than classically beautiful, Anne had striking dark eyes, a magnificent mane of dark hair, and an elegant carriage crowned by a long white neck. Her father Sir Thomas Boleyn's position as one of the king's most trusted diplomats had made it possible for him to place Anne first at the celebrated Brussels court of Margaret of Austria, widow of Catherine of Aragon's brother and now Hapsburg regent of the Low Countries, and then in the service of the queen of France, whose friend she became. This background, coupled with Anne's considerable intelligence, set her apart from the other women of Henry's court when the threat of war between England and France made it necessary for her to return home in 1521. She was about twenty-one years old by then, accomplished as a singer and dancer and instrumentalist, by the standards of the English court a paragon of fashion and taste. "No one would ever have taken her to be English by her manners," one observer wrote, "but a native-born Frenchwoman." As for her own aspirations at this point, too little is known to provide a basis even for responsible guesswork. In time she would champion ecclesiastical reform to the point of making herself an enemy of Rome, but this would happen only as it became obvious that she had no friends among the religious conservatives at court and the papal court was not going to clear the way for her marriage to the king. In the early going she was not so much Rome's enemy as Wolsey's, using her growing influence to cut off the cardinal's access to the king.

Her own allurements, combined with her status as granddaughter and niece of dukes of Norfolk, meant that Anne had no shortage of suitors. Her best chances for an advantageous marriage, however, had misfired one by one. A proposed union with the Earl of Northumberland's son and heir, Henry Percy, was blocked by Wolsey for complex political reasons having nothing to do with Anne herself. The cardinal may or may not have been acting on the king's instructions, but in any case his intervention caused Anne to distrust him forever after. By the mid-1520s Anne had seen her sister Mary become the king's mistress only to be pensioned off after a few years, had witnessed her father's elevation to the nobility as Viscount Rochford (whether in recognition of his services or as a reward for providing a royal mistress can never be known), and had found herself crossing the border into spinsterhood. But in 1526, just at the point when Henry was being overtaken by doubts about his marriage to a queen who no longer interested him, he suddenly fixed his attention on Anne to the exclusion of every other woman. In one of the many letters he sent her—letters rendered all the more extraordinary by the fact that throughout his life Henry almost never wrote to anyone else—he confessed to having been "struck by the dart of love." Setting aside the fact that in the eyes of the church and the law he was still a married man, he would not appear to have made a foolish choice. Anne was no giggling girl but a mature and accomplished woman, as worldly-wise a woman as the king had ever known. Nature had endowed her with an acid wit, a razor tongue, and a bold willingness to use both even with the king. Henry, long surrounded by fawning sycophants and female courtiers of limited experience and education, is likely to have found such a woman irresistible.

Be that as it may, from early in the relationship Henry wanted not only to bed Anne but to marry her, to make her the queen and mother of a royal family. It has generally been assumed that their relationship remained unconsummated for years because Anne, having seen in her own family how limited the benefits of becoming a royal mistress could be, refused to yield to Henry's advances. It is entirely possible, however, that he was as reluctant to proceed as she. Despite his posthumous reputation as a bluebeard, Henry was never a man of exceptional sexual appetite. His opportunities vastly exceeded the number of his mistresses, which was almost negligible compared to the tallies run up by other monarchs of the day. Anne herself, when their long courtship was over, would joke unkindly (and dangerously) about Henry's inadequacies as a lover. Where the king's greatest hopes were concerned, it would have been a disaster if Anne had become pregnant before he was free to marry her. At best that could have led only to the birth of another royal bastard. What Henry needed, what Henry wanted, certainly, was a *legitimate* son.

Consideration had been given, in the beginning, to having England's primate, the archbishop of Canterbury, declare the royal marriage null. The archbishop, William Warham, had long been close to the king and was likely to be amenable. But such an approach might not have been found acceptable either in Rome or at the court of Catherine's nephew, the emperor Charles, and in any case Henry wanted not just an annulment but the world's acknowledgment that he was entitled to an annulment. And so in 1527, on Wolsey's advice, he proposed that a special court be convened—in England, though by the pope's order—to consider and rule on his suit. This had to be a legatine court, meaning that the men sitting in judgment would be representatives of the pope, authorized to act with his authority. Henry proposed two such judges. His first choice was all too obvious: Wolsey himself, a logical candidate insofar as he had long been both papal legate in England and the kingdom's only cardinal, and a safe candidate because he was unquestionably the king's man. His second, seemingly almost as safe, was Wolsey's longtime friend Cardinal Lorenzo Campeggio, who was based in Rome but had been made absentee bishop of Salisbury in recognition of his services in representing the English Crown at the papal court. That Pope Clement readily agreed to the appointment of two men so obviously predisposed to favor Henry—that he did so in spite of his own sympathy for Queen Catherine as an entirely innocent victim—is early evidence of just how far this trouble-plagued and uncertain pontiff was willing to go to accommodate the king. Though a Medici and pope, he had little inclination to try to force his will on anyone.

Henry was not slow to give signs of just how far he was prepared to go to get what he wanted. As early as 1527, with Campeggio still months from arriving in England, the king was saying threateningly that he might, if not given the justice he knew he deserved, repudiate papal authority and thereby break the ancient connection between the church in England and its continental roots. The situation was not unique—there had been bitter struggles between kings and popes in the past—but Wolsey knew his master well enough to be alarmed. Both directly and through his agents in Rome, he began warning the pope that Henry was in dead earnest, and that if he were not placated the results could include the ruin not just of Wolsey but of the church in England. "I close my eyes before such horror," he would tell Clement in a pages-long, almost hysterical letter in 1528. "I throw myself at the Holy Father's feet." His appeals must have been one reason Pope Clement continued—though in ways so convoluted and hesitant as to be ultimately self-defeating—to do everything he felt he could to avoid offending the king.

As he waited for Campeggio, Henry began a campaign to get all of England on his side. He was savvy enough to understand that, however invincibly right he knew his position to be, in order to have any hope of carrying his subjects with him he was going to need the cooperation of men whose opinion the people respected. Catherine was a popular queen, much loved for her kindness and generosity and admired for the fortitude with which she had borne the disappointments of her life. Word that she was to be put away because Henry wanted a new, younger wife was already in wide circulation, and it was not being well received. The judgment of learned and esteemed Englishmen could change public sentiment if anything could, and so Henry turned early to two men to whom he had long been close, a pair known not only in England but across Europe. Bishop John Fisher had in the reign of Henry VII been confessor and counselor to the king's formidable mother, Margaret Beaufort, Countess of Richmond, who shortly before her death had urged her newly crowned young grandson to keep Fisher close at hand and heed his advice. Henry VIII himself, early in his reign, had boasted that no other ruler in Europe had a bishop to compare with Fisher—though the fact that in the following two decades the unpolitical and stubbornly independent Fisher was never promoted to a more important see than Rochester suggests that the king's enthusiasm may have had limits. Thomas More was younger than Fisher but already one of Europe's best-known thinkers and writers, author of the sensationally popular *Utopia,* a lawyer-politician whose company the king enjoyed and who had long since risen high in Henry's service. He was a friend of Erasmus of Rotterdam, the greatest exponent of the "new learning" sparked by the Italian Renaissance and a biting critic of clerical misconduct.

Asked for their views on the divorce question, More and Fisher responded characteristically. The cautious and lawyerly More declined to offer an opinion, asking to be excused on grounds that he was not qualified to judge such a matter. This was not the answer Henry wanted, obviously, but he accepted it with good grace. The answer that Fisher gave, on the other hand, must have ended any hopes that Henry might have had of getting through this business without a fight. Catherine was Henry's wife, the bishop declared. To claim otherwise was outrageous. If there had ever been reasons to question how the marriage was contracted, three decades and Catherine's many pregnancies had emptied those reasons of pertinence. This was definitely not what Henry wanted to hear. From that moment John Fisher was the king's most conspicuous adversary and a marked man.

Henry now entered upon the momentous part of his reign. It began with a slow sequence of years—it must at times have seemed an eternity—when all his energy and all his power as king were focused on securing the annulment but were not enough to make it happen. Everything seemed to conspire against him, both at home and abroad. May 1527 brought the previously mentioned pillaging of Rome; Clement VII took refuge in the ancient fortress tomb of Castel Sant'Angelo and soon found himself the prisoner of the emperor Charles, who had neither approved the destruction of the city nor even known that it was happening but did not decline to reap the benefits. On the face of it this was the worst possible news for Henry: the one man recognized across Europe as having the authority to free him from Catherine was now at the mercy of the one monarch who, in addition to being the most powerful on the continent, had committed himself unreservedly to her cause. Nothing connected with Henry's great matter was ever that simple, however. The rape of Rome, though not the emperor's doing, gave Clement abundant reason to hate him. It also underscored Clement's need for allies, and England, lacking as it did the means to pursue territorial ambitions in Italy, had always been a more dependable friend to the papacy than France, Spain, or the German states. Clement's need for support became all the greater when, toward the end of the year, he managed to escape from Rome only to find himself and his court living without furniture in three rooms of a derelict palace in the town of Orvieto. Historians have sometimes assumed that, after Rome fell into Charles's hands, Clement had no choice but to do the Hapsburg emperor's bidding. This is far from certain, and the opposite is not impossible. Clement, when his fortunes were at their lowest, wanted nothing from Charles except his removal from Rome and if possible from all of Italy—above all from Florence, the hereditary domain of the Medici.

No easy solutions were open to Clement. If he overruled the dispensation by which Pope Julius had approved the union of Henry and Catherine a generation before, he would compromise the authority of papal dispensations generally. If on the other hand he failed to do so, or to find some other solution, he risked losing nearly the best friend he had in all of Europe and compounding the problems rising out of the Lutheran revolt in Germany. From the beginning of the divorce case until his death, Clement repeatedly weakened his own position, risking betrayal of the principles by which justice required that the case be judged, in a fruitless effort to placate Henry. In the end the rupture between the two was caused not by obstinacy on the pope's part but by Henry's relentless escalation of his threats and demands even as the weakness of his case became more obvious. That weakness was so fundamental that—regardless of how much fear Charles V may have been able to arouse in the pope's breast—any ruling in Henry's favor would have been an act so transparently cynical as to constitute an indelible scandal. It would have seemed to confirm the worst things that any Protestant firebrand ever found to say about the papacy and its ways.

It was October 1528 when Campeggio arrived in England at last and preparations for a formal hearing could begin. The cardinal had moved northward from Rome in excruciatingly slow stages, so disabled with gout that he could travel only in a litter, in such pain that at times it was impossible for him to travel at all. He was a remarkable man, a legal scholar who had taken holy orders only after the death of the wife who had borne him five children, and an authority on canon law, a qualification rendered especially important by Wolsey's lack of background in the subject. He was known to be honest, fair, and wise in the ways of the world, and if he had often served England as an agent in Rome he had done so without compromising his integrity. The highest possible testimony to his stature is the fact that both sides in the divorce case—Henry and Wolsey as plaintiffs, Catherine and Fisher and others on the defense—initially welcomed his involvement.

Not all the cards were on the table, however. The king and Wolsey were privy to a secret not shared with Catherine and her advisers: Campeggio had brought with him from Rome a document declaring the case to have been decided in Henry's favor. Knowledge of this document, presumably to be disclosed at some propitious moment, bolstered Henry's confidence that everything would soon be settled to his satisfaction. To complicate the situation even further, however, Campeggio also had unwritten instructions, confided to him by the pope in person and not known to Henry or Wolsey. Clement had told him to search for a compromise solution that would make a formal hearing unnecessary and, if no such solution emerged, to delay a final decision by every possible means. With this in mind, Campeggio met repeatedly and at length with Henry, with Catherine, with anyone who might be able to influence Henry or Catherine or help him to do so. He tried every imaginable gambit, starting by assuring the parties that the pope would be pleased to issue a new dispensation correcting any flaws in the one that had permitted the marriage in the first place. This was obviously the last thing Henry wanted. Campeggio suggested to Catherine that she should enter a convent, take religious vows, and so free her husband to marry; the queen replied that she would do so as soon as Henry agreed to enter a monastery. Some of the things that Campeggio allegedly proposed could only have come from a desperate mind. He is supposed to have invited Henry to take Anne Boleyn as his mistress with a promise that Rome would legitimize their children— and to have suggested that Henry commit bigamy, marrying Anne without dissolving his marriage to Catherine. (Martin Luther, opposed to the annulment, would offer the same idea.) He is even supposed to have encouraged the king to ensure the Tudor succession by marrying Princess Mary to her half-brother, the king's illegitimate son Henry Fitzroy, an act of incest that would have stunned all Europe.

The whole affair seemed at times to be in danger of sinking to the level of farce. Henry sent a new petition to Rome, one distinct from the annulment suit, asking for a dispensation permitting him to marry Anne Boleyn in spite of the fact that her sister had, some years before, been his mistress. The issue here was the same as in the divorce: "consanguinity," a supposed blood relationship created by sexual intercourse. Canon law said that, because of his past relationship with Mary Boleyn, Henry was linked to Anne in a brother-sister relationship as real as the one that had joined him to Catherine before their marriage—*assuming that* Catherine's marriage to Prince Arthur had been consummated. If there had been no consummation, the barrier blocking Henry from marrying Anne was actually bigger than any between him and Catherine. It is curious, not to say ironic, that Henry would request a papal exemption in the Boleyn case while adamantly insisting that no pope could grant a similar exemption where Catherine was concerned. Clement quickly and cheerfully granted the king's request, at the same time rendering his own decision worthless by noting that the dispensation could be put to use only if the marriage to Queen Catherine were found to be invalid.

In another irony, that same year Henry's older sister Margaret, widow of King James IV of Scotland and mother of the young James V, secured an annulment of her second marriage in order to enter upon a third. Instead of congratulating her—instead of observing a disapproving silence, for that matter—Henry boiled over with indignation, accusing Margaret of violating the "divine order of inseparable matrimony." It is probably unfair to accuse him of hypocrisy in outbursts of this kind. Whatever his own behavior, however much the standards he applied to others diverged from those he applied to himself, he does appear to have sincerely regarded himself not only as a model of uprightness but as qualified to pass judgment on his inferiors—a category into which he would have put virtually every living human being.

Even so, making every possible allowance for the blindness produced in Henry by his limitless self-satisfaction, the performance he now put on for the benefit of a number of the kingdom's leading personages was nothing less than astonishing. In November 1528, annoyed by public demonstrations of support for Catherine (she was so loudly cheered whenever she appeared that Henry banned the gathering of crowds wherever she was in residence), he summoned to his court an august assembly that included members of his council, representatives of the nobility, and the mayor, aldermen, and other leading citizens of London. To this group he delivered an address much of which was devoted to praise of Queen Catherine, "a woman of most gentleness, humility, and buxomness," as Henry described her. "Yea," he added, "and of all good qualities pertaining to nobility she is without comparison."

"If I were to marry again, I would choose her above all women," Henry declared. "But if it be determined in judgment that our marriage is against God's law, then shall I sorrow, parting from so good a lady and loving companion." This was Henry VIII in one of his least attractive, most shameless manifestations: Henry the virtuous, the entirely innocent, ostentatiously shedding tears as he stated his determination to do what was right (and coincidentally most convenient to himself) no matter how deeply it pained him. It is difficult not to find him guilty of rank hypocrisy in this case.

He told the assembled dignitaries that he was prepared to accept the decision of the upcoming tribunal whatever that decision turned out to be—good evidence of his certainty that Campeggio and the pope were going to give him what he wanted. At the conclusion of his monologue, suddenly angered by no one knows what—a skeptical or sardonic look somewhere in the audience, or a sudden stab of fear that the tribunal might not end as he expected?—Henry began shouting about how he would respond if contradicted. "There was no head so fine," an ambassador observing the proceedings reported him as saying, "that he would not make it fly." This side of Henry would not be much in evidence for another five or six years but would thereafter become dominant.

The last little farce of 1528 came when Henry turned again to the thankless task of trying to make Rome and England and the wide world understand that his position was above rebuttal or reproach. He circulated among the kingdom's leading men—the nobility, the senior clergy, other persons of quality and note—a kind of petition stating that his suit should be granted because his marriage was void.

When it came back to him, it bore exactly three signatures.

One was that of the Duke of Norfolk. He was Anne Boleyn's uncle.

Another was that of the Viscount Rochford. He was Thomas Boleyn, Anne's father.

And the third was that of Anne's brother George, still a very junior courtier.

It was a humiliation, but Henry did not react. Perhaps he thought it didn't matter all that much. The new year would bring the tribunal at last, and the result of that, surely, was in the bag.

THE SPANISH CONNECTION

WEARING AS HE DID A CROWN TO WHICH HE HAD ONLY the most questionable of claims, from the start of his reign the first Henry Tudor had reason to worry about the place of his new dynasty among Europe's royal families. Acceptance was essential and could not be taken for granted. It was therefore a great coup, a breakthrough, when just a few years after the Battle of Bosworth Henry's diplomats were able to arrange the betrothal of his little son Prince Arthur to a daughter of the royal house of Spain.

The arrangement offered Henry a connection to one of the most brilliant political partnerships in history, that of Ferdinand II of Aragon and Isabella of Castile. Their 1469 marriage had united Spain's leading Christian kingdoms, and they spent the years that followed in a hard, ultimately triumphal campaign to drive the Moors—Muslims originally from North Africa—out of the southern kingdom of Granada. (Less gloriously, the pair also used the Inquisition to expel all Jews and Muslims who refused to convert.) Ferdinand and Isabella both belonged to the ancient house of Trastámara (and were also, incidentally, descended from King Edward III of England through his son John of Gaunt). At the time of their wedding Ferdinand was king of Sicily (which his father had given him) as well as Aragon, and in due course he began competing with the kings of France for domination in Italy.

Isabella was the most impressive woman of her time. She was a strong, skillful ruler and an active field commander in the war for Granada, along the way giving birth to the son and four daughters with whom she and her husband planned to perpetuate the Trastámara dynasty and link it to other important kingdoms. Having secured for their son and heir no less a bride than the daughter of the Holy Roman emperor, and having compounded this success by arranging to marry one of their daughters to the emperor's son and heir (two other daughters went to the Portuguese royal family), they could afford to send their youngest child, the Infanta Catalina, across the water to England. It was of course a strictly political arrangement. For Ferdinand and Isabella it was a way of keeping England from allying with France, their archrival. For the Tudors it was a confirmation of legitimacy.

More than a decade had to pass, however, before Arthur and Catalina would be old enough to live together as man and wife. Both children received superb preparation for the careers that lay ahead, but hers was the more impressive. In 1492, the same year that Christopher Columbus came upon the New World during a voyage to India financed by the Spanish Crown, the six-year-old girl rode with her parents and sisters and brother into the newly conquered city of Granada. The reunification of Spain being thus complete, Isabella was able to give full attention to readying her youngest child for a future as queen of England. The result, when the time came for Catalina to journey to her new home and become Catherine, Princess of Wales, was a refined, strong-minded young woman who knew the classics, knew history and the works of the church fathers, could converse easily in Latin, and had been taught by her mother to take her duties seriously and always be loyal to her husband and the church.

During the years of waiting Spain had gone from strength to strength. Its vast New World empire took shape with astonishing speed after Columbus's first voyages, promising to generate fabulous quantities of wealth. In 1494 the Treaty of Tordesillas drew a north-south line down the length of the Atlantic Ocean, conferring all the non-Christian lands on one side to Spain and those on the other to Portugal (which thereby acquired a Brazil that was probably not yet known to exist). King Ferdinand continued to pursue his ambitions in Italy, having so much success that in 1504 he added Naples to his string of kingdoms. All this was rendered nearly meaningless, however, by the death of his and Isabella's newly married son, John, at nineteen. The prince's bride was pregnant at the time of his death (which the royal physicians blamed on too much sex, the actual cause probably being tuberculosis), but the child was stillborn. Suddenly everything that Ferdinand and Isabella had built, the glorious legacy of the Trastámara, stood to be inherited by the family of their eldest surviving daughter's husband. For Ferdinand in particular, the thought that the fruits of his achievement would fall to the German Hapsburgs was almost too galling to be endured.

When the ship bearing Catherine arrived in England in 1501 at the end of a grueling four-month voyage through heavy seas, Henry VII insisted on violating Spanish protocol and having an immediate look at her face. He was delighted by what he was shown: an exceptionally pretty and self-possessed little lady, nearly if not actually a storybook princess, obviously a fitting progenitor for a mighty line of kings. He spent heavily to make the wedding a grand public event, a declaration that the Tudors had arrived. Throughout many of the festivities Catherine was escorted by her bridegroom's precocious brother Henry, who at age ten was Duke of York, earl marshal of England, lieutenant of Ireland, and warden of the Scottish marches and appears to have attracted far more notice than Arthur. Shortly thereafter the newlyweds were sent to their new home at Ludlow Castle, where Arthur, still only fifteen and destined to remain forever an indistinct presence in the chronicles of his time, died within a few months. The cause of death was possibly a mysterious disease called the sweating sickness that had only recently appeared in England, or possibly tuberculosis or influenza. Catherine, too, became gravely ill but recovered to find herself a widow—by her own testimony and that of her principal lady-in-waiting a virgin widow—at sixteen years of age.

Life became difficult for Catherine. She wanted to return home, but her father-in-law did not want her to go. Henry VII was on bad terms with France at the time, and fearful of losing his alliance with Spain. Never a man to part lightly with money, he had no wish to return the half of Catherine's considerable dowry that Ferdinand had sent with her. And he continued to be impressed with Catherine herself—so much so that he applied to the pope for the dispensation required for young Prince Henry to marry his deceased brother's wife.

By the time the dispensation was delivered in 1504—the year of Queen Isabella's death, which deprived Catherine of her best source of support and counsel—relations between England and France had improved. Now it was Ferdinand who, afraid of an Anglo-French alliance, was determined that Catherine must remain where she was and wed the

English king's son. King Henry began to regard her as a nuisance and to treat her disgracefully. She wrote home to complain that she had lost her servants, her clothes were in tatters, and she barely had enough to eat. When Prince Henry became fourteen, the age of consent under canon law, he signed a repudiation of his betrothal. He did so, we can be sure, on the instructions of his father, who had become interested in marrying him to a Hapsburg. Wherever the repudiation originated, it was a blow to Catherine, whose health began to fail. She was making preparations to depart England when, in the spring of 1509, the king sank into his last illness and died. In short order—it must have seemed a miracle—the new king declared his intention to marry her, possibly on the advice of his Council but just as possibly because he was a youth of healthy appetites, had no experience of women and no other marriage prospects, and preferred taking an attractive bride whom he already knew over waiting for whatever his diplomats might bring home from the international matrimonial sweepstakes. He was almost eighteen, Catherine twenty-three.

It was a good marriage for a long time. Catherine showed herself to be a devoted wife, sometimes begging Henry to change his mind but never defying him and certainly never speaking ill of him. She even personally embroidered his shirts. He for his part was clearly delighted to have a partner who was fully his equal in intelligence and learning and had far more knowledge of the world. To the extent that there was trouble, it came from Catherine's father. Ferdinand by this time was a sour and scheming old man, devoid of any reluctance to exploit and deceive even his own daughter's husband. In 1511, taking advantage of Henry's eagerness to make war on France, he allied their two kingdoms in the Treaty of Westminster. He joined the subsequent invasion of France only long enough to grab the little Kingdom of Navarre for himself. Having accomplished that, he made a separate peace, leaving Henry alone, exposed and looking like a fool.

Back in England, meanwhile, Catherine was serving capably in the post to which her husband had named her before his departure: that of "rectrix and governor of the realm." Not long after Henry's return, when four hundred Londoners were on the verge of being executed for rampaging in the streets and pillaging the homes and businesses of foreigners, she remained on her knees in front of the king until he granted clemency. In such ways, and with her piety and unassuming demeanor, she was becoming a beloved public figure. No one had ever heard of her doing a dishonest or cruel or selfish thing.

In spite of her father, her family connections were growing in value. Old Ferdinand, a lifelong lecher and father of many bastards, remarried late in life in the hope of generating another legitimate son. He succeeded, but the child lived only hours. And so in 1516, when Ferdinand himself died, the Kingdoms of Aragon and Castile and Sicily and Naples, plus New Spain in America and much else, all passed to young Charles of Hapsburg, the son of Catherine's apparently insane elder sister Joanna. When Charles's paternal grandfather, Maximilian of Hapsburg, died not long afterward, Catherine found that her nephew now loomed over Europe as ruler of the Spanish dominions *and* Holy Roman emperor.

She had only one real problem: children, or the absence thereof. In the first year of her marriage Catherine gave birth to a daughter, but the newborn died. A year after that she gave birth to a son, named Henry after his father, but after fifty-two days he died too. There followed in short order a miscarriage and then another short-lived boy. In February 1516 Princess Mary was born, a healthy girl with her parents' red-gold hair. She was followed by one or possibly two more miscarriages, the last of them in 1518, at which point Catherine entered her late thirties overweight and menopausal, the girlish beauty of her earlier years a memory. Henry by contrast was barely thirty, a fountain of vitality. In 1519 his dalliance with a woman named Bessie Blount resulted in the birth of a healthy boy. In traditional fashion the child was named Henry Fitzroy—Henry son of the king. Though his mother was sent off into a respectable arranged marriage, his royal father took pleasure in having a son at last.

He took pleasure in his daughter, too, an appealing and clever child, small like her mother, eager to please her mighty sire. There is little to suggest that the king was, at this point, greatly troubled about not having a legitimate male heir. The succession problem, to the extent that there was perceived to be one, appeared to be solved in the early 1520s when Princess Mary was betrothed to her cousin the emperor Charles. It delighted Henry to treat the Holy Roman emperor as his son, to give him advice (unwelcome though it may have been) on statecraft, and to think that one day, as a result of this glorious union, some grandchild of his would rule much of the world. It came as a shock to Henry and Catherine when, in 1525, Charles withdrew from the engagement. They should not have been surprised: Mary was only ten years old, Charles twenty-five. He had decided to marry another of his first cousins, the daughter of the king of Portugal. She was grown and brought with her a big dowry that he desperately needed.

Henry, in his anger and disappointment, lashed out at his wife and his daughter, using Fitzroy as a weapon. At age six the boy was brought out of the shadows, shown off at court, and made Duke of Richmond (that old Tudor family title), Duke of Somerset, and Earl of Nottingham. He was given lands commensurate with his new status, and there was talk that his father intended to make him king of Ireland, perhaps one day even king of England.

Now it was Catherine's turn to be furious, and for the first time in a decade and a half of marriage she allowed the court to see that she was angry with her husband. Henry was untroubled. What Catherine thought had never mattered so little to him. Their marriage was dead, England's connection to Spain and the Hapsburgs dead with it, and the stage set for all the troubles to follow.

3

Frustration and
Embarrassment

Getting rid of Catherine of Aragon was far from the only thing that
Henry and Wolsey had to worry about as the 1520s drew to a
close. They had a kingdom to manage and a not very happy one at that.
Its propertied classes were fed up with the Crown's incessant demands
for money, and the population at large was staggering under the effects
of several consecutive bad harvests. Relations with the continent required a good deal of attention as well. From January 1528 on into the
following year, England in alliance with France was at war with the empire of Charles V. It was a peculiar conflict in the way that most wars of
the time can seem peculiar to us: a tentative, distinctly limited affair in
which England sent no soldiers across the Channel to do any actual
fighting. But the stakes were not trivial. One of the ideas behind allying
with France and helping to finance its armies was to isolate Charles and
force him to join in the great pan-European peace that had long been
Wolsey's dream. Less loftily but no doubt more importantly from
Henry's perspective, the alliance was intended to weaken Charles to
such an extent that the pope need have no fear in annulling the king's
marriage. Thus much of Europe was at war at least partly because of
Henry's "great matter."

But alliances and treaties meant so little in sixteenth-century Europe
that one almost wonders why anyone considered them worth making.
War against Charles V meant war with a Hapsburg empire extending

from Hungary to Spain and on to the New World, but where England was concerned the most important part of that empire was the Duchy of Burgundy, which included the so-called Low Countries or Netherlands, today's Belgium and Holland. In the 1520s, the empire having grown far too unwieldy for any one man to manage, Burgundy was ruled by a regent, Archduchess Margaret of Savoy. Margaret, like Catherine of Aragon, was Charles V's aunt. But she was the sister of Charles's late father Philip the Handsome and therefore a true Hapsburg, whereas Catherine was the sister of Charles's mother and therefore without Hapsburg blood. In her youth Margaret had been married briefly to Catherine's brother, the short-lived Prince John. A bond of affection had formed between the two women; the archduchess supported her sister-in-law unreservedly and thereby made herself one of Henry's most troublesome adversaries. But money can talk more loudly than family ties, not least when whole national economies are at risk. Margaret and her imperial nephew found themselves faced with the hard fact that England, a leading source of wool for Burgundy's textile industry, was indispensable not only to the duchy but to the empire. North of the Channel, Henry and Wolsey came up against the other side of the same coin: if cut off from its markets in the Low Countries, a worrisome part of England's economy would be in danger of collapse. The situation posed political dangers as well: merchants, manufacturers, and workers were not likely to passively accept the loss of their livelihoods for the sake of a distant and arcane war with little real meaning for any of them (if indeed it made much sense in any objective way). Nor could the royal treasuries on either side afford to lose the revenues brought in by tariffs on the wool and cloth trade and the taxes that the industry generated. A deal was quickly cut to permit the wool and cloth trade to continue as if there were no war. The leading powers of the time never indulged in total war. The defeat of the enemy, not his total destruction, was always the point.

King Francis of France, as charmingly amoral a rogue as was to be found in all of Europe, was prepared as usual to pursue whatever opportunities he could find regardless of alliances or declarations of war. He had reason to hate Charles V, who had imposed a humiliating peace after destroying his army in the Battle of Pavia in 1525 and taking him prisoner. Charles still held Francis's two sons as hostages, and the strength of the Hapsburgs in Italy remained the one great obstacle to the expansion south of the Alps that Francis would lust after all his life. Nevertheless Francis now saw advantages in trying to come to terms with the empire, if only for the time being. If doing so might involve the betrayal (not for the first or last time) of his old friend Henry of England, that was a price that Francis, even more than most of the rulers of the day, would never hesitate to pay. And so by early 1529 representatives of France and Spain (Francis's mother and Charles's aunt Margaret prominent among them) were meeting to negotiate a peace. The English were not invited, and Wolsey was alarmed at finding himself excluded: the treaty being discussed would unite the two great continental powers, leave England without allies, and mean the ruin of everything he had been trying to achieve. Henry was little less troubled: by making peace with France, Charles would escape his isolation, and would be free to make himself the ally and patron, if perhaps not quite the master, of the pope.

Henry's only hope was to secure his annulment before France and the Empire came to terms. A new field of opportunity suddenly appeared to open up when, in February, word arrived of the death of Pope Clement. Henry went quickly into action, instructing his agents in Rome that everything possible should be done to secure Wolsey's election. He had attempted this same thing on earlier occasions; long before deciding to repudiate his marriage, he had seen the advantages of placing an Englishman on the throne of St. Peter. That Wolsey himself felt any compelling desire to become pope is not at all clear; his exalted position in England appears to have satisfied even his voracious appetite for power. But things had never gone as badly for him as they were going in 1529, and he seems to have sensed that unless he seized the papacy his career, even his life, might be over. So he prepared to campaign as never before. Henry, meanwhile, was telling his agents that if Wolsey's election proved impossible, they were to prevent the election of any of the several possible candidates answerable to Charles V. But then fresh news arrived: Clement was not dead at all, but only very sick. Several weeks passed before he recovered sufficiently to resume his meetings with England's representatives in Rome. The senior member of the embassy, Stephen Gardiner, was a youngish priest-courtier of the sort that had for centuries played a central role in the government of England. Earlier

Gardiner had served as Wolsey's secretary and had won the king's favor by energetically supporting the case for the annulment. Now, having traveled to Italy on Henry's behalf and accomplished nothing, he was desperate for a success of some kind to report back to England. To the papal court he repeated Wolsey's warnings that Henry, if thwarted, might ally himself with the reformers who were tearing the church apart in Germany. Audaciously, he urged Clement to consider the consequences for his own soul should he die without having given Henry the justice to which he, as king, was entitled. The pope, as he unfailingly did when pressed in this way, offered sincere but useless assurances that he wished to be as helpful to the English monarch as it lay within his power to be.

Henry and Wolsey were growing desperate too. Blocked in Rome, and frustrated by how badly their proxy war with the empire was going (the supplies of gold they were sending to France were not preventing Charles from winning one military victory after another), they once again focused their hopes on the tribunal for which Cardinal Campeggio had been sent from Rome months before. All was in readiness for the hearing—the trial—that Campeggio was still under secret orders to delay by every possible means. The king's case had long since been ready. Catherine, too, with the assistance of English advisers including Bishop John Fisher and canon lawyers sent from Flanders by Margaret of Savoy, had made extensive preparations. In the course of doing so, however, Catherine had lost whatever hope she originally had of receiving an impartial hearing. From Wolsey she could obviously expect nothing. And Campeggio, she now feared, was so eager to accommodate the king and had been so entangled in Wolsey's machinations as to be no longer capable of independent judgment. And so, early in March, arguing that the tribunal lacked the authority to hear the case and could not be expected to proceed without bias, she sent a letter asking Clement to recall the question to Rome. The pope, around whose neck the case now hung like a rotting corpse, did nothing in response. Catherine's appeal had no effect on Henry's determination to move forward, Campeggio could offer no justification for further delay, and on May 28 a license for the tribunal to begin its business was issued under the king's Great Seal.

The tribunal met for the first time three days later at Blackfriars

Abbey in London, a full seven months after Campeggio's arrival in England. It remained in session for a month, producing drama of the highest order. On June 18, the first day on which Catherine's representatives were expected to appear, the queen arrived in person. She repeated the complaints that she had already directed to the pope, telling the legates that their proceedings were inherently illegitimate and she herself was at a hopeless disadvantage, and that she therefore intended to offer no defense. She demanded that Wolsey and Campeggio send the case back to Rome.

When she and Henry were ordered to appear on June 21, both did so, the king no doubt eagerly and with high expectations, the queen under protest. The few accounts of that day's proceedings differ as to whether the king or the queen spoke first, but they agree about what was said. Henry delivered an oration, a reprise of the things he had said earlier to the dignitaries assembled at his court. He had asked the pope to commission a tribunal, he said, not because of any fault in Catherine—again he rhapsodized about what a good wife and queen she had always been—but because the promptings of his conscience left him with no choice. Perhaps because he knew he was rumored to be a mere pawn of Wolsey in this matter, more likely to assert Wolsey's ability to serve as an impartial judge, he claimed that from the beginning he had proceeded not on but against the cardinal's advice. To the extent that he had followed the counsel of anyone, he said, it had been that of his confessor and of certain learned (but unnamed) bishops in England and France. He repeated his transparently absurd assertion that nothing would make him happier than a finding in favor of the legitimacy of his marriage, saying again that he intended to accept the tribunal's decision whatever it turned out to be.

Wolsey's contribution that day was to announce that he and Campeggio had found against Catherine's protest, so that the case would not be returned to Rome—not, at least, by them. He assured all assembled that he was in no way prejudiced against the queen and wanted nothing except a just resolution of the case. Campeggio must have struggled to follow the proceedings; his knowledge of English was so limited that since his arrival he had had to communicate in French and Latin.

At some point, possibly before Henry gave his speech—though it makes a better story to assume (as Shakespeare later would) that she acted in response to what the king had said—Catherine rose from her chair, crossed the room to where Henry sat, and dropped to her knees before him.

"Sir," she began in the accent that had not left her in a quarter-century in England, "I beseech you to pity me, a woman and a stranger, without an assured friend and without an indifferent counselor. I take God to witness that I have always been to you a true and loyal wife, that I have made it my constant duty to seek your pleasure, that I have loved all whom you loved, whether I had reason or not, whether they were friends to me or foes. I have been your wife for years. I have brought you many children. God knows that when I came to your bed I was a virgin, and I put it to your own conscience to say whether it was or was not so. If there be any offense which can be alleged against me, I consent to depart with infamy. If not, then I pray you do me justice."

It was at least as much a challenge as an appeal. Catherine waited for a response, but Henry said nothing. Finally she stood, a short, stout woman, aging and careworn but totally in control of herself, her dignity anchored in the knowledge that she herself was descended from kings of England and was the daughter not only of a powerful king but of a great queen. After bowing deeply in Henry's direction she made for the exit. When an attendant attempted to call her back, she paused and spoke again. "I never before disputed the will of my husband," she declared to the silent chamber. "I shall take the first opportunity to ask pardon for this disobedience." With that she was gone, ignoring further demands for her return. Neither on that occasion nor at any other time did the king attempt to contradict Catherine's assertion that she had been a virgin on the day they were wed.

Catherine refused all future summonses to appear or to send representatives, and the tribunal declared her "contumacious" for doing so. The hearing therefore unfolded as an entirely one-sided affair, with the king's attorneys arguing his case and receiving no rebuttal. Basically that case rested on three main points: that the marriage of Arthur and Catherine had in fact been consummated (unproven at best); that the dispensation permitting Henry to wed Catherine had been obtained under false pretenses (the evidence for this complicated claim was even less impressive than the witnesses who testified to Prince Arthur's alleged boast, the morning after his wedding, that he had spent a hot night "in the midst of Spain"); and finally that a document produced by Catherine to prove that her father had known her first marriage to be unconsummated was a forgery (extremely improbable, and if true not possibly decisive). Weak as the king's position was, the fact that his was the only case being presented must have heightened Henry's expectation that the matter would soon be brought to a satisfactory conclusion. Poor Campeggio, largely dependent upon Wolsey and others to explain what was being said by the attorneys and witnesses, must have wondered how he was going to avoid making a final ruling. He wrote to Clement, plaintively adding his voice to those asking for a recall of the case to Rome.

On the mainland of Europe, meanwhile, the ground was shifting in ways that Henry could not have welcomed and must have cost Wolsey sleep. On June 21—the day of Catherine's challenge to Henry—the forces of the empire met a French army at Landriano and routed it. This was the second time in four years that Charles had inflicted a devastating defeat on Francis in Italy, and it convinced the French king to push the talks then in process forward to completion. The resulting Peace of Cambrai, signed on August 3, left Italy under Hapsburg control. The triumphant emperor, a canny diplomat as well as one of the best generals of the day, wisely began dealing not only gently but magnanimously with the pope, allowing his return to Rome and the rebuilding of the city's ruined defenses. Clement at this point had every reason for wanting the friendliest possible relations with Charles, who had never been less than respectful in his dealings with the papacy and was its strongest, most dependable ally in the endlessly difficult struggle with the Protestants of Germany. Among the forces drawing pope to emperor was the fact that Charles, once again master of Italy in the aftermath of Landriano, had it in his power to decide whether the pope's Medici kinsmen would be allowed to rule in Florence. Clement declared, not surprisingly, that he was now a committed "imperialist."

Therefore it was probably for a grab bag of reasons—the appeals not only of Catherine and her supporters but of Cardinal Campeggio, the complexities of the case and questions about the authority of the legatine tribunal, the shift in the continental balance of power in favor of the House of Hapsburg—that the pope signed an order recalling the case to Rome. Time would show, however, that this order did not signal any readiness on Clement's part to find against Henry. In any case, the order had not yet reached England when Campeggio adjourned the tribunal and, using the rather far-fetched excuse that the papal courts would not be in session until October and he and Wolsey must adhere to the Roman schedule, announced that it would not reconvene for nearly three months. This fresh delay intensified Henry's and Wolsey's frustration, but it became irrelevant as soon as they learned of what the pope had done.

Henry's life had turned into a series of setbacks and embarrassments. Even before being adjourned, and even in the absence of a defense by Catherine's counsel, the tribunal had failed utterly to advance his agenda. On June 28, one of the several occasions when the queen refused a summons to attend, there occurred an exchange that was almost as damaging as her last appearance to Henry's hopes of winning public opinion to his side. The king himself was present that day, and in the course of the proceedings he asserted that all the bishops of England had affixed their signatures and seals to a document calling for a formal inquiry into his marriage, thereby showing that they regarded the validity of that marriage to be questionable at least. When this was confirmed by Archbishop Warham, John Fisher angrily denied that it was true. "No, my lord, not so," he told Warham. "Under your favor, all the bishops were not so far agreed, for to that instrument you have neither my hand nor seal." Warham, pressed, admitted that he had signed for Fisher and used Fisher's seal, claiming that he had done so with Fisher's consent. "No, no, my lord," said Fisher again, "by your favor and license, all this you have said of me is untrue." He was ordered by the king to say no more. The impression left with onlookers was that the king and the archbishop had resorted to forgery in order to misrepresent Fisher's position, and that when caught out they had denied him an opportunity to put the record straight. In all likelihood there had been no intent to deceive. Old Warham, a man of good character and certainly no clumsy forger, had probably misunderstood Fisher's position before signing for him. In any case the public contradiction of the king's claim to the unanimous support of the bishops did his cause no good.

Fisher himself was deeply frustrated, and before the end of that same day's session he erupted. Henry had said that he wanted a just resolution of the question at issue and had asked his subjects to shed whatever light they could on it; therefore he, Fisher, owed it to the king to state openly what he had learned in studying the matter for two years. He felt obliged to do this (so Campeggio wrote to Rome a day later, describing Fisher's speech as "appropriate" and with that one word revealing a great deal about his own sentiments) "in order not to procure the damnation of his soul" and "not to be unfaithful to the king, or to fail in doing the duty which he owed to the truth, in a matter of such great importance." On the basis of what he now knew, he said, he was prepared "to declare, to affirm, and with forcible reasons to demonstrate to them that this marriage of the king and queen can be dissolved by no power, human or divine; and for this opinion he declared that he would even lay down his life." He described himself as prepared to die just as John the Baptist, in the New Testament, had sacrificed his life by condemning the marriage of Herod and Herodias. These were shocking words, especially from a man of Fisher's stature, a prelate long associated with the royal family. By unmistakable implication, the bishop was drawing a parallel between the king of England and a despot complicit in the death of Jesus. It is especially striking to see Fisher, at this stage in his long conflict with Henry, already speaking of his own death as a possible consequence of that conflict. Evidently he knew the king well enough to understand where this drama was likely to lead.

The time had not yet arrived, however, when refusal to believe what the king believed could result in death. That time would come, but just now it was Wolsey, not Fisher, whose life was in danger.

ENGLAND THEN

A CONSIDERABLE EXERCISE OF THE IMAGINATION IS REQUIRED, even of people who live in England today, to get a sense of what the kingdom was like during the reigns of the first Tudors.

It was economically simple, almost backward, even by the standards of its time. It had little manufacturing aside from the cloth and leather-goods industries that had arisen as offshoots of England's huge numbers of sheep (vastly greater than the human population) and the extraction, still on a minuscule scale, of its rich reserves of coal, tin, lead, timber, and stone. An overwhelming majority of the population grew its own food on land that it did not own, living in cottages that we would regard as hovels. Almost no specimens of the homes of ordinary people survive from the fifteenth century or earlier, because they weren't built to last much longer than their occupants. The walls, typically, were made of webs of interwoven sticks coated with mud or clay. Few houses even had chimneys; smoke from the cooking fires had to escape through holes in the thatched roofs.

Foreigners commented on the filthiness of English homes. The great humanist scholar Erasmus, who as an honored visitor from the continent would likely have entered few houses except those of the privileged, observed more than a generation after Bosworth that "the floors are made of clay and are covered with layers of rushes, constantly replenished, so that the bottom layer remains for twenty years harboring spittle, vomit, the urine of dogs and men, the dregs of beer, the remains of fish, and other nameless filth." The quantities of alcohol consumed (in the form of beer and ale mostly, wine being too expensive for the majority of people) also provoked comment. Bathing was scarcely feasible much of the year, but its absence does not appear to have been much lamented. In England as elsewhere, May was a popular month for weddings because, with winter well past, brides and grooms could be given a scrubbing without undue discomfort or perceived risk. Any odors not removed by a plunge into the nearest stream could be camouflaged, or such was the hope, behind a wedding bouquet.

As with so many aspects of life at the end of the Middle Ages, the extent of literacy is impossible to measure. Schools as we understand the term were uncommon except in cathedral towns and the larger market towns (a category that included any community with a few thousand inhabitants), where reading and even writing were often part of the training of choirboys. It would be a mistake, however, to conclude that illiteracy was nearly universal. The fifteenth century saw a great increase in primary education; it was provided by the parish churches to be found in all but the tiniest villages, by clergy connected with "chantries" (chapels, commonly attached to parish churches, established primarily to provide prayers for the souls of the families that endowed them), and the numberless guilds to which people throughout the kingdom belonged. By the first Henry Tudor's time, elementary schooling of this kind, a grassroots phenomenon neither promoted nor supported by the central government, was widespread. Grammar or secondary schools, though less common, also were spreading and attracting increased numbers of students not preparing for careers in the church.

Nothing worthy of being called medical science existed. The wealthiest classes probably had the worst of it, because they had the misfortune of being able to afford the services of university-trained physicians, whose education was focused on the works of ancient authorities and on acquiring a mastery of astronomy (it being considered essential to understand how the stars and planets affected various sicknesses and the efficacy of remedies). These worthies commonly prescribed without ever seeing their patients, depending instead on the examination of urine specimens. Below them were the surgeons, essentially craftsmen with no more education than, say, carpenters or stonemasons. In 1518 London's surgeons joined with one of their peer trades to incorporate as the royally chartered "Masters or Governors of the Mystery and Commonalty of Barbers and Surgeons." Even their services were generally beyond the financial reach of mere villagers, who were required to make use of folk remedies of which little is known; in all likelihood they were better off for it. Life expectancy was short. Thirty was the portal to middle age, and those who lived to fifty had reason to think of themselves as fortunate—and as old.

It is easy, and a mistake, to think of medieval society as static and unchanging. In fact it underwent steady, sometimes convulsive change. England, from the fourteenth century, was literally transformed by disease. Like all of Europe, but for some reason more than many parts of the continent, England in the late fifteenth century was still staggering from the effects of the demographic catastrophe known as the Black Death. This was not a single epidemic but a series of outbreaks that first struck in 1348 (when it may have wiped out a third of all the people in England), returning in 1361, 1369, 1375, and six more times between 1413 and 1485. It was not one disease, almost certainly, but a combination of bubonic plague, pneumonic plague, septicemia, and finally yet another mysterious and fatal affliction, sweating sickness or "the sweat," which arrived in England in the same year as Henry Tudor's invasion force and may have been brought across the Channel by it. The population, which in the year 1300 had reached a total of approximately six million, fell to about a third of that by 1450 and to perhaps only three hundred thousand in all of Wales. (By way of comparison, more than sixty million people lived in the United Kingdom at the start of the present century.) By 1485 the population was again growing, but as plague, smallpox (never seen in England until 1514), and pneumonia continued to return at unpredictable intervals, the rate of increase was held to perhaps three percent per generation. The deserted remains of hamlets in which everyone had died were still scattered across the landscape, and towns were studded with long-abandoned houses.

Occasional famines, too, were an inescapable part of the experience of the common people. When the population peaked toward the end of the thirteenth century, it did so in part because it had reached a Malthusian ceiling: the agriculture of the day was incapable of feeding more. Even after the demographic collapse, many people lived on the margins of survival, vulnerable to going hungry or even to starving when not enough rain or too much rain caused crops to fail. They responded by deferring marriage until their mid-twenties or even later (the same pattern of behavior would occur in Ireland centuries later, in the aftermath of the potato famine), and this too contributed to keeping the population down.

The consequences were dramatic and far-reaching. Wages rose as labor became scarce, and landowners suddenly faced a shortage of tenants. Serfdom disappeared without being formally abolished: families that for centuries had been bound to the land by the old feudal obligations found it possible to pack up and go, moving to wherever they found opportunities to rent vacant land at attractive rates. Suddenly if temporarily, upward mobility became widely possible. Onetime serfs became free laborers and even tenant farmers, the most industrious of their children could rise to become yeomen, and within a few generations grandchildren of yeomen would be sufficiently prosperous to claim the status of gentlefolk. Landowning families, meanwhile, began converting acres traditionally used for growing crops into pastures for sheep, which required little labor. They found themselves profiting handsomely as a result: Europe, the cloth-making centers of Flanders especially, proved to have an insatiable appetite for good English wool.

Great fortunes were made in the wool trade, but for most people the good times were short-lived. As more and more arable land was given over to sheep and the population slowly resumed its growth, good farmland would again become scarce, wages would fall, and the "enclosures" would become a cause of instability as resentful rural communities demanded that they be stopped or even reversed. The old iron law of population imposed itself once again; agricultural output proved sufficient for the exporting of grain only when harvests were bountiful, and when harvests were sparse those who suffered nothing worse than months on short rations could count themselves lucky. The Crown found itself occupying an uncomfortable middle ground, unable to ignore protests about the enclosures but also unable to balance its books without the income that the tariffs on the wool and cloth trade provided.

The political and economic life of the time is incomprehensible without some understanding of how rare money was, and how valuable. In the fourteenth century the imposition of a poll tax of twelve pennies per person gave rise to the Peasants' Revolt, because twelve pence equaled many workers' monthly wage. Things were not greatly different in the early sixteenth century: more than a decade after Henry VII's death the richest noble in England, the Duke of Buckingham, had a total annual income of £6,045. The incomes of most lords—and there were only about fifty in the entire kingdom—were little more than a fifth, even a tenth, of Buckingham's. The kingdom's five hundred or so knights received on average less than £200 per annum from their lands, but that was usually enough to make them the richest men in their localities. The thousand or so "esquires" (no more than one such personage existed for every ten villages) averaged about £80 annually. Landed income of £10 was enough to keep a family among the gentry, itself only a tiny part of the population. The wages of working people continued to be measured in pennies per day—a *few* pennies per day, and even less when a meal or two came with the job. Cash was universally necessary, however, if only in the smallest denominations. Most houses lacked ovens for baking bread, few people made their own clothes or beer, and so small exchanges of pennies for goods and services were essential to the functioning of even the remotest districts.

As had been true throughout the Middle Ages, land continued to be the primary source of wealth and political power and was concentrated in very few hands. The king had so much land scattered across England and Wales that his income from it, when combined with the duties collected on foreign trade and the fees generated by the royal courts, was expected by the wealthiest prospective taxpayers (who, being human, had no wish to pay any taxes at all) to cover the costs of government except in time of special need—which meant in time of war. The church, taken as a whole, owned even more land than the Crown, possibly as much as a third of all the acreage in England, with most belonging to cathedrals, parish churches, colleges, hospitals, and the like—not, as is commonly believed, to the monasteries. The extent to which this ecclesiastical wealth can be considered scandalous varies with the uses to which it was put, and those uses covered a broad spectrum. Much church income went to provide the population with the only semblance of a social security system then in existence—meals and shelter for those in need, stores of food for distribution when harvests failed, lodging for travelers, care for the sick—and to support a network of schools that included the nation's two universities. Conspicuous sums also went, however, to support those men at the top of the ecclesiastical hierarchy who chose to live in princely splendor.

England was hydrocephalic, its economic, political, and cultural life concentrated in London. By the late 1400s, thanks to its access both to the sea and to the exceptional prosperity and productivity of southeast-

ern England, London had a population in the neighborhood of forty thousand and was one of the leading commercial centers of northern Europe.
It was also growing fast. By the standards of England as a whole (only
Norwich and Bristol had as many as ten thousand residents), London not
only seemed to brim over with wealth but was uniquely cosmopolitan,
crowded with Flemings, Germans, Italians, French, and Spaniards, merchants and bankers and tradesmen most of them, who had come to England to do business. For reasons that are obvious today but baffled the
physicians of the sixteenth century, disease ravaged the city even more
severely than the rest of the country. But despite the appalling mortality
rate, London continued to grow as people displaced from the countryside were drawn to it by the magnetic power of money.

For most of the people of England, London must have seemed scarcely
less remote and mysterious than Rome or Constantinople. Going to the
big city meant going to Exeter, or Leicester or Leeds or York, and for many
even that was a rare adventure. To have seen London and returned home
was to have something to talk about as long as one lived. The great out-
let for those who yearned to see something of the world remained the
pilgrimage routes, of which there were several famous examples in England. The days of traveling all the way to the Holy Land, however, were
as gone as the High Middle Ages.

Though vast inequality of wealth and power was one of the defining
characteristics of the whole society, differences were narrowed by the
fact that even the elites lacked comforts and conveniences that today are
taken for granted throughout the developed world. The landless (and literally almost penniless) peasantry was, aside from the largesse extended
to it by the church, simply ignored. "The people here are held in little
more esteem than if they were slaves," a visitor from Italy observed.
"There is no injury that can be committed against the lower orders of the
English that may not be atoned for by money." That the two million people lumped together at the bottom of such a society might be tempted to
protest when their situation became desperate is hardly surprising. But
they were expected to know their proper place and accept it. Life had
inured them to hardship, and any who even appeared to threaten the
status quo could expect to be quickly and brutally cut down.

4

Radical Departures

If the recall of his divorce case to Rome was an infuriating setback for Henry VIII, it did have one advantage. It could easily be blamed on Thomas Wolsey. Easily but unfairly, because the king had given the cardinal a weak case to work with, at crucial junctures had gone around him in trying to influence the papal court, and had refused to consider compromises that might have put the entire matter to rest.

And if the Peace of Cambrai was a disaster for English foreign policy, one that turned France from an ally of England into an ally of the Hapsburg empire and closed the breach between empire and pope while leaving England isolated, that too was easily blamed on Wolsey. And more fairly this time, because it was Wolsey who had overreached and Wolsey's ambitious strategy that had failed.

What was worst for the cardinal, he was nearly without friends. That Queen Catherine held him responsible for the king's rejection no longer mattered, but Anne Boleyn and her family had, with even less reason, persuaded themselves that Wolsey was not only failing to pursue the divorce with all possible vigor but secretly undercutting Henry's efforts. The nobility had always despised and resented Wolsey for being not only a lowborn upstart but an insufferably haughty one, while the people at large, conveniently for the king, believed him to be at fault for the financial burdens imposed by Henry's wars. In 1525, when Wolsey attempted to levy what he laughably called an "Amicable Grant" to pay for a new continental campaign that the king was determined to launch (it was not a grant at all, of course, but a proposed confiscation of between a sixth and a third of the incomes and movable goods of almost every subject clerical or lay), protests came so close to turning into rebellion that Henry called off both the campaign and the levy. In doing so he pretended that the whole thing had been Wolsey's idea and that he himself had known nothing about it, cheerfully allowing the cardinal to take the blame. Later Wolsey drew both the king's wrath and that of Anne and her family by blocking the appointment, as abbess of the ancient convent at Wilton, of a Boleyn in-law named Eleanor Carey, a woman notorious for sexual promiscuity. The post went instead to the choice of the sisters of Wilton, an old woman known to be "wise and discreet." By doing the right thing, however, Wolsey had given the Boleyns fresh reason to regard him as their enemy, and by allowing the issue to become a royal domestic dispute he had deeply annoyed the king.

As for the world on the other side of the Channel, if the cardinal's many years in command of English diplomacy had won him any real friends there, those friends were, in the aftermath of Cambrai, unable or unwilling to do anything for him. On the contrary, all across Europe there were influential people who, if they were not exactly his enemies, could see little reason to lament his fall.

He had become eminently dispensable, a wonderfully convenient scapegoat. But for Henry, somehow, it was not enough merely to dismiss the man who had served him so faithfully and in most ways so effectively for two decades. The king wanted Wolsey's humiliation—his public humiliation and total ruin. On October 9, 1529, the day the cardinal was opening a session of the Westminster court over which he presided as chancellor, he was suddenly charged with several dozen crimes. Most strikingly, he was accused of violating the laws dealing with what was called praemunire, the interference by foreign courts—which in practice meant the papal court—in English affairs. These laws had been passed in the second half of the fourteenth century, mainly during the period when King Richard II was embroiled in a conflict with the pope, and after Richard was deposed they were almost never invoked though they were also never repealed. By making them his weapon as he now did, Henry underscored what would have been obvious in any case: that in throwing the book at Wolsey he was attacking not only the pope's legate but the papacy itself. He was taking a step the meaning of which could have been apparent only to those few English people who had any real knowledge of what Martin Luther and other reformers were doing in Germany. He was moving toward the separation of the English from the universal church. The fact that he was also destroying the most hated man in the kingdom, a man whose existence had become an inconvenience and whose ruin would deflect criticism away from the throne, was in the great scheme of things almost incidental.

The praemunire charges against Wolsey were true in a strictly literal sense but also absurd. Obviously the cardinal, by accepting his appointment as legate and then using his legatine powers, had made himself officially the pope's man in England; that was the very definition of the job. But all of it had been done with the king's knowledge and consent and often at the king's insistence—Henry had nagged at Pope Leo X to make Wolsey his legate, and at Leo's successors to renew the appointment and finally to make it permanent. For the king to now criminalize the very career that he himself had made possible was little less than an outrage. The cardinal would have had no difficulty in mounting a strong defense, had he chosen to do so. But he knew better than any man that he could have no hope of saving himself by opposing the king. He understood his sovereign's mind, and that resistance could only inflame the royal wrath. And so he surrendered immediately, without hesitation or argument, confessing himself guilty as charged. As the king demanded more and more of him, he continued to give ground. He handed over the Great Seal, and with it the office of chancellor, on October 17. He gave up the Bishopric of Winchester, and the handsome income that went with it, at about the same time. He also gave up his position as abbot of St. Albans, the wealthiest monastery in England. At the king's orders he withdrew to a rural manor house distant from any center of power.

For years Wolsey had been diverting part of his immense income to the creation of a college at Oxford (Cardinal College, it was to be called) and a grammar school in the town of Ipswich, where he had been born to a butcher's wife some fifty-five years before. In 1528 he had asked Pope Clement to permit him to shut down (to "suppress") twenty-nine small and presumably failing monasteries and use their revenues (mainly rental income from farmland) in the endowment of these projects. Assured that the monasteries in question were places "wherein much vice and wickedness were harbored," and eager as always to show as much friendliness to Henry and his chancellor as possible, Clement assented, cautioning only that the displaced monks must not be cast adrift but placed in other monasteries. In a seemingly trivial step that would have vast consequences, Wolsey gave responsibility for closing the monasteries and diverting their income to a resourceful new member of his retinue, a self-made lawyer named Thomas Cromwell. Soon after Wolsey's fall, the seized properties along with the other assets of his schools, which were to have been his legacy, were confiscated by the Crown. Cromwell moved with them as manager, thereby benefiting rather than suffering as a result of the cardinal's disgrace.

And so entered the service of Henry VIII the most remarkable figure of the entire Tudor era. Thomas Cromwell was sui generis—his own creation, like nobody else, about as self-made as it is possible for a human being to be. Born around 1485, the son of a blacksmith who was brought before the local authorities in his home village of Putney so many dozens of times that he must have been a troublemaker and probably was a drunk, young Thomas had grown up without connections, money, or much in the way of education. For reasons unknown he left England while still an adolescent, joined the army of the king of France and went with it to Italy where he may have been in a battle, and got himself hired by a banker in Florence. Later he worked in the cloth trade in Flanders. By the time he returned to England, aged about thirty, he spoke several languages, was an experienced businessman, and apparently had made enough money to set himself up in London and marry a widow of some means. He traded in cloth, became an agent for other merchants, and dabbled in moneylending and the providing of legal counsel. He must have made a powerful impression, because by 1523 he was a member of the House of Commons and a year later a fellow of Gray's Inn, part of the inner sanctum of the legal establishment. What most set him apart was his brainpower and his willingness to try anything. Once, on a business trip to Rome (where he inveigled an unscheduled appointment with the pope and supposedly used a gift of candies to win from him a favor sought by his client), he filled tedious weeks in the saddle by memorizing the New Testament in Latin.

He did not need long to get the attention of the king. His opportu-

nity came when Henry, in attempting to take over the revenues of the
suppressed monasteries, ran up against a legal complication. The pope
had allowed Wolsey to seize those revenues only on condition that they
be used for the endowment of his schools. By any reasonable interpretation of the law, the king had no right to them at all. Cromwell, characteristically, simply swept the problem aside, declaring that he had
"discovered" that Wolsey's agreement with the pope was in violation of
the praemunire statutes. Thus it was the cardinal who had no right to
the money, which therefore—somehow—became the property of the
Crown. As legal theory it may have been nonsense, but it satisfied the
king and no one dared to raise questions. Building on his strong start,
Cromwell began acting as liaison between the disgraced but still formidable Wolsey and the king, showing himself to be adroit enough to
avoid offending either party. Soon he secured a seat in the Parliament
summoned to meet for the first time in November 1529—the one that
would become forever famous as the Reformation Parliament. In short
order he was handling all the Crown's land transactions and overseeing
its many construction projects. His access to Henry attracted clients
eager to pay for his advice and support. There were complaints about his
methods—people said he extorted backroom payoffs whenever he
could—but if he was guilty it did him no harm.

As Cromwell rose, Wolsey continued his decline, surrendering one
by one all the things he had accumulated during his decade and a half of
power. Several years before, in a timely response to mounting criticism,
Wolsey had voluntarily handed over to the king the magnificent palace
that he had built for himself at Hampton Court. This palace was so
much grander than any of Henry's own residences that it had become
an embarrassment, a too-vivid example of the grandeur in which the
cardinal lived. Now, in giving up nearly everything else, he hesitated
only when ordered to sign over London's opulent York Place, soon to be
renamed Whitehall and to provide adjoining apartments for Henry and
Anne Boleyn. He explained that York Place was not his property but the
church's, belonging to the Archdiocese of York, so that he had no right
to give it to anyone. Told otherwise by the king's legal scholars, he
yielded with wry good cheer. "Inasmuch as ye, the fathers of the laws,
say that I may lawfully do it," he said, "therefore I charge your conscience and discharge mine. Howbeit, I pray you, show his majesty from

me, that I most humbly desire his highness to call to his most gracious remembrance that there is both heaven and hell."

Those were bold words to be addressed to Henry VIII, especially by a man who remained desperately hopeful, throughout his final tribulations, of being restored to royal favor. Henry encouraged Wolsey's hopes, periodically sending him little tokens of goodwill. Perhaps he was merely playing with his victim, as a cat will toy with a mouse. Perhaps, in spite of everything that Anne and her father and her uncle the Duke of Norfolk were doing to poison his mind against Wolsey, Henry was not yet certain that he could spare the cardinal. When he learned that Wolsey had fallen ill, he dispatched three court physicians to attend him. "God forbid that he should die!" Henry said. "I would not lose him for twenty thousand pounds."

But Henry had learned many things from Wolsey over the years, and now he was learning from Wolsey's destruction. He was even learning how to get along without Wolsey while making full use of his example. By achieving domination over the administrative machinery of church and state alike, the cardinal had demonstrated how the secular and ecclesiastical dimensions of English life might be pulled together into a single entity entirely subordinate to the Crown. By closing monasteries as a way of filling his coffers, he had demonstrated—Cromwell would soon show that he had understood this lesson best—how to tap a reservoir of seemingly limitless wealth. By not defending himself against ridiculous charges, Wolsey had shown the king how potent a weapon the praemunire statutes could be. By yielding without argument to the king's every demand, he had given Henry what must have been a deeply gratifying demonstration of how infinitely more powerful he was than even the mightiest of his subjects.

Henry was by this time developing a lofty conception indeed of the extent of his authority. On October 26, in conversing with an ambassador newly sent by Charles V, he concluded a monologue about the need for church reform, and the responsibility of rulers to effect reform, by stating that the clergy had no power over laymen except the power, through the sacrament of penance, to forgive sins. It can be difficult to grasp just how astonishing an assertion this was in the Catholic Europe of the 1520s. The word of the church had long been accepted as final in many areas of life, and in an age when religious faith was so nearly universal as to be taken for granted, those areas were widely regarded as more important than the ones under secular jurisdiction. The result was a division of power between church and state, a balance that by Henry's time had been in shifting and sometimes precarious equilibrium for hundreds of years. It had been sustained less by raw political (or military or economic) power than by an enduring consensus on how and for what purposes society should be organized. The papacy if not the church itself would have been extinguished many times over, between the end of the Roman Empire and the start of Henry's reign, except that an overwhelming majority of Europe's people were content to let it continue. Part of the consensus was an understanding, more often assumed than asserted or discussed, that the church must be free to govern itself, and that it was the church's responsibility to bring God and God's word to the people. Henry's comment to the ambassador provides a glimpse into a mind that was ceasing to believe such things, that wanted to move the boundary between church and state drastically in the state's (meaning in his own) favor. Over the centuries many European rulers, in England and elsewhere, had wanted something similar. Virtually all had failed, often paying a high price for their failure. None of those who succeeded had done so to such an extent as to overturn the ancient consensus.

But the world was changing. The foundations of the old equilibrium had grown brittle, and were more eroded than most people imagined. In the north of Germany the revolt of a single Augustinian friar, Martin Luther, had been enough to bring the whole traditional structure crashing down. Timbers were creaking in France and elsewhere. Everywhere people expressed discontent with the wealth and power of the church and its departures from its own standards, though the breadth and intensity of that discontent and the extent to which it was justified are impossible to measure. Throughout Europe, and for varied reasons, the general tendency of the sixteenth century was toward strong central governments dominated by monarchs who inevitably regarded the church skeptically, as a dangerous rival needing to be subdued. In country after country the church was on the defensive, and it would have been so even if the conduct of the clergy had been above reproach. It was under attack both by increasingly powerful princes and by religious reformers of many different kinds with widely differing aims.

Inevitably two of the great issues of the day, the condition of the church and the nature of kingship, became entangled. From an early age Henry had displayed an exceptionally keen appreciation of the powers and prerogatives of kings—exceptional even for the time, and even for a ruling monarch—while simultaneously making a great show of his Catholic orthodoxy and loyalty to the pope. As early as 1515 during a dispute with the clergy, he had angrily declared that "kings of England had never had superiors but God alone." Wolsey had defused that crisis by leading his fellow bishops in submission to the king, and by dissolving a Parliament that was raising unwelcome questions about the mysterious death of an accused heretic while in the custody of the bishop of London. But the idea of limitless royal authority to which Henry had briefly given voice continued to simmer not only in his own brain but in those of the most alienated and ambitious reformers. It also had the enthusiastic approval of some of the most powerful nobles in England, men who hated and feared Wolsey and after his fall directed their hatred at the ecclesiastical system that had produced him. In London and at Cambridge University and port cities like Bristol, those lawyers and merchants and scholars who were embracing the Lutheran ideas coming out of Germany supported this idea as well.

By 1529 those ideas were bursting into print, a still-novel phenomenon made possible by Johann Gutenberg's invention of movable type almost a century before. The year before, two remarkable works had been widely circulated and much talked about in London. The well-named *Obedience of a Christian Man* by William Tyndale, one of the first translators of the Bible into English, claimed for the king as much authority and as much right to the unqualified loyalty of every subject as any tyrant could have wished for. "God hath made in every realm [the king] judge over all, and over him there is no judge," Tyndale wrote. "He that judgeth the king judgeth God; and he that layeth hands on the king layeth hands on God; and he that resisteth the king resisteth God, and damneth God's law and ordinance." To justify these words, which would have raised the eyebrows of anyone familiar with English law and tradition, Tyndale invoked the example of the priest-kings of the Old Testament, chosen by God to rule Israel. Henry read Tyndale's book, possibly with the encouragement of Anne Boleyn, and of course was charmed. "This," he is supposed to have said, "is a book for me and for

all kings to read." Tyndale's time as a royal favorite would be brief:
within a year he infuriated Henry by condemning his efforts to rid himself of Catherine, dismissing the divorce case as the work of the papist
archfiend Wolsey, and rejecting items of church doctrine that the king
was determined to uphold.

Out of Antwerp there came at the same time *A Supplication for the
Beggars* by an English lawyer named Simon Fish. It was a depiction of
the abuses of the church so impossibly exaggerated as to be self-
defeating where credibility was concerned. England was crowded with
paupers, said Fish, because its wealth was being drained away into the
church. England was flooded with women turned into whores by a las-
civious clergy. The orders of friars that supported themselves by begging were draining £40,000 pounds or more out of the economy
annually. (This utterly impossible number rivaled the regular revenues
of the Crown.) Fish's diatribe was of course welcomed by those willing
to use any stick to beat the church, but what particularly pleased Henry
was his insistence that all these terrible abuses must be corrected *by the
king,* the church itself being too sunk in corruption. Henry is said to
have summoned Fish, extended assistance to him and his wife, and
shielded him from prosecution.

The ideas of Tyndale, Fish, and other reformers represented a radical
departure from traditional political thought in England. Certainly kings
had always been exalted above mere holders of high office. Their coro-
nations were quasi-sacramental occasions, centered upon an anointing
with holy oil that made the person of the monarch almost, if not quite,
sacred. From 1066, when William the Conqueror sailed from Normandy to win the English crown, to the first Tudor's capture of the
same crown at Bosworth Field in 1485, successful claimants had offered
the fact of their success as evidence that God wanted them to succeed.
Those who never had to fight for the crown similarly regarded their possession of it as proof of divine favor.

But none of this was the same as saying that kings were God's unique
representatives on earth and must be obeyed in exactly the same way
that God must be obeyed: absolutely, at all times, and in all things. What
the Tyndales and Fishes were preaching, what Henry and other princes
were eagerly professing to believe, required the repudiation of the pre-
vailing thought of the Middle Ages. If it had roots anywhere in the

Western past, they were to be found in the despotism of the Roman Empire and perhaps (as the most zealous reformers liked to claim) in the kings of the Old Testament. It is hard to know what could have motivated it except a burning hatred of the old religion.

For an expression of what was still Europe's living tradition, the tradition that the most radical of the new thinkers wanted to cast aside, one need look no further than to the man Henry chose as Wolsey's replacement in the office of lord chancellor. (The king's great friend the Duke of Suffolk had wanted the post, but the jealous opposition of the Duke of Norfolk made his appointment seem inadvisable.) Sir Thomas More was a prominent exponent of the so-called "new learning" but a traditionalist in every really deep sense—a man who loved and revered the church, England's heritage of individual rights under the common law, and the whole ordering of society that had taken shape in medieval times. He embodied nearly everything that the radical reformers sought to reject. For centuries he would be cast, throughout most of the English-speaking world, as the defender of precisely those things that had to be jettisoned in order for what is best in the modern world to emerge. Henry, by contrast, would long be seen as the man who had liberated his people from those same dark things. Today the truth appears to be very near to the reverse.

Henry, whose opinion of himself had always been grandiose (early in his reign he had boasted of not being able to see "any faith in the world, save in me," so that "God Almighty, who knows this, prospers my affairs"), was by 1529 arriving at the conviction that God intended him to have dominion over every aspect of the lives of his subjects, and that in ruling his kingdom he required the consent of no one other than God. But when on November 3 a new Parliament opened at Westminster, its members heard an opening address by More as chancellor that did not sit at all easily with what the king was coming to believe. Indulging the interest in philosophical questions that had already helped make him one of the best-known humanist thinkers in Europe, drawing upon ideas that he had earlier developed in his famous book *Utopia* and in a biography of King Richard III that would not be published in his lifetime, More invited his listeners to consider the question of where the princes of the world derive their power. His answer, which sounds startlingly modern, was based solidly on the mainstream thought of the preceding centuries. Genuine and legitimate power, More said, comes to the prince not from above but from below, from the community that is governed, "so that his people make him a prince." Society functions as it should when a prince, a monarch, acts in harmony with the will of the people. When on the other hand a prince acts at cross-purposes to what his people believe and want, the result is disorder.

These words were not thrown down as a challenge to the king, who stood at More's side as he spoke them. On the contrary, much of More's speech was a tiresomely commonplace exercise in political flattery. It praised Henry for his wisdom, his mercy, and most pointedly (if perhaps somewhat ignobly) for his ability to see through the schemes of Cardinal Wolsey and cast him aside. Henry loved flattery and easily mistook it for truth, and there is no evidence that he even noticed what More had said about the true source of his power. Nonetheless that part of the speech stands as an unmistakable early signal of just how far apart were the tradition represented by More, a tradition embodied in the Magna Carta and Parliament and indeed in the established relationship between church and state, and Henry's increasingly ambitious view of his place in the world.

It was a clear signal that, even at the start of his chancellorship, More was too far out of step with the king ever to become as powerful or even as useful as Wolsey had been. That the gulf between them was so wide that it would have been better for both if More had never become chancellor.

THE OLD CHURCH

THE ENGLAND OF 1530 CONTAINED SOME NINE THOUSAND parish churches, each a center of community life for the people living nearby. Each church had at least one resident priest, and attached to many were chantries, chapels with their own endowments for the support of additional clergy.

These parishes, along with those of Wales, were organized into twenty-one dioceses, each headed by a bishop or archbishop and supporting a cathedral with its chapter of canons and other clerics. The dioceses, in turn, made up two separate provinces: York in the north with only three sees, Canterbury with eighteen.

Additionally, nearly ten thousand monks and sixteen hundred nuns lived in more than six hundred monasteries scattered across the landscape. Nearly two hundred other houses, many of them situated in cities and towns, were occupied by the various orders of mendicant friars.

The kingdom's only universities, Oxford and Cambridge, were ecclesiastical institutions, administered by churchmen and dedicated chiefly to the education of clerics (many of whom, upon completing their studies, found employment in government or the service of leading men). The church operated an overwhelming majority of the lower schools and virtually every "hospital" (a broad category covering not just treatment of the sick but many charitable functions). Its courts had responsibility for everything from matrimonial law to the probating of wills.

The church was, in short, a massive and all-pervading institution, an essential and conspicuous part of England's public and everyday life. It was so big and so diverse, changing constantly as the society and economy with which it was intertwined changed, that evidence can be found to support almost anything said about it, whether in support or condemnation.

Was its leadership corrupt? Anyone wishing to say so need look no further than the greatest churchman of them all, Thomas Wolsey, archbishop of York, lord chancellor, cardinal, and papal legate. He had a bastard son, Thomas Winter, for whom he secured appointments as dean of Wells Cathedral, rector of several churches, and canon of still others. Together these offices generated annual income of £2,700, more than that of most bishops and many barons. And all while Winter was still a child. But to portray Wolsey as *only* corrupt would be an injustice. We have already seen him intervening to prevent a well-connected woman of bad character from becoming head of an important abbey. He spent years making the law courts more accessible to ordinary subjects and less biased in favor of the wealthy.

Nor was Wolsey's corruption typical. Other men, William Warham and Richard Fox among them, spent long years at the pinnacle of church and royal court without a whiff of scandal, cheerfully leaving the king's service as soon as they became free to do so and devoting themselves exclusively to their ecclesiastical duties.

Was the church the enemy of progress? Did it try, for example, to bar the door against the so-called "new learning" coming northward out of Renaissance Italy? This has often been alleged, but few charges could be more absurd. That the church contained conservatives who felt threatened by innovations such as critical analysis of the ancient sacred texts cannot be denied and is hardly surprising. But such men were not only balanced but outnumbered by the many prominent churchmen—Warham and other bishops among them—whose encouragement and support and own writings caused Erasmus to call England the great hope for the future of European scholarship.

Were the parish priests, especially those in the poorest and remotest districts, an ill-educated and brutish lot? Were the denizens of the convents and monasteries lazy, self-indulgent, and sexually licentious? Human nature being what it is, and considering that we are speaking of tens of thousands of people living under almost infinitely varied conditions, it would be a miracle if some were not. For centuries after the Tudor era it was taken for granted that many or even most were, but the writers who encouraged that assumption had axes of their own to grind. More recent scholarship, the kind that became possible only when sectarian passions cooled, has shown the reality to have been considerably less horrifying.

Anyone relying on movies and television for a depiction of England's bishops and abbots before the Reformation could come to no other conclusion than that their lives were devoted to oppression and denial, to forcing obedience to the most rigid orthodoxy on an unwilling but impotent people and crushing any departure from discredited ways of thinking. But it becomes clear, when one looks closely, that life in England before the 1530s could not have felt like that at all—certainly not for the vast majority of the people. "Heresy" was feared not only by the hierarchy but by people generally. It was feared because it appeared to threaten not just the prerogatives of the institutional church but the structure of society itself, even the meaning of life. But until the religious convulsions of the sixteenth century raised such fears to an unprecedented intensity, extreme measures for the punishment of heresy remained rare. Few English churchmen in positions of authority went out actively looking for trouble, at least where arcane questions of theology were concerned. One way in which Wolsey *was* typical of pre-Reformation English bishops was his lack of interest in searching out, never mind punishing, possible cases of heresy.

The documentary record—even the archaeological record—suggests that the people of England were strongly attached to their church in Henry VIII's time. The era was remarkable for the number of people remembering the church in their wills, endowing chantries, hospitals, and the work of the friars. Ordinary people contributed on an unprecedented scale—and, it must be said, voluntarily—to the improvement and adornment of their parish churches. The guilds that were an integral part of parish and therefore community and family life were not only active and prosperous but growing increasingly so.

Perhaps the most alien thing about England of the early sixteenth century, from a twenty-first-century perspective, is the extent to which almost the whole population believed—really *believed*—what the church taught. The result was not just consensus but something very close to unanimity, with all the advantages (a feeling of security, an immensely strong sense of community) and disadvantages (smugness, intolerance rooted in fear of the unfamiliar) that unanimity can bring. The "one true faith" encompassed not just every walk of life throughout the British Isles, not just all of Europe, but every past generation back to where history dissolved into legend. Few things could be more foreign to the sensibilities of the world we live in now.

England was not intensely anticlerical or anything of the kind. The church saw itself, and taught the faithful to see it, as a family of sinners rather than saints, of pilgrims making their way along the winding road to salvation. Its members generally accepted that in the family of faith, no less than in families of blood, there were drunken uncles as well as loving ones, that some uncles could be loving as well as drunk, and that even when their behavior was unacceptable, even when something had to be done about it, they were still part of the family. This is the spirit that suffuses *The Canterbury Tales:* some of Chaucer's clerical characters are absurd and some are unworthy of their positions, but they are not hated and the disappearance of their kind would be unthinkable. Such an attitude still prevailed in early Tudor times. England was not simply formally Catholic, affiliated officially with Rome; it was a deeply Catholic *culture.*

That culture came early to Britain—rather astonishingly so, considering the island's remoteness from the Holy Land and even Rome. At the end of the sixth century, when Pope Gregory I dispatched missionaries to Britain, he did so less to convert the inhabitants—he knew that many of them had been Christian for hundreds of years—than to make sure that the church already established there did not lose its connection to his own. That almost aboriginal church (sometimes called "British" by historians, more often "Celtic") had first taken root in the third or even the second century, when much of Britain was still a thriving province of the Roman Empire. During the generations following the departure of Rome's legions at the beginning of the fifth century, Britain's first Christians were able to maintain only informal, mainly commercial contact with the outside world. And though they clung with an odd stubbornness to ideas of their own on such questions as the proper dating of Easter, on essential doctrine they appear to have remained entirely orthodox. Recognition that the church was a unitary international community, and that the bishop of Rome was its leader, seems never to have been an issue: Britain was sending representatives to ecclesiastical councils on the continent even when the so-called Dark Ages were at their darkest. After the arrival of Gregory's missionaries, the indigenous church (which was especially well established in southwestern England and western Wales, the places most easily reached by traders sailing from the Mediterranean) was absorbed by gradual stages into the structures introduced by Rome.

By the time the future Henry VIII was born, Roman Christianity extended from the islands beyond Scotland to the islands of the eastern Mediterranean, and from the Atlantic Ocean to the western border of Russia. It was an essential element in Western civilization's understanding of itself, and England had been part of it much longer than it had been a kingdom, longer in fact than it had been "England." The first English diocese had been established in the year 597 at Canterbury (there were dioceses in Wales much earlier), which thereby became the home of the national church. Other dioceses soon followed—London and Rochester in 604, even York in the far north as early as 625.

It was a church with firm core beliefs, but it offered many different ways of living those beliefs—ways expressed, for example, in the very different rules of the various religious orders. It claimed to have been founded by Jesus Christ himself. It taught that Jesus had charged his apostles and their successors with bringing salvation to all the peoples of the world; that the bishops were those successors with the bishop of Rome as their chief; and that, as the instruments of salvation, Jesus had instituted seven sacraments—seven means by which the saving grace of God was conferred upon the faithful. One of these, the sacrament of penance or confession, was anchored in the belief that priests were empowered to forgive sin. Another, the Eucharist, was believed to return Jesus physically to Earth in the bread and wine that only priests could consecrate during the "sacrifice" of the mass. The church taught—and as the sixteenth century advanced would be reviled for teaching—that human beings were endowed with free will, so that they could accept or reject salvation, and that acceptance entailed earning divine favor by doing good and avoiding evil. It taught, too, that even most of the saved were at death not yet worthy of union with God, that to be made worthy they had to undergo purification in a process called "purgatory," and that the process could be speeded by the prayers of the living. It taught that the Bible was the word of God but not the only way of knowing God's will—that the core traditions of the church, teachings passed down orally from the apostles, carried comparable authority.

Of course, none of this could be "proved" on the basis of empirical evidence. All of it lay beyond the reach of scientific inquiry. It could be dismissed as pure invention, even as a conspiracy by which a cynically self-serving clergy had betrayed Christ and gained control over the minds and pocketbooks of Europe, and in due course it would. In the England of 1530, however, almost no one was prepared to see it in any such way.

Not that there was no trouble. There had always been trouble—how could there not be, with the church exercising so much authority at every level of English life? But the worst of it had generally occurred at a high level, with hierarchy pitted against Crown and the beliefs and practices of most people not affected. This happened in the twelfth century, with the murder in Canterbury Cathedral of Henry II's onetime friend and great adversary Thomas Becket. It happened later and in different ways under Kings John, Edward III, Richard II, and Henry IV. These episodes demonstrated that pushing the church too hard could be dangerous, but overall the monarchy more than held its own. Thus it came to be accepted that the king selected England's bishops, subject only to the formality of papal approval. And that the rules for the clergy of Canterbury and York were set neither by Rome nor by the Crown but by the convocations of the two provinces—regular clerical gatherings, divided like Parliament into upper and lower houses and usually dominated by friends of the king.

When Henry VIII set out to obtain the nullification of his marriage, there were already many points of friction between England's religious and secular authorities. Most of these involved old and even tiresome questions: whether cases of slander and libel really belonged in the ecclesiastical courts, whether it was necessary for the church's calendar to allow working people quite so many holidays, whether even holders of minor orders should be able to elude punishment by the civil authorities, how much priests should be allowed to charge for conducting funeral and other services. It can easily seem outrageous, today, that any church should have so much authority over so many things. There is, however, another way of viewing the subject. Twenty years into Henry's reign, the church was the only element of English society with any real possibility of opposing the Crown. Only it stood between the king and absolute power.

As for the king's subjects, no doubt many of them felt aggrieved. Many of them may have thought—and justifiably so—that it no longer made sense for the monasteries to own quite as much land as they did. Probably many of them resented the amounts of English money—amounts that tended to be comparatively trivial, actually—sent every year from England to a distant pope about whom they knew little and cared less. Those living in parishes where the rector was never seen would have understood that the practice of "pluralities," of granting one churchman the incomes of many offices, was much too widespread.

But any notion that the whole system was rotten at its core or was seen as such, or that England's people were eager or even willing to throw it off and start again with something radically new, is without basis in fact. In religion as in politics, the kingdom was in nothing resembling a pre-revolutionary state. A religious revolution, if there was going to be one, was going to have to come from the top down, not from the bottom up.

5

Another Way Devised

It is not at all clear why Henry VIII summoned a Parliament in December 1529. Such assemblies were not routine or regular events in those days. To the contrary, they were extraordinary: Parliaments met only when ordered by the Crown, and kings and their ministers rarely summoned them except when in urgent need of what only Parliament could grant—an emergency infusion of revenue. Under ordinary circumstances the Crown was expected to get by on the money generated by the king's own lands, the courts, and the tariffs, and so there was nothing resembling an annual tax on income or wealth. The calling of a Parliament was invariably a signal that the king was about to do what kings preferred never having to do: *ask* his subjects for cooperation. Such requests always created the danger that Parliament might make itself disagreeable by asking for something in return. Kings generally regarded themselves as fortunate if they could go for years, even decades, without having to deal with Parliament. Members, for their part, could have been excused for responding to a summons with a sense of dread.

Henry was seriously in need of money at the end of 1529, but that had been his usual condition for years, and it soon became clear that he was not intending to ask for more. Instead he and his agents began bullying the Lords and Commons to forgive the loans that Cardinal Wolsey had extracted from them in 1522 and 1523 to cover the costs of Henry's military adventures in France. All together these loans had totaled some

£352,000; that was a crushing sum, and it had fallen most heavily on the merchants and landowning knights and gentry from among whom the membership of the House of Commons was mainly drawn. The members of that house were not happy, naturally, when they learned with certainty what many of them had long suspected, that Wolsey's "loans" had not been loans at all but a confiscation; they were never going to see their money again. But the king's lieutenants had taken care, as usual, to assure that Commons was dominated by pliant and cooperative men—Henry's new lieutenant Thomas Cromwell probably conspicuous among them—and to exclude those who might prove resistant to the Crown's demands. No doubt the members were relieved at not being asked to vote new taxes or loans. In due course Henry got what he wanted: the loans were written off the books.

None of this explains why Parliament had been called. The king didn't really *need* a formal forgiveness of the debt he owed his subjects; he could more easily have simply continued to decline to repay. That he had something more in mind became apparent when other items of Crown business were brought to the members' attention. In the six weeks that it remained in session, after much disputation and considerable difficulty in the House of Lords, Parliament was presented with and ultimately approved three statutes laying down new rules for the clergy. One put limits on the fees that could be charged for the probating of wills, a traditional responsibility of the church's courts. Another specified how much could be charged for funerals. The third imposed restrictions on "pluralism" (the holding of multiple assignments or "livings" by a single churchman), on "nonresidence" (failure to be physically present at a living), and on the involvement of the clergy in trade and farming. Stern and unfamiliar penalties were imposed: a fine of £20 (a sum exceeding the annual income of many gentry families) for obtaining from Rome a license of the kind that traditionally had made nonresidence lawful, of £70 (plus the surrender of all income from the livings in question) for even requesting a dispensation to hold more livings than the new law permitted. These measures were entirely appropriate, being aimed at the correction of real abuses, but the bishops and abbots who made up a substantial minority of the Lords found them deeply objectionable. The problem was not that the hierarchy refused to acknowledge the need for change; many bishops and abbots were by this time imposing reforms of their own where they had the authority to do so, and the Canterbury Convocation was in the process of tightening the traditional rules. The problem, rather, was constitutional: the fact that the secular government—Parliament and the king acting through Parliament—was intruding itself into what had always been the business of the church.

In practical terms, the effect of the statutes would be limited, almost trivial. But the principle upon which they were based—that Parliament could set the rules by which the church operated—was potentially revolutionary. And because the kinds of dispensations that were being turned into crimes came from Rome (the reason for punishing those receiving the dispensations, rather than those who issued them, was that the recipients were within reach of English law), the ultimate target was the papacy. Though we do not know where the idea for this legislation originated—whether in a Commons venting its frustration with clerical practices, or with Henry and his advisers—it could not have been enacted without the king's consent. Frustrated by the failure of his divorce suit, he had been threatening for months to retaliate against Rome. Now he was doing so, albeit in a distinctly limited way that involved almost no risk. As soon as the statutes were approved—certain controversial provisions had to be removed to get them through the Lords—he sent Parliament home. He did not end it, however—rather, he "prorogued" it, declaring an intermission but leaving himself the option of recalling it whenever he wished without having to arrange another election. This suggests that he expected to be needing it again before very long—that he had something more in mind. It suggests as well that he was satisfied with the current membership of the Commons, which had shown itself willing to do his bidding.

Statutes of such limited immediate effect cannot have been intended to precipitate a showdown with Rome. By touching on fundamental constitutional issues, however, they demonstrated that Henry's threats were not empty. He was simultaneously asserting and testing his own strength, taking care not to overreach: when the possibility of closing some monasteries was raised in Parliament and drew a fiery response from Bishop John Fisher, the idea was quickly withdrawn. Meanwhile the king began applying pressure from other directions as well. He got a promise of support for his divorce case from Francis I of France, who had seen early on that it would be better for him if England's royal house ceased to be connected by marriage to the Hapsburgs. Henry's objective continued to be nothing more radical than the nullification of his marriage and the freedom to make Anne Boleyn his wife and with her produce children whom the world would accept as legitimate. When he learned that the emperor Charles and Pope Clement were together at Bologna—actually sharing the same palace, drawing together in the afterglow of the most recent expulsion of Francis's armies from Italy—he dispatched envoys to join them and try to achieve an accord that would include the annulment of his marriage. The talent that he put into this delegation suggests either that his hopes were high or that he was determined to leave no stone unturned to bring the pope around. At its head was the Earl of Wiltshire, who in addition to being one of the king's most experienced and trusted diplomats happened to be the father of Anne Boleyn (which explains why he had recently been promoted from viscount to earl). With him went the new bishop of London, chosen for that post because he had proved himself dependable on the divorce question, along with a clutch of legal scholars and lesser clergymen. One of the most obscure of these would soon emerge as a leading figure of the Tudor century.

This was Thomas Cranmer, an archdeacon and former Cambridge academic who just months before had been living quietly as a tutor and scholar. When Henry had made a visit to the abbey at Waltham and accommodations there were found to be limited, two court officers, the king's secretary Stephen Gardiner and his almoner Edward Fox, were lodged in a nearby house. Gardiner and Fox were priests (we earlier encountered the former as leader of one of the king's embassies to Rome), and at this point both were deeply involved in trying to help the king persuade the pope and the world that he was entitled to an annulment. When they fell into conversation with Cranmer, who happened to be living in the same house, he made clear his support of the king's position and offered an idea that caught their fancy. He suggested that, to bolster his position, Henry should get statements of support from university theologians. When Gardiner and Fox mentioned this idea to the king, he ordered that Cranmer be brought to him at Greenwich. When he had heard Cranmer out—heard his proposal for a shift from the arena of law, where Henry was making no headway, to that of academic debate—the king declared that here was a man who had "the sow by the right ear." At age forty Cranmer suddenly found himself vaulted from rural obscurity into royal service, assigned first to searching for texts supporting the king's suit, then to the Earl of Wiltshire's mission to Bologna. Thus was launched a career that would catapult Cranmer to the top of the hierarchy, change the character of the English church more profoundly than Henry himself could possibly have intended, and take many a strange turn before coming to its literally fiery end.

Thomas Boleyn and his retinue took with them to Bologna a rich array of offerings for the pope if he would see reason as King Henry saw it. From the start, however, things did not go well. Boleyn's suitability for this mission had been questioned—as Anne's father, he had a peculiarly intimate interest in the issues under discussion—but Henry had insisted that no other man could be so motivated to help him achieve his goal. Arriving at their destination, the Englishmen found pope and emperor ensconced together in friendship, Clement's outrage of a few years earlier buried and apparently forgotten. The pope showed himself, as always, to be not only friendly toward the English but eager to offer his cooperation. The generally good-humored emperor, by contrast, was stiff-necked and unyielding. He appears to have been motivated, throughout the long conflict over the divorce, less by affection for his aunt Catherine or concern for the honor of his extended family than by a visceral dislike for Henry, who over the years had shown himself to be a tiresomely overbearing and patronizing uncle-in-law and (during the period when Charles was betrothed to Princess Mary) prospective father-in-law. It is scarcely plausible that Charles cared enough about Catherine in any personal way to put himself permanently at odds with England for her sake; aunt and nephew did not know each other well, he having paid her little attention during his youthful visits to the English court. Throughout his life the long-faced, lantern-jawed emperor showed little inclination to be sentimental about his relatives on either side. When another of his aunts was cast aside by her husband the King of Denmark, he did nothing for her and took little interest in her case. Nor for that matter would Charles show much interest in Henry's continued bad treatment of Catherine after he divorced her and married Anne Boleyn. In fact, the vehemence and persistence of Charles's objections to Henry's divorce are somewhat mysterious. Pride may have been part of it: once he took a position, an emperor could not have wanted to be seen as backing down. The fact that during the years when the divorce was a live issue he had the upper hand over the nettlesome Francis of France, and so had no pressing need for the friendship of England, must also have been a factor. In later years, when his need was greater, Charles would actively curry favor with the English court. Henry for his part would respond positively to Charles's overtures whenever doing so suited his own interests.

Whatever his reasons, when faced with the visitors from England Charles assumed the mask of cold and arrogant emperor. He was offended by the presence of the delegation's leader, the father of the very woman—the "concubine," as Charles's ambassador to the English court called Anne in his reports—who was the cause of all the trouble. When Boleyn tried to speak, Charles brusquely cut him off. "Stop, sir," he said in French. "Allow your colleagues to speak. You are a party to the cause." Boleyn answered in the same language. He had come to Italy, he said, not as a father seeking favor for his daughter but as representative of the king of England, who hoped for the emperor's support but would continue to seek justice whether he received that support or not. In return for his friendship, he told Charles, Henry was prepared to pay him 300,000 crowns—the sum that had come to England as Catherine's dowry—and to support Catherine for the rest of her life in a fashion appropriate to her birth and her status as Dowager Princess of Wales. This proposal gave Charles a new excuse to take offense. He answered that he was not a tradesman and his aunt's honor was not for sale; that the divorce case was now before the pope where it belonged; and that he intended to accept the pope's judgment whatever it proved to be.

Things went more smoothly but no more productively with Pope Clement. Henry had authorized his envoys to offer Clement not only a substantial amount of money—at least as much as they had offered Charles, surely—but England's participation in a crusade against the Ottoman Turks. This last was no small point. Just months before, Sultan Suleiman the Magnificent had carried his penetration of central Europe to the very gates of Vienna, where he had been turned back after encountering not only masses of troops commanded by Charles and his brother Ferdinand but—what may have been more decisive—outlandishly bad weather. It is essential to keep in mind, in tracing the endless intrigues of Charles and Francis and Henry, that they took place at a time when the Turks, having overrun first Constantinople and then the Balkans and finally Hungary, seemed entirely capable of breaking through into Germany, possibly of overrunning the whole of central Europe. Clement was not the first pope to attempt to create a confederacy with which to oppose the Turkish threat and he would not be the last, but it had been generations since such an idea had had the power to pull Europe's leading powers together. In 1530 in Bologna it lacked the power to pull even the pope where he felt he must not go. Boleyn and his troupe returned to England with nothing more substantial than fresh assurances of the pope's goodwill.

Henry meanwhile was pursuing Cranmer's idea of showing learned opinion across Europe to be on his side. His agents, supplied with their master's theological arguments and abundant supplies of cash, were dispatched to the universities of Italy, France, and Germany. What ensued reflected badly on everyone, not least on Henry himself. Even in England, where to his offers of money the king could add an unrivaled power to make good on promises and threats, getting a favorable opinion out of the theology faculties of the two universities proved an awkward business. Fights broke out in Cambridge, and the women of Oxford stoned three of Henry's men. In Italy, where at Henry's request Pope Clement had issued a "breve" urging anyone who was consulted to express himself freely, the search went no better. In the end Henry claimed to have received the support of the universities at Bologna, Ferrara, and Padua, but the process had been so stained with bribery, and the reality of the support was so dubious, that no impartial observer could possibly have taken any of it seriously. In Germany the response was if anything worse: not only the universities in Catholic southern Germany but even the leading radical reformers declared against the divorce. Martin Luther himself, while insisting that the marriage of Henry and Catherine was valid beyond question, suggested that Henry might follow the example of the patriarchs of the Bible and take a second wife. (Even the pope at one point floated such a proposal, later conceding that he lacked the authority to approve any such thing.) None of this was of the slightest use, or interest, to Henry.

The great academic battleground turned out to be France, which had fourteen universities and a king who could always be depended on to fish in troubled waters. Henry's agents had spread out across the land-scape, dispensing money as they went, while Henry himself sought ways to put Francis's support to the fullest possible use. Francis professed his eagerness to help—what he really wanted, as always, was to keep Henry and Charles at each other's throats—explaining however that he dared not act too boldly so long as his two sons, who had been Charles's hostages since the French defeat at Pavia four years earlier, remained in custody in Spain. This was, in effect, an invitation to bribery. Charles wanted two million crowns in ransom. And, Francis having broken virtually every promise he had made in securing his own release, Charles demanded payment in cash. Two million crowns was more than the French treasury contained or could raise. Henry obliged by sending Francis 400,000 crowns (it was a loan, presumably) and allowing him to postpone indefinitely the repayment of a previous 500,000-crown debt. With this Francis got his sons back and, as good as his word for once, he joined Henry in seeking a favorable opinion from the theologians.

But even two kings applying pressure could accomplish little. In Paris months of struggle culminated in the issuance of a supposedly scholarly endorsement, but it was of highly questionable validity. Having been drawn up not by the theology faculty but at Francis's instructions, it had little impact anywhere. Similarly ambiguous results were all that could be extracted from the universities at Orleans and Toulouse, and a final humiliation occurred when a decree favorable to Henry was issued under the name of the university at Angers but repudiated by that institution's theologians. When it was all over, the king claimed to have a number of universities on his side. But the squalid means by which his support had been won were known to everyone, including the church authorities in Rome, who knew also that all the arguments in Henry's favor began with the assumption—unproved, unprovable, and denied by the queen—that Catherine's first marriage had been consummated. Nor were the other side's hands clean: Charles had spent heavily to neutralize Henry's bribes. The episode of the universities petered out in March 1530 when the pope, weary of the squabbling, ordered that nothing more was to be written about the English royal marriage. The scholarly judgments obtained at so much trouble and expense were so compromised that Henry never even sent them to Rome.

Blocked everywhere he turned, Henry by midyear was showing signs of deepening discouragement. According to one of his confidants, he complained of having been deceived into pursuing the divorce and said he would never have done so had he foreseen that it would bring him to this pass. Probably he was missing Wolsey at this juncture and finding himself badly in need of a strong new chief minister. Soon, however, he rallied—not only the Boleyns but the champions of radical church reform had good reason to fear the consequences if England and Rome were reconciled, and so they urged him on. By late summer he was again on the attack, possibly with Cromwell pointing the way. He somehow conceived or was given the idea, for which there was only the murkiest evidence, that a proper understanding of history revealed that no Englishman could rightly be made subject to a foreign court, even the papal court. In September he instructed his agents in Rome to inform the pope of this revelation and search the papal archives for supporting documentation. The ambassadors had never heard of any such principle and so were reluctant to present it to Clement. Their search for corroboration turned up nothing. Henry, meanwhile, the bit in his teeth now, issued on his own authority and without the involvement of Parliament a proclamation forbidding anyone in the kingdom, cleric or layman, to "pursue or attempt to purchase from the court of Rome or elsewhere, nor use, put into execution, divulge or publish anything . . . containing matter prejudicial to the high authority, jurisdiction and prerogative royal of this his [Henry's] said realm." Possibly this proclamation was intended to prevent anyone from protesting to Rome the statutes that Parliament had enacted late in 1529. Possibly it was intended to provide grounds for punishing those bishops, John Fisher most prominent among them, who had already sent such protests. Most certainly it was an act of defiance aimed at the pope, a gesture of a kind not seen before. Vague as it was in referring to "matter prejudicial" to the "prerogative royal," its implication that the church in England was independent of the international church was unmistakable. Not coincidentally, just at this time Henry began to assert that England was and had from distant times been no mere kingdom but an *empire*. He wanted to be regarded as equivalent to those Christian emperors of Rome—Constantine the Great foremost among them—who were supposed to have exercised absolute dominion over state and church.

At the end of September Henry took an even more shocking step. He instructed his attorney general to charge fifteen notable members of the English clergy with having violated the praemunire statutes by dealing, in the discharge of their ecclesiastic duties, with Cardinal Wolsey. The concept of praemunire had always been somewhat vague, and in the century since their passage the statutes had almost never been applied. Therefore the accused must have had difficulty understanding precisely what crime they were charged with. The general idea, however, was clear enough and brutally simple: Wolsey had broken the law by serving as a legate accountable to the papal court in Rome—his literal guilt could hardly be questioned, he himself having admitted it as soon as he was accused—and therefore anyone who had done business with Wolsey as legate had to be equally guilty. By extension, anyone involved in the administration of England's ecclesiastical courts was now subject to punishment in spite of the fact that those courts had been, for clergy and laymen alike, an integral part of life in England as far back as the records reached. In terms of simple justice the whole proceeding was even more ridiculous than the original praemunire charges against Wolsey. Even if there were reasons for eliminating the ecclesiastical courts (not even the king was suggesting any such thing—the courts performed essential functions and would continue to do so long after England's separation from Rome), to retroactively criminalize their operations was contrary to common sense.

The shabbiness of the whole proceeding was further apparent in the fact that almost all of the accused men (eight bishops and three abbots among them) were conspicuous opponents of the divorce. John Fisher was one of them, at the center of the fray as always. Being charged in this way must have been frightening all the same. Praemunire was a weighty offense: lesser treason, punishable with loss of freedom and possessions. And the difficulties of presenting a defense, already overwhelming with the king driving the prosecution, were compounded by Wolsey's decision, almost a year earlier, to throw himself on the king's mercy and hope for the best. In fact, Wolsey *was* treated with something like leniency after he submitted. Though expelled from the government and deprived of his most richly remunerative offices, he remained archbishop of York, traveled to York for the first time since becoming the city's primate a decade and a half before, and was making plans for a grossly belated but grandiose consecration ceremony there. But his acceptance of guilt created a presumption that his colleagues must also be guilty.

At least some of the accused—Fisher without question, probably others as well—would have defended themselves rather than follow Wolsey's example. And their defense would have been substantial, even if not successful in terms of the final judgment produced. Perhaps for that reason the matter never came to trial. Cromwell, in corresponding with Wolsey, reported that a trial was not going to be necessary because "there is another way devised." This is intriguing: another way had been devised for accomplishing *what*? The answer, almost certainly, is that by this point, October 1530, Henry had decided not to fight the church on the issues but instead to undermine its ability to resist. The way to do that—hit upon, in all likelihood, by the increasingly influential Cromwell—was to frighten the leaders of the church so badly that they became incapable of resistance. Convicting fifteen clergymen of lesser treason for doing nothing more criminal than carrying out their traditional duties would have been an impressive step in that direction. But before the fifteen could be brought to trial, someone—no one knows who with certainty, but again Cromwell is the best guess—came up with a more ambitious idea, one whose breathtaking scope would give it vastly greater impact. *The kingdom's entire clergy,* the church itself in effect, would be accused of praemunire. The idea appears to have been settled on by October, but then set aside to be sprung on the churchmen in the new year. Meanwhile Henry was postponing and postponing again the reconvening of Parliament. It was obvious to all that he had *something* in mind but wasn't yet ready to act. Fisher and his fellow defendants were let off with heavy fines.

Also in October, in a step providing further clues to his thinking, Henry called together a number of leading lawyers and clerics and presented a question for their consideration. The background to his question was a recent action of the pope's. Clement, warned repeatedly that Henry was prepared to act autonomously unless Rome nullified his marriage and no doubt weary of being bullied, had issued an edict stating that no one was to do anything about the divorce or a possible royal remarriage until the papal court issued its decision. To the lawyers and clerics he had assembled, Henry now posed the following: in light of his recently improved understanding of history—the insights enabling him to see that popes had long ago usurped rights belonging to English emperors and that no Englishman should ever be accountable to any external authority—would it not be permissible to ignore the pope? Couldn't the archbishop of Canterbury, primate in England for nearly ten centuries, proceed independently to set aside Henry's false marriage and allow him to take a legitimate wife?

The assembly discussed the question, which it must have found unsettling. Then, evidently assuming that it was being consulted in good faith by a king seeking to do the right thing, it delivered its answer. No, it said, Henry could do no such thing, and neither could the archbishop. This response was inherently uncontroversial: it arose in straightforward fashion from what virtually every European had understood for centuries about how Christendom worked and was organized. When the laws and governance of the church were at issue, the last word belonged to Rome.

Again Henry was blocked. And this time he was blocked not just by a faraway pontiff whom he had never seen but by some of the most learned and respected men in England. His options were narrowing. He could accept a humiliating defeat and yield, abandoning the idea of taking a new wife. Or he could teach his subjects to take him more seriously. Again it came down to a question of fear. If he were to get his way, people had to be afraid to deny him. He had to give them reason to be afraid.

That has to be why he embraced the idea of charging the whole clergy with praemunire. It also has to be why, more than a year after Wolsey had been exiled to the north of England, he was suddenly arrested, charged with high treason (a crime punishable with death), and ordered to return to London and meet his fate.

THE ROYAL HORN OF PLENTY

ONE THING ABOVE ALL ELSE WAS ESSENTIAL TO ANYONE WHO wanted to make his mark in the England of Henry VIII: *access*. Access to the king himself. Intelligence, courage, ability, sound judgment—such gifts were no less important than they are today, but they could have only a limited effect unless displayed before and approved by the man who wore the crown. Access, in turn, was rarely possible unless one went where the king lived, which meant to court. This was true whether one wanted to rise in the government, in the church, or in military service. Without access to the court, nothing out of the ordinary was possible. Thus the desperate lengths to which men would go, the sacrifices they would make, to get positions at court for themselves or for their children.

The power of access is demonstrated by the improbable importance, in the second half of King Henry's reign, of the office of groom of the stool. The core responsibilities of this position seem ridiculous to the modern eye: not only to assure that his majesty always had a "sweet and clear" place for his daily evacuations, not only to collect what he expelled and deliver it to the court physicians for examination, but to wipe the royal backside (using, for the purpose, small triangular pieces of paper). But performing such intimate services required a degree of access that not even the king's senior ministers and private secretaries could equal. Grooms of the stool were so close to the king that they became some of the most influential and therefore envied people in the kingdom. They were made, in effect, general managers not only of the king's toilet but of his private quarters and of everyone employed in those jealously guarded precincts: the knights and esquires of the body (also prized appointments) and the grooms of the chamber. They were entrusted with substantial amounts of Crown money and even, to a considerable extent, with the organization of the king's private life. If they were ever scorned or ridiculed for the nature of the duties that gave their job its name, it is unrecorded.

Access mattered so much because the whole political system was powered by royal largesse. It was the king (along with those to whom he listened) who bestowed the highest offices, the gifts of land, financial favors ranging from annuities and monopolies to exemption from the payment of tariffs, wardships like the one that had brought Plantagenet blood into the Tudor family, and pardons for virtually any kind of offense. Such gifts were the means by which the king built a following and rewarded faithful service. To be eligible for them one had to be known to the king or his most trusted friends, and there was little chance of becoming known except at court.

Admission to the court as most broadly defined—to the crowds that gathered wherever the king was resident—was not difficult. It required little more than a reasonably respectable appearance (meaning the attire appropriate to a gentleman), a plausible claim to have business with the Crown (anything from wares for sale to a dispute in need of resolution), and a sufficient supply of ready cash (bribery being routine). Merely being at court, therefore, was of limited value. Men spent years, even decades, hanging around the court and angling for preferment, only to see little of the king and come away empty-handed in the end. The trick was to get lifted out of the herd; this could be accomplished through good connections, an ability to charm or to make oneself useful, simple good luck, or some combination of these things. The goal was to become one of the lucky few likely to come to the royal mind when lucrative offices needed to be filled or patronage was available to be disbursed. Getting there could take years.

It is estimated that, at the start of Henry VIII's reign, there were at court some 120 positions that ambitious men of good birth could regard as worth having if only because they offered the *possibility* of visibility and advancement. By the end of the reign this number had increased by more than half. The bottom rungs on the ladder of upward mobility were entry-level positions for boys of good family—jobs as pages, for example—and though the ladder extended upward to the Royal Council (and yes, to the groom of the stool), relatively few of those who stood on it received a gentleman's living wage. All the same, at every level vacancies were hungrily fought over, because they could lead to almost anything.

Success at court—by no means always the same kind of success—propelled the careers of virtually every major figure of Henry VIII's reign including Thomas Wolsey, Thomas Howard, Duke of Norfolk, Thomas More, Thomas Cromwell, and Thomas Cranmer. And of yet another successful Thomas, Anne Boleyn's father. The story of the Boleyn family, in fact, illustrates just how fruitful access could be for people who knew how to use it. And how dangerous it could become when the political weather changed.

The Bullens or Boleyns were an old family, farmers in Norfolk for at least two hundred years, and by the early fifteenth century they were established in the capital and rising fast. Geoffrey Boleyn made a fortune in the cloth trade, married a baron's daughter, served as lord mayor of London, and acquired the kinds of rural estates necessary to be upper gentry. In the next generation William Boleyn lived as a country gentleman and married the daughter of an Anglo-Irish earl. By virtue of his wealth or family connections or the two things together, he got his young son Thomas admitted to the court of Henry VII.

Thomas, born in 1477, clearly was intelligent and must have been ambitious as well; he is not known ever to have wasted an opportunity. While still in his early twenties, he took a long step up the social pyramid by marrying a daughter of Thomas Howard, survivor of Bosworth Field, Earl of Surrey, and future Duke of Norfolk. Howard had an abundance of marriageable daughters and is likely to have been pleased to place one of them with a family as prosperous and respectable as the Boleyns. His son-in-law soon began to leave his mark in the records of the court: in 1501, probably the year of Anne's birth, he was present at the wedding of Arthur, Prince of Wales, to Catherine of Aragon, and two years later he was a member of the party that accompanied the young Princess Margaret Tudor northward for her marriage to King James IV of Scotland. As an esquire of the body—proof of excellent access, the body in question being the king's own—he became part of the circle of well-bred young gallants that gave the court of the aging and widowed Henry VII what little luster it retained. When the king died, Boleyn was among the favorites selected for knighthood by his successor. His penetration of Henry VIII's inner circle is not difficult to understand. He was skilled at things that Henry VIII admired—horsemanship, jousting, hawking, and the game of bowls—and by all accounts was a man of exceptional charm.

Sir Thomas, as he could now style himself, was fluent in both French and Latin. This was an essential credential in the world of diplomacy, and early in the new reign he was launched on the series of foreign missions that would punctuate his career. His widening horizons opened up opportunities, too, for his children, Mary, Anne, and George. When the king's younger sister, Princess Mary, embarked for France and marriage to King Louis XII, young Mary Boleyn joined her as a lady-in-waiting. Anne, barely an adolescent, was sent to Brussels in the service of Margaret of Austria, Hapsburg regent of the Netherlands. This last was a particularly coveted posting, as Margaret was a daughter of the Holy Roman emperor Maximilian and her court was among the richest and most elegant in Europe. Both girls were thus positioned to get the kind of continental finish that, when combined with their father's wealth and stature at court and the dash of royal blood that had come to them through their mother, could make them valuable commodities on the aristocracy's marriage market.

Anne had her father's ability to make use of whatever came her way, but her sister did not. The sketchy available information suggests that Mary Boleyn was not a model of chastity even when very young, and that while at the French court she acquired a reputation for easy availability. Whether for that or for some other reason, her sojourn abroad turned out to be short. When the decrepit Louis XII died just weeks after his wedding, his beautiful young widow impulsively married Charles Brandon, one of her brother Henry's closest friends and son of the William Brandon who had died carrying her father's standard at Bosworth Field. When the newlyweds prepared to return to England, it was decided that Mary would return with them and become a lady-in-waiting to Queen Catherine. Anne meanwhile had received high praise from Margaret of Austria, who had overseen the continuation of her education along with that of the four Hapsburg youngsters who were her wards at the time. At this point her father was able to arrange Anne's transfer from Brussels to the French court, where she became close to Francis I's Queen Claude. She remained in France for some six or seven years, until King Henry's 1522 decision to go to war with France made it impossible for her to remain. She took back with her to England a degree of sophistication that gave her a confidence bordering on brashness, arriving at about the same time her sister became the king's mistress. Anne was firmly established as the court's principal adornment when, a few years later, Henry returned Mary to her husband with grants of land as a gesture of thanks. Mary had not exactly been seduced and abandoned, but her example would not have impressed Anne with the benefits of yielding when the king sought a lady's favors.

Anne very nearly disappeared into Ireland. Her father had long been in a dispute with a noble Anglo-Irish family called the Butlers, with both sides claiming the Earldom of Ormond (which had belonged to Thomas's maternal grandfather). King Henry and Wolsey, grasping at a possible solution to this tedious but troublesome squabble, offered Anne to Sir James Butler as a way of uniting the two families and making it possible for them to share the inheritance. The Butlers refused, evidently because they expected a dowry bigger than Anne would provide. And so she remained at court—an exceptionally dazzling lady-in-waiting to Queen Catherine, a model for anyone wanting to keep abreast of the latest fashions—passing through a flirtation with the poet Sir Thomas Wyatt and the indignity of being kept from marrying Henry Percy by the interference of Cardinal Wolsey.

Thomas Boleyn, the value of his diplomatic talents augmented by the king's wish to make him a grateful rather than a resentful father, was ennobled as Viscount Rochford in 1525 and raised to the English and Irish earldoms of Wiltshire and Ormond in 1529. His son George had virtually grown up at court, taking part in the Christmas revels at age ten, becoming a page at twelve and the recipient of offices and even a manor while still barely grown; when Thomas became an earl, George, in his twenties by this time, already an esquire of the body and a junior diplomat, assumed the Rochford title. When the king entered into full pursuit of Anne, the Boleyns became for all practical purposes more the king's family than Queen Catherine and Princess Mary. All the Boleyns were heaped with honors. That their success may have gone to their heads is suggested by their attempt, thwarted by Wolsey, to secure the appointment of a disreputable sister-in-law of Mary Boleyn's as abbess of the convent of Wilton.

In the months just after Wolsey's fall, a triumvirate made up of Thomas Boleyn and the dukes of Norfolk and Suffolk stepped forward to fill the resulting power vacuum. Together the three became the king's most influential advisers, but only briefly; none of them had the political skill or the force of character to hold such a lofty position for long. It mattered little to Boleyn, who by this point had bet everything on his daughter. He and his son could hardly have been less eager than Henry himself for Anne to become queen and produce a royal heir. That would make them the grandfather and only uncle of the next king—positions from which they might aspire to almost anything.

6

A Revolution in the Making

In the weeks following his fall from power, Wolsey took up residence in a community of Carthusian monks not far from the royal palace at Richmond. Ever hopeful that the king would restore him to favor, he seemed determined to stay as close to the court as possible. He had reason for optimism: Henry would occasionally send him gifts, rings usually, and encouraging little messages. Seeking support among the king's peers, royal personages with whom he had dealt regularly while in high office, Wolsey wrote to Francis I and to Francis's mother, to the emperor Charles, and even, at some risk, to the pope. At the same time he involved himself in an apparently serious way in the religious life of his new companions, who "persuaded him from the vainglory of the world and gave him divers hair shirts to wear." He appears to have made a real effort to become a better priest, but the old hunger for power and pomp continued to gnaw.

His chances of rehabilitation were reduced by the number and influence of his enemies at court. Almost everyone with access to the king's ear—Anne Boleyn and her father and brother; Anne's uncle the Duke of Norfolk; Charles Brandon, Duke of Suffolk—detested Wolsey, had no use for the connection with Rome that he personified, and likely would have suffered grievously if he returned to power. Anyone friendly to the cardinal, on the other hand, would have hesitated to say anything in his favor in such an environment. The king is unlikely to have heard anything good about Wolsey, or to have been encouraged to do anything but distrust him and keep him at a distance. That Henry did distrust the cardinal is apparent in the government's interception of Wolsey's correspondence and the questioning of his physician by agents looking for evidence of disloyalty. The discovery that he was writing to foreign royalty did him no good.

It is hardly surprising, therefore, that in the spring of 1530 Wolsey was ordered to pack up and move north to remote districts where his chances of crossing paths with the king would be virtually nil. He went for the first time in his life to York, there taking up with unexpected earnestness the ecclesiastical duties that he had so long ignored, visiting country churches every Sunday and holy day, dispensing alms to the poor, seeing to the repair of decrepit properties, and making it his special interest to counsel troubled families. But in his letters he described himself as profoundly miserable. That he continued to be regarded as one of the most important men in the kingdom—possibly *the* most important after the king himself—was evident in June, when an official letter demanding nullification of the royal marriage was prepared for delivery to Rome. This document, addressed to the pope and intended to show that everyone of importance in England supported the king, was sent to Wolsey before anyone else had signed it, so that his name would appear on it first. It is in the Vatican library in Rome today, dripping with ribbons and seals, Wolsey's name atop all the others. Notable by their absence are the signatures of John Fisher, of other bishops who would soon be complicating the king's life, and of Wolsey's successor as chancellor, Sir Thomas More.

Wolsey made elaborate plans for the ceremony in which he was to be formally installed as archbishop on November 7. On that same day, he ordered, the Northern Convocation (the assembly representing that part of the English clergy under the authority of York rather than Canterbury) would also convene. It was to be a great occasion, an echo of the cardinal's days of glory. But on November 1 a rider set out from the king's palace at Greenwich, bound for York with a warrant for Wolsey's arrest. It charged him with high treason—with engaging, presumably because of his wide-ranging correspondence, in "presumptuous sinister practices." Wolsey, upon being served with the warrant, understood that this was the end. He stopped eating for a time, saying that he preferred a natural death to what awaited him in London. His health was bad (he was afflicted with edema, or dropsy), and though he set out under guard as ordered, traveling on muleback, he made only slow progress. Near Shrewsbury he came down with dysentery and was unable to continue for two weeks. When he reached his next stopping place, the abbey at Leicester, the end was at hand. "Father Abbot," he said upon arrival, "I have come to lay my bones among you." He was put to bed, and a day or two later he opened his eyes to see a familiar face, that of the lieutenant of the Tower of London, who had been sent north to escort him to prison.

"Master Kingston," said the cardinal to this gentleman, "I pray you have me commended to his majesty, and beseech him on my behalf to call to mind all things that have passed between us, especially respecting good Queen Catherine and himself, and then shall his grace's conscience know whether I have offended him or not. He is a prince of most royal courage. Rather than miss any part of his will, he will endanger one half of his kingdom, and I do assure you, I have often kneeled before him, sometimes for three hours together, to persuade him from his appetite, and could not prevail. And Master Kingston, had I but served God as diligently as I have served the king, he would not have given me over in my gray hairs. But this is my just reward for my pains and study, not regarding my service to God but only my duty to my prince."

He died a day later, sixty years of age. He was buried in a nearby church, coincidentally next to the tomb of King Richard III, thereby creating a curiosity that the local people would come to call "the tyrants' sepulcher." In Wolsey's case at least, the name is unfair. He was a gravely flawed man, vain and proud and in love with power and its trappings, but his legacy was far from black. Over many years he had tried repeatedly to bring peace to a Europe endlessly troubled by futile wars, and more than once he had risked his own position in doing so. He had done much to improve the delivery of justice, and he had tried without much success to curtail the enclosures of farmland that were depriving rural families of their livelihood. He had served one of the most willful and self-centered monarchs ever to draw breath, and if the difference in Henry's conduct before the fall of Wolsey and after is any fair measure, Wolsey deserves to be judged, for all his weaknesses and failures, a force for good.

Whatever Henry had planned (a show trial leading to a public execution, probably), the cardinal's passing deprived him of it. If Wolsey had lived to speak in court as he had spoken on his deathbed, he might have given the king cause to regret calling him back from York. Be that as it may, a new year was approaching and the king was laying plans for bigger things than the destruction of his old lieutenant. His time of uncertainty, the period of some three years when he acted by fits and starts and sometimes reversed himself and often seemed paralyzed, was drawing to a close. It had begun with Henry wanting the annulment of his marriage and the freedom to take Anne as his wife. It would end when he showed himself to be openly and unambiguously set on separating his kingdom from the ancient communion of Europe and on making himself a kind of national pope, the supreme spiritual authority over England and its people. Historians disagree as to exactly when Henry stopped wanting just the first thing and started wanting both, which is another way of saying that no one can say for sure. It seems reasonable to conclude, however, that by the time of Wolsey's death, he was seriously considering, if not yet quite committed to, a break with Rome. This would explain the severely hard line that he now began to take, setting out not only to destroy a sickly and ruined old man who almost certainly wished him no harm and could not have done him harm if he did wish it, but to destroy whatever independence the English church actually possessed. A hypothesis in three parts—that by the end of 1530 Henry had decided to separate England from Rome; that he thought it necessary first to break the English hierarchy to his will; and that until the clergy had been subdued, he wanted to keep the divorce proceedings in Rome from moving to a conclusion—makes his actions at this time more intelligible than does any other explanation.

It explains, among other things, the otherwise curious fact that by late 1530 (probably even before the Boleyn delegation's visit to Bologna was known to have ended in failure) Henry's strategy had shifted from trying to get Pope Clement to issue a favorable ruling to trying to keep the pope from doing anything at all. Delay, long a source of frustration, now became an objective. His success in achieving it is reflected in Pope Clement's response to the appeal for action sent to him with Wolsey's signature preceding all the others. This petition, composed before Henry changed tactics, complained that the postponements, equivocations, and evasions of the papal court were depriving England's king of the justice to which he was entitled. It said that Rome's failures could expose England, in the event of the king's death, to the dangers of a disputed succession (his daughter by Catherine of Aragon now being, by the king's reckoning, a bastard). It accused the pope of being biased in Catherine's favor, and it repeated the by-now-familiar threat that the Crown's only recourse might be to proceed independently. By the time this missive reached the pope, Clement was able to reply that he was entirely ready to bring the case to trial, that he had not yet done so because Henry had not appointed anyone to represent him in court, and that the Boleyn party, in departing Bologna, had asked not for action but for more time. All these things were true, and they shed interesting light on the question of who was actually responsible, by this point, for the failure to proceed.

The case remained unsettled as 1531 began and the king put into motion the plan that had taken shape the previous autumn—the threat to charge the whole of the English clergy with violations of the praemunire statutes. The Canterbury convocation was in session at Westminster, and news of the king's threat threw the churchmen first into confusion, then into frightened and angry debate. They had before them the uninspiring example of the late cardinal, who had submitted without complaint when faced with the same charge and in doing so had left them all vulnerable. And they were being urged to submit by their own leader, William Warham, a respected figure after almost thirty years in the see of Canterbury. To his threat of prosecution, Henry added a demand that convocation, as the embodiment of a church that had caused him so much undeserved trouble, should reimburse him for the expenses of the divorce case (all of which had been incurred, as he saw it, because of the pope's refusal to do what was right). It was to do so by repeating a subsidy of £100,000 that Wolsey, in desperate need of money because of Henry's war on France, had wrung out of it in the early 1520s.

After days of debate, convocation offered Henry, in effect, a deal. It would pay him the £100,000 that he demanded (another £18,000 was being extracted from the much smaller York Convocation) in five annual installments, there being no tolerable way of coming up with such an immense amount of cash at once. In return Henry was asked to do two things. First, he was to issue a general pardon so that the praemunire charge would not hang over the heads of the churchmen forever, and provide a written explanation of just what praemunire was, so that in future they would know what actions to avoid. Second, he was to reaffirm the traditional liberties of the church as previously upheld by the Magna Carta and other precedents reaching even further back in time: the clergy's right to operate their courts under their own system of laws, for example, and to provide sanctuary to fugitives.

In the message that conveyed their offer and request to the king, convocation's leaders referred to Henry as the "protector and highest head" of the church in England—generous words, one would have thought, in light of the church's theoretical freedom from secular control. Henry soon let it be known that this was not enough. He wanted to be called "*sole* protector and *supreme* head of the English church and clergy." Here was a revolution in the making, and the terms this time were far more portentous than any mere quibble over pluralities or the cost of funerals. Henry was demanding what no king of England, no monarch of any European kingdom, had ever dared to claim. And there was more: he wanted an acknowledgment that he had "cure" of the souls of his subjects—that responsibility for delivering those souls to God rested not with the bishops, not with the pope, but with him. This was an entirely new theory of kingship, one that turned upside down what every Englishman had been taught about the relationship of church and state.

Four days after Henry made these demands, convocation accepted them in a way that left everything shrouded in ambiguity. In its final form, the clergy's message to the king described him as supreme head "as far as the law of Christ allows." It would have been just as clear if it had declared that the king is supreme head except if he isn't; its meaning depended entirely upon what "the law of Christ" was, and that of course could be a matter of opinion. It is unclear whose words these were. If they came from John Fisher or someone like him, they must have been intended to neuter the king's flamboyant claim without being unnecessarily combative. If they were Thomas Cromwell's words, or the words of some other member of Henry's inner circle of advisers, they were a subtle way of trying to seduce the clergy into abandoning a thousand years of tradition. Possibly they were the work of someone like old Archbishop Warham, someone not definitely on one side or the other, in which case they were simply an attempt to avoid or at least postpone a showdown. On the whole, the result appears to have been something approaching a victory for the clergy in all respects except financial. The king got his £100,000, but his new title of supreme head had been so hedged as to mean anything or nothing. Other changes left him with less than the cure of souls—convocation's final draft, accepted by a silent king, restored that responsibility to the clergy—and some of the things that he had demanded were omitted altogether.

In the end Henry granted the requested pardon. In doing so, he explicitly approved the continuing operation of the ecclesiastical courts, thereby confirming the lawfulness of the very activities for which the churchmen had been threatened with prosecution. Significantly for the future—the omission must have seemed ominous—he ignored convocation's request for a reaffirmation of its traditional rights and liberties.

The churchmen, if confused and frightened, had not been entirely cowed. They had shown themselves to be unwilling to yield to whatever the king demanded. Cuthbert Tunstal, a bishop known for his learning and virtuous personal life and so high in the king's regard that he had recently been promoted from London to the wealthy northern diocese of Durham, sent Henry a letter in which he pointedly objected to the royal claim of supreme headship. He argued—with the evidence of history overwhelmingly on his side—that the kings of England had always been masters in the temporal realm, never in the spiritual. Departure from this tradition, Tunstal warned, would destroy the unity of the Christian world. The king responded cordially but in startling terms. Of course I am not the head of the church, he said; Christ is the head of the church. I as king merely have jurisdiction over the church in England in Christ's name. Specifically, Henry said, his supremacy gave him final authority over the election of bishops, the property of the church, and the "courts Christian." He blithely assured Tunstal that there was nothing revolutionary in any of this, that he was simply stating what was obviously true: that "we and all other princes be at this day chief and heads of the spiritual men." Tunstal must have been taken aback. Though almost from time immemorial England's kings had enjoyed the right to nominate bishops, in principle such appointments were the pope's business, and no one chosen by the king could actually be consecrated until the necessary approvals were received from Rome. And though over the centuries innumerable disputes had erupted between Crown and church over property and jurisdiction and other matters, not even the most ambitious kings had ever claimed to be able to overrule the pope on every question. Henry, in his letter to Tunstal, was expanding his role in nearly the most radical way imaginable.

The churchmen understood that, though they had survived a skirmish, further and probably more dangerous struggles lay ahead. A letter signed by seventeen members of the Southern Convocation's lower house provides a rare glimpse (it survives only because Charles V's ambassador to England procured a copy and sent it to Spain) into how unsettled the situation of ordinary members of the clergy had become by this time. The letter takes much the same line as Tunstal's, affirming the independence of the church, the authority of the pope, the traditional arrangements between the temporal and spiritual powers, and the importance of preserving unity. The seventeen signatories say that, in conceding to Henry the title of supreme head, they had intended no repudiation of tradition. They conclude, oddly and rather pathetically, by disavowing in advance anything that they might later say or do to repudiate what they are here affirming. Any such later words or actions, their letter says, will be the work of the devil or the result of their own weakness. Such sentiments could have been put into writing only by men of passionate conviction who were almost desperately afraid both of what lay ahead and of how they themselves were likely to respond to retribution. That their fears were justified soon became clear: several were arrested not long after their letter arrived at court, and all who survived imprisonment (some did not) ultimately accepted all the king's claims.

Though Henry had accepted the insertion of the words "so far as the law of Christ allows," from the start he either ignored them or interpreted them in his own favor, displaying more and more boldness in his approach to religious issues. He fancied himself a majestically knowledgeable theologian, loved to engage in discussions of doctrine and dogma, and invariably concluded such discussions by proclaiming the truth to everyone involved. Soon after his exchanges with the Canterbury Convocation, he attended and actively involved himself in the heresy trial (such proceedings, historically rare in England, would occur with increasing frequency in the superheated environment of the early

1530s) of a preacher who had got into trouble by echoing the beliefs of the German reformers, most of which Henry abhorred. Examining a list of the accused man's alleged heresies, Henry saw at its top the statement that the pope was not the head of the whole church. "This proposition cannot be counted as heretical," Henry declared, "for it is both true and certain." Paying no attention to the rest of the list—it would inevitably, being Lutheran, have contained many items that the king regarded as intolerable—he ordered the lucky man set free. Thus did he exercise his new authority and shed a confusingly distorted light on the kinds of opinions he was and was not prepared to approve. For the first time in history the king was defining heresy and deciding who should be punished for it.

With similar aplomb he refused to allow a French abbot of the order of Cistercians to enter England for the purpose of visiting and inspecting the houses of the English Cistercian monks. The abbot's mission could hardly have been more routine: it was to determine whether his order's strict rule was being sufficiently observed and whether corrective measures might be in order. Such visitations had been a familiar and essential element of monastic life since the time of Saint Benedict early in the sixth century. The fact that the English houses were to be inspected by a French abbot reflected the international character of the order and indeed of the church, and it was mirrored by the use of English monks to inspect houses in France and elsewhere. But now Henry declared that no foreigner could have jurisdiction in his kingdom. If anyone was going to pass judgment on English religious houses, it would be Englishmen acting on his authority. It was yet another way for him to broadcast the fact that the old rules no longer applied, and that the new rules would be of the king's making and entirely in his favor.

The success of every such gesture demonstrated to Henry and to his subjects lay and clerical that he could do very nearly whatever he wished. The absence of serious resistance must have added to his growing self-assurance and to his willingness to go further. Rome offered no objections because Pope Clement—irresolute by nature and faced with the near-disintegration of the German church, plus the Turkish threat in eastern Europe and the Mediterranean, plus the ongoing conflict between Charles and Francis—still hoped to avoid provoking him. Henry had quieted the English clergy—which was receiving no leadership, not so much as a word of guidance, either from Rome or from Warham—by alternating between intimidation and confusion while casting an artful veil of ambiguity over his own intentions. As for the people at large, little had happened thus far to cause them serious concern. Squabbles between the Crown and the pope were a centuries-old story, and thus far they had always left the traditional order intact. This latest unpleasantness—which in any case had had no impact on everyday worship or on what was taught by the parish priests—could be expected to end in the usual way.

Suddenly the tide was running strongly in Henry's favor. In a stroke of sheer good luck for the king, a remarkably high number of bishoprics were now becoming vacant, thirteen between 1529 and 1536, along with the position of abbot at several of the most important monasteries. Any pope would have hesitated to deny any English king his choice of candidates to fill these positions, and Clement was still looking for every opportunity to make Henry think of him as a friend. And so Henry encountered no difficulty in filling the sees of England with men who had proved their loyalty to him. Stephen Gardiner, his secretary, became bishop of Winchester. Edward Lee, his almoner, replaced Wolsey as Archbishop of York. The dependable John Stokesley became bishop of London, and so forth. These and the king's other nominees applied to Rome for the traditional bulls signifying approval. When the bulls arrived in England, Henry accepted them without comment. Here again the interested parties must have been confused. Henry was already claiming, as he had done in his response to Tunstal, that as a matter of principle he had the authority to appoint England's bishops. But he was continuing to follow the old forms. He was either unsure of how to proceed—which would have been justified, considering the consequences that a conclusive break with Rome might bring down on his head—or simply biding his time.

Things were also turning in Henry's favor on the continent. If he was in fact determined by this time to break with Rome, he was also, necessarily, considering the possibility that such a step would lead to war. As a schismatic king, he could expect to be excommunicated, and as an excommunicated king he would be fair game for invasion by whatever forces the pope and the emperor Charles and possibly Francis I might send against him. He had good reason to be grateful, therefore, for the friendliness that Francis was continuing to extend. He could rejoice that Charles was adrift in a sea of troubles, so threatened by the Turks and overextended in Italy that he was forced to make peace with the newly Lutheran princes of northern Germany—heretics, as the Catholic Charles saw them, badly in need of being disciplined.

Henry became forty that year—still a strong, hearty man but past his physical prime. He was troubled now with the thigh ulcers that would plague him intermittently, at times causing excruciating pain, for the rest of his days. He was also suffering from severe headaches. Though his treasury continued to be painfully low in funds—the Crown was able to meet its obligations only because of the money extorted from the church and the "pension" that Francis was once again paying to keep the English out of France—Henry still regarded all the money in the kingdom as his to do with as he chose. His extravagance was remarkable: he wore a jacket that cost as much as a farm; bought a thousand pearls in a single day; lost thousands of pounds betting on cards, dice, tennis, dominoes, and bowls; and was building and expanding more palaces—Whitehall, Richmond, St. James's, and many others—than any king could possibly have needed or even used.

At the center of his life was Anne Boleyn, living though supposedly not sleeping with him. (This can strain credulity, considering that they had by this time been waiting for the divorce for four years and were at a level of intimacy that had Henry rhapsodizing about kissing Anne on her "pretty dukkys"—her breasts.) She was a high-spirited, temperamental woman, beginning to feel the strain of the king's long struggle to become free to marry, so uninhibited in her arguments with Henry as to reduce him to baffled exasperation. He complained that Catherine had never spoken to him as brazenly as Anne did, but he remained in her thrall. Through the first half of 1531 Henry and Anne and Catherine all lived under the same roof, Catherine stubbornly following along as the court moved from place to place. Anne found this intolerable, not surprisingly, and treated Catherine and her retainers with excoriating contempt. Anne was given lavish living quarters adjacent to the king's and allowed to spend freely. She could not have dominated the court more completely if she were already married to Henry and the mother of a royal son, but she was popular neither with the public (rumors circulated that gangs of commoners were plotting to murder her) nor with those members of the court who were not part of her family-centered, ardently antichurch faction. The comptroller of the king's household, Sir Henry Guildford, earned a small share of immortality when Anne became angry with him and said that when she became queen she would have him dismissed. Guildford replied that he would save her the trouble and quit on the spot. He refused to relent even when Henry asked him to pay no attention to "women's talk."

Early one morning in July Henry rode off from Windsor Castle, leaving Catherine behind and not saying goodbye. They would never meet again. When she wrote, he became apoplectically angry, shouting that she should be ordered not to send any more letters. But if this was a nerve-rackingly tense time for the king, for his subjects it was becoming dangerous. Anyone whose beliefs did not conform exactly to the king's was likely to find himself in trouble. To continue believing things that all Englishmen had been expected to believe since Christianity first came to their island was suddenly to put oneself in jeopardy, because the king no longer believed all those things and was determined that everyone should follow his lead. On the other hand, to repudiate too many of the traditional beliefs was to risk another kind of trouble, because the king still believed strongly, and would continue to believe strongly, that most of those things remained true and whoever denied them should be subject to the penalties prescribed for heresy. Anyone with serious religious beliefs of any kind would have needed nerves of iron not to feel unsettled.

No one's situation was more difficult than that of the man who had replaced Wolsey as lord chancellor, Sir Thomas More. He had not wanted to become chancellor, understanding from the start that his thinking about the divorce was irreconcilable with that of the king. But Henry had assured him that their differences on that one subject would not matter and prevailed on him to accept. But it *did* matter, as did More's conviction that without the old church Christian civilization would dissolve. He had never been a fervent papalist; early in his public career, when Henry was writing enthusiastically in support of the pope and against Luther, More had cautioned him to be more restrained in his language. In addition to being head of the church, More had observed, the pope was the ruler of a state and therefore a potential adversary. But More was a committed Roman Catholic all the same—Henry did not yet know how committed.

Because he was completely lacking in Wolsey's craving for power and also out of step with the king's thinking, More as chancellor never achieved a fraction of the influence that his predecessor had long wielded. By late 1531 he was not even part of the king's inner circle and barely had a voice in the making of policy. He focused instead on the judicial responsibilities of his office—the chancellor was a judge among other things, and More's background equipped him superbly for the bench—and on doing what he could to turn back the flood of heretical ideas that had been coming across the Channel since the advent of Martin Luther. Those ideas, as More saw it, were putting millions of souls in danger of damnation.

His role as a suppressor of heresy put More further at odds with the king because their views on what constituted heresy were diverging radically. And Henry compounded his chancellor's difficulties—we can only wonder if he was acting with malicious intent—by requiring him to present arguments to Parliament that More himself did not accept. More did as instructed, but he did it in a coolly impersonal way, refusing to answer when asked for his own opinion.

It was an impossible situation, an explosion waiting to happen.

WINDOWS OF OPPORTUNITY

THAT THE ENGLAND OF THE LATE MIDDLE AGES WAS A society of rigid class distinctions is hardly a secret. The nature of those distinctions, however, is considerably less obvious. Though a baron was not the equal of an earl, and a yeoman was not quite the same as a farmer, differences of this kind were subtle and of limited importance. Basically there was just one great line of separation, but it was a chasm so deep and wide, dividing the population into such grossly unequal parts, that the people on the two sides might almost have been living on different planets.

At the pinnacle, below the royal family but above everyone else, were the fifty-odd holders of hereditary titles. Dukes were highest of all (the name derives from the Latin for "leader" and was long reserved for the sons of kings), followed in descending order by marquesses (so called because they were supposedly responsible for governing marks or marches or borderlands), earls (an Anglo-Saxon word, the equivalent of count), viscounts, and finally mere barons. The proudest of these dignitaries were those with Norman forebears who had come to England with William the Conqueror (the Percy earls of Northumberland, for example, and the de Vere earls of Oxford) and those whose family trees had been injected with royal blood via marriage (the route that carried the Howards from obscurity to the Dukedom of Norfolk in just a few decades).

Below the titled nobility, but not always far below in wealth or even status, were the landowning families that made up the local elites ("lords of the manor" in spite of not actually being barons) in every part of the kingdom. They called themselves the gentry—people of "gentle" birth—because they thought of themselves as having, and in fact often did have, antecedents quite as good as the titled families; many were descended from the daughters and younger sons of nobles. This is a crucial fact about English society not only in the Tudor era but for centuries after: the closest thing to a middle class identified with—regarded itself as related to and descended from—those above it on the pyramid of rank. This was true even of those families that had climbed to wealth through the window of opportunity that opened briefly when the Black Death wiped out half the population, and of families that got rich in business and (like the Boleyns) used their winnings to buy country estates. Such families wanted no reminders of their origins and would have recoiled at any suggestion that they might ever have had any connection with the masses of landless workers. The word "gentleman," accordingly, carried a potency that it has long since lost, at least in America. It bore no necessary relation to wealth or position or even to having good manners (though all those things were prized). Rather its use was a claim to being special by birth, special in ways that only ancestry made possible.

This was the great divide: the line separating not just the rich from the poor or the powerful from the weak but the few who were inherently superior from the many who, having no family at all by the standards of the time, did not matter. To achieve a position of prominence in public life, it was not necessary to be noble—nobles were far too few for that much exclusivity to be possible. But it was *absolutely* necessary to be "gentle." Without that qualification, all the best doors remained shut.

With one conspicuous and important exception: the church. For centuries, and well into the reign of Henry VIII, it had been the one ladder by which young men of virtually any background could rise even to positions of the greatest power.

The pattern was set early, if not in the most appealing of ways. Ranulf Flambard began life in Normandy as the son of a simple parish priest (marriages of clergymen still being arguably lawful) but rose to become the strong (and brutishly ruthless) chief agent of King William II as well as bishop of Durham. Roger, bishop of Salisbury, had origins so obscure that no one knows where he was born, or when or to whom; but in the twelfth century he became Henry I's chancellor and most trusted adviser. Thomas Becket grew up as the sports-loving son of a London tradesman and took holy orders only after his father's financial ruin made it necessary for him to find employment, and he, too, became both chancellor and archbishop.

There is no mystery about the rise of men like these to heights that were utterly inaccessible to laymen of similar background. For centuries after the Conquest, education remained almost exclusively the domain of the church: even the universities were founded by clerics and operated by clerics mainly for the purpose of training more clerics. The aristocracy, by contrast, continued to live by a code that exalted martial values above all others; in their world, education beyond the rudiments long seemed to have little point or purpose. It was in the church alone, therefore, that kings could find the levels of literacy and intellectual sophistication needed for diplomacy, the creation and functioning of a system of justice, financial management, and general administration. And priests offered the further attraction of not having to be paid, no small consideration as money was always in short supply; they could be rewarded with appointments to ecclesiastical livings, any number of which might be held by a single churchman. The most valuable of the king's servants could be made bishops, which had the great advantage of putting the church itself, with all its wealth and influence, in the hands of men whose loyalty to the Crown rarely had to be doubted.

The church, for its part, kept the ladder of mobility in good working order by offering nearly unlimited opportunities, first in education and then in educational and ecclesiastical management, to the most able and ambitious of its recruits. Noble and gentle credentials were useful, inevitably, but rarely to the exclusion of talent. Communities of monks and nuns even elected their own leaders, commonly making their choices on the basis of merit. The almost egalitarian character of many of the church's institutions must have been rooted at least in part in the belief, integral to Catholic doctrine, that no human being is more or less a child of God than any other and the mighty have no better chance of salvation than the destitute. In part, no doubt, openness to the advancement of the lowborn was also a function of institutional self-interest: both the church itself and the Crown obviously benefited when talent was given the fullest possible scope. Aristocratic resentment at the rise of clerical leaders with roots in the peasantry, to the extent that it existed, was tempered by the clerical commitment to celibacy. An archbishop might dispense more money than a duke, but neither his title nor his wealth could be made hereditary, even if he had children.

As the amorphous phenomenon known to us as the Renaissance burst upon Italy and spread north, the scholarly apparatus of the church became the conduit through which it was introduced to England. And it found fertile ground there, thanks mainly to the ecclesiastical meritocracy. The most respected English bishop of Henry VIII's reign, John Fisher, became a member of the King's Council, founded two colleges at Cambridge, and by the time of the king's separation from Catherine of Aragon was known throughout Europe as an advocate of reform from within, a champion of the new humanist learning, and a man of impeccable probity. All this after starting life as the son of a Yorkshire cloth merchant. England's first great scholar of classical Greek, Thomas Linacre, was one of a number of eminent scholar-churchmen of whose family background virtually nothing is known. As for William Warham, the man who headed both church and government just before Thomas Wolsey's emergence, we know his father's name but nothing of his occupation. We know only that the family included a carpenter and a maker of candles.

With all this as background, there could be nothing truly astonishing about the emergence of the butcher's son Wolsey as chancellor of England, archbishop of York, member of the College of Cardinals, candidate for the papacy, and master of international politics. He was in fact a familiar kind of figure, having received his first degree at such a precocious age—fifteen—that he became known as "the boy bachelor," proceeded from there to an M.A., to ordination at twenty-five, to doctoral studies in theology (an unusual choice even then for a young cleric hoping for a career in government, suggesting that the young Wolsey had no such aspirations), and finally to the obscure jobs that led him into royal service. It is impossible to doubt that every step of his rise had been the result of ability and hard work.

If Wolsey was a great manager and administrator, he was certainly not the first churchman of whom that could be said. If for more than a decade he exercised so much power as to be called *alter rex,* the other king, again he was not unprecedented. If he became a great patron of education and the arts, if he showed serious commitment to the improvement of the justice system, and if he even tried to address abuses of the church's prerogatives (an area in which he was gravely handicapped by the burden of his own bad example), in all these things he was typical of the English church's hierarchy at the time. That hierarchy included many men of talent and learning. If few were as saintly (or as pugnacious) as John Fisher, virtually all set a better example than Wolsey.

It was his flaws, his failures, that really set Wolsey apart. His way of life was magnificent on a scale never before seen in England. It centered on a court of some five hundred persons (his kitchens alone employed seventy-three men and boys), and it shifted back and forth between palaces at Hampton Court and York Place that surpassed any of the royal family's homes. His every public move became a procession, a display of opulence, with gentlemen and nobles carrying before him the gold and silver emblems of his great offices and waiting on him at table. Some of this was appropriate to the king's chief minister in an age when royalty was expected to offer constant proofs of its wealth and power, and a man in Wolsey's position *needed* an army of assistants to deal with an unending stream of visitors and all the business of church and state. But inevitably it drew mutterings from almost every direction. And some of Wolsey's indulgences were simply indefensible. If it was not scandalous of him to hire an Italian sculptor to build his tomb—and to insist that that tomb surpass the one in which the remains of Henry VII and Elizabeth of York had been laid to rest in Westminster Abbey—it was not far short of being so.

Nor can anything be said in defense of Wolsey's private life. He had a mistress and children, and on his son and namesake, ordained a priest before he was grown, the cardinal lavished a cornucopia of church livings. When he vacated the rich see of Durham in order to become bishop of Winchester and abbot of St. Albans (grabbing the latter plum in defiance of canon law, which barred nonmonks from becoming abbots), he did so partly in the hope of inserting his son as Durham's new bishop. But even he was unable to get away with that.

Perhaps his ultimate failure grew out of his chief strength, his brilliance as an executive. In the king's name Wolsey ruled virtually alone, refusing to share power, reducing the council to a shadow of what it had been before his rise. This further inflamed the resentment of those members of the higher nobility who already hated the cardinal for his arrogance, for his constant rubbing of their noses in the outward signs of his greatness, for the intolerable presumption of this escapee from the wrong side of the class divide. Wolsey alienated everyone. Those loyal to the old church—Catherine of Aragon most visibly—regarded his way of life as a disgrace. Those drawn to the ideas of Luther and other radical reformers—the Boleyns and their faction at court, for example—pointed to him as proof that the whole Roman connection was corrupt beyond hope of repair. Wolsey had left himself with no powerful friends except Henry VIII, surely the least dependable and most dangerous friend in all of England.

By 1530 England had changed to such an extent that it no longer needed Wolseys. Education was no longer almost exclusively the province of the church. Laymen such as John More were becoming eminent jurists, and in the next generation lawyers such as More's son Thomas were among Europe's leading humanist scholars. A few years at university were now a rite of passage for sons of the nobility and the gentry, and some were even using those years to get educations. Only once after Wolsey would a power in the government become a power in the church as well, or vice versa, and that sole exception would be Wolsey's onetime protégé, Stephen Gardiner. With the old ladder of mobility destroyed, England's class divisions would become more rigid, more impermeable, than ever.

7

A Thunderbolt Falls

A crisis appeared to be near as 1532 began, but it was impossible to know for sure. Everything depended on the king, on what he intended to do, but the signals he was sending were so self-contradictory as to be indecipherable. That the king himself knew what he wanted is unclear.

In the year just ended he had given numerous indications that he no longer hoped for a favorable judgment from Rome, that his sights were on something much bigger than a mere annulment. But now he sent a delegation of nobles to Windsor Castle to call on Queen Catherine, to offer yet another solution to the old deadlock. The idea this time was that the divorce question should be referred to a panel of eight men, four lay lords and four bishops or abbots, with the understanding that whatever judgment they rendered would be final. It is not known whether her visitors informed Catherine that something very similar to their proposal had already been floated in Rome, that Pope Clement had responded positively, but that in doing so he had added that no such arrangement could be acceptable without the queen's assent, as it was she who had appealed to Rome. What they were offering, Catherine's visitors told her, would be of great comfort to the king's troubled conscience. "God grant him a good conscience," she replied. "But this shall be your answer: I am his wife, lawfully married to him by holy church, and so I will abide until the court of Rome, which was privy to the beginning, shall have made thereof an end."

She was ordered to leave Windsor for a smaller, more remote residence where there could be no possibility of her intercepting Henry and Anne as they made their royal rounds. "Go where I may," she said, "I shall still be his lawful wife." In the months that followed she would be moved again and again and would not be allowed to see her daughter. She wrote often to the princess, always advising her to honor her father and be properly submissive.

And so the king's great matter hung in the air unresolved, a vexation to everyone it touched, a force powerful enough to push even the queen to the outermost periphery of public life while drawing others toward the center against their will. Among those others were Henry's cousins the young Pole brothers, grandsons of that Duke of Clarence who had been the brother (and was killed on the orders) of Henry's maternal grandfather, Edward IV. Being of royal blood was a very mixed blessing in the England of the sixteenth century; the tenuousness of the Tudors' claim to the throne inclined them to see kinsmen as potential threats, which is why Henry VII had had Clarence's harmless son put to death. The Poles (a family entirely distinct, by the way, from the king's other and more obstreperous cousins the *de la* Poles) were already acquainted with the cutting edge of Henry VIII's distrust and anger. In 1521 their mighty relative the Duke of Buckingham, a man all too haughtily proud of his Yorkist blood and conspicuously unwilling to curry favor with the upstart Tudors, had arranged the marriage of his son and heir to Ursula Pole. Henry reacted to this union of two families that had plausible claims to the throne with unexpected savagery. Buckingham was convicted of treason and executed; Ursula's mother, Margaret, Countess of Salisbury, lost her place as lady governess to little Princess Mary; and the countess's two eldest sons were imprisoned in the Tower. Later the family won its way back into favor, Henry Pole achieving a prominent place at court as Lord Montague, but they lived with the knowledge that careless displays of ambition could prove fatal.

With this history—his grandfather put to death by one of the last Plantagenet kings, his uncle killed by the first Tudor and his sister's father-in-law by the second—it is hardly surprising that the youngest of the Pole brothers, Reginald, grew to adulthood with no wish to be involved in the court or its politics. In spite or perhaps because of this, Henry VIII took a fatherly interest in him, providing five hundred crowns a year for his education. In five years at the University of Padua, the bookish and unambitious youth won favorable notice for his devotion to his studies, his pleasing manners, and his excellent moral character. After two years back in England, during which he took up residence in a monastery and continued his preparations for a career in the church, he was permitted by the king to return to the continent for further study at the University of Paris. In departing he turned his back on the certainty that, had he remained at home, the king would have showered him with offices and other signs of favor.

Pole's quiet life in France was first interrupted when Henry set out to get support for the annulment of his marriage from the continental universities. Considerable intellectual gifts, excellent contacts in the academic world, and a growing reputation made Pole a potentially valuable agent in the king's campaign, and he received instructions to become involved. When he claimed to be too young and lacking in experience to be of any use—much later he would write that his real reason for begging off was discomfort with the king's position—he was ordered home. There the Duke of Norfolk, England's most powerful magnate as well as Anne Boleyn's uncle, confided to him that Henry had marked him out for a high place in the church but expected a clear statement of where he stood on the divorce. (The Archbishopric of York, Wolsey's old sinecure, was still vacant when this conversation took place and is almost certainly what the king had in mind. It would have been a surprising and even inappropriate appointment in light of Pole's youth and the fact that he was not yet even an ordained priest, but the pope doubtless would have given his assent even if Pole had not been so favorably regarded in Rome. Clement would soon be accepting from Henry an at least equally surprising nominee for the even more exalted see of Canterbury.)

When Pole confessed that on the basis of what he then knew he was unable to support the king, Norfolk advised him to take a month to learn more about the issues involved. In the weeks that followed he studied the relevant commentaries on Scripture and canon law and discussed the matter with scholars. Finally, perhaps in part because of his brothers' fears of conflict with the king, Pole announced that he had

thought his way to a position that Henry was likely to find acceptable.
He was summoned to see the king, who was eager to receive him as an
ally and ready to reward him. Once in the royal presence, however, Pole
found the arguments he had constructed in his mind collapsing under
the realization that he was not being honest even with himself. He tried
to explain why, to his own intense regret, he could not agree with Henry
on the divorce. The king, furious, walked out on him, leaving him in
tears. Lord Montague and Sir Geoffrey Pole, too, were furious when
they learned what their brother had done. They accused him not only of
destroying his own prospects but of putting the whole family at risk.
Reginald wrote to the king, trying to explain why he had found himself
unable to be more helpful and asking permission to go abroad once
again. Lord Montague, expecting the worst, went to see the king to say
how much *he* regretted his brother's conduct.

"My lord," a surprisingly good-humored Henry told Montague, "I
cannot be offended with so dutiful and affectionate a letter. I love him in
spite of his obstinacy, and were he but of my opinion on this subject, I
would love him better than any man in my kingdom." This was the king
at his magnanimous best, and a demonstration of Reginald Pole's ability, which only a tiny number of men would ever possess, to somehow
bring out that best. Pole was allowed not only to leave England for
Italy—where he must have hoped to stay well clear of the king's matrimonial troubles—but to keep his allowance. His brothers and their
mother, all of them descended from kings stretching back to William
the Conqueror, must have breathed easier when he was gone. But if
they thought the worst was over for any of them, they could not have
been more wrong.

When Parliament and the Southern Convocation assembled yet
again in January 1532, no one outside the king's innermost circle had
any way of knowing what to expect. That something extraordinary was
in the air, however, must have been made obvious by the selective character of the royal summons. Cuthbert Tunstal, the bishop of Durham
who had disputed Henry's claim to be supreme head, was not present
because he had received no call. John Fisher, the scrappy old bishop of
Rochester, was among the others not summoned, but he traveled to
London all the same. The general sense of anticipation had sharpened
his readiness for a fight.

Henry remained impossible to read. Pope Clement, who a year earlier had forbidden the king to remarry while the divorce case remained unsettled, received a letter from Queen Catherine reporting that she was no longer allowed to be under the same roof with her husband and asking for a ruling on the marriage. This prompted him to write to Henry and tell him that he dishonored himself in treating his wife as he did. He added that reconciliation with Catherine would be the greatest favor that he, Henry, had ever done for the papacy. Henry scoffed at this as he had scoffed at an earlier order from Clement to send Anne Boleyn away. The pope was giving signs of running out of patience, and the king was responding in kind.

On February 8 Henry showed his hand. He had sixteen clergymen and six laymen, all of them men in positions of considerable authority, indicted on charges that required them to explain to the King's Bench by what right or authority—*quo warranto*—they claimed to be able to appoint coroners, take possession of discovered treasure, and supervise local trading in bread and beer. Here again the clergy (the inclusion of six laymen in the indictment remains unexplained) found themselves accused of breaking the law by doing things that men in their positions had been doing for centuries. It made no sense except as harassment and intimidation, an attempt to add to the pressure applied earlier through the threat of praemunire. What was stunning was the identity of those indicted. The list began with the name of William Warham, a dignitary of unimpeachable reputation and unquestionable loyalty to the Crown. Also listed were a bishop and the heads of seven monasteries and several colleges. Obviously no one was safe from the king's displeasure.

These indictments seem almost childishly petty today, and probably they seemed so when they were issued. The supreme oddity, in any case, is that the charges were never pressed and no bill was ever proposed in Parliament for the criminalization of the acts—the supposed offenses—that had been the basis of the indictments. Instead, Henry changed course and delivered a different, harder blow from an equally unexpected direction. His agents in Parliament introduced a bill abolishing annates, one of the principal means by which England and the other countries of Europe had for centuries provided financial support to the papal court in Rome. In accordance with ancient practice, whenever a new bishop was appointed to a vacant see his first year's net income went to the pope as an annate—payment of what was called "first fruits." The sums involved could amount to several thousand pounds in a single year, especially when the wealthier dioceses were involved. It was not difficult to rouse the taxpaying knights and gentry of the House of Commons to a state of indignation over the sending of this money out of the kingdom at a time when the financial demands of the Crown had become so burdensome.

The scholars whom Henry had put to work searching for historical evidence of his supreme headship had turned up documents indicating that annates had originated as a way of providing the papacy with the means to defend itself against the barbarian invasions that followed the collapse of the Roman Empire. The transformation of such presumably temporary assistance into an eternal entitlement, the king and Cromwell now argued, was an example of how the bishops of Rome had, over the centuries, taken things to which they had no right. The annates bill was the most radical attack yet on the prerogatives of the church, and its introduction may have reflected Cromwell's growing influence and his willingness to push the king to new extremes. As originally proposed, it would have required any bishop who paid first fruits to Rome to forfeit everything he owned and the income from his diocese for as long as he remained in office. It would have established a new procedure by which any bishop-elect whom the pope refused to approve could be consecrated by his archbishop or two other bishops, and it would have ordered that anything attempted by the pope in the way of retribution—anything up to and including excommunication, which had always been the papacy's ultimate weapon—was to be ignored.

Such a bare-knuckles assault on ancient practice was too much for the bishops of 1532 to accept, and they along with several of the abbots who sat with them in the House of Lords declared themselves opposed. The bill was too much even for many in the Commons, where resistance proved formidable. Clearly rough tactics would be needed if the bill were to have any chance of passage. Henry showed himself ready to use them. He made three bullying visits to Commons, finally going so far as to order the members to divide themselves physically into two groups: those who supported his bill were to line up beside him on one side of the room and those opposed were to withdraw to the other. Even this exercise, intimidating as it must have been for country gentry, proved to be not enough. Henry did not secure passage until the proposal was considerably softened. Most important, it was made provisional: it would not take effect until Easter of the following year, and even then it would not become law unless Henry issued the letters of patent necessary for implementation.

The king's position remained ambiguous. In its original form the annates measure had been without precedent, overturning every Englishman's understanding of the kingdom's connection to the see of Rome and imposing ruinous penalties on anyone who attempted to maintain the old ways. But by delaying implementation for a year, thereby giving the king ample opportunity to change his mind, Parliament left a door open for reconciliation with the pope. Probably the king accepted this compromise less because he still harbored hopes of reconciliation, or would have accepted reconciliation if it became possible, than because doing so was the only way of getting the needed majorities: Parliament had not yet been pummeled into docility. Cromwell at this point had neither won Henry's full confidence nor brought Parliament under control, and he may have been trying to move faster than either king or Parliament was prepared to go. Henry, for his part, appears to have been adopting some but not all of Cromwell's ideas, trying them out, measuring the reaction.

Even as the king hesitated, however, Cromwell was helping him to see Parliament in an entirely new light. In the first twenty years of his reign, Henry had followed his father's example, doing his best to govern without Parliament, summoning it only in times of dire necessity. Wolsey had certainly favored this approach, all the more so as his money-raising expedients earned him the hatred of both houses. For two years Henry got little out of the Parliament first summoned in 1529, the one destined to be remembered as the Reformation Parliament. But then Cromwell, once his star had risen and his genius had ripened, showed him how to transform Parliament from a nuisance, an obstacle, into a tool of immense value. Together the two of them began using Parliament, at first almost against its will, to spread a canopy of legitimacy, of legal propriety, over their most radical initiatives. They maneuvered it into approving, or at least *appearing* to approve and sometimes even to initiate, the things they wanted done. By this means they could claim to be doing nothing beyond what the people of England wanted. It was in opening such new vistas to the king that Cromwell, a self-described onetime "ruffian" who even at the height of his power never lost the savage instincts of a backstreet knife-fighter, first showed himself to be one of the most brilliant political operators that England has ever produced.

Transforming Parliament required meticulous and skillful management. It required carrots and sticks—a balanced application of the Crown's power to reward and its power to destroy. Above all, in the beginning especially, it required creating the illusion that Crown and Parliament were in agreement even when a majority in Commons could not be depended upon to vote with the king. Thus even more attention had to be paid than in the past to finding the right kinds of men to sit in positions of leadership in Commons, and to culling candidates who were not likely to conform. Luckily for Henry, Cromwell was not only as painstakingly careful a manager as Wolsey had ever been but also, where Parliament was concerned, far more adroit. He was also more ruthless and much less inhibited by established law and custom. Once again Henry had been blessed with a lieutenant into whose hands he could confidently place full responsibility for the achievement of his own most urgently desired objectives.

If Cromwell was still learning early in 1532, he was learning fast and becoming capable of dazzling moves. On March 18 Parliament formally presented to the king a document called the Supplication Against the Ordinaries (an "ordinary" being, in ecclesiastical parlance, a bishop or archbishop—someone with jurisdiction over church courts and administration). It was a supplication in the sense that, after making numerous complaints about the church hierarchy's abuse of its rights in such areas as the handling of heresy cases, excommunication, and fees and tithes, it asked the king to take corrective action. It was radical in looking, contrary both to law and to tradition, to the Crown rather than to the church itself for correction of the alleged abuses. Although supposedly a spontaneous work of Commons, in actuality it was mainly Cromwell's doing. (Several early drafts, all in Cromwell's hand and dated before March 18, are among his surviving papers.) By having his allies in Commons offer the Supplication as an expression of popular discontent, Cromwell was able to raise Henry above the fray. Now the king, rather than attacking the church and challenging the traditions of the realm, was being called upon as an impartial judge. He was asked to consider the grievances of his people against a church that had, presumably, conducted itself so disgracefully as to give rise to deep and widespread unhappiness. Henry was no longer in the position of having to prod Parliament to act on his instructions; Parliament in presenting the Supplication had taken the initiative, and Henry was free to respond if and as he chose.

It was a neat trick, and Cromwell had pulled it off in spite of the fact that serious discontent with the church or its hierarchy was *not* widespread among the people or even dominant in the Commons. Resentment certainly existed, but with nothing like the intensity found in Germany, where a church immeasurably more entangled than England's in secular politics had in many places made itself the object of burning popular hatred. Anticlericalism in England was centered mainly in London, especially among the lawyers and merchants of the city's growing middle class. It was the representatives of these professions, together with Londoners serving as members for boroughs far from the city, who had pressed their complaints about the church in the Reformation Parliament's first session at the end of 1529 and been satisfied with a small number of limited reforms. It was those same men who now, under Cromwell's firm direction, asked the king to give his attention to the Supplication's fresh complaints. By involving the speaker of the house—an appointee of the Crown—Cromwell was able to create the impression that the Supplication represented the thinking of the majority. In fact, the membership at large had been given no opportunity to express an opinion.

Henry forwarded the Supplication to convocation and invited it to respond. On the face of it, this was an eminently fair and reasonable thing to do. But it was also tactically astute. It put the hierarchy in the position of having to acknowledge the accusations of some of its most intemperate critics, and to dignify those accusations with a reply to the king.

Though the Supplication complained of many things, its focus was on the ecclesiastical courts. It echoed Henry's claim to "imperial jurisdiction" (evidence of Cromwell's domination of the drafting process), arguing that Englishmen could not be held to account by any authority beyond the cliffs of Dover. It thereby delivered a fresh challenge to the old idea of a universal church and to the leadership of the pope. Initially, possibly because it believed itself to be responding to Commons rather than to the Crown, convocation displayed a determination to yield no more ground. It delivered to the king a Defense of the Ordinaries, much of which was written by Stephen Gardiner, who was Henry's secretary as well as bishop of Winchester. It offered one significant compromise, agreeing that during Henry's lifetime any new laws passed by the hierarchy would be subject to royal approval. Otherwise it rejected all the Supplication's complaints and claims. It reiterated the old idea, familiar to all, that the church had been given its authority by God and that not even a king—or an emperor, for that matter—could interpose himself between it and God. No part of this response could have surprised anyone; it was the settled orthodoxy of Catholic Europe. In saying anything else, Gardiner and his fellow bishops would have been repudiating beliefs that lay at the core of their clerical vocations. They would have been declaring unconditional surrender in their unwanted struggle with the king.

Nor should anyone have been surprised, however, that the king was unhappy with convocation's response. But he held his fire, passing the Defense of the Ordinaries to the speaker of the House of Commons with the wry comment that "we think their answer will smally please you" and asking the bishops to amplify on some parts of what they had written. That was where things stood, with Commons and clergy apparently entering upon an exchange of arguments as sterile as the endless dispute over the divorce, when suddenly a thunderbolt fell.

It came on May 10 in the form of a royal demand surpassing anything the king had thus far attempted. Convocation was given not a question to discuss or a complaint to answer but an ultimatum, and it came not from Parliament but from the king himself. The churchmen were ordered to give formal assent to three things. They were, first, never again to enact ecclesiastical laws except with the approval of the Crown—and not just during Henry's lifetime but ever. Second, all ecclesiastical laws then in effect were to be reviewed by a committee of thirty-two members, half clerical and half lay, all appointed by the king. Finally, even those laws found by the committee to be acceptable would remain without effect unless the king gave them his personal approval.

The climax had arrived at last: the moment, so long feared but so slow in coming, when the clergy were left with only two possible courses of action. They could stand up to the king, insisting on the rights that had been handed down to them through generations beyond numbering, or they could relinquish those rights forever.

PARLIAMENT

THE FIRST THING TO BE UNDERSTOOD ABOUT PARLIAMENT in the time of the Tudors is that it had nothing to do with democracy and was a "representative" body—representative of a substantial part of England's population—only in a sense so broad as to be practically meaningless.

Parliament under the Tudors remained what it had been since its origins three centuries before: an instrument of the Crown first, and then of regional, local, and commercial elites. It was closed to all but the king's wealthiest and most influential subjects, with limited room for individuals who were neither wealthy nor powerful but enjoyed royal favor. It had always been a malleable institution, used for different purposes at different times, and in the sixteenth century it evolved into something radically if not at first obviously new. By using it to cast a cloak of legitimacy over Henry VIII's unprecedented expansion of royal power, Thomas Cromwell not only established Parliament as an essential element in England's government but laid the foundations upon which, a hundred years later, it would become more powerful than the Crown.

Parliament had grown out of simple political realities: even the most powerful rulers find it easier to govern if they have the support of their most important subjects, if they provide some mechanism through which such subjects can be involved in the formulation of policy, and if they at least pretend to have the consent of the people they tax. Even William the Conqueror, whose victory in 1066 made him literally the owner of virtually every square foot of England (even the greatest of his nobles were merely his "tenants in chief"), found it advantageous to create and confer with his Magnum Concilium, or Great Council. It was made up of the mightiest of William's barons, the magnates, and its role was limited to settling disputes and managing whatever the king instructed it to manage. Its members—as well as the members of the Curia

Regis or King's Court, made up of individuals (often senior clergy) better qualified than warrior-barons to deal with challenging legal questions— were chosen by the king and could claim to represent no one beyond themselves and possibly their fellow lords. The existence of council and court signified very little beyond the obvious fact that William himself could not do everything.

Power as nearly total as William's could never be sustained, and after a century and a half his great-great-great-grandson King John took a great fall in trying to sustain it. The result, famously, was his signing under duress of Magna Carta. Though not exactly the birth of liberty that it is often represented as being, it did shift power away from the Crown in favor of the higher nobility. It committed the king to levying or collect- ing no taxes except with the consent of his council. Thereafter meetings of the Great Council and the King's Court began to include, if only occa- sionally, knights chosen by the leading families of every county. The idea of a Parliament (a "talking") made up of the king and his council, the barons and bishops, and representatives of influential (meaning wealthy) families of less than noble rank gradually began to take shape. Any no- tion that the non-nobles represented the people at large, however, would be grossly anachronistic. Just to vote in parliamentary elections one had to own property worth at least forty shillings, a threshold so high that in some counties fewer than a dozen men qualified. To sit in Com- mons, a "knight of the shire" needed an annual income of £600, and "burgesses" or townsmen needed £300. These were enormous sums.

John's son Henry III, too, found himself at war with the barons. The issue, as before and since, was money, and the conflict arose out of Par- liament's new importance as the vehicle for approving royal requests for taxes. The leader of the baronial party, Simon de Montfort (himself not only a magnate but married to the king's sister) broke new ground in 1265 by summoning a Parliament without Henry's approval. He invited each county to send four knights and each borough to send two burgesses, thereby placing the Commons on something approaching an equal footing with the baronial Great Council. His aim was to use wide participation as a way of building support, and to use Parliament as a medium to communicate with all parts of the kingdom. A generation later Henry III's son Edward I (the first king since the Conquest, inciden- tally, to bear an Anglo-Saxon rather than a Norman name) followed

Montfort's example in recognizing Commons as a part of Parliament. His motive was not to weaken but to strengthen the Crown, using Parliament both to fund his wars and to demonstrate that he had the support of the kingdom.

As long as true feudalism lasted, with the barons able to function almost as little kings in their own domains and to demand military service of their subtenants, struggles for power were waged almost exclusively between the nobility and the king. The advantage shifted from one side to the other depending upon the personality of whoever happened to occupy the throne at any particular time. The main point of contention continued to be money: the kings' military adventures imposed a heavy financial burden upon the nobles. Important precedents were set as nobles and Crown alike paid lip service to the role of Commons in their efforts to attract support. A turning point as important as Magna Carta came early in the reign of the weak and pleasure-seeking Edward II, when the baronial party took control and issued the Ordinances of 1311. Whereas Magna Carta had taken the form of a royal proclamation, thereby recognizing the authority of even a gravely weakened king, the Ordinances were issued as the work of the barons, who merely claimed to be acting with royal approval. Having been driven to rebellion by the costs of the first Edward's wars and his son's reckless generosity to his favorites, the barons reasserted their right to limit the collection of taxes and control appointments to important royal offices. Though Commons was given no active role in any of this, the Ordinances enhanced its legitimacy by requiring the king not only to summon a Parliament annually but to include the lower house. Edward II, when he later repudiated the Ordinances, did so on grounds that they had been enacted without the approval of Commons. Thus both the Ordinances themselves and the grounds on which they were set aside helped to entrench the Commons in the government.

It came to be accepted that Parliament had three elements: the king and two houses, Lords and Commons, that met separately and were jointly responsible for raising the money required by the Crown. Parliament was also a mechanism for redress of grievances—the Ordinances of 1311 had asserted the right of subjects to appeal to it—and it came to be understood that any "petitions" (later they were called "bills") that both houses approved became the law of the land if accepted by the

Above left: 1. Henry IV and Joan of Navarre from their tomb at Canterbury Cathedral. Henry IV's usurpation of the crown caused the turbulent Wars of the Roses.

Above right: 2. King Henry VI depicted *c*.1500 as a saint on a screen at Ludham in Norfolk. He died in the Tower of London in May 1471 and was succeeded by Edward IV.

Right: 3. The marriage of Catherine of Valois to Henry V in the parish church of St John, Troyes, 2 June 1420.

VIII and Henry VII, by Holbein, from

, queen consort of Henry VII and moth

6. Margaret Tudor, daughter of Henry VII and Elizabeth of York, and Henry VIII's sister.

7. Perkin Warbeck, the false Plantagenet chosen by disaffected Yorkists to impersonate Edward VI's son Richard, Duke of York, the younger of the two 'Princes in the Tower'.

8. Matriach of the Tudor dynasty, Lady Margaret Beaufort, mother of Henry VII. She married Edmund Tudor, the first son of Catherine of Valois and Owen Tudor. Owen Tudor was Catherine's second husband, she had previously been Henry V's queen.

Opposite: 9. Henry VIII in about 1540 by Holbein.

10. Henry VIII processes to the opening of parliament in 1512.

Opposite: 13. Title page of the first edition of 'The Great Bible', 1539. Enthroned as God's vicar, Henry symbolically hands out the Word of God to the spiritual and temporal hierarchies of his realm, headed respectively by Thomas Cranmer on his right and Thomas Cromwell on his left.

11. Henry VIII, from a window in the chapel at Sudeley Castle.

12. Henry VIII portrayed in all his magnificence at King's College, Cambridge.

¶ The Byble in
Englyshe, that is to saye the content of all the holy scrypture, bothe
of ý olde and newe testament, truly
translated after the veryte of the
hebrue and Greke textes by ý dy-
lygent studye of dyuerse excellent
learned men, expert in the forsayde
tonges.

¶ Prynted by Rychard Grafton &
Edward Whitchurch.

Cum priuilegio ad impzimen-
dum solum.
1539.

Above and above opposite: 14. & 15. The Field of Cloth of Gold, 1520. Two bas reliefs from the 1520s.

16. Act of Six Articles, 1539.

17. Golden Bull of Pope Clement VII. This one was affixed to Clement VII's bull confirming Henry VIII's title as *Fidei Defensor*.

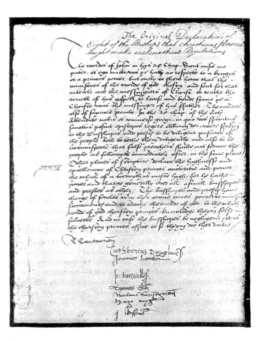

Above: 18. Act of Succession, 1544. This section of the act spells out the oath that must be taken by all clergymen and royal officials, renouncing the 'Bisshopp of Rome' (the Pope).

Right: 19. Declaration by the bishops, c.1536.

The Lady Henegham

Above left: 20. Bessie Blount, one of Henry VIII's earliest mistresses who bore him a healthy son in 1519.

Above right: 21. The tomb of Henry Fitzroy, Duke of Richmond, Henry VIII's bastard son by Bessie Blount.

Left: 22. Mary Shelton, later Lady Heveningham, thought to have been one of Henry VIII's later mistresses.

Opposite: 23, 24, 25, 26. English Ladies, by Holbein.

KATHERINA VXOR HENRICI .

27. *Divorced.* Catherine of Aragon, Henry VIII's first wife.

Top: 28. Henry VIII riding at the tilts on 12-13 February 1511, with Catherine of Aragon looking on. From the Great Tournament Roll of Westminster.

Centre: 29. The grave of Catherine of Aragon in Peterborough Abbey (which Henry converted into a cathedral in 1541).

Right: 30. A letter from Queen Catherine, acting as regent while Henry VIII was in France, to Thomas Wolsey, the King's Almoner. 2 September 1513, concerning the imprisonment of the Duke of Longueville, taken prisoner at the 'battle of the spurs' in the 17 August.

31. *Beheaded 1536*. Anne Boleyn.

32. Thomas Howard, Anne Boleyn's uncle.

33. A letter from Cranmer at Dunstable, informing Henry VIII of the date when his 'grave grete matter' will be resolved.

34. One of a series of friendly letters which Anne Boleyn wrote to Cardinal Wolsey during the summer of 1528, when she was still looking to him as the man most likely to untangle the king's first marriage. She thanks him for the 'grete payne and trobell that yr grace doth take' about the matter (BL Cotton MS Vespasian F.XIII, f. 73.).

35. Letter from Anne Boleyn to Stephen Gardiner, then in Italy pursuing the king's quest for an annulment of his marriage, 4 April 1529.

36. Queen Anne Boleyn was executed on 19 May 1536.

37. Hever Castle, the family seat of the Boleyns.

38. Design for a pageant tableau, by Holbein, staged on in honour of Anne Boleyn on the eve of her coronation, 31 May 1533.

39. *Died 1537.* Jane Seymour.

40. Jane Seymour's badge of the phoenix, together with the Tudor Rose, from a stained glass window at the Seymour family home of Wolfhall, near Marlborough. It was moved to Great Bedwyn Church following the destruction of Wolfhall.

Top right: 41. *Divorced 1540.* Anne of Cleves.

Above: 42. Anne of Cleves, by Barthel Bruyn.

Left: 43. Anne of Cleves House.

Opposite: 44. *Beheaded 1542.* Catherine Howard, Henry's fifth wife. Detail from the window of King Solomon and the Queen of Sheba in King's College Chapel, Cambridge. It is believed that the image of the Queen of Sheba is modelled on Catherine Howard. This stained glass was created during Henry VIII's reign and paid for by Henry himself.

46. Cardinal Thomas Wolsey (1471 or 1475-1530).

47. A letter from Wolsey to the king, October 1529, written in the wake of his fall from favour.

49. Thomas Cranmer (1489-1556). He was appointed Archbishop of Canterbury following the death of William Warham.

Opposite: 45. *Survived*. Catherine Parr.

48. Archbishop Warham (1450-1532), by Holbein.

Top: 50. The Family of Thomas More, by Holbein.

51. Thomas More (1478-1535), by Holbein.

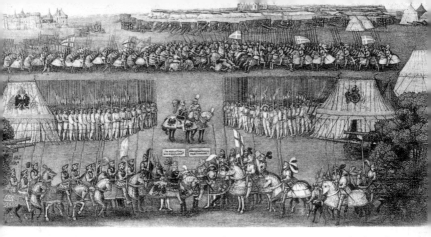

52. Henry VIII meets the Emperor Maximilian I. Henry's tent is marked with the royal arms, Maximilian's with the Habsburg double-headed eagle.

53. Henry VII's chantry chapel in Westminster Abbey. This elaborate bronze structure houses the tombs of Henry VII and Elizabeth of York.

54, 55 & 56. Henry VIII's Great Seals. The Great Seal was the ultimate instrument of authentication for acts of royal power in Tudor England, and was affixed, for example, to treaties and charters. It depicted the king enthroned in majesty on the front, and riding into battle on the back, symbolising his power as fount of justice and leader in war.

Above left: 57. Erasmus. This iconic woodcut by Dürer depicts the greatest scholar of the age, Desiderius Erasmus of Rotterdam, at work in his study.

Above right: 58. Holbein's design for a jeweled pendant for Princess Mary.

Right: 59. Thomas Boleyn, Earl of Wiltshire. Despite the executions of his son George and his daughter Anne in 1536, Thomas Boleyn himself died in his bed at Hever Castle in 1538. His funeral brass in St Peter's Church there, the only known likeness.

Anglici Matrimonij

Sententia diffinitiua

Lata per sanctiss.imum . Dñm Nostrum . D. Clementem . Papã . vij . in sacro Consistorio de
Reuerendiss.morum Dominorum . S . R . E . Cardinalium consilio super Validitate Ma
trimonij inter Serenissimos Henricum . VIII . et Catherinam Anglie Reges contracti.

PRO.

Eadem Serenissima Catherina Anglie Regina,

CONTRA.

Serenissimum Henricum . VIII . Anglie Regem.

Clemens Papa. vij.

Hristi nomine inuocato in Tróno iustitie pro tribunali sedentes, et solum Deum pre oculis habentes, Per hanc
nostram diffinitiuam sententiam quam de Venerabilium Fratrum nostrorum Sancte Ro . Ec . Car . Consistorialiter
coram nobis congregatorum Consilio, et assensu serimus in his scriptis, pronunciamus, decernimus, et declaramus,
in causa, et causis ad nos, et Sedem Apostolicam per appellationem, per charissimam in christo filiam Catherinam Anglie Reginam Illustrem a nostris, et Sedis Apostolice Legatis in Regno Anglie deputatis interposi
tam legitime deuolutis, et aduocatis, inter predictam Catherinam Reginam, et Charissimum in christo filium Henricum . VIII .
Anglie Regem Illustrem , super Validitate, et inualiditate matrimonij inter eosdem Reges contracti, et consumatis rebusæ alijs in
actis, cause et causarum huiusmodi latius deductis, et dilecto filio Paulo Capissucho causarum sacri palatij tunc decano et pro
pter ipsius Pauli absentiam Venerabili Fratri nostro Iacobo Simonee Episcopo Pisaurien. vnius ex dicti palatij causarum Auditori
bus locumtenens , audiendis instruendis , et in Consistorio nostro Secreto referendis commissis, et per eos nobis , et eisdem Car
dinalibus Relatis , et mature discussis , coram nobis pendentibus , Matrimonium Inter predictos Catherinam , et Henricum An
glie Reges contractum , et inde secuta quecunq fuisse, et esse validum, et canonicum validaæ, et Canonica , suosæ debitos de
busse, et debere sortiri effectus , prolemæ exinde susceptam , et suscipiendam fuisse , et fore legitimam , et prefatum Henricum Anglie Regem teneri, et obligatum fuisse , et fore ad cohabitandum cum dicta Catherina Regina eius legitima coniuge , illamæ
maritali affectione , et Regio honore tractandum , et eundem Henricum Anglie Regem ad premissa omnia, et singula cum
effectu adimplendum condemnandum ommbusæ iuris Remedijs cogendum , et compellendum fore , prout condemnamus, cogimus, et
compellimus, Molestationesæ, et denegationes Per eundem Henricum Regem eidem Catherine Regine super inualiditate, ac se
dere dicti Matrimonij quomodolibet factas, et prestitas fuisse, et esse illicitas, et iniustas, et eidem Regio Regi super il-
lis ac inualiditate matrimonij huiusmodi perpetuum Silentium imponendum fore, et imponimus, eusdemæ Henricum Anglie Regem in expensis in huiusmodi causa pro parte dicte Catherine Regine coram nobis, et dictis omnibus legitime factis condemnandum fore, et condemnamus , quarum expensarum taxationem nobis imposterum reseruamus .

Ita pronunciauimus ·I·

Lata fuit Rome in Palatio Apostolico publice in Consistorio die . XXIII . Martij .   M . D . XXXIIII .

Blosius.

60. Clement VII's judgment against Henry. After calling in vain upon the
king to leave Anne and take back his first wife, Clement VII finally issued his
'definitive sentence' in favour of Catherine of Aragon on 23 March 1534.

Henry VIII's will (30 December 1546).

62. The 'Lady Elizabeth' of Henry VIII's later years.

63. Oatlands (Surrey), one of Henry VIII's many palaces, where he married Catherine Howard on 28 July 1540.

64. Greenwich Palace. Massively and expensively rebuilt by Henry VII, Greenwich Palace was the birthplace of Henry VIII and a favoured residence of all the Tudors.

65. Whitehall Palace.

66. Hampton Court Palace, once the country home of the fallen Cardinal Wolsey.

67. Henry VIII's lock for his private apartments. Henry travelled from palace to palace with this lock and held the master key.

68. Richmond Palace as built by Henry VII.

Tennis court
G

Great Ha
by Wolse

The court

F The court yard

Preaching
place

'Holbein' gate

H

Pri

King St Gate
F

F

Court

Kinges street

Charton row

C

B

Wesmynster Hall (the seat of the law courts)

A

E

Starre Chamber

Abby

House of Commons
(formerly chapel of St Stephen
from 1547 until the fire of 183

E

House of Lords

Court of Requests

The Queens bridge

Henry VII's chapel

E

70. Nonsuch Palace. Built by Henry VIII, Nonsuch was a far more intimate royal residence without the space for the entire court. From an old English engraving in the late Emperor of Austria's private library.

Opposite: 69. Plan of the palaces of Westminster and Whitehall *c.* 1578.

71 & 72. The keep of Windsor Castle and the St George's Chapel. A fortress rather than a favoured residence, but Henry VIII chose to be buried there alongside Jane Seymour.

king. Thus Parliament continued to develop as a legislative body even as the judicial functions that had come to it through the Great Council and the King's Court were gradually taken over by other institutions.

By the time the first Henry Tudor became king in 1485, no one questioned the need for parliamentary approval of taxes and legislation. Indeed, it was accepted that Parliament could deny the Crown's requests for money if it chose to do so—something that it had already shown itself capable of doing when a king refused to consider its wishes. Like his predecessors, therefore, Henry VII preferred to do without Parliament, summoning it only when financial necessity left him with no alternative. This remained true through the first two decades of Henry VIII's reign, though his foreign adventures made meetings of Parliament far more commonplace. Both the Lords and the Commons remained the domain of the landed aristocracy, along with representatives of the wealthiest residents of the cities and largest towns. To Cardinal Wolsey, they were unavoidable evils that had to be placated in order for the Crown to pay its bills.

Everything changed with Henry's claim to supremacy and Cromwell's emergence as the man responsible for giving him what he wanted. That Henry was likely to be able to overpower the leaders of the church and bully the nobility soon became clear. What he lacked, and urgently needed, was a basis for claiming the *right* to overturn the traditions of a thousand years. Cromwell's genius was to use Parliament as it had never been used before. He coopted such authority as it had accumulated over the generations, driving it to pass statutes that acknowledged the powers that Henry was claiming for himself and thereby giving tyranny a footing in the law. In doing so he crushed whatever autonomy Parliament might have claimed to possess, arranging the election to the Commons of enough men under his (and the king's) control that later, when his innovations finally provoked an uprising, one of the protesters' complaints would be about the number of Crown employees and dependents sitting in Parliament as members.

Part of Cromwell's craft was to use Parliament without empowering it: in drafting his bills he was careful to include language stating explicitly that Parliament was not itself conferring powers on the king but merely recognizing that the king possessed the powers in question by divine right. The preambles to his most revolutionary statutes assumed the truth of propositions that were at best debatable: that England had long been an "empire," for example, and therefore could be subject to no external authority, ecclesiastical or otherwise. Cromwell has been credited with being the father of parliamentary government, in which sovereignty came to be shared by Crown and Parliament. The lengths to which he went to keep Parliament submissive while using its prerogatives to achieve a radical expansion of royal power, however, make it difficult to believe that he intended any such thing.

Whatever Cromwell's intentions, his actions permanently transformed Parliament's role. He would call it into session seven times in eight years, changing it from Wolsey's regrettable nuisance into an indispensable part of the machinery of government. What perhaps mattered most, he prepared the way for Parliament itself, Commons especially, to see itself in a new light. When he was finished, it was no longer the king who was supreme in England but "the king in Parliament"—a subtle distinction, but ultimately an epic one.

8

Submission

By the time King Henry delivered his ultimatum to convocation, almost everyone with a connection to his court was tangled in a web of hostility and dread.

Old friendships were being sundered by the tension. Even Charles Brandon, Duke of Suffolk, close to the king from boyhood and now his brother-in-law, was ordered to withdraw to his country home and take his family with him. Suffolk himself was loyal enough, but his wife, Henry's sister Mary, was too open about her contempt for the Boleyns.

The Tudors were not the only family being torn apart. Thomas Howard, Duke of Norfolk, though he kept his place at court, was compromised by his wife's outspoken opposition to the divorce and tormented by the angry outbursts of his high-strung niece Anne Boleyn.

Careers were being made and ruined. Stephen Gardiner, royal secretary and bishop of the rich diocese of Winchester, had damaged himself irretrievably by insisting, in his response to the Supplication Against the Ordinaries, that church law was above the reach of the secular authorities. He was now an outsider, still officially secretary but no longer trusted. The eagerness of Thomas Cranmer to find scholarly support for the king's every act and desire, by contrast, had lifted him into the bright sunshine of royal favor. He was back on the continent now, taking up new duties as Henry's ambassador to the court of Charles V.

Strange things were happening. One morning the whole household of Bishop John Fisher became violently ill. One of the bishop's servants died, as did an indigent woman who had come to Fisher's door for that day's distribution of free food. The bishop himself escaped, saved by his practice of not eating until the beggars had been fed.

It was discovered that the morning's batch of porridge had been poisoned. According to some of the surviving accounts, someone had given a powder to Fisher's cook, one Richard Roose, who thought it was a laxative and put it into the porridge as a practical joke. By other accounts Roose claimed complete innocence, saying that he knew nothing about any powder and that if anything had been added to the porridge, it must have been done while he was away from the kitchen, possibly by a nameless stranger who had shown up that morning and later disappeared. Rumors arose to the effect that the poisoning had been arranged by the king, whose motive would have been to put an end to Fisher's unceasing criticism, in writing and in person, of his pursuit of a divorce and his attacks on the church.

What is most interesting is the king's reaction to these rumors—a reaction so extreme that it stirred up further suspicion. He visited the House of Lords and delivered an impromptu speech on the evils of poisoning, a subject of which he appears to have had a deep horror. He then hurried through Parliament a bill that made the use of poison an act of high treason, and he had Roose attainted (a step, to be much used in the years ahead, that made it possible to punish and even execute a suspect without holding a trial). The unfortunate Roose, whose degree of complicity can never be known, became the first person to suffer the penalty prescribed for poisoners. He was deep-fried alive in a cauldron of boiling oil.

Next Henry himself became a target, though of words only. On Easter morning he attended mass in the church of the Observant Franciscans adjacent to the royal palace at Greenwich. The Observant friars, so called because they were stricter than other Franciscans in adhering to the rule laid down by their order's founder, Francis of Assisi, were respected throughout Europe as a model of how men in holy orders should conduct themselves. They had been invited into England by Edward IV, Henry VII had taken them under his patronage early in his reign, and their connection to the royal family remained strong. Catherine of Aragon had always been especially devoted to the Observants, choosing John Forest of the Greenwich friary as her confessor. Henry VIII on more than one occasion had written to the pope to commend their blameless way of life and their "hard toil day and night" to bring souls to God.

The preacher at this year's Easter mass was William Peto, former warden of the order's house at Richmond (another place where a Tudor palace stood side by side with an Observant friary), newly elected head of its English province and onetime confessor to the king's daughter Mary. Henry must have been expecting an edifying homily appropriate to the holiest day in the liturgical calendar and attuned to his lofty understanding of matters theological. What he got instead must have stunned him; it is difficult to believe that he would have set foot in the church had he known what Peto was intending. The friar addressed him directly, personally, telling him in so many words that he had no right to end his marriage, that there was no way to do so except by proving, contrary to what the queen continued to swear, that her marriage to Prince Arthur had been consummated. Moving into even more shocking territory, Peto compared Henry to Ahab, the Old Testament king who had been enchanted by the wicked Jezebel, was seduced into thinking himself above the law, and so had come to a terrible end. "I beseech your Grace to take good heed," Peto said in conclusion, "lest if you will need follow Ahab in his doing, you will surely incur his unhappy end also, and that the dogs lick your blood as they licked Ahab's, which God avert and forbid." Henry showed impressive sangfroid, not only sitting stoically through what must have sounded to him like incredible insults but staying behind after mass to talk with Peto, hoping perhaps to win him over with the royal erudition. Peto proved immovable, however. He warned the king that all England was restless because of his actions and that if he persisted he could put his very throne in danger.

Within the next few days Peto departed Greenwich for a general conference of the Observants' English province. As soon as he was gone, Henry issued instructions for one of the royal chaplains, Dr. Richard Curwen, to preach the following Sunday at the friars' church. This was irregular because Curwen was not a Franciscan, and it was unwelcome because he was known to be willing to do or say anything to win the king's attention and favor. Henry Elston, warden of the Greenwich friary, objected but was ignored. Curwen appeared on Sunday as instructed, and as he rose to speak the king was once again in attendance.

Things did not go according to plan. Curwen, knowing what was expected of him but going perhaps a bit far in his eagerness to please, not only repudiated Peto's words of a week earlier but denounced him as "dog, slanderer, base, beggarly friar, closeman, rebel and traitor." The friars in his audience absorbed this in silence. The king did the same, no doubt with considerable satisfaction. But when Curwen went on to accuse Peto of being absent out of cowardice—"not to be found, being fled for fear and shame as being unable to answer my arguments"—a voice called out from the loft above the king. "Good sir," said Elston the warden loudly, "you know that Father Peto, as he was commanded, is now gone to a provincial council held at Canterbury, and not fled for fear of you, for tomorrow he will return again." Elston declared himself ready to "lay down my life to prove all those things true which he hath taught out of the holy scripture, and to this combat I challenge you before God and all equal judges." Noisy confusion ensued, and quiet was not restored until Henry himself ordered everyone to be silent.

Peto and Elston were called before the King's Council. There they were roundly chastised, the Earl of Essex exclaiming that they deserved to be bundled up in a sack and thrown into the Thames. Elston was not impressed. "Threaten these things to rich and dainty folk who are clothed in purple, fare delicately, and have their chiefest hope in this world," he replied. "For we esteem them not, but are joyful that for the discharge of our duties we are driven hence. With thanks to God we know the way to heaven to be as ready by water as by land, and therefore we care not which way we go." The two were taken into custody, and Henry petitioned Rome for license to have them tried by the compliant provincial of a different order, the Augustinians. Before anything came of this they were sent into exile on the continent. They went to Antwerp, where they took up the production of books rebutting Henry's claims on the divorce and supremacy. Their persistence did nothing to encourage the king to allow those who disagreed with him to leave England and remain at liberty.

Just days after Elston's clash with Curwen, an outbreak of violence showed that tension was reaching dangerous levels even inside Henry's court. The dukes of Norfolk and Suffolk were by this point less influential with the king than the upstart Cromwell, and were disgruntled and perhaps even fearful as a result. The pressure they were under put them and their followers at odds to an extent that soon threatened to get out of hand. One day, after an altercation of some kind, one of Suffolk's retainers took refuge in Westminster Abbey to escape pursuit by a group of Norfolk's men. The abbey was a recognized place of sanctuary, but the pursuers entered anyway and killed Suffolk's man. When Suffolk learned of this (he was back at court, though without his wife), he assembled an armed gang of his own and headed for Westminster in pursuit of vengeance. The king was alerted in time to dispatch a messenger with an order for Suffolk to stop, and the duke and his men were obliged to swear that they would refrain from violence. They did so unhappily, and their mood was not improved by news that the murderers of their comrade had been let off lightly.

This was the atmosphere that hung over the Southern Convocation as it struggled uncertainly to respond to the king's ultimatum. The bishops in particular were in an excruciatingly difficult position. Most of them held their positions less because of any special piety or wisdom or devotion to the church than because over the years they had demonstrated an ability to make themselves agreeable to the king. They were better trained in obedience to the Crown than in loyalty to a distant, unseen papacy, they had more reason to fear their prideful and determined king than a pope who sometimes must have seemed little more than an abstraction, and if any of them had looked to Rome for guidance since the start of the divorce crisis the only response had been a troubled silence. Archbishop Warham, who since the fall of Wolsey had stood alone at the top of the hierarchy, only added to the confusion. Many years before, he had expressed doubts about the propriety of a marriage between Catherine of Aragon and her late husband's brother, but of course he accepted the pope's decision on the matter and even presided at the wedding. From the start of the crisis he had seemed lost in irresolution, sometimes questioning but at least as often appearing to accept the king's arguments. Not long before Henry delivered his ultimatum, Warham had publicly criticized some of the king's more aggressive initiatives. But after receiving the ultimatum and getting a taste of the Crown's hard tactics, he withdrew into silence.

Convocation as a whole, however, was showing signs of willingness to resist. The lower chamber especially, less accustomed than the bishops to the compromises required for political preferment, displayed an angry understanding of what was at stake in this latest confrontation. Henry, aware of its restiveness, reacted indirectly but pointedly, summoning a group of his most dependable parliamentary supporters. Among them were thirteen members of Commons, the king's handpicked speaker among them, and eight lay lords. Their function that day was to provide an audience for a theatrical performance in which the king would play not just the starring but the only role. "Well-beloved subjects," Henry told them (it is easy to imagine him expressing innocent surprise followed by righteous indignation), "we thought that the clergy of our realm had been our subjects wholly. But now we have well perceived that they be but half our subjects—yea, and *scarce* our subjects!"

This would have been the listeners' cue to feign astonishment and indignation. How was such a thing possible? How could the clergy not be true subjects of their glorious king? Henry then revealed the supposedly shocking truth (which of course had been obvious for centuries): "All the prelates, at their consecration, make an oath to the pope, clean contrary to the oath that they make to us, so that they seem to be his subjects, and not ours. The copy of both the oaths I deliver here to you, requiring you to invent some order that we be not thus deluded of our spiritual subjects." The opacity of the king's second sentence is likely to have been intentional: it leaves unclear exactly what Henry was threatening, but there could be no doubt that he was accusing the bishops of something serious, something smelling of treason, and that he would welcome the involvement of his friends in Parliament. In delivering this little talk, however, he may have been bluffing; it would have been far from clear at this point that Parliament as a body was prepared to support his most radical demands. If his words were a bluff, however, the bluff worked. Two days later convocation offered a compromise that had been hashed out between the bishops and the lower chamber, with the latter continuing to show more firmness than the lords of the church. The response to the king's ultimatum conceded much of what he had demanded, promising that the clergy would not legislate without royal permission. However, it repeated a familiar qualification along with a familiar request. The new rule was to be effective only during

Henry's lifetime (the bishops had been willing to make it permanent, but the lower house would not agree), and as before, the king was asked to confirm the traditional liberties of the church.

Again Henry was not satisfied. Having no further need for Parliament at this point, and probably not wanting its more restless members to remain together at Westminster as he pushed his conflict with the clergy to a climax, he sent it home. Convocation was told that it, too, was to adjourn—not quite immediately but in twenty-four hours—but that he wanted a better answer before it did so. He sent envoys including the Duke of Norfolk and the Boleyns, father and son, to make certain that the churchmen understood that he meant business—that failure to cooperate would bring consequences.

Thus it was that May 15 became one of the most significant days not only of the Tudor century but in English constitutional history. It was the day on which, in the person of Archbishop Warham, the clergy of the Southern Convocation utterly, absolutely, and forever surrendered such independence as their church possessed to King Henry VIII and his heirs. In doing so, they abandoned rights and immunities that reached back into the dimmest early years of Christianity in England, prerogatives that their predecessors had fought repeatedly and sometimes sacrificed much to maintain. The question that arises is how such a momentous surrender could have happened so quickly and apparently so easily—how the stewards of an institution rooted so deeply in English society and culture came to agree unconditionally to even the most extreme of Henry's demands less than a week after he first made them.

The answer is that it didn't happen that way. The whole process of surrender was little more than a sham. In fact, only three members of convocation's upper house—three out of all the bishops and leading abbots in England and Wales—signed the document of submission without adding reservations. Two refused outright, and more absented themselves from the proceedings than showed up either to sign or refuse. The lower house was even less cooperative; so many members refused to vote that there was no way even to pretend that the king's demands had been accepted. When the "submission of the clergy" was presented to the king, therefore, it bore the signatures of only a tiny minority of those men whose positions gave them at least some right to act on behalf of the church. As an expression of the will of the hierarchy or the whole clergy, therefore, it had an extremely dubious legitimacy. This fact appears to have troubled the king not at all. He had what he needed: an official document, bearing the signature and seal of the archbishop of Canterbury and a few others, that proclaimed him to be the ultimate master of ecclesiastical law in his kingdom. He still did not have a divorce, and difficult questions about the relationship with Rome remained to be resolved, but Henry had won one of the great victories of his life. He held in his hand a basis for claiming that the clergy now lay prostrate at his feet. That this is what he had wanted all along—that he had no real interest in a comprehensive revision of canon law—is clear in the fact that though Warham's submission agreed to the creation of a review committee, no such body was ever appointed. As for the troublesome fact that most of the clergy had not *really* submitted, that detail could either be corrected later, if necessary, or simply forgotten.

On the day after Henry received the submission, the Duke of Norfolk escorted Thomas More to the gardens of York Place, the great London palace that had previously been the residence of Cardinal Wolsey and was now home to the king and Anne Boleyn. There the chancellor met briefly with Henry, handed over the Great Seal that symbolized his office, and quietly ended his career in government. It is natural to suppose that More had decided to resign upon learning of the submission, realizing that he could not serve a monarch with whom he was in deep disagreement about matters of such great importance to both of them. But in fact May 16 was merely the day on which More, after an extended and unhappy wait, was at last *allowed* to resign. His position had become untenable long before, first because of the lengths to which the king was going in pursuit of his divorce and then because of his threats to the unity of the church. More had recruited Norfolk, with whom he had maintained an uneasy friendship in spite of the duke's impatience with the idea of papal authority, to ask the king to allow him to resign. For a long time Henry turned a deaf ear. He could not permit his subjects and the whole world to see the highest-ranking officer in his government quitting in protest of royal policy. Such a spectacle was especially impossible at a time when the king was seen to be locked in conflict with convocation and Parliament and neither could be depended upon to obey his instructions.

But now the annates battle was won, the hierarchy had surrendered if only in a formal sense, and neither Parliament nor convocation remained in session and capable of raising protests. If More remained in office, he could only be an awkwardness, and if he were still in office when Parliament or convocation reconvened he might become a figure around whom others could rally. It was the right time to let him go. The king accepted the Seal, and More withdrew gratefully to his home in Chelsea, saying that he hoped to spend whatever time remained to him preparing his soul for the hereafter.

OTHER REFORMATIONS

IT SEEMS AN EXCEEDINGLY STRANGE COINCIDENCE THAT the greatest turning point in the history of the church in England, the crisis after which nothing would ever be the same, occurred at almost precisely the same time that the religious life of central Europe was also being violently transformed. What is strange is that these two simultaneous revolutions happened independently of each other, rose out of radically different circumstances and causes, and ultimately unfolded in distinctly different ways.

Certainly at some deep level having to do with the spirit of the age, this wasn't a coincidence at all. Be that as it may, when Martin Luther fastened his ninety-five theses to the door of Wittenberg Cathedral in 1517 he set off a powder keg of a kind that simply did not exist in England. His revolt was neither the cause of nor the inspiration for the upheaval that Henry VIII put in motion a decade and a half later. Henry in fact loathed what he knew of Luther, and loathed many of the defining ideas of Luther's theology. Long before declaring war on the pope, Henry made himself the avowed enemy of Friar Luther and *his* war on the pope. For the book in which he responded to Luther's heresies (he had help in writing it, especially from Thomas More and John Fisher), he was rewarded with the title Defender of the Faith by—it would become the ultimate irony—the pope in Rome himself.

Luther repaid the king in full. First he declared in a book of his own that Henry was a villain and fool and tool of the Antichrist, a "damnable rottenness and worm." Later he denied that Henry had any right to divorce Catherine of Aragon, suggesting instead that he commit bigamy.

And yet, though both would have been pained to think so, Henry and Luther were intimately linked. Such intellectual support as Henry found for his revolution came largely from Englishmen whose thinking had been strongly influenced by Luther's. And Luther's impact could never have been as widespread as it finally proved to be if not for the resources that Henry's revolt made available to the Protestant cause.

There is irony in all this. From the beginning of his reign to the end, Henry thought of himself as not only a good Catholic but literally the best and most orthodox of Catholics—better than the pope, in the end, because better connected to God. Hence his revulsion toward the books, written in Latin mainly and reproduced in great numbers thanks to the recent invention of movable type, that Luther was turning out with dazzling speed and spreading to every corner of Europe as his dispute with the papacy escalated into schism. His beliefs as they matured—that man is so corrupted by original sin as to be incapable of acting freely, that therefore he can do nothing to merit salvation, that therefore faith alone can "justify" him or free him from the consequences of sin, and finally that acts of charity and self-denial and prayers for the dead must all be without effect—added up to a blunt repudiation of Henry's very Catholic views. Luther insisted that the Bible is the sole source of truth, that baptism and the Eucharist are the only valid sacraments and priests have no more power than any layman, that people are predestined to salvation or damnation and can do nothing to alter their fate—ideas no less offensive to the English king than to Rome. They were no more consistent with Henry's expanding view of his own role than with the most ambitious assertions of the popes.

Luther's first moves onto radical theological ground were viewed with enthusiasm, even with excitement, in a Germany where many people had long regarded Rome as an alien force, remote, exploitive, and corrupt. The accusations that he leveled against the institutional church received so much support and encouragement, even from powerful nobles and influential members of the clergy, that Luther himself must have been taken by surprise. Certainly he was emboldened to carry his attack further. When the emperor Charles tried and failed to silence him and even had him outlawed without effect, Luther found himself free to follow his ideas wherever they led. What he found, in developing them, was release from agonies experienced during years of struggle with an intense sense of his own sinfulness. The resolution at which he arrived, the conviction that neither he nor anyone could do anything to merit salvation but salvation was possible all the same as an undeserved gift from God, persuaded him that his struggle had always been not only futile but unnecessary. He thereby brought that struggle to an end. But this answer also reduced to futility his monastic vocation, which he had always pursued so rigorously, so self-punishingly, that his Augustinian superiors had warned him against excessive scruples. In fact it rendered the church itself futile—left no place for the church as it then existed. Thus it left no place for a pope. The gulf that opened between Luther and Henry VIII never narrowed even as Henry changed from one of the pope's most dutiful sons into one of his most implacable enemies. Luther, having crossed swords with Rome and emerged not only unharmed but a German national hero, became contemptuous of the very idea of ecclesiastical hierarchy. He decided that the papacy must be the shadowy enemy of Christ that the New Testament's Book of Revelation calls the Whore of Babylon. This took him down paths where the king of England had no intention of following.

One trait that Henry and Luther shared was a conviction that the whole world should agree with them, reinforced by an expectation that it would. The resistance that both encountered should not have surprised them but did. What was worst for Luther, what enraged him because it made a mockery of his determination to construct a new religious unity on the ruins of the old, was the way the reform movement itself began to fragment and fragment again as men who had begun by rejecting Catholic doctrine went on to reject Lutheran doctrine as well.

The first aberration was the most dangerous, and the most horrible in its consequences. By 1524, only seven years after Luther had first challenged Rome's practice of selling "indulgences" (which were rather like get-out-of-Purgatory-free cards), common people across Germany were inspired by his example to mount challenges of their own not only to the ecclesiastical authorities (hated in Germany to a degree unimaginable in England) but to the secular rulers as well. The result was the Peasants' War, as large an uprising by an underclass as Europe had ever seen. The aims of the rebellion were more secular than religious—an end to enclosures of farmland long held in common, for example, and a restoration of the feudal rights of the peasantry—but the rebels looked to Luther as their natural leader. This put him in a severely awkward position. The peasants were doing what he himself had done: not only questioning but defying traditional authority. But if he endorsed their rebellion he would alienate the many princes who, by separating their domains from Rome and confiscating church lands, had helped to make his revolt a world-changing event. He took the safer course, condemning the rebels in the most hateful terms imaginable and urging their rulers not only to suppress but to exterminate them. What followed was the butchering of an estimated one hundred thousand people, many of them armed only, where they were armed at all, with farm implements. The idea that Christians owe unqualified obedience to the state became at that point deeply implanted in Lutheranism and therefore in the psyche of Protestant northern Germany. What was implanted in southern and western Germany and Austria, where the rebellion had been most widespread and the reprisals most savage, was a deep popular antipathy for the whole Lutheran phenomenon. In Switzerland, too, where the reformist leader Huldrych Zwingli had supported the rebels, the Peasants' War opened up new divisions.

Zwingli would have been lost to Luther in any case, because in Luther's eyes he went too far in his rejection of established dogma and practice. Luther believed, in almost the same way as Catholics, that the living Jesus really was present in the Eucharist, holy communion; Zwingli believed that the Eucharist was merely symbolic. Luther believed that religious art—paintings, statues, crucifixes, stained-glass windows—fostered piety and should be encouraged; to Zwingli such things were idolatrous. Zwingli separated himself from Luther on the question of free will, arguing that with the help of God people are capable of choosing to live in accordance with the commandments. Luther believed no such thing: in his view, Scripture offers its admonitions to do good and avoid evil only to impress upon believers how impossible it is for them to do either, so that they will put all their faith in God's undeserved mercy and attach no value to the actions of their unworthy selves.

Thus did reform separate first into two main branches, German Lutheranism and a more austere, puritanical Swiss variant, and then, after surprisingly few years, into a multitude of sects. The most notorious were the Anabaptists, so named because they rejected the ancient practice, which Luther had retained, of infant baptism. Some of the Anabaptists were radical to the point of lunacy. In 1534 they seized control of the German city of Münster from the Lutherans who had recently expelled the local Catholic bishop. Under the leadership of a man named Jan Beuckelson, who declared himself king of the new Jerusalem and said he was following the example of the Old Testament patriarchs in taking sixteen wives, they announced that the second coming of Jesus was imminent and that it was the duty of believers to make war on their oppressors. They were considered such a threat that Catholics and Lutherans joined forces to take Münster back from them, after which Anabaptists everywhere were ferociously suppressed. Those who fled to England were rounded up and jailed, and those who refused to recant, Henry had burned.

As it broke into divergent and even warring factions, the evangelical movement—a name signifying elevation of the Bible over other authority—lost the momentum of its rapid early growth. The violent rise and fall of the Münster Anabaptists worsened the fear of innovation to which the Peasants' War had given rise. Even in England, as early as 1531, a king already at loggerheads with Rome was putting evangelicals to death. Thomas Bilney, a popular young preacher who attached more importance to Scripture than Henry found acceptable, was burned at the stake at Smithfield. John Frith, another young evangelical with many admirers, met the same fate for his Zwinglian views on the Eucharist.

Luther and his followers had long entertained hopes of winning over Europe's leading humanist and scriptural scholar, Erasmus of Rotterdam. They had reason to do so: like Luther a disaffected Augustinian friar, Erasmus was for years a vocal and influential critic of a church that he saw as badly in need of reform. But he had not left the church, and for years he did not respond to appeals from evangelicals and traditionalists alike that he enter the fray on their side. When he finally did so, it was in a way that gave Luther fresh cause to be furious. In an austerely scholarly treatise, carefully limiting himself to only one of the issues separating Luther from Rome and to evidence taken from Scripture because he knew that Luther would accept no other authority, Erasmus argued that the father of the Reformation was wrong—that man does have free will. It was a restrained testament to say the least, but it put an end to any thought that the greatest humanist of the age would be joining forces with the greatest reformer. Protestantism continued to split into so many factions over so many issues that it seemed, in Luther's words, to have "nearly as many sects as there are heads."

As for England, from where Luther sat it must have been a very hard place to understand. The church of Henry VIII was not evangelical and it was not Roman Catholic. No one in either camp could have imagined that in the next three decades it would become first the former, then the latter, and finally go off in a third direction of its own devising.

9

Consummation

In August 1532, three months after receiving the submission of the clergy, King Henry learned of the death of William Warham. He must have been pleased with the news. Though both as primate of England and as onetime chancellor Warham had long been a friend to the Crown, his great age had reduced his ability to be useful even when he wished to be so, his swings of opinion since the start of the divorce case had brought his dependability into question, and his unhappiness with the direction of royal policy was becoming increasingly worrisome.

His passing meant that Henry was now free, assuming that he met with no interference from the pope, to fill the highest clerical office in the kingdom with a man of his own choosing. He would not have been slow to appreciate the potential benefits.

But Warham's death was an even bigger stroke of luck than Henry appears to have realized. The archbishop had been a man of exceptional abilities and great learning, with doctorates in civil and canon law, and his early performance in the royal service had caused him to be singled out for advancement by no less demanding a judge than Henry VII. And unlike Wolsey, who eventually succeeded him in the chancellorship (possibly but not certainly by elbowing him aside—Warham appears to have been genuinely happy to focus exclusively on his ecclesiastical responsibilities), he had always maintained the highest standards in both his professional and his personal life. Erasmus, an unsparing critic of clerical politicians, called him "a man worthy of the memory of all posterity." Though age had diminished his ability to provide consistent and decisive leadership, he remained a formidable potential adversary, and after his death it was discovered that he had been preparing to speak out. He had been drafting, presumably for delivery in the House of Lords when Parliament reconvened, a speech invoking the example of his most celebrated predecessor in the seat of Canterbury, the martyr Thomas Becket. A canonized saint whose tomb was a pilgrimage site that drew thousands of visitors from around England and the continent, Becket had been murdered in 1170 by a trio of knights who thought, probably mistakenly, that they were carrying out the wishes of King Henry II. Becket and the king, once the closest of friends, had come to be bitterly at loggerheads over the latter's insistence on trying clerics in his own courts and blocking appeals to Rome. The reaction to Becket's murder was so powerful that Henry, one of the most forceful and dynamic monarchs of the English Middle Ages, was not only defeated in his challenge to the church but forced to do public penance. The veneration in which Becket was held explains why such an extraordinary number of fifteenth-century Englishmen had been given the name Thomas. His legend was a potent one for Warham to draw upon.

Warham's draft referred also to other kings who had tried and failed to challenge the rights of the church, and it ended on a note of defiance. At the time of his death Warham had hanging over him a praemunire charge laid against him earlier in the year—another of the king's acts of harassment, this one accusing the archbishop of having failed to obtain royal permission before installing a new bishop in a small, obscure Welsh diocese. (The difficulty Henry's researchers must have had in finding a "crime" in Warham's past is suggested by the fact that the alleged offense had been committed a decade and a half before.) In his undelivered speech, Warham declared his refusal to pay the bond that was being demanded of him in connection with the charge. The Crown had no right to make such a demand, he wrote, or to take action against him for refusing to comply: anyone who arrested or assaulted a bishop committed a mortal sin, and any kingdom where such a thing happened could be—as England had been after the murder of Becket, until Henry II begged forgiveness—placed under an interdict forbidding the exercise of the sacraments. Implicit in these words was the threat that, if Henry continued on his present path, he too might be excommunicated. Had the archbishop lived to utter them, they might have had a powerful impact on churchmen whose refusal to accept the document of submission had shown them to be hungry for leadership. Their effect on the people, and even on a king still hesitant to complete the break with Rome, could likewise have been immense. Excommunication and interdiction had, in centuries past, stopped ambitious monarchs in their tracks. No one could be certain whether they retained their old power, but Henry had reason to be concerned. It was a boon to his cause that Warham went to his grave when he did.

The prestige of the see of Canterbury made finding the right replacement crucial. If Warham had died just a year earlier, he probably would have been succeeded by Bishop Stephen Gardiner, an early and vigorous champion of Henry's divorce suit. (An interesting sidelight on Gardiner is an old assertion, utterly unprovable, that he was a son of Jasper Tudor's illegitimate daughter and therefore Henry VIII's second cousin.) But Gardiner's part in writing the bishops' response to the Supplication Against the Ordinaries had been, in the king's eyes, an act of betrayal. Other likely candidates presented similar problems. Edward Lee had been chosen to replace Wolsey as archbishop of York after helping substantially with the preparation of the king's divorce case, but thereafter, while never daring to defy his royal master, he had become a halfhearted and almost grudging advocate. Cuthbert Tunstal was among the most respected bishops in England, and Henry's decision to promote him from London to Durham in 1530 had been widely applauded. But by now he too was out of the question, having put himself on the side of Catherine of Aragon in the divorce controversy and objected in writing to Henry's claim to be supreme head.

Other bishops had proved more pliant than Gardiner or Lee or Tunstal, but for one reason or another none seemed quite satisfactory. Thus the king's attention turned to a man who was not a bishop, had never before been considered for a bishopric, and was unknown even by reputation to most of the clergy of England. Henry appointed a new ambassador to the court of Charles V and ordered Thomas Cranmer to return home, where his opinions and willingness to cooperate could be given a final examination. All the auguries were encouraging, certainly. Cranmer came with the endorsement of the Boleyns, who had sponsored him earlier in his career and encouraged his membership in that circle of Cambridge clerics whose reformist ideas extended as far as a questioning of Catholic doctrine including the authority of the pope. The king himself, by this point, had had considerable opportunity to observe Cranmer and take his measure. He had used him as a researcher, an envoy to the universities, and finally a diplomat. He had found him to be intelligent, learned, industrious, and conscientious, and to give no evidence of seeking either to enrich himself or to push any personal religious agenda. Instead he seemed happy to embrace the king's objectives, and to acknowledge that the setting of priorities was the king's province exclusively. If Henry was hoping to find a lieutenant who could be as useful to him in the ecclesiastical sphere as Cromwell was proving in the council, he should have seen the emergence of the amiable, unassuming Cranmer as his latest stroke of good fortune.

There was an obstacle, however: in contravention of his clerical vows, Cranmer was married. During his time as Henry's representative in Protestant Germany, where his reformist and antipapal inclinations had been reinforced by exposure to leading Lutheran thinkers, he had made the acquaintance of a Nuremberg theologian who called himself Osiander and had won fame by persuading the head of the religious order of Teutonic Knights to break with Rome. This Osiander, himself a married former priest, persuaded Cranmer—who appears to have needed little convincing—that his vow of chastity was papist nonsense. Thus liberated, Cranmer married Osiander's niece; it was actually his second marriage, an earlier wife having died years before, thereby making it possible for him to resume his career at Cambridge and in the church. Cranmer kept the German marriage secret, and with good reason: King Henry was, and all his life would remain, rigidly insistent on the celibacy of the clergy, forbidding matrimony even to the monks and nuns released from their vows of poverty and obedience after the destruction of their monasteries. Eventually there would be stories— one hopes that they were the invention of his Catholic adversaries— about how, when Cranmer returned to England, his wife accompanied him upside-down, hidden in a trunk into which airholes had been punched. A decade would pass before Cranmer finally confessed his marriage to the king. There is no better evidence of Henry's unique affection for him, an affection anchored in the certainty that in Cranmer he had found an absolutely loyal servant, than his decision to allow him to keep both his job and his spouse so long as the latter remained secret.

As the end of 1532 approached the pace of events began to accelerate. The king's divorce case and his attack on the church, which until now had been distinct battles fought on separate fronts, came to be inextricably entwined. Barely a week after Warham's death, Henry raised Anne Boleyn to the high rank of Marquess of Pembroke with a suitably munificent income (land worth a thousand pounds per year, plus an annuity of another thousand pounds exacted from Stephen Gardiner's diocese of Winchester) and the right to pass title and wealth to the "heirs male" of her body. Never before had an Englishwoman received a noble title other than by inheritance or matrimony. Perhaps Henry's sudden generosity was intended as an inducement for Anne to surrender at last; it provided some assurance that, even if she and the king never married, she would be handsomely provided for, and that any son born out of wedlock would be heir to a title and a fortune. The title she was given had had special meaning for the Tudors ever since Jasper was made Earl of Pembroke three-quarters of a century before and the future Henry VII spent most of his childhood at Pembroke Castle.

Not coincidentally, Anne's title enhanced her suitability to serve as the king's companion at a meeting with Francis I in northern France. Both kings had been eager for this meeting, which took place in October first at Boulogne (which belonged to France) and then at Calais (English), because each wanted to make sure that the other did not enter into an alliance with Charles V. Henry in particular had to be concerned that a conclusive break with Rome might cause the pious Charles to want to invade not only to avenge his aunt's honor but to rescue England from schism and heresy. The gathering was a grand occasion, as such events invariably were. The new Marquess of Pembroke (she did not have the female form of the title, marchioness, because she held it in her own right rather than as a spouse) had the satisfaction of dancing with Francis and later of receiving from him the gift of a costly diamond. To be presented to the king of France as the king of England's all-but-wife was no small thing, and it must have added to Anne's confidence that she was in no danger of being cast aside. The only disquieting note was the failure of any of the female members of the French royal family to appear: evidently they found the relationship between

Anne and Henry insufficiently respectable. Concerns on that score were not assuaged by the refusal of Henry's own sister Mary, herself a one-time queen of France, to join the festivities in Calais; she remained infuriatingly loyal to Catherine.

The substance of the conference had less to do with Charles V— Henry and Francis were satisfied for the time being with reaffirming the defensive alliance that already bound their two countries—than with the recalcitrant Pope Clement. Francis professed sympathy with Henry's anger and frustration. When Henry proposed that the two of them call a general council of the church as a way of overriding and neutering the pope, Francis was not enthusiastic, perhaps out of fear of Charles's possible reaction. He offered excuses: a council would be too difficult, would take too long to arrange, would be unpredictable in the final result. As an alternative he said that he was attempting to arrange a meeting with Clement in the new year, and he offered to include Henry in this meeting and use it to try to effect a resolution of the issues dividing England and Rome. Henry agreed; the thought of the French king meeting separately with the pope, of his possibly being drawn into an alliance with Clement and Charles, would have given him severe discomfort. He promised to do nothing in the meantime that might make reconciliation with the pope impossible. Francis for his part pledged not to proceed with a plan to marry his second son to the pope's niece Catherine de' Medici until Clement nullified Henry's marriage. Henry and Anne then returned home by slow stages, making leisurely stops along the way.

It was at about this time that Anne, if she had never done so previously, admitted Henry to her bed. We know this for the best of reasons: she was, by late January, incontrovertibly pregnant. Several things could have caused her to yield at this point. Her prominence during the visit to France, and her new status in the upper reaches of the hereditary nobility, obviously would have served as positive inducements. On the negative side were the French king's unexpected offer of a meeting with the pope and Henry's alarming (from Anne's perspective) acceptance. This raised the spectre of a rapprochement between England and Rome, a development that could mean ruin for Anne, her family, and their whole following including the religious reformers with whom the Boleyns were allied. If Henry decided to abandon the divorce—that could not have seemed likely, but no one knew better than Anne how unpredictable he could be—everything that had come to them with the king's favor would likely be lost. On the other hand, the promise of a royal son could secure the future for all of them.

Anne's pregnancy further accelerated the pace of everything the king was doing. It immediately gave rise to a need to ensure that her child, the king's son, would be legitimate. This led to an impromptu wedding at York Place early on January 25. The ceremony was performed by one of the royal chaplains, Rowland Lee, who as he hurried to the palace's western turret that morning knew only that he had received an unexpected order to go to a specific room to say mass. When he arrived, he was surprised to find waiting for him King Henry, Lady Anne, and a lady and two gentlemen of the court. Told that Henry and Anne wished to be married, Lee, mindful of the unresolved state of the divorce case, expressed concern about whether he was free to proceed. The king assured him that the necessary papal permission was in safekeeping in his privy chamber. At best, he was referring to the bull with which, long before, the pope had set aside the impediment created by the king's affair with Mary Boleyn, granting him permission to marry Anne *if* the marriage to Catherine were found to be invalid. At worst, Henry was simply lying. Lee, whether or not his mind was put at rest, had little choice but to take the king at his word.

The wedding was kept secret so that, later, it would be possible to fudge the date and make it appear that Anne and Henry had been married when their child was conceived. Anne's father, however, was sent across the Channel to inform Francis I, who did not abandon his hopes of including Henry in a meeting with the pope but did feel free, now that the English king had broken his promise, to resume negotiations for the marriage of his son to Pope Clement's niece. Under other circumstances a Medici might not have been considered an acceptable bride for a prince who was second in line to the crown of France. But Francis, obsessed as always with his ambitions in Italy, would have sacrificed more than family pride in order to keep pope and emperor apart.

Henry now had the wife he had craved, and she was delightfully pregnant. The only remaining need was for the marriage to be declared valid, which would remain impossible until the marriage to Catherine was nullified. As he had no hope by now of getting the pope's help, he had to find another way, and quickly. Inevitably, his attention and Cromwell's focused on the Archbishopric of Canterbury. More than five months had passed since Warham's death, and the two had used that time to work out a plan of action more detailed and ambitious than anything they had thus far attempted. Cranmer was central to that plan and, in the days after he arrived home from the continent, had shown himself to be as eager to assist as Henry and Cromwell could have hoped. In mid-January the king dispatched riders to Rome with a politely submissive request that Thomas Cranmer be appointed to Canterbury. A heavy curtain of secrecy remained in place around Henry's marriage to Anne and her pregnancy so that the papal court would have no idea that something new was afoot. To further ensure the pope's good will, he continued to be sent his traditional share of England's ecclesiastical revenues. He like the king was of course unaware that the candidate had a wife.

The nomination of an obscure archdeacon to such a high post would have raised eyebrows in any case, but Cranmer's candidacy provoked alarm. Well-placed Catholics on the continent and even in Rome had had dealings with Cranmer, whose assignments had taken him at one point to the Eternal City. His doctrinal inclinations were therefore fairly well known if his marital status was not, and Clement was warned not to agree to his appointment. The pope, however, lived in fear of a break with England as damaging to the church as the Lutheran rebellion that had already engulfed half of Germany. Though he was satisfied that Henry's marriage to Catherine was valid, and though he was mortally sick of the king's ham-handed attempts to bully and cajole him, he remained willing to do almost anything short of approving the divorce to heal the breach between them. Knowing little of who Cranmer actually was and nothing of the uses to which Henry intended to put him, Clement dispatched the documents required for the new primate to be consecrated exactly as his predecessors had always been.

Henry and Cromwell's plan was to have Cranmer, as soon as possible after he was installed, declare the king's first marriage null and his second valid. It was a simple plan as far as it went, but there was one complication. Catherine was certain to appeal to Rome, just as she had appealed years earlier. This would lead to delays even more intolerable than those the king had already suffered, and there could be no hope that Catherine would be denied. The legitimacy of the prince whose birth now approached would be compromised, and Henry would stand in increased danger of being excommunicated, his kingdom put under an interdict.

Cromwell was ready with an answer, and as usual his solution was to cut the Gordian knot. Long before the end of 1532 he had had in preparation a draft bill that would become famous as the Act in Restraint of Appeals (not to be confused with the Act in Restraint of Annates). Once approved by Parliament, it would use England's supposed status as an empire and the English king's consequent autonomy as a basis for forbidding any of his subjects to ask any foreign power (the bishop of Rome most emphatically included) to overrule him on any question. Cromwell revised his draft and revised it again as he waited for Cranmer's bulls of appointment to arrive from Rome, and sought advice on how to maximize support in Parliament. As soon as the bulls were in hand, he was ready to move. The years-old deadlock would be broken at last.

The next necessary step was to consecrate the new archbishop. This happened on March 30, and it happened in a way so peculiar that it might not have been possible had Cranmer not already shown himself to have a relaxed view of vows. The ceremony for installing bishops had always included the taking of an oath of loyalty to the pope. Until Henry turned this oath into a weapon with which to charge the bishops with praemunire, this procedure had never posed a problem. Except on those few and usually brief occasions when kings had clashed with the church over questions of jurisdiction, everyone had understood the distinction between royal and ecclesiastical authority and accepted the legitimacy of both. But Cranmer came to his new position with no such understanding. On the contrary, he believed sincerely that neither the king nor he nor any Englishman owed anything to the bishop of Rome, and that where religion was concerned the monarch's wish and will provided the answers to all questions.

The papal oath, therefore, presented Cranmer with a problem of ethics. He resolved that problem, just minutes before his consecration, by taking four selected witnesses and a notary aside to a place where they could hear him privately declare that, although he was about to complete the traditional formalities, nothing that he swore publicly should be construed as an intention to violate the law of God, disobey the king, or fail to do whatever must be done for the good of the church in England. The installation ceremony then began. Cranmer took the very oath that he had minutes before repudiated, an oath in direct contradiction to the work he was preparing to undertake.

That work was multifaceted but went forward with lightning speed. Six days after Cranmer's consecration, with the new archbishop presiding, the Southern Convocation approved a resolution declaring that the king's marriage to Catherine of Aragon had never been valid. This victory was easily won; many churchmen had never been strongly opposed to the divorce, and many who had been opposed, faced now with the demoralizing presence of Cranmer as their ostensible leader, saw no point in resisting. Two days after that, in spite of stubborn resistance, the Restraint of Appeals bill was passed by Parliament and became law. After another six days Anne's marriage to the king was announced in such a way as to create the impression that it had occurred in mid-November, before the expected child was conceived. By all accounts the news was not well received; at one London church on Easter Sunday, upon being told that Anne was now queen and asked to pray for her, the entire congregation got to its feet and walked out. The lord mayor was ordered to make certain that there would be no more such displays of discontent, and the city's professional guilds were told to keep silent on the subject and make their apprentices do the same.

The stage was now set for the final act, an ecclesiastical hearing at which Cranmer and a selected panel of his fellow divines would hear arguments on the validity of Henry's marriage to Catherine and pass final judgment. The result was a foregone conclusion. A procedural difficulty arose, however, in connection with Henry's new status as supreme head of the church: with the pope out of the picture, so that Cranmer could not claim to be acting in the name of any higher ecclesiastical authority, on what basis could he *order* the king to appear before the court and allow his case to be judged? Seeing that there was no such basis, the archbishop prudently decided not to order but to beg. But when he wrote to the king saying that "most humbly on my knees" he requested permission to convene his court, his words were found to be insufficiently abject. In the final version of his request, poor Cranmer described himself as "prostrate at the feet of your Majesty."

On May 23, to the surprise of no one, Cranmer's court declared that Henry and Catherine had never been married. Five days later, equally unsurprisingly, it declared that Henry and Anne were very married indeed. Just three days after that, at huge expense and amid great fanfare intended to inflame the enthusiasm of a public that in the event showed no enthusiasm at all, Anne was crowned queen of England at Westminster Abbey.

All of it had gone almost exactly according to plan, and everything continued to do so. On July 11, the same day that Henry signed the letters needed to implement the long-deferred Act in Restraint of Annates and terminate all payments to Rome, Pope Clement declared Henry's marriage to Anne invalid and warned him that unless he recognized Catherine as his wife he would be excommunicated—but not until the following September, and only *if* he failed to mend his ways. Henry responded with a fury that must have been fueled in part at least by fear, recalling his envoys and cutting off communications with the papacy. His participation in the planned meeting between Clement and Francis was now out of the question, but when that meeting finally took place in September Francis remained hopeful of somehow effecting a reconciliation. He had little difficulty persuading Clement to delay the excommunication again. In fact it would never be promulgated, so that neither Henry nor Clement ever found out whether it was still a weapon that could hurt.

Only one thing remained for the scenario to be complete. Anne still had to give birth to her son.

The child, when born on September 7, was named Elizabeth, after Henry's mother.

PART TWO

Monster

1533–1547

10

First Blood

Two dams broke in 1534. One was in Parliament, where resistance to the Crown snapped at last under Cromwell's relentless pressure and a torrent of revolutionary new laws began to change the character of English government and society. The other was inside the mind of a monarch who, perhaps swept away by the ecstatic realization that in the whole kingdom there was no force capable of keeping him from doing exactly as he wished, threw off all restraint and showed himself ready to destroy not only anyone who opposed him but anyone withholding approval of whatever he wanted to do.

The first victim, both of the newly docile Parliament and of the newly savage king, was a twenty-seven-year-old nun named Elizabeth Barton. Possibly epileptic, Barton, while a servant girl still in her teens, had been mysteriously healed of some affliction and begun falling into trances, having visions, and predicting the future. This caused her to become famous first locally, in her home county of Kent, and then more widely. She came to be revered as the Holy Maid of Kent and then, after she entered a convent, as the Nun of Kent. By all accounts she lived a blameless life and made a favorable impression on practically everyone who met her, including skeptical clergymen assigned to question and report on her. But, tragically for herself, eventually she was making pronouncements on the king's efforts to divorce Queen Catherine and warning that evil would befall him if he did not desist. She sent a message to the pope, saying that he too would be cursed if he did as Henry asked. The attention that she attracted is evident in the fact that at various times Cardinal Wolsey, Archbishop Warham, Bishop Fisher, Chancellor More, and even the king himself all met with her. All who had firsthand exposure to her and left a record of their impressions said that Barton seemed virtuous, humble, and possibly even holy. Even Henry was favorably disposed until she began to talk about the divorce.

Barton's fame, and the increasingly inflammatory nature of her opinions, made trouble inevitable. Cromwell's power and confidence were in full flower by this time—he had been given a seat on the Royal Council before the end of 1532 and made chancellor of the exchequer the following April—and in July 1533 he had Barton arrested. He and Cranmer questioned her at length, after which she was confined in the Tower along with a half dozen of the churchmen (an assortment of parish priests, Benedictine monks, and Franciscan friars) who had made themselves her supporters and, so it was said, her manipulators in the national debate over the divorce and the king's claim to ecclesiastical supremacy. The idea, clearly, was to discredit Barton and make her a frightening example of the price to be paid for opposing the Crown.

In November the Nun and her adherents were put on public display, made to listen to a preacher who ridiculed and vilified them, and finally, according to accounts left by people in the pay of Cromwell, required to confess that her entire career had been a fraud intended to mislead the gullible. It is not certain that these reported confessions actually occurred; no record of them was left by witnesses who can be considered impartial. Even if the accused did in fact confess, the men in whose custody they had been for months were quite capable of using torture to get what they wanted. Barton's own confession, as recorded for posterity, was obviously not the work of a barely literate serving girl but of a ghostwriter of some sophistication.

The confessions were not the end of the story, in any case. An effort was mounted to convict Barton and her companions of high treason by establishing that she had prophesied the death of the king and so had effectively threatened his life—and to draw in other, bigger prey on grounds that anyone who had encouraged her or even listened to her without reporting her words was guilty of treason as well. This effort came to nothing. The king's judges reported that the case was too weak even for them—there never was a shred of evidence that Barton at any time encouraged anyone to oppose the king actively or to use violence for any purpose—and there was at this point no basis in English law for charging someone with treason because of what he or she had said. Treason was still an *act*. Remarkably, some of Barton's judges were reported to have declared that they would die themselves rather than find her guilty.

Cromwell responded by finding yet another new way to make Parliament useful to the Crown. At his direction both houses approved a bill of attainder that declared Barton and her six closest associates guilty of high treason. Six others, Thomas More and Bishop Fisher among them, were attainted for misprision of treason—that is, for knowing of another person's treason and failing to report it. From the king's standpoint, this simplified everything beautifully. Not only Barton and her cohorts but several of the most eminent personages in the kingdom could be disposed of without the inconvenience of a trial, attainder being a legislative rather than a judicial device. The fact that no one including Barton herself could possibly have committed treason as the word was then understood in English law became irrelevant.

More and Fisher defended themselves, or tried to. More requested permission to appear before Parliament to address the charge against him. Upon being refused he wrote to Cromwell and the king, explaining how, in his meetings with the Nun of Kent, he had refused to hear her opinions of political matters and had advised her to share those opinions with no one. He told them also that when visited by admirers of Barton who wanted to discuss her visions, he had not allowed them to do so. Cromwell advised Fisher to throw himself on the king's mercy—good advice where saving his own skin was concerned, as Henry was always most likely to be generous when his victims submitted abjectly—but predictably the bishop refused. He said, sensibly enough, that he had been told by men he trusted (Archbishop Warham for one) that Barton was an honest and virtuous woman, and that his willingness to believe them, whether wise or foolish, could not possibly have been a crime. He said he had talked with Barton on three occasions, but only because she visited him uninvited. He had not reported Barton's dark predictions, he said, because he knew for a fact that she herself had already shared them with the king.

None of this had any effect on Henry, who obviously was interested not in the guilt or innocence of the accused but in their elimination. His friends, however, saw that he was in danger of overreaching; in the end More's name was removed from the bill of attainder, but only because Cranmer, Cromwell, and the Duke of Norfolk literally got down on their knees and implored the king to permit its removal. The three were willing to beg less because they wished to save the former chancellor than because, as they warned Henry, even a supine Parliament could not be depended upon to destroy a man of More's reputation on such thin evidence.

Fisher's name remained on the bill, and after its passage he was imprisoned. After a while, however, he was allowed to pay a fine of £300, the yearly income of his little Diocese of Rochester, and set free. Barton and five others—two Benedictine monks, two Observant friars, and Barton's confessor—were taken to the royal killing ground at Tyburn. There Barton, perhaps because she was a woman and allegedly confessed to being "a poor wench without learning" and having fallen into "a certain pride and fantasy with myself," was shown the mercy of simple death by hanging. The priests endured a good deal more. They too were hanged, but then they met the full fate of traitors: cut down while still alive and brought back to consciousness, they had their genitals cut off and stuffed into their mouths, their intestines torn from their bodies and thrown into a fire, and their beating hearts pulled out of their chests and held up where they could see them. Finally their bodies were cut into four quarters for display in different parts of London, their heads boiled and put on stakes. As they had never been tried, it was impossible for anyone to know how, exactly, they had committed treason, or whether, given the opportunity, they might have been able to establish their innocence. The public was left free to conclude that they had died for displeasing the king. The king, no doubt, wanted it to conclude exactly that.

Henry, meanwhile, was occupied elsewhere. The future of his dynasty was a question that never went away, the birth of the baby Elizabeth had done nothing to answer it, and now that he was in his forties the king was giving evidence of being more seriously concerned about his lack of a male heir than he had ever been before. The previous November he had married his only living son, the illegitimate fourteen-year-old Henry Fitzroy, to Mary Howard, who as a daughter of the Duke of Norfolk was also Anne Boleyn's cousin. This was another coup for the Howard family, another joining of its blood to that of the Tudors, potentially of vast importance because of the possibility, which had been in the air for years, that Henry might choose in the end to make the playful young Fitzroy, on whom he doted, his heir. By January, however, Anne was pregnant for the second time. As preparations began anew for the arrival of a crown prince—Henry was always touchingly certain that his next child would be a boy—the king took as his mistress yet another young Boleyn cousin, a girl named Madge Shelton. The magic was going out of the royal marriage by this time; the increasingly insecure Anne upbraided her husband for his dalliances, and Henry turned his back on her in mute disbelief. The situation was not improved when Anne miscarried. This happened in the middle of a remarkably busy spring, when the Nun of Kent was being readied for execution, the papal court in Rome was taking up the divorce case at last, and Parliament was pouring out laws that would have been unimaginable a few years earlier.

Pope Clement, under pressure from Charles V and provoked into action at last by Henry's taking of a second wife without being released from his first, assembled a council of cardinals—a consistory—to consider the divorce case. On March 23, rather to the pope's surprise (he knew that agents of the king of France had been lobbying hard to line up support for Henry, spending the English king's money freely), nineteen of the twenty-two assembled cardinals voted to deny the annulment, uphold the validity of Henry's marriage to Catherine, and declare that Catherine had been dealt with unjustly and should be restored to her place as queen. The remaining three voted not in Henry's favor but merely for further delay, at which point, after so many years, the king's great matter was settled even in Rome. But Clement, his hopes of somehow avoiding a final break with Henry being practically inexhaustible, postponed issuing a formal judgment.

Rome was no longer relevant, however; things had gone too far in England for papal rulings to matter. By coincidence March 23 was also the day on which Parliament, with Cromwell issuing the instructions, passed an Act of Succession that not only gave the force of civil law to Cranmer's nullification of the king's first marriage and validation of his second but erected around the archbishop's findings a protective barrier of punishment for anyone who failed to assent. The act's assertion that Henry was to be succeeded on the throne by the children of his "most dear and entirely beloved lawful wife Queen Anne" (the sheer number of adjectives heaped upon the lady's name is suggestive of royal defensiveness) could have surprised no one by 1534. Its failure to mention Princess Mary, implying that she was illegitimate and therefore excluded from the succession, would have offended many but surprised few. Much more startling, for anyone who knew the law, was the act's broadening of the crime of high treason to encompass anyone acting or writing in defiance or rejection of the Boleyn marriage. Even speaking against the marriage was made misprision of treason. With these provisions the king closed the loopholes—it would be more accurate to say he destroyed the protections—that had made it impossible to bring the Nun of Kent's case into a court of law.

The Act of Succession did not stop even there. Not satisfied with forbidding criticism, Henry had added a requirement that every subject "observe, keep, maintain and defend the act and all the whole contents and effects thereof, and all other Acts and Statutes made since the beginning of this present parliament"—since, that is, December 1529, when the king had ventured his first hesitant attack on ecclesiastical privilege. To ensure compliance, every subject was to take an oath of loyalty not only to the king but to his heirs by Anne, and refusal to swear was made treason. Conveniently, Parliament neglected to specify what the words of the oath should be. This left Henry and Cromwell free to put it into whatever form best pleased them and even to require different people to swear to different things.

This was not the only law approved by Parliament in furtherance of the king's agenda that spring. An Act for the Submission of the Clergy gave statutory form to, and therefore enhanced the legitimacy of, the submission so dubiously wrung out of convocation two years earlier. An Act in Absolute Restraint of Annates removed the conditional aspects of the earlier annates legislation, diverted the payment of annates from Rome to the Crown rather than eliminating them as might have been expected, and laid down curious new rules for the selection of bishops. The king would henceforth send the name of his nominee to the clergy of the diocese involved. The clergy would then be accorded the privilege of approving the king's candidate. If somehow such approval was not forthcoming, the royal choice would take office anyway and the clergy of that diocese would lose the honor of being consulted in future. Yet another act took the awarding of dispensations away from Rome and gave it to the archbishop of Canterbury, assigning two-thirds of the fees thus generated to the Crown. Anyone appealing a ruling by Canterbury was to turn henceforth not to Rome but to the King's Chancery Court, and of course it was no longer heresy to refuse to recognize the pope—the bishop of Rome, as he was now to be called—as head of the English church. Those monasteries which until now had been under the jurisdiction of the orders with which they were affiliated rather than their local bishops were put under the authority not of the bishops but of the Crown.

What it all added up to was a wholesale chopping away of the English church's traditional connections to Rome and their replacement with new obligations to the king. Henry was creating, not a church free of domination by any external power, but a church that he himself would dominate totally. Parliament, too, was being made newly subordinate to the Crown. Cromwell continued to take care, in preparing the latest statutes, to make clear that Parliament was merely recognizing the king's supremacy rather than conferring supremacy upon him. The king's authority was acknowledged as coming directly from God, not from any earthly source and certainly not (as Thomas More had dared to suggest years before, in his first public appearance as chancellor) from his subjects. To oppose the king was to oppose God. This was the highwater mark of royal authority in England, the opening of an era—it would not last long—in which the Crown claimed, and for a while actually possessed, mastery over the lives, the property, and even the consciences of its subjects. Cromwell's reward for making it happen was to be appointed, that spring, King Henry's principal secretary. He would turn the position into the most powerful in the government. From it he would reach out to control both houses of Parliament, the courts, and the council.

The destruction of ecclesiastical authority was final: after the 1530s the bishops as a body never again played a major role in the political life of the kingdom. It is arguable, some would say certain, that this and the other changes of the spring of 1534 were an improvement over traditional arrangements. Most of them were, in any case, irrelevant to the everyday lives of the overwhelming majority of English men and women. Few of them could ever have had occasion to appeal to Rome or even to Canterbury, to request a dispensation or become involved in questions of heresy. Aside from being required to take an oath that must have struck many of them as more odd than important, most people would have had little reason even to be aware that new laws had supplanted the old. Parish life, the age-old Latin Mass, the seven sacraments, beliefs that had been part of the heritage of every man and woman in England through more centuries than most of them had knowledge of—none of this had been altered at all.

Still, the popularity of Catherine of Aragon and the widespread sense that she had been dealt with unfairly ensured that the Act of Succession would not be well received. And many, almost certainly most of the best-informed and most influential of the king's subjects, those who had some sense of the significance of the new laws, would have been uneasy at least about what was happening. The making into treason of things that had never been treason before—had never even been crimes before—would have unsettled any reasonable mind. The requirement that everyone swear to defend and uphold innovations condemned by some of the best men in the kingdom could easily have seemed an outrage. Henry was discarding beliefs and customs and understandings that his people had been raised with. To require those people not simply to accept his changes but to champion them, to swear that they believed them to be right, was an assault on the integrity of the individual of a kind never before seen in England. It was inevitable that the people would be skeptical. Outbreaks of popular discontent, too, were probably inevitable, though they would not be quick in coming.

Further initiatives by the king *would* be quick in coming. The butchering of the Nun of Kent and her group was barely the beginning.

THE TOWER

MAKE A CHRONOLOGICAL LIST OF ALL THE NOTABLE ENGLISH men and women who were ever imprisoned in the Tower of London and then put to death there, and a remarkable fact leaps out: such executions were overwhelmingly concentrated in the Tudor era, with few happening afterward and even fewer earlier, during the supposedly terrible Middle Ages. There is no better measure of just how big a deviation from the norm the Tudors were—of how much more savage their politics were than anything seen before or since.

Though the Tower had loomed ominously over London for four and a half centuries by the time Henry VIII had Elizabeth Barton and her associates locked up in it and then killed, throughout almost all of its history it had not been a particularly bloody place. In its earliest manifestation it was an improvised motte-and-bailey affair—a wooden stockade on a hilltop—hurriedly erected shortly after the Norman Conquest of 1066 not as a defense against possible invaders but to intimidate the Anglo-Saxon population of the adjacent and still tiny city of London. After ten years William the Conqueror decided to rebuild it in stone and began work on the massive keep that came to be known as the White Tower. It, with the four "onion domes" added by Henry VIII in 1530, became the centerpiece of a complex of surrounding fortifications and remains one of England's most familiar landmarks down to the present day. Here as elsewhere the Normans built for eternity: constructed of stone carried by ship from northern France, the White Tower was ninety feet high with a 118-by-107-foot foundation and had walls that were fifteen feet thick at the base and eleven feet thick at the top with towers at each corner. The entry was well above ground level, and the stairs leading to it were removable in case of attack.

When completed by William II in 1097, the Tower was by far the most impressive structure ever seen in London. Though its location near the lowest bridgeable point on the River Thames would make it increasingly important as a defensive stronghold in case of invasion, as the twelfth century began its prime purpose continued to be to give the Normans an impregnable base from which to dominate a subject population. From the start it served multiple purposes—fortress, royal residence, place of worship, armory, prison—and as the generations passed so many kings expanded and altered it in so many ways that it became, as it remains today, a kind of museum of medieval castle architecture. Three generations after the completion of the White Tower, King Richard the Lion-Hearted returned from the Third Crusade with new ideas about defensive stoneworks and ordered the construction of so-called "curtain walls" around the original tower. Even more extensive additions, the most important by Richard's nephew Henry III and Henry's son Edward I, extended the perimeter out farther and farther until finally what was still called "*the* Tower" covered eighteen acres and included twenty-one distinct towers, all behind two concentric walls of overwhelming height and a broad moat filled with water from the Thames. There was no more powerful fortress anywhere in Europe. It retained all of its original functions, becoming an increasingly opulent home for the royal family, and also provided a virtually impregnable home for the Crown jewels, the mint, the government's records, and even a royal zoo complete with lions.

Though its radically increased size and strength made the Tower an ideal place for the confinement of important prisoners, it remained remarkably free of political violence for almost four centuries. Within a few years of the White Tower's completion and King William II's death, his hated minister Ranulf Flambard (Ranulf the Torchbearer) was imprisoned in it, but he escaped by climbing down a rope smuggled to him inside a wine cask. Richard II was forced to abdicate in the Tower in 1399, but his death took place elsewhere. The climactic years of the Wars of the Roses brought the Tower's first major eruption of mayhem: the 1471 murder of Henry VI; the 1478 execution of Edward IV's and Richard III's brother George, Duke of Clarence; the 1483 killing of Edward's chamberlain Lord Hastings by Richard; and the disappearance of Edward's two young sons in that same year. Things were again quiet for a decade and a half until, as we have seen, Henry VII had both the imposter Perkin

Warbeck and Clarence's son the earl of Warwick taken from their cells and put to death.

The Tower was still a royal residence when Henry VIII was a boy (it would remain one into the Stuart dynasty in the seventeenth century), and he must have known it well while growing up. When he was not quite six years old, he and his mother, Queen Elizabeth, took refuge in the White Tower when a force of rebels professing support for Warbeck came out of the west and threatened London. Six years later Elizabeth died in the Tower shortly after giving birth, and her body lay in state there before being taken to Westminster for interment. A year after Henry inherited the throne he reached into the Tower to deliver to the executioner his father's hated henchmen Dudley and Empson, and three years after that, before leaving England for his first war in France, he did the same with his cousin Edmund de la Pole. But then quiet returned for two decades—the last bloodless decades that the Tower would know until the Tudors were no more. The change came in 1534, when Elizabeth Barton and her five associates were sent to their deaths and replaced in the Tower by Sir Thomas More, the onetime lord chancellor, and John Fisher, the bishop of Rochester. From then on, to be a significant character in the Tudor story—even to *be* a Tudor—would be to run a high risk of being sent first to the Tower and from there to a gruesome death.

11

Supremacy

King Henry was driven—by his compulsion to dominate, by his hunger for admiration and approval, and by the dangers into which his needs were drawing him—to become an early practitioner of the art of political propaganda. What he was demanding was obviously not going to be easily achieved, and the price of failure was potentially high. Discontent could turn into rebellion, and Henry's new status as an outlaw in the eyes of the Roman church could become an encouragement for the continental powers to invade. His survival might very well depend on the acquiescence of his subjects, for whom he seems to have felt little except contempt.

Those subjects had to be won over. Where they could not be won, they had to be frightened into conformity. In the spring of 1534 Henry undertook to do both things: to convert his people and to terrify them. A national propaganda machine was erected for the purpose: instructions went out for churchmen, on Easter Sunday and thereafter, to preach the new truth—that the pope was an imposter and a usurper, and that in religious as in secular matters there was no authority higher than the king. Cranmer, free at last to give vent to the hatred of Rome that appears to have been boiling deep inside his otherwise placid nature nearly all his life, showed the way by telling his congregation at Canterbury Cathedral that the bishop of Rome was "the Antichrist of the Apocalypse." Such words would have shocked and offended many of the clergy whose leader Cranmer now was, not to mention his conventionally Catholic lay listeners. That his example was not followed as widely as he wished is apparent in the fact that he soon resorted to the novel idea of requiring all the priests in his archdiocese to obtain licenses to preach, suspending the licenses for a year, and instructing all the bishops of the Southern Convocation to do the same. Everything possible was being done to silence a recalcitrant clergy, but resentment became almost palpable. A monk who laughed at Cranmer, calling him "a fool archbishop," was thrown into prison; it was reported that guards were needed to ensure the archbishop's safety when he was in Canterbury. Justices of the peace around England and Wales received instructions to arrest any preacher who spoke in favor of papal authority. Propaganda was reinforced with the police powers of the Crown.

In the days following Easter the royal hammer began to descend on anyone whose words, acts, or omissions might, in the opinion of the king or his ministers, serve to encourage disobedience. The Crown's principal weapon was the oath prepared for use under the Act of Succession. In the form approved for general use, this oath acknowledged that the king was right about the divorce, his marriage to Anne, and his imperial authority—about everything. Agents fanned out across the kingdom, to the universities and to distant villages, seeing to it that the oath was taken everywhere. Some targets, however, had higher priority than others. Anyone in a position of authority, anyone whose decision was likely to become known to substantial numbers of other people, was automatically a prime target. Any such person likely to be perceived by the public as not in agreement with the king received an even higher priority. No one had higher priority than Thomas More, who had left the chancellorship rather than assent to the king's supremacy and had since then maintained a silence that was obviously heavy with meaning, and John Fisher, who from the start had been anything but silent and was all the more dangerous because so widely admired.

Both Fisher and More received summonses to appear at Lambeth Palace, the London residence of the archbishop of Canterbury, on Monday, April 13. They knew what to expect. More spent time with his family before leaving home that morning, telling them that he was likely bound for prison and might never return. Upon their arrival at Lambeth he and Fisher found themselves in a long procession of men being marched one by one into the presence of Cromwell, Cranmer, Thomas Audley (the nonentity who was More's replacement as chancellor), and the abbot of Westminster. All were asked, when their turns came, to sign the succession oath. Almost all did so and were sent on their way. Fisher refused and was escorted to the Tower. More asked for time to read what he was being asked to sign and, having done so, observed that by signing he would be accepting not only the succession rights of Henry and Anne's offspring but the ecclesiastical supremacy of the king in England. He too refused. When asked to explain himself, he declined to do that as well, saying only that in signing he would be violating his conscience and thereby endangering his soul. Clearly he had already offended the king, he said, and in giving his reasons he could only give further offense. Even when standing on principle, he remained the crafty lawyer.

More was told that every member of the House of Commons had sworn the oath. He was shown the signatures and asked how he could oppose his conscience to those of so many others. He answered that he had no quarrel with those who elected to sign, but that he himself could not do so, and that he had on his side most Christians living and dead. After that the discussion had nowhere to go. More was put under arrest. He spent the next four days in the custody of the abbot and then joined Fisher in the Tower. The two were kept apart in fairly comfortable accommodations (More was allowed to keep his manservant), and in the days following both offered to swear to the succession. The king and Parliament had the right to decide such matters in whatever way they chose, More and Fisher said, and they could have no difficulty in acknowledging that right if they were not required at the same time to repudiate the authority of the pope and, by extension, the international community of Christians. Cranmer looked favorably on this offer. He urged the king to accept it, and to make much of the fact that More and Fisher had done as he required while ignoring their refusal to do *everything* required. Cromwell, however, was opposed, and Henry agreed with him.

Faced with the grim consequences of refusal, and receiving from Rome no word of guidance or encouragement and from Canterbury firm instructions to conform, most of the clergy subscribed. Where resistance appeared, it was generally hesitant, isolated, and susceptible to modest applications of pressure. The exceptions, those instances where resistance was bold and not quickly dissolved by threats, brought down the full wrath of the Crown. Those who resisted were seen as both a danger to the king and an opportunity for him and his henchmen to show that they would not be defied. From this followed, with a speed that might have surprised even Henry himself, the extinction of the Observant Franciscans, as respected a religious order as any in England.

The Observants, the reader will recall, were the order of William Peto, the priest who, from his pulpit at Greenwich, had dared to chastise King Henry on Easter Sunday 1532. Founded a century and a half earlier by a breakaway group that believed the Franciscans were becoming too lax, the Observants won recruits and admiration for the austerity of their lives and their dedication to their preaching mission. Invited into England in the early 1480s, they soon had six flourishing friaries. Henry VIII himself had been baptized in one of the friars' churches, as were the short-lived son to whom Queen Catherine gave birth in 1511, Princess Mary, and—rather surprisingly, considering all that had transpired by the time she was born—Anne Boleyn's infant daughter.

Not surprisingly, considering this background, the Observants' refusal to accept the divorce became a major source of annoyance for Henry. The diatribe that Friar Peto directed at him, and Friar Elston's withering treatment of the preacher sent to answer Peto, had been startling acts of defiance. Observants from the order's house at Canterbury had been involved with Elizabeth Barton, too, and a pair of them died with her at Tyburn. The frequency with which Observants denounced the king's innovations in their sermons, along with the writings being sent across the Channel by Peto and Elston from their place of exile, made it inevitable that the Crown would move against them.

By the spring of 1534 Henry and Cromwell had no reason to delay. A special version of the succession oath was prepared for the friars' exclusive use. It was even more comprehensive, and from the conservative perspective even more objectionable, than the version that More and Fisher had been unable to accept. It required the Observants not only to swear allegiance to Henry and Anne and the offspring of their union (none of them disputed the king's right to require that), not only to recognize the king as the supreme earthly authority under whom they followed the Franciscan rule, not only to deny that the bishop of Rome had more authority than any other bishop, but to pledge themselves to do everything possible to persuade others to do likewise. In demanding so much, the king was requiring that the friars actively repudiate much of what they had vowed in becoming Franciscans.

To humiliate the Observants and underscore his unhappiness with them, Henry ordered that the oath be delivered to their six houses by visitors selected from other, more cooperative orders of friars, the Augustinians and the Dominicans. This too was provocative. There being, inevitably, a degree of rivalry among the orders, sending representatives of one to make demands of another came close to being an insult, all the more so as the original encouragement of the Observants in England by Edward IV and Henry VII had implied dissatisfaction with the orders already established there, the Augustinians and Dominicans included. The results of the visits were, in any case, infuriatingly unsatisfactory from the king's point of view. At the Canterbury friary, a house traumatized by the ghastly killing of two of its members with Elizabeth Barton, only two members of the community refused to take the oath. But at Richmond, though the prior was willing, almost all the friars refused. At Greenwich, the Observant establishment with the closest connection to the royal family, refusal was again almost unanimous. Overall the results were ambiguous; at some houses a solid majority was opposed but after much persuasion agreed to let four senior members decide for all. The one thing that would satisfy the king, unanimous acceptance, the Observants could not be induced to give him. And so Henry settled for second best: another chance to show just how high the price of refusal could go.

One day in June two carts loaded with friars were seen rumbling through the streets of London en route to the Tower. Others followed, and by the end of August every one of the order's houses had been emptied out and some two hundred of its members were in prison. They did not get the gentle treatment accorded to Fisher and More. Many were chained to the walls of their cells, many were tortured, many were starved. Some fifty eventually died in confinement. After several years, the king's attention having moved on to other things, those still alive would be permitted to slip away quietly to exile in France, Scotland, and Ireland. There has never been evidence that any of them had been involved in sedition, in attempting to overthrow the king, or in encouraging others to do anything of the kind. Not one was ever charged with any crime. The extermination of their order was simply an eloquent demonstration of the king's power, and of his willingness to use it.

The lesson was not lost on the bishops, none of whom followed Fisher's example. Several were clearly unhappy with what the king was doing, and some would eventually regret their failure to resist. The reason for that failure lies partly in the starkness of the choice that Henry laid out for them: they could do things his way and prosper, or they could be locked away. It also lies partly in the bishops themselves. They had been chosen for their positions not by the pope, not by other ecclesiastics or any other element of the clergy, but by Henry or (as was true of a few of the oldest of them) by Henry's father. And most had been chosen because of their service to a Crown to which, in consequence of how they had been rewarded, they felt a heavy obligation. They were administrators and diplomats. They had political skill. They lived in a time increasingly dominated by the idea that princes ruled by the grace of God, and that to disobey one's ruler was akin to disobeying God. Nothing in any of this had prepared them for martyrdom, and few of the decisions out of which they had shaped their careers had shown them to be inclined in that direction.

Even so, some of them had to be wrestled into submission, and some paid a price for resisting as much as they did. Cuthbert Tunstal appeared for a time to be destined to follow Fisher into the Tower. When at the start of 1534 he set out for London and the next session of Parliament, he received an order from the king to turn around and return home—not the first time his criticism of the king had made him unwelcome at Westminster. It was not until the parliamentary session had concluded, with its flood of statutes cutting off England from Rome, that Tunstal was summoned. He arrived in London to find Fisher in prison amid reports of the killing of Elizabeth Barton, and soon his London residence was invaded and ransacked by Cromwell's agents. At this point Tunstal capitulated. He took the oath of succession, supposedly with reservations that have been lost to history. As usual the king wanted more. He made certain that Tunstal was not merely subdued but made to crawl, requiring him to visit Catherine of Aragon in company with the archbishop of York and explain that he no longer believed her marriage to be valid. Catherine of course was hurt and angry, all the more so because at about this same time she learned that her former confessor, the Observant friar John Forest, also had taken the oath. (He was in prison at the time.) For Tunstal the experience must have been excruciating. He was allowed to return to his ecclesiastical duties but was never again trusted by the king.

It was much the same with Stephen Gardiner. Though originally one of the most active supporters of the king's campaign for a divorce, Gardiner was deeply conservative, and he had immense difficulty in leaping from a simple belief that the king's marriage was invalid to the vastly bigger idea that the papacy had no right to the authority it had always exercised. After being passed over for the see of Canterbury in 1532, Gardiner got back into line and tried to show himself to be the king's man first, but he did so too late. His expulsion from the court's inner circle became official when Cromwell replaced him as secretary.

November brought news—accurate this time—of the death of Pope Clement. Surprisingly in light of the lengths to which he had already gone to put an end to papal jurisdiction in England, Henry ordered one of his agents in Italy, Gregory Casale, to go to Rome and do what he could to promote the election of a candidate likely to be friendly to his cause. He could not have been disappointed by the emergence of Cardinal Alessandro Farnese as Pope Paul III; before his election Farnese had expressed his eagerness to bring the English monarch back into the fold, and soon afterward he was asking Casale for advice on how to make that happen. He was unable to grasp that Henry would no longer consider conceding anything—that though he would have been delighted by papal acknowledgment that his marriage to Catherine was null and his marriage to Anne valid, he had no intention of undoing any of his anti-Roman statutes. Thus the new pope, like Clement, continued to nurse empty hopes.

The sterility of those hopes should have become obvious even as far away as Rome when Parliament reconvened in November and in short order passed three more momentous laws of Cromwell's devising. The Act of Supremacy was, strictly speaking, nothing new. It summarized and put into statutory form much of what Henry had previously and successfully claimed for himself: supreme ecclesiastical jurisdiction including authority over convocations of the clergy; the power to issue injunctions to which the clergy were obliged to conform; and the power to declare, through Parliament, what his subjects should and should not believe. Like the statutes passed in the year's first session, this one conferred no powers on the king; instead it acknowledged the powers presumably conferred on him by God. Its importance, Cromwell's reason for drafting it and pushing it through to approval, lay in the simple fact that statutory expression of the king's authority gave Parliament a basis for punishing anyone who denied that authority. Thus it became impossible—or less possible, at least—to accuse Henry and Cromwell and their agents of acting unlawfully when they killed or imprisoned the likes of Barton, Fisher, More, and the Observant friars. Such acts would henceforth be in accordance with the law.

The king's powers having been thus laid out systematically and in some detail, all that remained was to establish what exactly the king's subjects owed him in this connection and what kinds of behavior would put them in violation of the law. This was accomplished by a new measure that extended the state's definition of treason into areas that even the Act of Succession had left untouched, fundamentally changing that definition for the first time in 182 years. If the Supremacy Act was little more than a codification and legitimization of things that Henry had previously done, the Treasons Act of 1534 was without precedent. Until it was passed, no English man or woman could be found guilty of high treason and therefore be made subject to a penalty of death except as a result of attempting to end the king's life, making war against him, or allying with his enemies. And there had had to be at least two witnesses to the commission of treason. But now, and most ambiguously, it was made treasonous to deprive the king, the queen, or their heirs of "the dignity, title or name of their royal estates." To be guilty of high treason, it was no longer necessary to try to do harm to the royal family but only to "wish, will or desire by words or writing, or by craft imagine" such harm. Mere words, even mere thoughts, could now be punished with execution, and only one witness was required. Finally and absurdly, the new law made it a capital offense to call the king a tyrant (or for that matter a heretic, a schismatic, or an infidel).

Though records of the parliamentary proceedings of this period are sparse and often of questionable accuracy, these provisions appear to have shocked a good many members, and to have moved some to resistance. This probably explains the insertion into the bill, at two places, of the word "maliciously"; Cromwell is believed to have had to agree to this in order to get the bill passed. It meant, presumably, that one could wish to deprive Henry and his queen and children of the "dignity" of their "royal estates," or even call the king a tyrant, so long as one did not do so with evil intent. It was another unfathomable ambiguity, and it would prove to be no check on the king as he went about bending the law to his purposes.

The third major statute passed by this session was a stone that killed two birds. It conclusively cut off the flow of money from England to Rome, not only diverting it to the Crown but increasing it substantially. It was called the Act of First Fruits and Tenths—first fruits because it required anyone appointed to an ecclesiastical office to give the king the year of income previously sent to the papal court; tenths because it gave the king, for the first time, ten percent of the income of every "archbishopric, bishopric, abbacy, monastery, priory, archdeaconry, deanery, hospital, college, house collegiate, prebend, cathedral church, collegiate church, conventual church, parsonage, vicarage, chantry, free chapel, or other benefice or promotion spiritual, of what name, nature or quality soever they be, within any diocese of this realm or in Wales." By this single stroke the Crown's income was majestically increased, and the supposedly unconscionable burden that Rome had long been imposing was abruptly made bigger. The numbers are impressive: the average amount sent to Rome annually between 1485 and 1534—£4,800—was replaced by payments to the Crown of £46,052 in 1535 and £51,770 the year after that.

In 1534, for the first time in a decade, Henry asked Parliament for taxation. He was given a traditional levy: two "fifteenths and tenths" (percentages of certain assets of different classes of subject) and also a subsidy. When everything was taken into account, therefore, the year brought the Crown a massive inflow of gold. It was not enough, however, to remove the financial difficulties that Cromwell now had the duty to manage. The king's gambling, his many luxuries, the expansion and improvement of Hampton Court Palace and Whitehall and his other residences, the building of the new St. James's Palace in London—taken together, these things were almost more than the treasury could bear.

The year had brought astonishing things: proof of Henry's ability to make Parliament deliver practically anything he demanded, the enshrinement of his ecclesiastical supremacy in the law of the land, the crushing of domestic opposition, a conclusive repudiation of Rome, and a great deal of badly needed money. But all of it seemed merely to whet the king's appetite. He wanted more. He became more determined than ever that everyone in England was going to conform to his will and embrace his definition of the truth.

Queen Anne, tragically, was failing to conform: her second pregnancy ended in miscarriage. Henry was still hopeful, still trying, still sleeping with the queen for whom he had waited so long, but he was becoming weary of her tantrums and her jealousy and her failure to produce the expected heir. He began to wonder if something was wrong—not with himself, of course, but with Anne, or with their union. He began to suspect that his second marriage must be as displeasing to God as his first had been. Evidently he also—as Anne would be heard to complain— began to have difficulty performing sexually. A long time would pass before Anne became pregnant again.

Fisher and More were still refusing to conform. Maddeningly, they sat in their stone cells in the Tower and under the closest scrutiny said nothing and did nothing that could make it possible to have them put to death. Henry therefore resorted to what was becoming a favorite way of destroying those he saw as his enemies when they were not within reach of the law. He had them attainted for misprision of treason, and this time the penalty would be no mere fine. Attainder provided a basis for keeping them in prison for the rest of their lives if that was what the king wished, and for confiscating everything they owned. More's Chelsea household, which included a large extended family, was reduced to destitution. More himself was no longer allowed visitors or access to the Tower gardens.

As one of his last acts of the year, Henry appointed Cromwell to serve as his vice-regent, empowered to administer the church on his behalf. Even the most reform-minded of the bishops, the ones most antagonistic toward Rome and most eager to cast off the old ways, found this hard to accept. Suddenly they were subordinate not only to their king but to a rough upstart commoner who had never taken holy orders at even the lowliest level and had no training in theology or canon law or anything of the kind.

Cromwell and Henry, of course, knew exactly what they were doing.

They were positioning themselves to use for their own purposes a power that traditionally, virtually from time immemorial, had belonged to the bishops and the heads of the religious orders. This was the power of visitation—the right and responsibility to enter the religious houses of England and Wales, examine their operations, and impose such corrective measures as might be found necessary.

For the first time in history, thanks to the parliamentary enactments of 1534, this power now resided in the king.

And the king had in his vice-regent a man who understood what kinds of opportunities this created, knew how to exploit them to the full, and would feel no hesitation in doing so.

Cromwell was now ready, as one of the most momentous years in the history of England came to its end, to begin using the king's new powers in ways that the king himself may not yet have imagined.

MONKS, NUNS, AND FRIARS

FOR AT LEAST FOUR CENTURIES AFTER HENRY VIII'S DEATH, British conventional wisdom insisted confidently that his assault on the religious orders and their houses was not only justified but little short of imperative. The people of England were taught that by the 1530s monasticism was dying, was sunk in a moral decay too awful to be discussed in mixed company—fabricated stories about secret tunnels connecting the sleeping quarters of nuns and monks had become part of the national folklore—and needed to be put out of its misery.

About one thing, at least, this national mythology was right. Monasticism in England *was* dying when Henry decided to kill it—in fact, it had been dying for centuries. But that is only part of the story, and not the most interesting part. What is equally true, and more significant because so greatly at variance with what is commonly believed, is that England's monasteries had also been reviving, reinventing, and renewing themselves all through the centuries of their decline. Which is simply to say that the institution of monasticism, in the sixteenth century no less than in the fourteenth or the twelfth or long before that, remained a living, multifaceted, endlessly changing thing—a *dynamic* thing. If in some ways it was not entirely healthy when Henry launched his attack on it—and it certainly was not—in others it had rarely been more robust. Some parts of it were withering even as others flourished, and up to the end it appears to have been changing for the better in at least as many ways as it was changing for the worse.

It had always been so. Recurrent, frequently radical reform had been one of the main threads in the history of European monasticism from its beginnings. Monasticism had arisen out of an urgent impulse to create something new—to find a way by which people in pursuit of the transcendental might organize themselves into supportive communities—and naturally it was the seekers themselves who did the creating. The waves of reform that followed one after another were almost without exception the work not of some disapproving outside authority but of the monks and nuns themselves. There should be nothing surprising in any of this. The monastic vocation being almost by definition a way of life for men and women wanting something not easily found in ordinary experience, it is only to be expected that some of the people who enter it will be dissatisfied with what they find and that some of those will insist upon going deeper. It has always been inevitable that the very success of different varieties of monasticism would spark a desire to experiment with other, newer (and sometimes older) forms.

Britain's first great experience of monastic reform came as early as the tenth century, the time of the Anglo-Saxons, when the perhaps two hundred small monasteries then functioning on the island agreed to organize themselves in a new way and subject themselves to a new system of discipline. Throughout the preceding four centuries, during what later times have named the Dark Ages (they were distinctly less dark north of the English Channel than on the European mainland), the monasteries of England and Wales and even more so those of Ireland had been very nearly the only institutions in all of Western Christendom to preserve the cultural and intellectual heritage that had collapsed with the Roman Empire. Many of these earliest monasteries were, in addition to unique centers of learning, bases from which parties of monks set out to carry the gospel, and with it literacy, to barbarian tribes on the continent. Each was organized and governed according to whatever system it had worked out for itself or borrowed from some convenient source. Each adopted whatever practices and purposes it chose, and the differences between houses could be extreme and controversial. Through many generations there was no widely accepted answer to the question of how religious communities might best manage their affairs, and the extent of dissatisfaction with this situation can be inferred from the readiness with which a remedy was embraced as soon as a potentially workable one became available.

What crossed to England in the tenth century was the so-called Rule of St. Benedict, a system of monastic governance that had been drawn up by an obscure abbot in Italy fully four hundred years before. This set of regulations, rigorous but not fanatically severe, proved to be the most workable of many early efforts to show people wanting the religious life how to form communities that would not fall apart under the strain of human interaction. Benedict of Nursia's plan met so many needs so well that it was adopted throughout Italy and from there spread north. Eventually it became so universal a standard that, for a time, nearly every monastery in Europe was "Benedictine." In 970, at a church synod at Winchester, the abbots and abbesses and priors and prioresses of England accepted Benedict's system as their "one uniform observance." A form of monasticism that would remain familiar across the island for the next five and a half centuries began to take shape. It was a simple system and not easily abused. Men and women were strictly segregated. The members of each community elected their superiors, who exercised absolute authority but could be removed for unsatisfactory performance and were adjured in Benedict's writings to consult with the members before making decisions. The monastic day began at two A.M. (three A.M. in summer, when darkness fell later) and was divided into periods of prayer, labor, and study. The schedule varied only with the seasons and the demands of the liturgical calendar of "feast days" and fasts. There were two meals a day in summer, when more daylight hours were available for work, but only one in winter, and only the sick were allowed meat. All visitors were to be offered food and shelter, and providing for the local poor and sick became a primary responsibility of every house. This was not a life likely to attract anyone without a serious commitment to spiritual pursuits. A system of periodic visitations by authorities from the outside helped to ensure fidelity to the rule, and in the centuries following its adoption there were strikingly few grave or systemic failures of discipline. Problems did not go unaddressed. A typical problem, one characteristic of the time, was the practice, carried forward from pre-Benedictine days, by which wealthy families not wishing to divide property among multiple heirs would deposit their surplus children at the abbeys, presumably for life. The worst consequences of this were removed by a rule forbidding anyone to take monastic vows before reaching the age of consent, which was usually eighteen.

Success bred prosperity and complexity. Some of the houses grew large and rich: forty-five (eight of them communities of women) were important enough to figure in the public records of 1066, the year of the Norman Conquest, and the Normans in their turn endowed new establishments on a sometimes lavish scale. The Benedictines—now formally an international order—grew increasingly sophisticated. The abbots of the greatest houses sat in the House of Lords. It came to be the norm for the monks to be ordained as priests, whereas Benedict himself had not regarded monks as being clergy in the strict sense, and when the first universities were founded one of their primary purposes was to educate young men sent from the monasteries. The religious observances of the houses became so elaborate that little time was left for work or solitude. A growing perception that all this marked an unacceptable departure from the spirit of the rule led first to discontent and then to the establishment, in France initially, of the breakaway order of Cistercians, whose garments of unbleached wool caused them to be called the "white monks" in contrast to the black-robed Benedictines. (The "black monks," not pleased with this implicit criticism of their presumably more comfortable attire, accused the Cistercians of making an ostentatious display of humility and austerity. Members of different religious orders were not above jealousy and resentment.)

The emergence of the Cistercians was a real revolution, and from their arrival in England in the twelfth century they attracted astonishing numbers of recruits. They settled in wild and unpopulated districts, set out to support themselves by draining marshland and converting it to pastures for sheep, and gradually grew rich by doing so. Within a generation the order had almost a dozen English houses. Its growth was only part of what is called the twelfth century's Monastic Renaissance, during which more than 250 new houses for men were opened in England along with more than 100 for women. Among them were the first English houses of the so-called canons regular and also of the Carthusians, a hybrid order of hermits-in-community that would grow to nine houses, only to be singled out for early destruction by Henry VIII and Cromwell. These and other orders—Norbertines, Bridgettines, the English Order of Sempringham, Knights Templar, and Knights Hospitalers—adhered to orthodox doctrine (though disputes about how well they did so were common) while pursuing their different missions in their distinctive ways.

The thirteenth century brought yet another revolution: the arrival of the friars, new mendicant (the word means "begging") orders that had started on the continent, spread with startling speed, and were focused not on maintaining houses of prayer and seclusion but on outreach to the laity—especially the growing and increasingly sophisticated urban laity, an emerging social force that had received much attention at the Lateran Council of 1215. The Order of Preachers, or Dominicans, first appeared in England in 1221, the year that its founder, the Spaniard Dominic, died. When the Friars Minor or Franciscans followed three years later, their founder Francis of Assisi was still alive. Both orders emphasized poverty and simplicity of life along with helping ordinary people to live Christian lives in a world of towns and cities. They proved popular wherever they settled, though in doing so they often attracted the unfriendly attention of the secular clergy—the diocesan and parish priests who belonged to no order.

Soon there were Dominican and Franciscan houses for women, and still other orders of friars, Augustinians and Carmelites, also arrived from the continent. Both within the oldest Benedictine houses and among the more recent arrivals, the old struggle over how best to live the religious life went on as ever. The problem was perhaps most acute among the Franciscans. We have already encountered the Friars Observant, especially favored by the royal family until they refused to accept Henry VIII's annulment suit and his claims to be supreme head. They called themselves "observant" to distinguish themselves from those Franciscans who, in their opinion, were no longer sufficiently faithful to the precepts of their founder. Such splinterings were far from unusual, and they were hardly evidence of decay. They were evidence, rather, that the monastic impulse had not grown cold—that people drawn to the religious life still regarded themselves as on a quest that had to be taken seriously.

The English church that Henry inherited was, at least in part because of its monastic element, scarcely less diverse than the broader society of which it was part. Monasticism reached across the whole culture, from humanist scholars at Oxford and Cambridge to Charterhouse hermits growing vegetables outside their cells, from abbots in the House of Lords to friars ministering to the poor in the filthy streets of London and solitary Cistercians tending sheep on the windswept moors of Yorkshire. Vitality was probably lowest where monasticism was oldest, in some of the hundreds of Benedictine houses that dotted the landscape. All the religious orders had lost devastatingly large numbers of their members in the Black Death of the fourteenth century, but the ranks of the Benedictines were especially slow to refill. Because new kinds of opportunities were emerging in the lay world, and also because the most adventurous spiritual seekers now had so many other options, their appeal was not what it once had been. Increasing amounts of Benedictine land were being worked by tenant farmers, who generally found monks to be better landlords than their counterparts among the nobility if only because they were less desperate for cash, and the monasteries were showing an increasing tendency to allow their tenants to become freeholders. Some sort of adjustment of the place of the Benedictines in the life of the nation was obviously advisable and becoming increasingly likely.

But it would be claiming too much to say that even the Benedictine rule had arrived at the point of exhaustion. That was proved by the willingness of some of the leading Benedictine abbots to die rather than surrender to Henry's demands. It is proved in the twenty-first century by the fact that Benedictine houses are again prospering in England and have been doing so since they ceased to be illegal.

12

"We Will All Die"

The full viciousness of the new regime that Henry and Cromwell had brought to perfection by the end of 1534 is not to be seen in the execution of the Nun of Kent, the destruction of the Friars Observant, or the fate of John Fisher and Thomas More. What was done to them was, if horrible, at least understandable. Elizabeth Barton, by ignoring friendly warnings not to meddle in politics in a dangerous way at a dangerous time, had made her own ruin all but inevitable. The Observants, if as innocent as Barton of anything that could reasonably be construed as a capital crime, had certainly gone out of their way to challenge the king and provoke his wrath. The stature of Fisher and More, two of the most esteemed Europeans of their time, made their refusal to acquiesce in the royal supremacy not only gallingly frustrating but an incitement to anyone else inclined to resist. There were reasons for destroying such people.

Nothing of the kind can be said in the case of John Houghton, a man who by his own choosing was so obscure as to be practically invisible, offered Henry all the loyalty that any other king of England had ever required of his subjects, and asked for nothing except that he and the men who had chosen him as their leader should be left alone. If Barton and the others were victims of judicial murder—and they were—Houghton's murder was of a singularly atrocious kind. His story is a vivid demonstration of the lengths to which Henry and Cromwell were prepared to go, the depths to which they were willing to descend, to break the will of England.

Houghton, when the Act of Succession became law, was in his late forties and his fourth year as prior, elected head, of the London monastery of the Order of Carthusians. This order, unique in the austerity of its rule, had been founded in a remote valley of the French Alps late in the eleventh century for the purpose of permitting its members to live both in community and as hermits. These two aims, if apparently contradictory, were achieved with impressive success. In four and a half centuries Carthusian houses were established all across Europe, so that by the sixteenth century there were more than two hundred. The order had been invited into England by Henry II as part of his effort to show contrition for the murder of Thomas Becket, and by the time of Henry VIII it had nine English houses. These were known as Charterhouses, their inhabitants as Charterhouse monks—an Anglicization of the name of the order's motherhouse at La Grande Chartreuse in France. The Carthusians were remarkable in never departing from their original rule and so never giving rise to reformist offshoots. In the sixteenth century, in England as elsewhere, they preserved a way of life focused on solitary prayer, contemplation, study, and work. Their daily routine remained identical in every detail to that established by their founders. Even a century and a half after Henry VIII, Pope Innocent XI would say of the Carthusians that they were *numquam reformata, quia numquam deformata:* never reformed because never deformed.

John Houghton, the son of a family of gentry or near-gentry in Essex, earned a bachelor's degree at Cambridge University as a young man and, to the intense disappointment of his parents, decided to take holy orders rather than embark upon the kind of career likely to raise the family's fortunes. Obliged to leave home, he lived with a parish priest while continuing his studies (eventually he would receive three degrees from Cambridge) and at around age twenty-five was ordained into the secular priesthood—meaning that he was a member of the local diocesan clergy, the source of most parish priests. In his late twenties, feeling himself called to something more demanding, he entered the London Charterhouse. Here, apparently, he was content. Like his brother monks he lived alone in a "cell" of three small rooms (one for storage, one for study and sleep, the third for prayer) adjacent to a small walled garden for growing flowers and vegetables. There was one meal a day in winter—always meatless, with each monk cooking foodstuffs delivered to his door—and two in summer, the diet limited to bread and water on Mondays, Wednesdays, and Fridays. The monks said daily mass alone in their cells but gathered twice a day for worship in common. Like all monasteries, the Charterhouses were required to be financially self-sufficient, and work of some kind was a prescribed part of the daily routine. For most Carthusians this meant making, by hand, scholarly and devotional books for sale. Sundays and the major feast days of the liturgical calendar were special: the monks had mass and a meal together, afterward meeting in chapter to conduct the business of the house and enjoy a period of free conversation.

It was a life stripped down to essentials. Only the roughest cloth was used as clothing and bedding, no silver or gold ornaments were permitted aside from the chalices in which the bread and wine of communion were consecrated, and monasteries were kept small to avoid the complications and distractions of managing large institutions. It was a life that could make sense only to men prepared to sacrifice everything in pursuit of spiritual experience, but the number of such men was not insubstantial in England and on the continent in the late Middle Ages. The London Charterhouse had an abundance of young members in the time of John Houghton, a number of them from noble families. Thomas More, at the start of his career, had thought long and seriously about giving up the law and joining the Carthusians, finally and with real regret deciding that he was not suited to celibacy. As late as 1534 Sir John Gage, a member of Henry VIII's council described by Charles V's ambassador as "one of the wisest and most experienced in war of the whole kingdom," resigned his post as vice-chamberlain and became a Carthusian.

Houghton had entered the order two decades before Gage, progressing in the customary way through a year as a postulant and two or three years as a novice. He then would have taken "simple" (nonperpetual) vows of poverty, chastity, and obedience, and later the "solemn" vows that bound a man for life. Almost nothing is known, naturally, of his first dozen years as a Carthusian, years spent in training and solitude, but it is clear that he won the respect of his superiors and peers. In 1523 he was made sacristan of the London Charterhouse, with responsibility for the vestments and paraphernalia used in worship services. Three years after that he was elevated to procurator, supervising the monastery's business dealings with the outside and managing its little corps of lay brothers, nonpriests who performed the labor needed to keep the establishment in good working order. He must have become known beyond London, because in 1531 the monks of the house of Beauvale in Nottinghamshire elected him prior. Later that same year, however, he returned to London after receiving word that his former associates had unanimously elected him prior there. Years later one of the monks of the London Charterhouse—a man who was still alive because under threat of death he had sworn the supremacy oath—recorded his memories of Prior Houghton. He was "short, with a graceful figure and dignified appearance; his actions modest, his voice gentle, chaste in body, in heart humble, he was admired and sought after by all, and by his community was most loved and esteemed. One and all revered him, and none were ever known to speak a word against him. . . . He governed rather by example than precept, and his subjects were influenced as much by the fervor of his preeminent sanctity as by the burning exhortations he addressed to them in their chapter. . . . Once at least each month, in his exhortation to the religious, he would cast himself upon his knees before them and with tears bewail his shortcomings, and ask pardon of his brethren."

It is hardly surprising, considering the nature of their rule, that the men of the Charterhouse did not follow the example of the Friars Observant in raising objections when King Henry cast off his first wife and took a second. The friars were a preaching order whose mission took them into the public arena and engaged them with the issues of the day. By contrast the Carthusians, modeling themselves on the desert fathers of the first Christian centuries, avoided any such engagement. They would have been content to allow the storm over the king's great matter to blow itself out at a distance.

No such thing was possible, however, under a monarch who felt entitled to the active support of everyone in the kingdom and was determined to have it. In April 1534 two of Thomas Cromwell's agents called at the London Charterhouse and demanded to see the prior. They told Houghton they wanted his signature on the succession oath. Houghton, in the most inoffensive way imaginable, declined to sign, saying simply that the king's matrimonial affairs were the king's business and had nothing to do with the Charterhouse or its monks. This was not the response the royal commissioners were looking for—their assignment was to get the agreement of everyone they visited—and so they demanded to meet with the house's full chapter of monks. The result was a community discussion in the course of which Houghton said more than he had ventured to say earlier: that he could not see how the king's marriage to Catherine, having been approved by the church and continued for so many years, could now be judged invalid. When the assembly expressed its agreement, Houghton and the monastery's procurator, Humphrey Middlemore, were taken away under guard.

For a month the two were kept in the Tower under the harsh conditions that were becoming standard for clerical prisoners—neither warmth nor bedding nor sanitation, scarcely enough food to sustain life—but at length they were visited by Archbishop Lee of York and Bishop Stokesley of London and persuaded, apparently after much discussion, that if royal marriages were not a monk's business they were also not something that a monk should sacrifice his life over. Having accepted this line of reasoning, and having indicated their willingness to encourage the other members of their community to accept the oath, Houghton and Middlemore were allowed to return home.

Back at the Charterhouse, Houghton told his fellows that he believed signing the oath would save neither him nor them for long—weeks in prison left him with no illusions about what lay ahead. Their response was to argue that in that case there was no reason for any of them to sign. Their resolve weakened, however, when the king's commissioners not only returned but brought with them the lord mayor of London, a company of armed men, and the threat that if they did not sign they would all be taken into custody. Houghton, Middlemore, and fourteen others signed with little or no delay, and the rest signed a day later. In doing so, however, they tried to create for themselves the same kind of loophole that the bishops had earlier attempted when faced with King Henry's demands, attesting that they accepted the Act of Succession "so far as it was lawful."

In the months that followed, the Carthusians, like other religious communities across the kingdom, were kept under constant pressure: those men who seemed most likely to yield were sent off in pairs to be interrogated and preached at by senior churchmen who had accepted the king's claims. The passage of the Act of Supremacy, bringing with it a new and even more demanding oath, sealed the fate of those unwilling to comply. The men of the London Charterhouse understood this from the start. When Houghton lamented that he didn't know how to save them, they replied that all of them should prepare to die together so that "heaven and earth shall witness for us how unjustly we are cut off."

"Would indeed that it might be so, so that dying we might live as living we die," Houghton replied. "But they will not do to us so great a kindness, nor to themselves so great an injury. Many of you are of noble blood, and what I think they will do is this: me and the elder brethren they will kill, and they will dismiss you that are young into a world which is not for you. If therefore it will depend on me alone—if my oath will suffice for the house—I will throw myself for your sakes on the mercy of God. I will make myself anathema, and to preserve you from these dangers I will consent to the king's will. If, however, they have determined otherwise—if they choose to have the consent of us all—the will of God be done. If one death will not suffice, we will all die."

From Houghton's perspective, that is, a forced return to the outside world was more to be dreaded than death. He was prepared either to take an oath he did not believe or to sacrifice his life if in either way he could save his brothers, but he did not expect any such solution to prove possible. According to the sole surviving account of what was happening inside the London Charterhouse at this time, the other monks agreed that escape was improbable and began to prepare themselves for death. There was one exception: a monk who wrote to Cromwell to acknowledge the royal supremacy and beg release from his vows, complaining that "the religion is so hard, what with fasting and with the great watch, that there is not six whole monks within this cloister but that they have one infirmity or other." Such eager surrenders were rare. It is surely ironic, considering the accusations of laxity that in due course would be leveled against all the orders, that from the beginning of Cromwell's campaign the harshest punishments were meted out to those houses where the strictest rules were most faithfully observed. And that the only complaint known to have been made against

Houghton by one of his own monks was that discipline was *too* strict under his leadership.

While waiting for the next display of kingly power, Houghton was visited by two other Carthusian priors, Robert Laurence of Beauvale and Augustine Webster of Axholme. No doubt they too were expecting the worst, and it would have been natural for them to look for direction not only to London but specifically to Houghton, who since 1532 had been "visitor" of the order's English province and therefore its senior member. For reasons unknown (possibly they thought that by taking the initiative they could demonstrate their wish to be cooperative, or perhaps Laurence and Webster had taken up Houghton's idea of trying to sacrifice himself for the sake of the community) the three decided not to await the return of the king's commissioners but to go and see Cromwell. There was, however, no meeting: as soon as he learned of their arrival, Cromwell had his visitors taken to the Tower and locked up. In the days that followed, they refused to take the oath and were joined in their confinement by a fourth prisoner, Richard Reynolds, a monk of Syon, the Bridgettine order's only English establishment. Reynolds was a noted humanist scholar, said to be the only English monk conversant in Latin, Greek, and Hebrew. He had helped to make Syon one of England's leading centers of Renaissance learning, and his order like the Carthusians and Friars Observant was noted not only for its high standards but for its long advocacy of church reform. Thus Syon, like the London Charterhouse, had been singled out by Cromwell for special attention, and that attention had focused on Reynolds because of his renown. Under questioning he had said that he "would spend his blood for the king" but could not deny that the pope was head of the church.

On April 28 the four priests were indicted for refusing the supremacy oath. They pleaded not guilty at the start of their trial, which did not go smoothly for the authorities. The jury declared itself unable to find the defendants guilty because, following as they did the dictates of their consciences and not seeking to persuade anyone to agree with them, they could not have been acting maliciously—"maliciously" being the word that Cromwell had had to insert into the Treason Act to get Parliament to approve it. The judges then instructed the jurymen that none of this mattered: that to refuse the oath was, ipso facto, to act maliciously. Even after this the jury continued to balk, so that finally Cromwell had to make an appearance and batter the members into submission with threats. On May 4 the four convicted men—joined now by a fifth, a parish priest named John Hale who was a friend and neighbor of Reynolds's—were tied to hurdles (flat rectangular forms made of wood and similar to sections of fence) and dragged from the Tower to Tyburn Hill, the place of execution for traitors. There they were given a final offer of pardon in return for swearing the oath, and all refused.

Remarkably, all were dressed in clerical garb; until now it would have been unthinkable to execute a priest in the habit of his vocation—or for that matter, to execute a priest without first degrading him from his clerical status. Even more remarkably, among those in attendance were Henry Fitzroy, Duke of Richmond, the king's illegitimate son; Queen Anne's father Thomas Boleyn, Earl of Wiltshire, and his son, George Lord Rochford; the mighty Thomas Howard, Duke of Norfolk; and in fact virtually the entire royal court including the council. This must have happened at the king's instructions, and its purpose was almost certainly to discourage expressions of discontent from the large crowd that an occasion of this kind was sure to attract. It is possible that the king himself was present, though in disguise: five horsemen whose faces were covered with visors arrived on the scene, and when one of these visors fell open it revealed the face of Norfolk's brother, an intimate of King Henry's. As the five approached the killing ground, the members of the court deferentially stood aside.

Houghton died first, and in keeping with custom he was allowed to speak before doing so. "I call almighty God to witness, and all good people, and I beseech you all here present to bear witness for me in the day of judgment, that being here to die, I declare that it is from no obstinate rebellious spirit that I do not obey the king, but because I fear to offend the majesty of God. Our holy mother the church has decreed otherwise than the king and the Parliament have decreed, and therefore rather than disobey the church I am ready to suffer. Pray for me and have mercy on my brethren, of whom I have been the unworthy prior." It was later reported that the king was angry with Norfolk, Wiltshire, and the other nobles because none of them had offered any response. But as he probably knew—he certainly knew if he was present—the mood of the crowd had been hostile not to the men being executed but to their being killed. It might have been dangerous to try to belittle Houghton in the moment before his death.

Perhaps because so many distinguished guests were on hand to be edified and impressed, the usual work of butchery—an interrupted hanging, followed by emasculation, evisceration, and the rubbing of a still-beating heart in the victim's face—was carried out with exceptional energy that day. Reynolds was last to die, offering encouragement to the others as they climbed the scaffold, and before presenting himself for execution he asked the crowd to pray for the king. He like the others was quartered, his head and the sections of his body put on display around London. One of Houghton's arms was nailed above the entry to his monastery, a warning to everyone associated with the place. In the weeks that followed, four more monks and lay brothers of the London Charterhouse would die at Tyburn, among them the procurator Humphrey Middlemore and a man named Sebastian Newdigate who before entering religious life had been a member of the royal court. In the subsequent months fifteen would be starved to death in prison; iron collars around their necks, their feet in shackles, they were chained to upright posts in such a way as to be unable either to sit or lie down and left to slowly die. A new prior, one friendly to the king's cause, was introduced by Cromwell to replace Houghton. With armed force he imposed a new regime that made it impossible for the monks to follow their rule and transformed their monastery into a prison. They were allowed to do almost nothing except listen to sermons delivered by preachers sent by Cromwell and wait for their fate to be decided.

It had been arranged, on the morning of Houghton's execution, that Thomas More would be visited in the Tower by his daughter Margaret, who had long been asking him to accept the oath of supremacy and so save his life. From a window, and obviously not by coincidence, the two were able to observe the condemned priests as they were taken off to be killed. It was all part of the continuing effort to use every tool at the Crown's disposal—terror, persuasion, the promise of a swift return to royal favor—to induce More and John Fisher to submit. This latest gambit worked no better than the others. It became an occasion for More, not to lose his resolve, but to offer comfort to the young woman to whom, of all his large family and circle of friends, he was closest. "Lo, dost thou not see, Meg, that these blessed fathers be now as cheerfully going to their deaths as bridegrooms to their marriage?" he asked.

> Wherefore thereby mayst thou see, mine own good daughter, what a great difference there is between such as have in effect spent all their days in a strait, hard, penitential, and painful life religiously, and such as have in the world, like worldly wretches, as thy poor father hath done, consumed all their time in pleasure and ease licentiously. For God, continuing their long-continued life in most sore and grievous penance, will no longer suffer them to remain here in this vale of misery and iniquity, but speedily hence taketh them to the fruition of his everlasting deity. Whereas thy silly father, Meg, that like a most wicked wretch, hath passed forth the whole course of his miserable life most sinfully, God thinking him not worthy so soon to come to that eternal felicity, leaveth him here yet still in the world, further to be plunged and turmoiled with misery.

He wanted his daughter to see his own death, which pretty clearly was not far off, as a deliverance, even a cause for celebration.

It is fair to say that the king did not want More's death and did not want Fisher's. What he wanted was their submission, their acknowledgment before the whole Christian world that from the beginning of his conflict with Rome he had been right and the two of them had been wrong. But if he could not have that he would take their lives instead, as yet another warning to anyone who had not paid sufficient attention to the fate of the Observant Franciscans and the Charterhouse priors. And by May 1535 his patience was wearing thin. A long procession of eminent churchmen had been sent to reason with his two most famous prisoners—at least half a dozen bishops are known to have called on Fisher—but all their arguments and commentaries upon ancient texts had accomplished nothing. The conditions of More's and Fisher's confinement, as well as the state in which More's household had to live, had been made progressively worse until by winter the aged Fisher was literally begging for help, declaring that he had neither enough clothes nor sufficient food to keep himself alive. But harshness, too, had produced no results. The prisoners continued to refuse to submit, but continued also not to do or say anything that would allow the Crown to condemn them to death. Under repeated questioning—they were always interrogated separately, just as they were kept apart in the Tower—they refused to express any opinion of the Act of Supremacy. Fisher was straightforward in his refusal: not even the Act itself, he said again and again, required any man to reveal his innermost thoughts. More was more careful if no less consistent. Because he had been attainted, he said, he no longer enjoyed the protection of the law and so had no reason to concern himself with it. "Now I have in good faith discharged my mind of all such matters," he said, "and neither will dispute kings' titles nor popes'." It was a sterile, agonizing standoff for everyone involved.

The new pope, Paul III, unwittingly broke the deadlock with an announcement that, when it reached England on May 20, astounded everyone and pleased no one: John Fisher had been named to the College of Cardinals, becoming the first Englishman since Wolsey to be so honored. Paul was a reformer, among the first pontiffs to recognize that the excesses of the Renaissance were not merely wrong but intolerable. In putting together a list of men to be made cardinals he had selected candidates known for scholarship, for exemplary personal conduct, and for upholding high standards in all areas of ecclesiastical life. Fisher was an obvious choice in every respect, a charismatic figure known across Europe for his theological writings and life of simple virtue. The pope is said to have believed that King Henry would be pleased to see the mentor of his youth, a man he himself had described as one of the ornaments of England, honored with a cardinal's red hat. If so, he was incredibly ill informed. It seems more plausible that he hoped by singling Fisher out to give him some measure of protection against the royal wrath, but even here any such thoughts would have been badly mistaken.

Henry interpreted the news from Rome as an intentional provocation. He took the announcement as an insult to his own man Thomas Cranmer, who as England's primate would, under ordinary circumstances, have been made a cardinal long before any mere bishop of Rochester. He warned that the pope could send Fisher a hat, "but I will take care that he have never a head to wear it on." Fisher, for his part, was reported to have told the man who brought him news of his appointment that if the red hat were lying at his feet "he would not stoop to pick it up, so little did he set by it." There is no reason to doubt the sincerity of those words, or that Fisher could have uttered them. He was the antithesis of Thomas Wolsey, never in the course of his long life showing the slightest interest in personal advancement or political power. Nor is it possible to doubt that the king meant what he said. The pope's initiative settled the fates of Fisher and More alike.

Though further interrogations failed to draw anything new out of Fisher, in June, enfeebled by two years of imprisonment under conditions that almost seemed calculated to kill, he was put on trial for treason. His conviction was a foregone conclusion, the judges and jury having been handpicked by Cromwell and the king, but for purposes of propaganda it was important to make the proceedings seem as legitimate as possible. The Crown's best weapon was its key witness, the lawyer Richard Rich. Now in his late thirties, Rich had risen to become solicitor-general by attaching himself to Thomas Audley, himself such an unfailingly dependable servant of the Crown that Henry had made him first speaker of the House of Commons and then, after More's resignation, chancellor. Rich's testimony was, after all the long months during which the Crown had repeatedly tried and failed to induce Fisher to express himself on the supremacy, nothing less than a bombshell. He told the court that when the king sent him to meet with Fisher, the bishop told him that he "believed in his conscience and by his learning knew that the king neither was nor by any right could be supreme head in earth of the church of England."

What was perhaps even more surprising, Fisher did not challenge the truthfulness of Rich's testimony. He erupted with the furious indignation that had been characteristic of him for years now, ever since the king had begun claiming that his marriage to Queen Catherine was not valid, but his anger here was aimed less at what Rich was saying than at his daring to say it in court. Rich, it turned out, had in his visit to the Tower told Fisher that he had been instructed by the king to ask for the bishop's opinion of the Supremacy Act, and to promise that nothing he said would be used against him in court or otherwise. He had added, Fisher told the judges, that the king sincerely wanted to know what he thought "for the great affiance [trust or confidence] he had in me, more than in any other." There had followed—again according to what Fisher told the court—an explicit suggestion that Henry, after taking Fisher's position into account, "was very like to retract much of his former do-

ings and make recompense for the same, in case I should so advise him."
To all this Rich had added his own promise not to repeat anything Fisher
told him to anyone except the king. Fisher had responded as any honest,
trusting, and even moderately courageous subject would have under
such circumstances. For the first time since coming under suspicion, at
the king's request and for the king's sake, he unburdened himself. In
doing so he committed treason.

It is impossible to know anything about the characters of the two
men involved in this exchange—or for that matter, of Henry VIII—and
doubt Fisher's account. This is all the more true because even Rich himself, who was building a phenomenally successful career on a willingness to do and say whatever was likely to be most pleasing to those more
powerful than himself, never challenged what Fisher had said. And because Fisher, who to his dying day never lost a profound if exasperated
respect for Henry as king and an equally deep affection for him personally, would certainly have responded to even an indirect appeal from him
for guidance. He may have had little opportunity to get to know Richard
Rich or to learn what kind of man he was. He would have been reluctant to think any man capable of making the kinds of pledges that Rich
made not only on his own behalf but on the king's and then breaking his
word in the most destructive way imaginable.

"What a monstrous matter is this!" Fisher cried.

To lay now to my charge as treason the thing which I spake not until
besides this man's oath, I had as full and sure a promise from the king,
by this his trusty and sure messenger, as the king could make me by
word of mouth, that I should never be impeached nor hurt by mine
answer that I should send unto him by this his messenger, which I
would never have spoken, had it not been in trust of my prince's
promise, and of my true and loving heart towards him, my natural
liege lord, in satisfying him with declaration of mine opinion and conscience in this matter, as he earnestly required me by this messenger
to signify plainly unto him.

Rich, accused not only of disgracing himself but of suggesting disgraceful behavior on the part of the king, might well have responded by
calling Fisher a liar. Instead he accepted Fisher's version of what had

transpired between them, probably in order to keep the Crown's case intact. Rich and Fisher were together in testifying that the bishop had—regardless of his reasons, whether or not he had been deceived—denied the supremacy. That was enough; it gave the king's judges all they needed. Tacitly accepting that Henry had, in effect, promised Fisher immunity, they set aside Rich's assurances to the bishop as making no difference. Every other argument that Fisher offered in his defense was likewise swept aside. Inevitably (the jurors understood that they had no choice if they valued their own liberty and livelihoods) he was convicted, sentenced to death, and returned to the Tower. Perhaps because of his wretched physical condition, perhaps because the king still felt some of his old affection, Fisher was told that he would merely be beheaded, not subjected to the horrors that had been visited upon the Carthusians.

June 22, the day of his execution, found him prepared and at peace. He was awakened at five A.M. and told that this was the day he had been expecting—that he was to be killed at ten. His response was to ask to be left to sleep longer. When he arrived at Tower Hill, the scaffold on which he was to die was still under construction, so that he had to spend an hour on muleback, waiting for the preparations to be completed. The assembled crowd was large and, being sympathetic to the old man, markedly subdued. Before putting his head on the block Fisher asked for the prayers of the crowd, telling them that though up to this point he had remained unafraid, he feared that his faith might fail him at the last moment. He asked the people to pray for their king, too, and to love and obey him, "for he was good by nature."

When it was all over, Fisher's head was set atop London Bridge. A story was circulated—an expression of the esteem in which he had been held—that every day that head grew pinker and healthier and more lifelike. He was the first English bishop ever to be condemned in a judicial proceeding and put to death by authority of the Crown. There had been no death remotely like his since Thomas Becket's murder more than three centuries before. England was shocked by it. Europe was shocked. Henry and Cromwell were now at liberty to turn their attention to Thomas More, who was still in the Tower and still refusing to share his thoughts with anyone.

BEST SELLERS

THE EXECUTION OF JOHN FISHER AND THE IMPRISONMENT of Thomas More electrified not only England but all of Western Christendom, and for a reason that was entirely novel. The two men were phenomena of a type that had only recently appeared on the world stage: famous living authors, and therefore international celebrities. The books they had written, and the books written about them and sometimes against them, had spread through Europe's fast-growing reading public with a speed that would have been impossible just a few generations earlier. They had created the kind of sensation that only the news of the day can generate.

It was all part of the revolution sparked by the invention of the printing press—of movable and reusable type, one of the most world-altering technological breakthroughs in history. By the time Henry decided to discard Catherine of Aragon, printing was Europe's leading growth industry. The new ability to mass-produce long texts at low cost was transforming everything: education, religion, the economy, the very character of civilization. It was affecting everyday life more dramatically and profoundly than the automobile would in the twentieth century, or the Internet in the twenty-first. It had so accelerated the movement of new ideas, and so magnified the impact of those ideas, that all Europe was left almost literally dizzy. At a time when being educated meant reading Latin, a controversialist like Martin Luther—or like Fisher or More—could become famous from Vienna to Lisbon in a matter of months.

Difficult though it is to measure something as amorphous as fame at a distance of four and a half centuries, Fisher at the time of his death was probably better known than More. He had been early to involve himself in the religious disputes that evolved into the Reformation, and his deep learning and the firmness of his opinions made him a formidable advocate. His book *Assertionis Lutheranae confutatio* appeared in 1523, just

six years after Luther first raised his voice against Rome, and was so
widely reprinted and held up so well under rebuttal that it came to be regarded as *the* standard statement of orthodoxy. Within the next two years
Fisher produced two additional responses to Luther—both were published in Cologne rather than England, an indication of Fisher's international reach—and they were followed in 1527 with a treatise on the
Eucharist that would have a formative effect on Catholic thinking for
many years. All this work had the enthusiastic approval of Henry VIII, but
the attention it received explains why Fisher's subsequent objections to
the king's divorce and claim to supremacy brought such wrath down
upon him. His researches had placed him among the leading authorities
on the history of church doctrine, and his flagrant refusal to accept the
king's interpretation of that history was genuinely dangerous. There was
no way that the man Henry had become by the 1530s could have found
Fisher's resistance anything other than intolerable.

More's fame was of a different character than Fisher's, if no less likely
to cause trouble when he declined to approve Henry's innovations.
Outside England it was based mainly on his "novel" (as it is sometimes
anachronistically described) *Utopia,* which he began writing in 1516
while on a diplomatic mission to Flanders and spending much time with
his friend Erasmus. Written in Latin, the description of a visit to an imag-
inary island, the book *appears* to function on two levels: as a satirical
commentary on contemporary life, and also as More's vision of how society (even a non-Christian society, one lacking revelation and therefore
obliged to depend upon natural law for guidance) might best be organized. However, it is so complex, containing so many intentional ambiguities and possible red herrings (the name of the character who brings
news of Utopia translates as "dispenser of nonsense") that critics and
scholars still disagree about where More was being serious, where he
was joking, and what the whole thing actually means. It definitely expresses a yearning for a simpler, less materialistic society than Tudor-era
Europe—much the same kind of yearning, interestingly, that would be
characteristic of the kinds of evangelical reformers whose rejection of
the Roman church later horrified More. There is no private property in
Utopia, the laws are so straightforward that the legal profession does not
exist, and all people do manual work and wear the same plain clothing.
The book also expresses the reverence for tradition and order, the almost

obsessive fear of disunity and disruption, that later would turn its author into a determined persecutor of those people whose beliefs and practices he regarded as heretical: premarital sex is punished with enforced lifelong celibacy in Utopia, adultery with enslavement.

Surely More must have been joking in making it a capital crime to discuss politics anywhere except in Utopia's government buildings (one way to eliminate tedious conversations!). And it is curious, in light of his later history, that although belief in the immortality of the soul is mandatory (because essential to mortality) on the island, unbelievers are not punished but converted through instruction. More appears to have written the book for his amusement and that of his friends rather than for publication, and when Erasmus published it in Louvain in 1516 he did so without the author's knowledge or consent. It was a huge success from the start, establishing the thirty-eight-year-old More among the best-known writers of the day. Some of the book's most sensitive elements—its discussion of why kings are so inclined to start pointless wars, the suggestion that republics are the best-governed states—may explain why More, though he revised *Utopia* before republishing it in Switzerland in 1518, never translated it into English or allowed its publication in England. The elusiveness of its meaning foreshadows his later behavior when, under attack by the king, he refused to explain himself to anyone. In any case it was nothing that *Utopia* said but simply the fame it had brought to its author that drove Henry VIII to the belief that he had to make an example of More one way or another.

Printing's effects on the lives and careers of Fisher and More were nothing compared to what they did to and for Martin Luther. Without the magnifying power of the press, the disputes that Luther triggered might never have become anything more than what Clement VII called them: a dreary argument among monks. It can almost seem that printing arrived just in time to serve Luther's purposes; the last of the ingredients that made it possible fell into place only shortly before his birth. Astonishingly, paper (which originated in China and long remained the secret of Arab producers) was never seen in Europe until the twelfth century and was not produced there until the thirteenth. And although movable type first appeared in China by the eleventh century and in Europe three centuries later, no one knew how to produce raised letters that were hard or durable enough to make mass production possible. Only in the fifteenth century did the goldsmiths, silversmiths, and jewelers of Germany and the Rhineland take up the challenge, slowly developing the alloys and production methods with which Johannes Gutenberg was able to produce his magnificent two-volume Bible in 1455. That was only twenty-eight years before Luther's birth, and, as great an achievement as the Gutenberg Bible was, it was just the beginning. (For one thing, a single copy cost as much as a common laborer could earn in three years.) But from that point the refinements came one after another at a quickening pace. By 1517, when Friar Martin posted his complaints about papal indulgences on the door of Wittenberg Cathedral, the technology of printing was very nearly as advanced as it would remain for the next several centuries. Luther the writer proved to be as prolific as he was powerful, churning out books with almost unbelievable frequency, shifting from Latin to the vernacular and shaping the German language at least as much as Thomas Cranmer with his Prayer Book would soon be shaping English. Much of Europe was hungry for his words, and now it was possible to deliver them quickly wherever they were wanted.

13

"Preserve My Friends from Such Favors"

On Thursday, July 1, 1535, dressed in a plain robe of the coarsest wool, his once clean-shaven face covered by a long gray beard, filthy after long confinement and leaning heavily on a staff, Thomas More emerged from the Tower of London like some terrible vision out of the Old Testament. A week had passed since the killing of John Fisher, and now it was More's turn to stand trial for high treason. He was led under guard through the capital's busiest streets to the seat of government at Westminster—put on display, in effect, so that the people could see yet again the price of failing to believe what the king believed.

At Westminster More was taken before a panel of eighteen judges, among whom were Thomas Cromwell, Chancellor Thomas Audley, the dukes of Norfolk and Suffolk, and Anne Boleyn's father and brother. No longer able to stay on his feet as he had through the innumerable interrogations to which he had been subjected during his imprisonment, More accepted the offer of a seat. Promised release if he would affix his signature to the oath of supremacy, he thanked the gentlemen and politely declined. He then listened as the indictment was read aloud. It was ridiculously long, piling item upon item and burying each in a heap of explanatory verbiage, but essentially it boiled down to four charges: that More had committed treason by refusing during interrogation to acknowledge the king's supremacy, by conspiring with Fisher while both were prisoners, by describing the Act of Supremacy as a double-edged sword that killed either the body or the soul, and finally by telling Richard Rich—that name again—that the act was not legitimate.

More would have understood, even more clearly than Fisher, that this was a show trial, the outcome of which could not have been more certain. In defending himself, therefore, he focused not on trying to save his life—he could have entertained no hope in that regard—but on creating an indelible record of the absurdity of the proceedings and his reasons for declining to swear as ordered. His best weapons were the power of his own mind and the fact that his case really *was* being handled in an outrageously unfair manner. One by one he was able to dispose of the charges. He invited his accusers to show that he had ever uttered a word in opposition to the Act of Supremacy, and they were unable to do so. He asked for evidence of any conspiracy between Fisher and himself and was shown none. He acknowledged having described the Supremacy Act as a sword that would destroy the soul of anyone who *falsely* swore to it—swore without believing it to be true—but repeated that he had never spoken against it. He turned the judges' attention to the fact that even under the king's new laws it was not possible to construe silence as treason. On point after point the prosecution was stymied.

Which left Richard Rich as the Crown's last hope not of convicting More—his conviction remained inevitable—but of making the trial seem something less ignoble than a lynching. What Rich had to say was similar in significant respects to his testimony in the Fisher trial. Again he told the court of having visited the defendant in the Tower, and of a conversation that culminated in a statement—an undeniably incriminating statement—of opposition to the Act of Supremacy. There were important differences this time, however. Rich said that on June 12 he had gone to the Tower not with a message from the king but simply to take away the last of More's personal belongings, his books and writing materials. (Obviously this had been done as part of the steadily intensifying effort to make life in prison unbearable. Until deprived of the means to do so, More had devoted his empty hours to composing two books, devotional works titled *A Dialogue of Comfort Against Tribution* and *On the Sadness of Christ*.) While waiting for More's things to be bundled up, supposedly just to pass the time, Rich had engaged the prisoner in a kind of lawyerly word game. Suppose, he had said, that Parliament declared that I,

Richard Rich, were king. And suppose Parliament declared also that it would be treason to deny that I were king. Would you then agree that I was king? More said that he would, because Parliament had the power to declare who was king of England. Then he offered a question of his own. How would Rich respond if Parliament declared that God was not God and made it treason to say otherwise? Would he accept that? Rich replied that he would not—that "no parliament may make any such law."

This was Rich's account of the first part of the conversation, and More never disputed it. What happened next, however, has been a puzzle ever since. According to Rich's testimony, he threw another question at More—a question that the surrounding circumstances loaded with all-too-obvious significance. What, he claimed to have asked, if Parliament declared the king to be supreme head of the English church? What would More say to that? Rich swore that More replied that Parliament could do no such thing, because England was forever part of the Christian community that had always recognized the bishop of Rome as its head. Such words were clear and certain treason as Parliament had defined treason in 1534—assuming that More spoke them.

But at this point More's story diverges radically from Fisher's. Whereas Fisher never denied saying the things that Rich had reported him as saying, complaining instead that he had opened himself in response to the king's request and under a promise of confidentiality, More vehemently denied having said anything to incriminate himself. There is of course no documentary evidence to establish who was and was not speaking truthfully. Two potential witnesses—the men who were packing More's books while he and Rich had their exchange— were called to testify but claimed to have paid no attention to the conversation. (It would be understandable if they had no wish to get involved in such a foul and dangerous business.) Be that as it may, More was unquestionably the more credible witness. He knew that he faced certain death, nothing could be more obvious than his determination to prepare himself for a "good" death, and for a man of his convictions lying under oath would have been tantamount to self-damnation. Nor is it easy to believe that a man as intelligent and careful as More, a man of his skill in the law, could have fallen into such an obvious trap. More himself asked his judges if they found it credible that he would have allowed himself to be drawn by Richard Rich, of all people, into revealing thoughts that he had been keeping from the whole world, even from his own family, from the beginning of his troubles.

"Can it therefore seem likely unto your honorable lordships," he asked,

> that I would, in so weighty a cause, so unadvisedly overshoot myself as to trust Master Rich, a man of me always reputed for one of so little truth as your lordships have heard, so far above my sovereign lord the king or any of his noble counselors, that I would unto him utter the secrets of my conscience touching the king's supremacy—the special point and only mark at my hands so long sought for? A thing which I never did, nor never would, after the statute thereof made, reveal either to the king's highness himself or to any of his honorable counselors, as it is not unknown to your honors, at sundry several times sent from his grace's own person unto the Tower unto me for no other purpose. Can this, in your judgments, my lords, seem likely to be true?

Regardless, he was that same day found guilty. Before sentence was passed, he requested and was granted the customary right of a convicted prisoner to address his judges, the usual strategy at this point being to argue that there should be no punishment because the conviction had been illegitimate. Being a good lawyer, More did exactly this, saying that the acts of Parliament that had brought him before the bench were "directly repugnant to the laws of God and his whole church." But he did so in a way that offered not the slightest possibility of saving him from execution. He was speaking now not to the men who had judged him but to posterity, hoping to put himself on record forever. He said that no layman, not even a king, could be supreme head of the church even in a single country. He said that England was one part of the great thousand-year-old community of Christendom, and that it could make no laws contrary to the ancient understanding that bound that community together. He spoke for an ideal that was even then passing out of existence. When he had finished he was condemned to die, exactly as he and everyone present had known he would be from the start of the day's proceedings.

Later he was informed that the king, as a special favor, had ordered him like Fisher to be beheaded rather than hanged, drawn, and quartered. "God preserve all my friends from such favors," he said cheerfully. On the Tuesday following his conviction he was awakened early and informed that he was to die at nine o'clock. He was advised that the king wished him to say little before dying. He said he was grateful to be so informed, because although he had planned to say nothing that would displease the king, he had intended to speak at some length. "I am ready," he said, "obediently to conform myself to his grace's commandments." When his hour came round, he found himself too weak to climb the stairs of the scaffold unassisted. "I pray you, master lieutenant," he told the man in charge, "see me safe up, and for my coming down, let me shift for myself." Hoisted to the chopping block, he kissed the executioner, telling him that "thou wilt render me today the greatest service in the power of any mortal." He asked the crowd of onlookers to bear witness that he was dying "in and for the faith of the Catholic Church," and that he died "the king's good servant, but God's first." His last words came as he lowered himself to the floor, placed his head on the block, and moved his beard out of the way. The beard had committed no treason, he said, and did not deserve to be cut in two. His head joined Fisher's on London Bridge.

Cromwell now turned his attention to one of the main pillars not only of the church but of English society as it had evolved through the Middle Ages, the more than eight hundred monastic institutions that dotted the landscape from the cliffs of Dover to the Irish Sea. In January he had been given, as an addition to the offices he already held, that of vice-regent, first "for the sole purpose of undertaking a general ecclesiastical visitation" but later and more broadly as "vicar-general and principal commissary with all the spiritual authority belonging to the king as head of the church, for the due administration of justice in all cases touching the ecclesiastical jurisdiction and the godly reformation and redress of all errors, heresies and abuses in the said church." It was not only a lofty commission but an improbable one, conferring virtually absolute authority over the practices and beliefs of the church in England on a man with no background in theology, canon law, or related disciplines and no experience in ecclesiastical administration aside from the financial work done years earlier for Wolsey. The king had demonstrated the fact of his supremacy, the extent to which the church was now subordinate to the civil government and the civil government to his every whim, by placing Cromwell above every clergyman including the archbishop of Canterbury, every nobleman including even the dukes, and every other officer of the Crown including the lord chancellor. To drive home the point, he next suspended by royal edict all the traditional powers of the bishops—the authority to ordain priests, for example, as well as to administer the ecclesiastical courts and probate wills. The bishops were required to petition the Crown for permission to resume their work, and by doing so they would acknowledge that they derived their authority solely from the king. As a final insult, the bishops were told that their petitions were being granted not because they were essential to the proper functioning of the church but because the vicar-general was unfortunately unable to do everything himself. That the lords of the church submitted to this humiliation virtually without complaint shows what they had learned from the examples of Fisher and More: to resist was to die, to protest was to die, even to do nothing was, if the king wished it, to die.

Whether any action on Rome's part might have made a difference is a moot question, because Rome did not act. In the aftermath of Fisher's execution, members of the papal court had demanded that Pope Paul do *something*. A bull was drawn up giving Henry ninety days in which to admit his errors and either appear in Rome personally or send representatives. The penalties for failing to comply were to be weighty if theoretical: excommunication, loss of the English crown, loss of the right of Henry's descendants by Anne Boleyn to inherit the crown, the withdrawal of all clergy from the kingdom, a papal order for Henry's subjects to rebel, and more. But the pope, when the bull was ready for publication, thought better of it. He realized that the only men in Europe who might conceivably back it up with force were the emperor Charles and Francis of France, and that neither was likely to prove able (or for that matter willing) to do so. He realized also that to issue such a document under current circumstances could only underscore the impotence of the papacy and expose it to ridicule. Thus it was locked away. The new pope remained, as far as anyone in England could tell, as passive as his predecessor Clement.

There was a second reason, one more substantial than a symbolic demonstration of the king's might, for suspending the powers of the bishops at precisely this time. The Reformation Parliament, in taking from the bishops their ancient responsibility to make occasional visits of inspection to the monastic houses, had placed a new and potent weapon in the king's hands. Visitation was now the Crown's business, which meant it was Cromwell's, and no man of the new vice-regent's vitality, ambition, and determination to please the king could have been given such an opportunity without finding use for it. By the time of More's death, Cromwell was ready to move against the religious orders and their houses. Aside from the monks and nuns living in those houses, the people most likely to object were those men who until recently had regarded the monasteries as theirs to oversee, to protect, and sometimes to exploit: the bishops. Suspension of their authority deprived them of even an historical basis for protesting: what had traditionally been regarded as their rights were no longer rights at all but privileges conferred by the king. The requirement that they ask the Crown to restore their ability to function made it indelibly clear to the bishops themselves, to the whole of the church including the religious orders, and to anyone else inclined to take an interest that none of them had any rights except those the king might choose to grant them.

Commissioners appointed by Cromwell were dispatched to make formal visitations to religious houses across the kingdom and to the two universities, Oxford and Cambridge, which were still so focused on the education of the clergy by the clergy as to be essentially religious establishments themselves. What Cromwell and the king intended in undertaking this program of visitation has been a matter of controversy ever since. Students of the subject who approve of what Henry VIII did to and with the church have tended, understandably, to argue that the visits were necessary and well intended. On the most practical level their stated purpose was to find out what the various monasteries owned and owed and what their annual income amounted to, so that the government could determine how much they should be required to pay under the new statute of First Fruits and Tenths. From a loftier perspective they were intended to search out and eradicate the many and supposedly horrible abuses of which the church's most radical critics had long been complaining.

Other factors, too, help to explain why Henry and Cromwell turned their attention to the monasteries as soon as their grip on the church was assured. The old religion was still a force to be feared: no student of Henry VIII's reign will deny that in the 1530s and for decades afterward the break with Rome was incomprehensible where not outright repugnant to very large numbers of the English people. The religious houses were symbols and instruments of a way of life that the population had not rejected even if the king had. If few of the leaders of those houses had thus far shown much inclination to follow the Friars Observant and the Carthusians to violent deaths, neither were many of them overly careful to conceal their dislike of what the king was doing. Thus they were natural, conspicuous targets for anyone determined that there should be no restoration of the connection with Rome—and exactly that determination was shared by everyone from Cromwell to Queen Anne, from Cranmer to the dukes of Norfolk and Suffolk. The more Lutheran or Protestant of the reformers (the word *Protestant* was just then being born in Germany) wanted the monasteries condemned as cesspits of hypocrisy, sexual deviancy, and general moral corruption. They saw them as unconnected to the true spirit of Christianity, and therefore to require elimination.

Cromwell was aware that the church—the monasteries perhaps most obviously, but the dioceses, colleges, hospitals, and other clerical institutions as well—owned a great deal of land and controlled the revenues generated by that land. He had seen this firsthand while in Wolsey's service, where he had been among the first Englishmen to taste the fruits of shutting down religious houses and seizing their assets. And it happened that the mid-1530s were a singularly hard time financially for the English nation and its government. The grain harvest failed almost completely in 1535 (people said it had been raining almost without stop since the killing of the Carthusian priors), and this was but the latest in a series of seriously lean years. Thousands were literally on the verge of starvation, and in June riots broke out in London over the scarcity and price of wheat. The people who farmed the king's lands were unable to pay their rent, owners of land were unable to pay their taxes, and the treasury was so empty that officers of the Crown went without their meager pay. The men responsible for guarding Catherine of Aragon reported being unable to keep her household supplied with food. The king, meanwhile, remained as financially insatiable as ever, spending freely on his varied pleasures and seemingly oblivious to the suffering of his subjects. No one in Cromwell's position could have been unmindful of the immense sums of money represented by the church whose master he now was. Nor was he unaware of the religious eruptions taking place in Germany, or of how Germany's elites were gorging on the property of the church. On the other hand, no one could have cared less than Cromwell and his master about the extent to which church revenues were used for the benefit of the population, or how important the benefactions of the monasteries became when conditions were as hard as they now were.

However appropriate it may have been for the Crown to examine the monasteries, however noble the motives of the king and Cromwell may conceivably have been in launching their program of visitations, as executed that program was a sordid affair. The men Cromwell chose for the job were largely a brutish lot, bent not on informing themselves about the state of the monasteries but on collecting or even fabricating as much negative information as possible as quickly as possible and hurrying it to court. It soon became clear that nearly their only aim was to give Cromwell what he had made clear he wanted—a quick harvest of money in the short run, a basis for harvesting vastly greater amounts later—so that they, in their turn, could be rewarded with a share of the spoils. Several of them became hugely wealthy in just a few years. The details of how they succeeded are almost comic in what they reveal about the malice and greed driving the whole project, tragic in their consequences for hundreds and ultimately thousands of blameless people.

Monastic visitations, whether by the local bishop or by officials of the order to which a particular house belonged, had traditionally been painstaking affairs in which residents and their superiors were interviewed separately about their daily routine, their perceptions of the orderliness of the community or its lack thereof, their questions, suggestions, problems, and complaints. Reports of misconduct or lapses of discipline were investigated to establish their accuracy and seriousness, and eventually the results of all this became the basis of an overall evaluation—a report card, in effect—that prescribed the changes that the visitors regarded as desirable or necessary. Follow-up visits ensured that corrective action was actually taken. The visits by Cromwell's people in 1535 and early 1536 were different: hurried and cursory, with all the emphasis on tallying alleged misdeeds, no exploration of the accuracy of what was reported, and no attempt at correction as opposed to condemnation. Two of the most active and prominent visitors, Richard Layton and Thomas Legh, traveled more than a thousand miles and supposedly visited 121 houses in two months—more than fifteen miles and two monasteries per day, on average. They carried with them eighty-six "articles of inquiry" (questions to which they were supposed to get answers everywhere they went) and twenty-five injunctions or rules to which every house was being required to subscribe. Obviously none of this could be done with even minimal care or thoroughness in the time available.

But it was not their purpose to be thorough or careful. Their mission was to make trouble, blacken reputations, and spread fear. Some of the injunctions could only have been intended to weaken the houses visited and make the maintenance of discipline impossible. It was ordered, for example, that any residents of religious houses under the age of twenty-four, and any who regardless of their current age had taken their vows before the age of twenty, should be discharged into the world whether that was what they wished or not. This had a devastating impact on the manpower (or womanpower) of many houses, the smaller ones especially, and it became a nightmare for individuals unprepared to be sent out into society and wanting nothing except to remain in the communities that had long been their homes. Some of the discharged men were given or at least promised small payments of money and, in the case of the old and infirm, small pensions. Discharged nuns, on the other hand, were given only gowns before being sent away. Those not forced to depart were encouraged to do so voluntarily (the number who agreed to do so appears to have been very small) and—in a step surely calculated to undercut good order and discipline—were told that if they had problems with their superiors they could appeal directly to Cromwell. Any costs incurred in connection with such appeals were to be paid by those same superiors. Another injunction forbade anyone to leave or enter a monastery without the permission of the royal commissioners. When used to stop all traffic in or out—and some of the commissioners used it in exactly this way—this could prevent a monastery from conducting essential business or even supplying its members with food. The new restrictions were rendered all the more odious by the introduction of preachers selected by Cromwell and Cranmer for their eagerness to propound ideas that the residents of the monastic houses were almost certain to find repellent.

The results of all this were sometimes as ridiculous as they were ruinous to the houses. Increasingly, Cromwell received letters from monks complaining not of immorality in their houses but rather of the strictness with which the rules were observed. He encouraged complaints of almost any kind and bestowed favors on those who complained. "Thanks for excusing my getting up for matins at midnight," John Horwoode, a monk of the Benedictine abbey at Winchcombe, wrote to him. "The abbot says this has given cause to some murmurs and grudging among the convent. The truth is, I do not like the burdens and straightness of religion, such as their accustomed abstinence, the 'frayer' (recreations), and other observances of the rule." Before the start of the visitation program, William Fordham, a monk of the priory of Worcester, had been removed as procurator on grounds of extravagance and dishonesty. When he and a former subprior who also had lost his position because of misconduct appealed to Cromwell, the vice-regent responded (one can imagine his glee) by putting the two in charge of the house over the protests of the other monks and throwing the prior in prison on a charge of treason. When Chancellor Audley could find no basis for putting the prior on trial, it was decided to let him rot in confinement. Complaints were rare—surprisingly so, considering the rewards that Cromwell was prepared to bestow on anyone willing to help stir up trouble—but their nature was ironic all the same. A frenzied hunt for evidence of monastic laxity more frequently produced evidence that discipline was often so strict as to offend the less zealous religious.

Among the unstated objectives of the visitations was to harass the superiors, making their lives so unpleasant that finally they would give up and voluntarily surrender their establishments to the Crown. There is no reason to think that Eustace Chapuys, Charles V's ambassador to England, was misunderstanding the situation when, in September, he sent the emperor his report on what was happening: "Cromwell goes round about visiting the abbeys, making inventories of their goods and revenues, instructing them fully in the tenets of the new sect, turning out of the abbeys monks and nuns who made their profession before they were twenty-five, and leaving the rest free to go out or remain. It is true they are not expressly told to go out, but it is clearly given them to understand that they had better do it, for they are going to make a reformation of them so severe and strange that in the end they will go, which is the object the king is aiming at, in order to have better occasion to seize the property without causing the people to murmur." Chapuys was an alien at the English court of 1535, a man known to be hostile to Henry's whole religious program and to represent an emperor who was equally hostile. That even he knew not only what was happening but why, and that he knew it long before Henry made his real intentions explicit, indicates rather strongly that the king's and Cromwell's objectives, if they were secret at all, must have been the worst-kept secret in England.

In any case, Cromwell's hopes of bullying the heads of the religious houses into giving up came to almost nothing. By the end of the winter of 1535–36, in spite of incessant interference, threats of worse to come, and promises of pensions for those religious who agreed to depart, only five monasteries had gone out of existence. All five were poor, tiny establishments forced to yield to the hard fact that, after the expulsion of some of their members and the financial exactions of the Crown, they simply had no way of surviving. Still, the visitations had been far from a waste of Crown resources. The government had been able to intrude itself deeply into the internal affairs of every monastery in the kingdom. One house after another had seen the number of its residents reduced, with few except the aged left behind in some instances, and almost all had been weakened financially. In a number of cases it had proved possible to remove superiors unfriendly to the work of the visitors and to inject new leaders of Cromwell's choosing. Every such change had been another assertion of royal mastery, and as such had deepened the demoralization of men and women who were finding it increasingly difficult to believe that they were going to be permitted to continue living in the old way. Cromwell and his men, meanwhile, had taken a first big step down a road that promised to lead them to great wealth. Cromwell had long since shown himself to be expert at extracting money from the people with whom he did business. Now he was able to apply his skills on an immeasurably expanded scale. Money fell into his coffers from terrified abbeys and priories hoping to buy their way out of destruction, from people eager to buy their way into the leadership of abbeys and priories and thereby gain control of their assets, and from his own agents as they moved across the country shaking down their victims and taking care to send their master a share of the booty.

Most important for the long term, the visitations led to the creation of documents that Cromwell could offer to the king and Parliament as proof of the horrifying state of monasticism in England. That this report had been assembled with impossible haste, that it was the work of men interested only in negative findings, that it had involved no serious effort to distinguish fact from fiction—none of this was given the slightest attention. Nor was there any acknowledgment that in some cases the truth had been grossly distorted; masturbation was classified as "sodomy," for example, and when nuns admitted to having illegitimate children no effort was made to determine whether they had borne those children before entering religious life or after.

The fact that the visitors had been able to turn up evidence of *possible* immorality among only a tiny percentage of the monastic clergy was absolutely irrelevant as far as Cromwell was concerned. He had his report in hand—not a coherent report in any serious sense, but a jumbled assortment of mainly vague and unsubstantiated accusations—and it was up to him alone to decide what it actually meant. Whatever he decided, neither Parliament nor the bishops would be likely to disagree. He had planned to recall Parliament late in 1535, but widespread sickness related to continuing famine made a postponement necessary. When Parliament did reconvene, he would be ready to use it for a new and far more ambitious attack on the monastic houses. The report on the visitations, crooked though it was, would be his weapon.

One other event of 1535 merits attention. A group of zealous religious reformers arrived in England from the continent that year. They were Anabaptists, regarded as dangerous radicals even by the Lutherans because of their rejection of infant baptism and much traditional doctrine. They must have traveled to England in search of refuge, their movement having come under intense persecution in Germany, Switzerland, and elsewhere. Immediately upon arrival, however, they were taken into custody. The fourteen of their number who refused to renounce the tenets of their sect were promptly burned at the stake. Obviously it was not sufficient in Henry VIII's England to be anti-Rome. Safety was going to require being anti-Rome in whatever way Henry himself decided to find acceptable.

POPES

WHAT IS CALLED THE RENAISSANCE PAPACY WILL STINK IN the nostrils of history to the end of time. Its story is a litany of violence and deceit, of greed and pride and murderous ambition—finally of a corruption that reached such depths as to defy belief. It is an embarrassment to every Catholic who knows about it, a gift to anyone wanting to believe that the Catholic Church really is the Whore of Babylon.

However, it had essentially nothing to do with Henry VIII's destruction of the old church. Tudor England was too far away to be much affected by or even very aware of it, and in any case the worst was already over when Henry came to the throne. By the time he was killing the likes of John Fisher and launching his attack on the monasteries, a new era of reform was dawning in Rome itself.

The papacy had touched bottom when Henry was a child, during the dozen years when the Spaniard Rodrigo Borgia ruled as Pope Alexander VI. A man so vile that when he died in 1503 the priests of St. Peter's Basilica refused to bury him, Alexander had begun his career as the nephew of an earlier Borgia pope thanks to whom he became a bishop, a cardinal, and finally vice-chancellor of the whole church. (He really was Calixtus III's *nephew,* by the way; the word was not always an oblique way of referring to a pope's illegitimate son.) Once he was pope himself, Alexander devoted his reign to advancing the fortunes of the favorites among his numerous bastard children, the most notorious of whom were his son Cesare (a ruthless adventurer who became archbishop of Valencia at age seventeen, and for whom Machiavelli wrote *The Prince*) and his oft-married daughter Lucrezia, rumored though never proven to have been a skilled poisoner and to have committed incest with her brother. Alexander tried to turn vast expanses of church property in central and northern Italy into private domains for his sons, not hesitating to start wars for this purpose or to involve Spain, France,

Venice, Milan, and Naples. At one point he was in such serious trouble that he appealed to the Ottoman Empire, which by that time posed a threat to the very survival of Christianity in eastern Europe, for help. His rather mysterious death, sometimes said to have been the result of an accidental poisoning by his son Cesare, came as a relief to everyone except his offspring. His successor refused to have masses said for him on grounds that it was blasphemous to pray for the damned.

If Alexander's reign was the worst, it differed from what came just before more in degree than in kind. The degradation of the throne of St. Peter had begun in the fourteenth century, during the seventy-three years when seven consecutive popes, all of them French, resided not at Rome but in Avignon and were under the control of the kings of France. This was followed by the Great Schism, four decades during which there were never fewer than two popes, each with his own court and college of cardinals. By the time the Council of Constance resolved this mess and reestablished a single pope at the Vatican, the reputation both of the papacy and of the city of Rome (its population down to twenty-five thousand) was in ruins. From that point, however, the popes began to rebuild their economic and political power, steadily increasing the size of the Papal States and making themselves major players in the cutthroat world of Italian politics. (They were less assiduous in attempting to rebuild their moral authority.) Each new pope tried to outdo his predecessor in restoring the Eternal City to its former splendor, in the process making the papal court Europe's leading source of patronage for artists and the new humanist learning.

The negative aspects of all this success were evident by the reign of Sixtus IV, which began in 1471. Sixtus had risen from modest beginnings to become a Franciscan friar, a university lecturer, minister-general of his order at age fifty, a cardinal at fifty-three. At the time of his election he was regarded as a reformer, so that great things were expected of his reign, but he devoted himself instead to power politics and to making his relatives rich. Though he had no children (like some other Renaissance popes he was probably homosexual), he went to outrageous lengths to advance the interests of his family, the della Roveres. He was implicated in a plot not merely to defeat but to exterminate the rival Medicis of Florence. (In fairness it must be acknowledged that there is no proof that Sixtus himself approved the committing of murder.) Though the scheme fell short of its objective, it did result in the stabbing death, in Florence's cathedral, of the Medici whose then-still-unborn son would one day have the misfortune of serving as Pope Clement VII when Henry VIII sued for his annulment. Perhaps Sixtus's greatest achievement was arranging the marriage that brought the Dukedom of Urbino into the possession of the della Rovere family, his greatest shame that he permitted Ferdinand of Aragon to launch the Spanish Inquisition. He started work on the Sistine Chapel, which is how it got its name.

Nothing much changed under Sixtus's successor, the ludicrously misnamed Innocent VIII. He was yet another assiduous nepotist, marrying the eldest of his numerous illegitimate children to an illegitimate daughter of Lorenzo the Magnificent of Florence and raising Lorenzo's thirteen-year-old son, Giovanni, to the College of Cardinals as part of the deal. (The boy would grow up to become the first Medici pope, Leo X.) Innocent was followed by the monstrous Alexander VI, of whom enough has already been said, and then by Sixtus IV's nephew Giuliano della Rovere, who as Julius II presided from 1503 to 1513 over what is often called the Renaissance papacy's golden age and in fact was, at a minimum, a gilded age. Della Rovere had been Alexander's bitter enemy— so much so that he spent the latter's papacy in exile—and upon becoming pope himself he made it his first priority to recover the papal territories controlled by Cesare Borgia and his brothers. That accomplished, Julius went on to make war on a much grander scale, organizing the so-called Holy League against France, inviting England to join, and thereby giving young Henry VIII a supposedly religious reason to pursue his dreams of military glory. As a ruler Julius was an epic figure: warrior, builder, patron of great artists. As a religious leader, he was perhaps the last of Rome's sick jokes.

Julius's death brought an end to the worst of the outrages. Leo X, the onetime thirteen-year-old Medici cardinal, was elected in 1513, and though he possessed none of the majesty of his predecessor he was also not a bad man. He raised the quality of the College of Cardinals (one of his appointees was the respected Lorenzo Campeggio, who much later would be sent to England to judge King Henry's annulment suit) and even tried without success to convene a council for the purpose of effecting reforms. It was during his eight-year reign that the Lutheran revolt erupted in Germany, which is one reason his death resulted in the election of a scholarly and almost saintly Dutchman, Adrian VI, who died before being able to accomplish anything (and would prove to be, incidentally, the last non-Italian pope for more than four hundred years). Next came another Medici, Clement VII, the intelligent, conscientious, but also indecisive and unlucky pontiff whose whole reign turned into a stalemated struggle with problems among which the English king's wish to be rid of his wife was far from the most difficult or dangerous. If Clement solved none of those problems, he also never disgraced his office. He had been a champion of reform long before becoming pope and recognized the need for reform on the largest possible scale, but he declined to call a general council of the church out of fear that such a body might become yet another threat to papal authority.

The 1534 election of Alessandro Farnese as Pope Paul III must have been a troubling development for at least some reformers. Early in his career Farnese had been a protégé of Alexander VI, who made him a cardinal in 1493 when he was only twenty-five, and almost his first major act upon becoming pope was to bestow red hats on two of his own grandsons, both of them barely out of childhood. After that appalling start, however, he changed course, making the papacy not only friendly to the reform cause but its driving engine. He set remarkably high standards for his subsequent appointments, looking for men of unquestionably good character, impressive intellectual credentials, and a demonstrated commitment to the purging of abuses. It was he who added John Fisher to the College of Cardinals in 1535, and he would do the same to Henry VIII's cousin Reginald Pole a year later. Pole was also named to, and became a conspicuously active member of, a commission responsible for identifying areas where reform was most urgently needed. Paul had begun his reign believing that it was still possible to close the rifts that in less than twenty years had shattered the unity of Western Christendom, and unlike Clement VII he saw a general council as a possible way of achieving reconciliation. In this he was perhaps naïve: when he announced plans for a council to meet at Mantua, the German Protestant states declared that they would attend no assembly held in Italy under papal auspices. A council remained one of his highest objectives, however, and with the support of the emperor Charles he would continue to try to convene one.

Paul definitely thought, in the early going, that reconciliation with England was still possible. His years as dean of the College of Cardinals had persuaded him that Henry VIII was well disposed toward him—the impression was probably not wrong when originally formed, Cardinal della Rovere being rich in the skills of diplomacy and Henry at first eager for friends at the papal court—but he appears never to have understood the island kingdom of the distant north. He even believed, evidently, that Henry would welcome his decision to make John Fisher a cardinal. News of Fisher's execution set him straight soon enough, and the killing soon afterward of Thomas More left no room for doubt. Obviously Henry would never voluntarily reconnect with Rome on anything resembling traditional terms, and henceforth Paul would shape his English policy accordingly.

14

All but Godlike

At the start of 1536 Catherine of Aragon, hidden away at Kimbolton Castle far from London, was on her deathbed. She asked that her daughter be permitted to visit, but though the two had not seen each other in years, the king once again refused. He had been as unsuccessful in getting Mary to accept his supremacy and her illegitimacy as he had been in persuading Catherine of those two things, and perhaps he feared that if the two met they would strengthen each other's resolve. Possibly he was motivated by nothing more calculating than a mean-spirited desire to punish his onetime queen by denying even her dying wish. Certainly his current queen could have had no argument with Henry's refusal: understandably, Anne regarded the very existence of Catherine and Mary, now a marriageable woman of twenty, as a threat to her own position and the futures of her daughter Elizabeth and the additional children she expected to bear. She had had Mary sent away from court and placed in the custody of her—Anne's—aunt, who pestered her daily with demands that she stop claiming that she was a royal princess and her little half-sister was not.

No longer strong enough to take pen to paper, Catherine dictated a last letter to the man she continued to regard as her husband. She touched on many subjects, gently calling Henry to account for having "cast me into many calamities, and yourself into many troubles," forgiving him for everything and asking God to forgive him also. She asked him to be good to Mary, and to provide the three ladies remaining in her service with dowries so that they could marry, and her servants with a year's pay. "Lastly, I make this vow," she said, "that mine eyes desire you above all things. Farewell." A few days later she was dead, an aged, worn-out, heartbroken woman just three weeks past her fiftieth birthday. An autopsy revealed that she apparently had been in good health except for a growth, "completely black and hideous," on her heart. Centuries later pathologists would conclude that this growth was a secondary cancer, a reflection of the apparently undetected sarcoma that must have been the actual cause of death. But in 1536, inevitably, a rumor traveled through England to the effect that Henry had had her poisoned. Catherine had asked to be buried at one of the houses of the Observant Franciscans, but thanks to her husband no such houses remained. Three days after her death he decided that she should be buried at Peterborough Cathedral. Her tomb was decorated with the arms of Spain combined with those of Wales rather than England. She could be honored as Princess of Wales, but not as queen of anything.

Henry was reported to have shed a tear or two upon reading Catherine's letter, but to be so jubilant when this was followed by news of her death that he dressed in yellow with a white feather in his hat and ordered up a banquet and a tournament in celebration. He and Anne— she too was festively adorned in yellow—brought little Princess Elizabeth to court that day and ostentatiously showed her off. To her parents she must have seemed an augury of still better things to come: her mother was once again pregnant. Anne and the king would have been ecstatic, Henry because once again he could look forward to the arrival of his long-yearned-for son, Anne because by giving birth to the next king of England she could make herself secure.

Ironically, the death of Catherine left Anne more vulnerable than she had been before. In the eyes of the Roman church Anne was the king's mistress rather than his wife, whereas Henry was now a widower, free to wed whom he chose. If he put Anne aside, he would be free to take a Hapsburg bride or a Valois bride or whatever bride he preferred. And he was obviously no longer as enchanted with Anne as he had been before their marriage. For months now he had been openly flirting with one of Anne's ladies-in-waiting, Jane Seymour. Anne, quick to notice, must have wondered if history might be repeating itself. In her anger and fear she had lashed out both at Henry, whose complaints about his wife's flaming temper were taking on a sharper edge, and at the apparently unoffending Jane. Henry, remembering the restraint with which Catherine had carried herself when faced with evidence of a romantic entanglement involving her husband and one of her ladies, could not have been pleased to hear of "much scratching and by-blows between the queen and her maid." But none of that mattered compared to the fact of Anne's latest pregnancy. If she could bring this child to term, if it proved to be male and survived, she would have nothing to fear from any woman in England and little to fear even from Henry himself.

But it was not to be. On January 29—the day of Catherine's burial—Anne miscarried a fetus that appeared to be in its fourth month of development, and to be male. Anne of course was deeply, wretchedly, almost hysterically unhappy, but when Henry visited her bedchamber he displayed more self-pity than concern for his wife. According to one story, she tried to arouse his sympathy by telling him that the miscarriage had been triggered by the force of her love: six days before, he had been unconscious for two hours after a hard fall from his horse, and Anne is supposed to have claimed that her fear for his life had caused her to lose the child. An alternate story has it that Anne went into labor after discovering Henry with Jane on his knee. Whatever the truth, the end of the pregnancy was the end not only of the marriage but of Anne. She now became a victim of history, of domestic and international politics, and of course of her husband.

Much more was in play now than Anne's failure to produce a son or the king's latest infatuation with one of the ladies of his court. Anne was also dangerously exposed because, for the first time, she was seriously at odds with Thomas Cromwell. What separated the two was the question of the monasteries: not whether to continue the attack on them, because she as an evangelical was no more sympathetic to the religious houses than he was, but what to do with the riches that the attack was making available. Parliament, obediently accepting the king's assurances that Cromwell's visitations had shown the smaller monasteries to be sinkholes of degeneracy sexual and otherwise, passed in March a bill authorizing the seizure and closing of all religious houses (the bill said they were to be "converted to better uses") with annual revenues of less than £200. All the larger and richer houses, the "great and solemn monasteries," were spared on the grounds that "(thanks be to God) religion is right well kept and observed" by them. Obviously it was implausible that all the smaller establishments were so corrupt as to be beyond saving while all the larger ones were above reproach, but targeting only the weakest allowed Cromwell to win the acquiescence of those abbots of great houses who sat in the House of Lords. As for the lay lords and the Commons, quite apart from their fear of the king, they could be brought along by the twofold hope that the liquidation of the smaller monasteries might spare them from being taxed and possibly even enable them to share in the spoils. Cromwell, responsible as he now was for paying the bills of a financially irresponsible monarch, naturally intended to claim the property and income of the monasteries for the Crown (which would, of course, make it possible to divert some part of the resulting windfall into his own hands and those of his henchmen). Queen Anne, more nobly if naïvely, proposed that the money in question, once it had been cleansed of papist corruption, should continue to be used for religious or at least quasi-religious purposes—for education and charity. The stakes were high, and feelings were correspondingly intense on both sides. One result, a fateful one for the queen, was that Cromwell now had a positive reason to fear her continued influence over Henry. The most powerful man in England after the king thus became the enemy of a queen who already had too many enemies—all those numberless people who harbored resentments over how Catherine had been rudely discarded and Mary was even now being shabbily treated. Cromwell had chosen a good issue over which to break with Anne and her party. Where the disposition of the wealth of the church was concerned, he could be confident of his free-spending king's support.

Internationally, too, events were unfolding in ways that seemed almost calculated to leave Anne alone and vulnerable. The greatest danger to Henry was the possibility that Francis of France and the emperor Charles V would put their differences aside, ally themselves with the pope, and launch a military crusade aimed at driving the English apostate from his throne. This was not inconceivable: Charles was an ardent Catholic who might easily be persuaded to see such an undertaking as his duty if it had any real chance of success, and Francis was ambitious and restless enough to be drawn into almost any adventure that carried the promise of gold or glory. England's great need—Henry's desperate need—was to keep Charles and Francis apart. The best way to accomplish that was to enter into an alliance with one of them so as to neutralize both with a single stroke.

He could hardly have been luckier in this regard. For nearly eight years Francis had been biding his time, waiting for France to recover its strength sufficiently for him to avenge the humiliations inflicted after the battles of Pavia and Landriano. By the spring of 1536 he felt ready. Charles having sailed off to North Africa to attack the Turkish stronghold of Tunis, Francis invaded and overran part of the Hapsburg dominions in northern Italy. Charles returned to find that he had good reason to repair his relationship with England, and he was pleased to learn that Cromwell was receptive. The old obstacle, Henry's divorce of Charles's aunt Catherine, had been removed by Catherine's death; though Charles had apparently found it necessary to be mortally offended by the insult done to his mother's sister, he was too much of a realist and in 1536 too badly in need of friends to allow policy to be determined by what had been done once upon a time to his insane mother's dead sister. Now the problem was on the English side: it was Henry's insistence that everyone, not just everyone in England but *everyone,* recognize his marriage to Anne. In the case of Charles, this was asking too much. He could only have seen such a step as compromising his honor.

But Henry was no longer as devoted to Anne as he once had been. He was definitely less disposed to put his throne at risk for her sake. Perhaps his marriage was not something the whole of Christendom must be made to accept but a problem, a source of danger even, a barrier standing between himself and safety. He suspected that Anne's miscarriages, like Catherine's, must be signs of divine displeasure. Knowing that God could not be unhappy with him, he reasoned that Anne or the marriage must be the cause of the trouble. He began to complain that Anne had somehow bewitched him into marrying her "by means of sortileges [sorcery] and charms." He ordered the same churchmen who had provided him with grounds for annulling his first marriage to find reasons for annulling the second. Henry Percy, who years earlier had been in love with the young Anne Boleyn and would have married her if not for Wolsey's interference, was asked to testify that he and Anne had been bound together in a precontract of marriage that rendered her ineligible to marry the king or anyone else. Percy's refusal put an end to what might have been an easy solution, but it freed Cromwell to pursue a more ambitious course. He saw a way not only of ridding the king of another marital problem but of fortifying his own position by eliminating a whole power bloc, the court's Boleyn party.

He was able to make his move early in May: Anne was arrested on charges of adultery and locked in the Tower. Accused with her were five men: a court musician, three members of the king's inner circle including a knight who had long been one of Cromwell's rivals for royal favor, and Anne's own brother. She could not possibly have been guilty; her alleged lovers were offered pardon if they would confess, but only one did so and he had probably been tortured. Nor could Henry possibly have believed her guilty, unless he had sunk so deep into paranoia as to be out of touch with reality. That is unlikely: Henry was vicious by this point, but far from insane. Anne's destruction is adequately explained by Cromwell's opportunism, her husband's weariness with her, possibly his wish to punish her (it was revealed at her trial that she had ridiculed his sexual performance), and the changing international landscape. At times during her imprisonment (nothing could be more understandable) she broke down in fits of hysterical laughter or weeping, but during her farce of a trial she displayed regal composure and firmly maintained her innocence. On May 19, in the moment before being beheaded, she called upon Jesus to "save my sovereign and master the king, the most godly, noble and gentle prince that is." George Boleyn and the other accused men, the one who had been promised mercy for confessing included, had been executed two days before. Thomas Boleyn had been excused from sitting as a judge at his children's trials (their uncle the Duke of Norfolk presided and passed sentence), but he lost his position as Lord Privy Seal (Cromwell took the title for himself) and withdrew permanently to his country home.

Anne just missed out on the distinction of being the first queen of England to be executed; on the day of her death she was no longer Henry's wife and therefore not queen. Shortly after her arrest Henry had instructed the infinitely flexible Archbishop Cranmer to nullify the marriage. Even for Cranmer, this must have been an unwelcome assignment. It was he, after all, who had at the king's behest undertaken to review the two royal marriages and solemnly proclaimed the first to have been invalid and the second to be sound and true. Now he had to undo his own work. He went dutifully through the necessary motions, summoning Anne and inviting Henry to appear before him and offer, if they wished, reasons why their union should not be annulled. At the appointed hour a representative of the king presented arguments not in support of the marriage but against it. Two men claiming to represent the queen confessed themselves to be unable to answer such a convincing case, and all asked for a speedy judgment. Two days after Anne was found guilty of treason—an event celebrated with a pageant on the Thames, where "the royal barge was constantly filled with minstrels and musicians"—Cranmer declared that she was not married to Henry and never could have been, because of the king's relationship with her sister Mary. His master was content. The child Elizabeth, like her half-sister Mary, was now illegitimate. Henry was once again a bachelor with no legitimate offspring, free not only to marry but to generate children who would have an uncontestable right to succeed him.

He wasted no time. On the morning following Anne's execution, after a short delay that allowed Cranmer to issue a dispensation permitting Henry to marry Jane in spite of the fact that both were descendants of King Edward III and therefore distant cousins, it was announced that the two were betrothed and would be wed on May 30. Once again Henry was besotted with a bride-to-be. He had established Jane in apartments at Whitehall, with her brother Edward Seymour and his wife quartered nearby to act as chaperones when Henry made his frequent visits. The Seymours were a vigorous and ambitious clan—Jane had many brothers and sisters—and by captivating the king she had created thrilling opportunities for all of them. She herself was an intelligent woman in her late twenties, not beautiful but experienced in the ways of the court, modest in her demeanor and far more submissive than the temperamental Anne had ever been. As a longtime lady-in-waiting she had witnessed the fall not only of Anne but of Catherine before her, and she had seen the Boleyns raised high by their king only to be destroyed. She could not have been unaware of what dangerous waters she and her siblings would have to navigate when she became queen, and one can only wonder how she felt about having been singled out in this extraordinary way. Certainly her bridegroom was not, in physical terms, the stuff of which dreams are made. The onetime golden young king had become grossly overweight, afflicted with chronic headaches and stinking ulcers of the thigh and leg.

With Catherine and Anne both dead and Henry truly and entirely unattached for the first time in a quarter of a century, there was no longer any reason—any matrimonial reason, in any case—why Henry and his kingdom should not be reconciled with the papacy and the universal church. The marriage to Jane presented no problem at all: it was a valid union by anyone's reckoning, and Jane herself was known to be, in her quiet way, more drawn to the old religion than to the reformist party that the Boleyns had so energetically championed. Jane even, as the suppression of the smaller monasteries got under way, attempted to intervene with her husband on the monks' behalf, drawing back when Henry warned her that her predecessor had not benefited from injecting herself in matters that were none of her affair. Pope Paul and Charles V were not only hopeful that Henry could be brought back into the fold but expectant that it was going to happen. Both were prepared to make it as easy for Henry as possible. Paul was prepared to forgive and forget such inconvenient matters as the killing of Cardinal-designate John Fisher.

Which simply went to show that neither understood what kind of man Henry had by now turned into, or where things stood in England in the summer of 1536. Henry had taken immense risks in claiming supremacy over the church, and his success had been profoundly satisfying to his unfathomably needy ego. He would have seen little reason to relinquish any substantial part of all that he had won even if other factors had not complicated the situation. Foremost among those factors was the suppression of the monasteries and the seizure, by and for a Crown that desperately needed money, of their lands, revenues, and treasures. The information gathered by Cromwell's visitors indicated that 372 religious houses in England and another 27 in Wales—somewhat more than half of all the monastic institutions in the kingdom—had annual revenues below £200 and so were subject to liquidation under the statute enacted by Parliament in March. A new Court of the Augmentations of the Revenues of the King's Crown was established to manage the torrent of income that soon followed, and the administration of that court was entrusted to a man who would show himself capable of exploiting its full potential on the king's and Cromwell's behalf and also on his own: the same Richard Rich whose testimony had provided legal cover for the killing of Fisher and More. By April fat trunks were being hauled into London filled with gold and silver plate, jewelry, and other treasures accumulated by the monasteries over the centuries. With them came money from the sale of church bells, lead stripped from the roofs of monastic buildings, and livestock, furnishings, and equipment. Some of the confiscated land was sold—enough to bring in £30,000 in the first two years—and what was not sold generated tens of thousands of pounds in annual rents. Taken all together, it was a tremendous boost to the Crown's revenues, though as great as it was it failed to close the deficit. The longer the confiscations continued, the smaller the possibility of their ever being reversed or even stopped from going further. The money was spent almost as quickly as it flooded in—so quickly that any attempt to restore the monasteries to what they had been before the suppression would have meant financial ruin for the Crown. Nor would those involved in the work of suppression—everyone from Cromwell and Rich to the obscure men whose work it was to strip the monasteries bare and haul away what they contained—ever be willing to part with what they were skimming off for themselves.

Parliament's suppression bill had reserved to the king the power to allow any religious houses of his choosing to continue in operation. In practice this power rested with Cromwell as vicar-general, and in his hands it became another potent tool for self-enrichment. Desperate to save their houses by any possible means in spite of being offered pensions in return for cooperation, the heads of scores of abbeys and priories offered to pay not to be shut down. In many cases they had nothing to offer except the very treasures that would be confiscated if their houses were seized, or whatever money they could raise by leasing or borrowing against the land that was their chief support. The Crown stood to gain nothing by accepting such payment rather than taking possession of everything; Cromwell and his people, by contrast, stood to profit tremendously. The number of houses that survived in this way was surprisingly large—more than a hundred, ultimately—and the extent to which the king's men benefited was no less impressive.

All the same, the suppression was disruptive on a painfully large scale. The number of monks and nuns expelled from the seized houses was probably on the order of two thousand, and taking into account servants, dependants, and tenants makes it likely that as many as ten thousand people were displaced. It is impossible to believe, on the basis of the available evidence, that all or most or even a substantial minority of the closed houses were morally corrupt, unable to sustain themselves financially, or of no use to the broader society. In the archives there survive many letters written from members of the gentry to Cromwell and his agents, explaining why some establishment should not be destroyed and begging that it not be. "We beseech your favor," one such letter states, "for the prior of Pentney, assuring you that he relieves those quarters wondrously where he dwells, and it would be a pity not to spare a house that feeds so many indigent poor, which is in a good state, maintains good service, and does so many charitable deeds." Interestingly, the same prior who was defended in these terms had earlier been singled out for particularly harsh criticism in the visitation reports that preceded the suppression. Similarly, a letter asking mercy for the priory at Carmarthen in Wales asserted that its revenues exceeded £200 per annum, but that the total had been understated by the visitors in order to make suppression possible. This same letter describes the Carmarthen house as well built and in good repair, and the conduct of the twelve monks living there as impeccable. It adds that "hospitality is daily kept for poor and rich, which is a great relief to the country, being poor and bare . . . alms are given to eighty poor people, which, if the house were suppressed, they would want . . . [and] strangers and merchantmen resorting to those parts are honestly received and entertained whereby they are the gladder to bring their commodities to that country." Such documents provide a more objective picture than the reports of Cromwell's agents of the true state of the smaller monasteries and their role in the life of the kingdom. The appeals of the writers, however, were less effective than cash payment in determining which houses were closed and which were allowed to continue.

The appeals of the monks, begging not to be thrown out, were ignored except where enough gold could be found to touch the consciences of the king's commissioners. The suppressions proceeded with such speed that by early July 1536 Ambassador Chapuys was writing that "it is a lamentable thing to see a legion of monks and nuns, who have been chased from their monasteries, wandering miserably hither and thither seeking means to live; and several honest men have told me that, what with monks, nuns and persons dependent on the monasteries suppressed, there were over twenty thousand who knew not how to live." Chapuys's number may have been high, but the picture he painted was accurate. A new kind of pauperism was being created across England as a direct consequence of the actions of the king. It was a pauperism for which, with the disappearance of the monasteries, there could be no adequate relief. It would plague the reigns of Henry's children. As the government began to seek remedy by punishing the paupers themselves, yet another dimension would be added to the horrors of the age.

The response of the religious orders to the destruction of their houses was almost uniformly passive. They were, after all, communities of monks and nuns, not of politicians or soldiers, and they were receiving no support from their bishops or even from the larger, more influential houses. A striking exception occurred in late September in the north. As the four men charged by Cromwell with shutting down monasteries in Northumberland approached the town of Hexham, they found armed men blocking their way. The townsfolk had turned out to stop them, and had turned the local monastery into a fortress. The monks inside, informed that the commissioners had been sent in the king's name to execute the bill of dissolution, replied that "we be twenty brethren in this house and we shall die all, or that ye shall have the house." The visitors withdrew and did not return. Hexham was left in peace—for the time being. The fact that this act of defiance had taken place in the north would soon prove symptomatic of that whole region's hostility to the king's program.

Henry had other things to concern himself with than a small community of recalcitrant monks and their supporters in a distant corner of the kingdom. For many months, through his court chaplain, he had been badgering his young cousin Reginald Pole to provide a written statement of his position on the annulment of his first marriage and, especially, the supremacy. Pole was still on the continent, buried in the studies to which he had been allowed to return after infuriating the king and alarming his own family with his refusal to take Henry's side. During his absence the king had grown more confident than ever that no intelligent, informed, and open-minded person could possibly fail to see the irrefutability of his claims, and he had not stopped thinking of young Pole. By 1537, apparently, he was sure that Pole's years of reading and reflection must have brought him around. He sent him books refuting the idea of papal primacy (such works were being written in great numbers by clergymen eager to win the attention of the king), learned that he had begun researching and writing a book of his own on the question, and was eager to see the result. Winning over Pole would be a victory, a vindication, of international consequence.

But the fruit of Pole's labors, a work that he titled *De Unitate Ecclesiastica,* turned out to be the opposite of what Henry expected. Assuming the role of Old Testament prophet, casting the king as a tyrant in desperate need of being saved from the consequences of his own errors, Pole expressed himself recklessly, in terms that could hardly have been better chosen to offend a man of Henry's immense pride. After comparing Henry not only to Richard III—the archfiend in the Tudor version of English history—but to the emperor Nero as well, Pole charged that he "did not merely kill, but tore to pieces all the true defenders of the old religion in a more inhuman fashion than the Turk." Henry's actions, he said, made a mockery of his papal title Defender of the Faith, and without quite saying so explicitly he suggested in unmistakable terms that Henry's actions were so repellent to his own subjects as to make a revolt likely if not inevitable. Compared with this invective, Pole's scholarly denial that any secular ruler could claim to be supreme head of the church even within his own realm was familiar almost to the point of being merely tiresome. If at any point there had existed a real possibility that Henry might opt to settle his differences with Rome, Pole's little work (which he had not had printed, claiming that it was intended for the king's eyes only) ended that possibility absolutely. Pole's mother and brothers, when they learned of what he had done this time, denounced his actions as "folly." Though Henry took no action against them, he lashed out in other directions.

No longer satisfied merely to make the life of his daughter Mary a hell of humiliation and deprivation, he sent representatives to her place of confinement with a demand that she do what her late mother had taught her to regard as unthinkable: take the oath of supremacy and, the crowning blow, acknowledge that she herself was illegitimate. Mary refused, was threatened, and refused again. The screws were tightened further. The woman who was her closest friend, almost the last companion she was still permitted, was taken away to the Tower. Two men suspected of being sympathetic to her were purged from the Privy Council, and Cromwell himself began to fear that he was going to suffer for efforts he had made earlier to reconcile father and daughter. He wrote to Mary, calling her "an obstinate and obdurate woman, deserving the reward of malice in the extremity of mischief." He provided her with a draft letter that he suggested she transcribe in her own hand and send to her father; it recognized Henry as supreme head, repudiated the pope, and described her parents' marriage as "incestuous and unlawful." Rumors reached Mary of the king's intention—what better way to increase the pressure on a daughter with little fear for herself?—to move not only against her but against everyone regarded as friendly to her. Finally even the one man of any importance who had remained unflinchingly loyal to her and her mother, her cousin Charles's ambassador Eustace Chapuys, urged her to submit. And so she copied out Cromwell's draft word for word, signed it, and sent it to her father. In doing so she abjectly denied her own deepest beliefs, but she was not utterly crushed: later, when ordered to give up the names of those persons who had encouraged her to resist the king's demands, she said she would die before doing any such thing. Still later, sufficiently rehabilitated to be permitted to dine in her father's company, she heard him jokingly rebuke members of his council because "some of you were desirous that I should put this jewel to death." This revelation of just how close she had been to losing her life caused her to faint.

When Lord Thomas Howard, half-brother of the Duke of Norfolk, neglected to obtain royal permission before contracting to marry Lady Margaret Douglas, the king's sister Margaret's daughter by her second husband, Henry chose to interpret this, absurdly, as an attempt on Howard's part to make himself king of England. Howard was attainted for treason, and along with his bride-that-might-have-been he was imprisoned in the Tower, where he would remain until his death. (Lady Margaret survived to become the mother-in-law of Mary, Queen of Scots, and so paternal grandmother of England's King James I. Unlike Henry—who, one suspects, would be deeply chagrined if he knew—she is therefore an ancestor of all the subsequent kings and queens of England down to the present day.)

Henry used his expanding powers not only to blight lives but to bend

England's unwritten constitution into bizarre shapes. A new Act of Succession, pushed through Parliament without difficulty, voided the statute that had declared Anne Boleyn to be the king's only wife and their descendants to be the only legitimate heirs to the throne. Now Jane Seymour was the only wife, her (as yet unborn) children by Henry the sole line of succession. In a truly extraordinary step, one without precedent in law or tradition, Parliament bestowed upon the king the power, if he left no legitimate children, to name as his heir and successor "such person or persons in possession and remainder as shall please your Highness." At the same time the definition of treason was again broadened to make it easier to ensnare anyone bold or mad enough to follow the examples of Fisher and More. Now it became a capital crime not only to reject the new Succession Act but to remain silent when asked for an opinion. The act also provided—whoever thought this up must have smiled at his own ingenuity—that anyone who attempted to repeal it would be guilty of high treason by virtue of having done so.

The 1530s being a period of such astonishing religious ferment, with Protestantism taking firm root on the continent and splintering into sects virtually all of which found adherents in England, it was inevitable that Henry would set about to impose his will in the realm of dogma and doctrine. His confidence in himself as England's one source of truth, and his determination to cast aside the old connection to Rome, were accompanied by an equally strong determination to make all his subjects not only believe but actively profess exactly what he believed. This presented no small number of challenges. Being essentially conservative in his approach to questions of dogma, Henry was repelled by such defining Protestant beliefs as justification by faith alone (a rejection of the notion that individuals could improve their chances of salvation through prayer and good works). Likewise he was infuriated by the reformers' rejection of purgatory and transubstantiation (the belief that, in the mass, the bread and wine of the Eucharist become the flesh and blood of Jesus). But many of the people who at various times were closest and most important to him—Cranmer and the Boleyns among others—gradually came to embrace the very ideas that Henry himself most abhorred. From the time of his break with the papacy until the end of his life, Henry had to walk an often fuzzy and crooked line between Roman Catholicism and an evolving evangelical Protestantism. In doing so he had to remain mindful that there were politically powerful forces on both sides of that line. On the whole he was skillful at playing the factions off against one another, balancing conservative (but not necessarily Roman) Catholic interests against the evangelicals, allowing the two sides to neutralize one another to his advantage. But in the strictly religious dimension, in his efforts to explain what he wanted his people to believe and get them to believe it, he was not only less successful but ultimately a nearly complete failure. His problems in this regard began in the summer of 1536 with the issuance of the so-called Ten Articles, officially the work of convocation but really an expression of Henry's thinking at the time, the first in what would become his increasingly confusing efforts to tell England what to believe and how to worship. The Articles were wordy and ambiguous, and at points they were nearly self-contradictory in dealing with the issues that most sharply separated Catholic doctrine from the various Protestant and evangelical subgroups. Even today scholars disagree as to whether and to what extent they show Henry to have been holding to a firmly conservative line or leaning in a radical direction.

About one thing there can be no uncertainty. Henry wanted everyone in his kingdom to agree on religion, and he expected agreement on his terms. This is unmistakable in the preface to the Ten Articles, which states that it is the king's responsibility to assure "that unity and concord in opinion, namely in such things as doth concern our religion, may increase and go forthward, and all occasion of dissent and discord touching the same be repressed and utterly extinguished." Shortly after the Articles were published, Cromwell issued a set of injunctions ordering the clergy to preach and promote them in their Sunday sermons. At the same time, however, he forbade the churchmen to say anything about such inflammatory subjects as images, miracles, and relics—popular aspects of the old religion that the evangelicals despised as superstitious. No doubt this enforced silence was partly a reflection of Cromwell's (and the king's) reluctance to stir up unnecessary trouble. But it may have been rooted also in uncertainty on Henry's part about what he himself currently believed. He was determined to have uniformity, but he was not in every case sure what uniformity should entail. In shattering the consensus on which the old religion had been based, he had let a whole flock of doctrinal genies out of the bottle. To expect all of them to reassemble in a new bottle of his choosing was to expect a great deal, all the more so as Henry remained unclear about what he wanted the shape of that bottle to be.

Where Henry knew what he wanted, however, he had little difficulty translating his wishes into civil law and church doctrine. His all-but-godlike status under the new dispensation was captured vividly on the title page of a new translation of the Bible. The woodcut drawing that the court artist Hans Holbein created for this page under Cromwell's direction has as its dominant figure not God the Father or Jesus Christ, not the prophets of the Old Testament or the apostles of the New, but Henry VIII. He is shown seated center stage on his throne, the sword of justice clutched firmly in his right hand, passing the Sacred Scriptures to a cluster of bishops kneeling not before their creator but at the feet of their king. The dedication offered to that king by the new Bible's translator—"He only under God is the Chief Head of all the congregation and church"—is so modest by comparison with the illustration that one wonders if Henry found it disappointing.

But the real world had not been abolished. It lurked in the background mainly, but occasionally it intruded into the world of Henry's making with a reminder that the king was *not* God and could not bend *everything* to his will. In July his sixteen-year-old son Henry Fitzroy, Duke of Richmond, the possible successor on whom he had doted and lavished honors and riches, died of tuberculosis. And the months were passing without any sign that Queen Jane was with child.

And then the kingdom itself, to all appearances so submissive, so worshipful of its great ruler, suddenly exploded.

THEY WERE WHAT THEY ATE

SIXTEENTH-CENTURY EUROPE WAS A WORLD IN WHICH conspicuous consumption really mattered. It wasn't just that wealth meant power—has there ever been a society in which that wasn't true?—but that wealth had to be *seen* to be believed. Emperors and kings, nobles and bishops, landowners and merchants all understood that they could never be more important than they were able to *appear* to be. Appearance was reality. Only a man rich enough to *look* rich could expect to be taken seriously in the great marketplace of patronage and influence.

Hence all the emphasis, in England as elsewhere, on wearing extravagantly expensive clothes, and living in extravagantly grand houses, and trying to win friends by giving extravagantly costly gifts.

And on eating—more important, on serving—extravagant quantities of extravagantly expensive food. In dining as in all things, it was an age of excess for everyone who could afford it.

The roots of all this went back to early feudal times, if not further. When society was utterly dominated by the warlords, a man's importance was a function of the amount of land he controlled and the number of fighting men his land could support. To be of the highest importance, one needed a large following of lesser nobles, knights, and soldiers, a great hall in which these subordinates could be sheltered, and food and drink for all of them. If the Norman kings and barons fed their liegemen with deer and wild boars that they themselves had killed in their own hunting parks, that simply added to the aura of power that stayed with them everywhere they went.

None of this changed under what historians call the "bastard feudalism" of later centuries, when the old sacred oaths of loyalty to an overlord came to matter less than how much cash a man could raise and how big a following he could *buy*. Leaders were still expected to maintain and feed extensive households, and to receive and feed steady streams of guests, and to do so in a style that made a statement. Those lesser men who aspired to rise, to establish themselves as leaders, naturally tried to do the same. If the amounts of cash required could be painfully, even dangerously high (they inevitably were, food being much more expensive relative to income than it is today), that had to be accepted as part of the cost of doing business.

The most conspicuous consumers of all were the kings. Their responsibilities made an extensive administrative apparatus necessary, so their courts had to be larger than those of even the greatest nobles. They also had to surpass even their mightiest subjects in grandeur; anything less would have compromised their dignity and raised questions about the reality of royal power. Even Henry VII, that supposed miser, expended huge sums to impress England and the world with the splendor in which he lived. Following the French example to which he had been exposed during his years in exile, he established a personal bodyguard of uniformed "gentlemen pensioners" and put his pages, grooms, and other staff in green and white livery. His court became the setting of elaborate rituals, processions, and ceremonies, with much bowing, scraping, and genuflecting whenever royalty appeared. Hospitality remained, as it had been for the Plantagenets, a central element in Tudor ostentation: as many as seven hundred people would dine simultaneously in Henry VII's great hall (the royal family sitting apart on a raised gallery), and on the most special occasions as many as sixty different dishes might be served.

In the next generation the young Henry VIII's hunger for grandeur and indifference to cost raised court and kitchen to levels previously unimagined. Most of the royal household was managed by a lord steward whose annual budget was, at least in peacetime, the largest in the kingdom. His 225 subordinates (virtually all of them men, incidentally; the Tudor "serving wench" is a mythical figure) staffed not only enormous kitchens but such satellite operations as the bakehouse, pantry, saucery, spicery, wafery, confectionery, scullery, boiling house, and scalding house. The sheer numbers of people being fed made all this necessary; the record survives of a single day when, though the royal household was smaller than usual because temporarily in Calais rather than in England, it consumed six oxen, eight calves, forty sheep, a dozen pigs, 132 chickens, seven swans, twenty storks, thirty-four pheasants, one hundred ninety-two partridges and an equal number of cocks, and many other things. Waste and pilferage were inevitable in an operation of such enormous dimensions and occurred on a scale commensurate with the quantities being prepared. Effective financial management was somewhere between difficult and impossible, and as Henry added more and more embellishments—eventually he employed sixty court musicians, compared with five in the reign of his grandfather Edward IV—the household sometimes teetered on the brink of being completely out of control.

At court as elsewhere, what one ate was largely a function of one's position in the social pyramid. As the list of things cooked one day in Calais indicates, courtiers like other people of wealth and prominence subsisted to an extraordinary extent on meat and poultry, which may have made up as much as eighty percent of the elite diet. The harvest (and eating) season for fruit and vegetables was short in England, it was difficult to import most such produce, and in any case ancient medical authorities including Galen had pronounced it unhealthful. People of means could afford to keep and butcher livestock throughout the winter and thus had year-round access to fresh meat. Where preservation was necessary it was accomplished through drying, smoking, or immersion in granular salt or brine. Salt was expensive, however, and so was used only with varieties of fish and meat that had demonstrated a capacity for surviving the preservation process in a reasonably appetizing state and were therefore regarded as "worth their salt." Cod from the abundant fisheries of recently discovered Newfoundland was an increasingly important example.

The Crusades had long since exposed western Europe to the spices and condiments of the East, and by the sixteenth century the trade in commodities ranging from pepper, cinnamon, cloves, nutmeg, ginger, saffron, and caraway to cardamom, coriander, mustard, and garlic was a major element in international commerce. By Tudor times, as a result, recipes like the following for stew had become possible:

> Take a necke of mutton and a brest to make the broth stronge and then scum it cleane and when it hath boyled a while, take part of the broth and put it into another pot and put thereto a pound of raisins and let them boyle till they be tender, then strayne a little bread with the Raisins and the broth

all together, then chop time, sawge and Persley with other small hearbes
and put into the mutton then put in the strayned raysins with whole prunes,
cloves and mace, pepper, saffron and a little salt and if ye may stew a
chicken withall or els sparrowes or such other small byrdes.

Other culinary delights, including some that would soon transform
European cuisine, were beginning to arrive from the New World. Among
them were corn and sweet peppers, potatoes and tomatoes, turkey and
peanuts and vanilla, and still other things so familiar today that their absence is almost unimaginable. In the lifetime of Henry VIII, however,
most such commodities remained unknown. Chocolate and coffee,
when they first arrived, were used for medicinal purposes only. Potatoes
were not seen in England until almost a century after Henry's death.

The high price of spices and other exotic foodstuffs was one reason
for the so-called sumptuary laws that were first introduced in England in
the fourteenth century and, with frequent revisions, would remain in
effect for hundreds of years thereafter. These laws, difficult to enforce,
were a somewhat oblique attempt to limit costly imports and thereby reduce the outflow of capital. Another of their purposes was to preserve
class distinctions by prohibiting the unworthy from presuming to imitate
the lifestyles of their betters (for a time only high nobles were allowed to
wear fox fur, for example), and they could become remarkably detailed
in what they prescribed. In 1517, probably at the direction of a Thomas
Wolsey eager to emphasize his superiority over everyone in England except the royal family, it was decreed that whereas cardinals could be
served nine dishes in the course of a single meal, dukes, archbishops,
marquesses, earls, and bishops were to have no more than seven each,
and nobles below the rank of earl a mere six. Gentlemen with annual incomes of between £40 and £100—was there ever a time when such
careful attention was paid to exactly how much money a man had?—
were to receive only three. Pains were taken, at banquets, to seat people
in precisely the right order of precedence, and the most eminent guests
received not only the most but the costliest dishes. Table manners were
better than is often supposed today, and for the most practical of reasons.
Guests wore the most expensive clothing that the law and their purses or
credit permitted, with laces and ruffles not only around their necks but
on their cuffs as well, and they had no wish to carelessly spoil costumes

that sometimes cost more than a laborer could earn in years. Forks were still exotic, rarely seen, and when dining out people knew that they were expected to bring their own knives and spoons. Even high nobles expected to share the dishes they were served with at least one person of equal rank.

Such was the life of the elite and near-elite only, and it would be a mistake to suppose that it had any connection with the lives of the common people. With food as with so many things, the mass of the population lived in virtually a parallel universe, one in which spices and sugar were so expensive as to be unattainable and even meat and salt were rarities. A working family's typical meal might consist of dark bread made of rye or barley rather than more expensive wheat flour (often a slab of this bread would be used as a "trencher" or edible dinner plate), cheese or the whey that is a by-product of cheese-making, a "pottage" or soup of oats or barley, perhaps a portion of curds or whatever fruits or vegetables happened to be in season. Though vitamin deficiencies were commonplace, especially in winter and early spring, and though crop failures could lead to malnutrition, outright starvation was almost unheard of except in the far north during the worst years. Perhaps the ultimate irony—the term "poetic justice" comes to mind—is that except in times of exceptional shortage, the diet of the plain folk was much more healthful than that of their meat- and sugar-devouring masters. Possibly that explains why so many of the Tudors were so worn out and sick at such early ages. Elizabeth, the longest-lived of them, was notably abstemious in her diet.

15

Rebellion and Betrayal

The story of how Henry VIII extracted himself from the most dangerous crisis of his life by lying to his subjects and betraying honest men who had put their fate in his hands is essentially the story of Robert Aske.

A lawyer and fellow of Lincoln's Inn in London, Aske was one of several sons in a modestly distinguished family in the north of England. His father, a landowning knight, was related by marriage to the mighty Percy clan. His maternal grandfather had been a baron, and Robert himself, early in his career, had served as secretary to the Percy who was then Earl of Northumberland. He was thirty-seven years old early in October 1536, when he set out from his Yorkshire home for London and the opening of the autumn term of the royal court at Westminster. It was a routine business trip of a kind that Aske had been making at this same time of year almost since boyhood, first as a student and then as a practicing attorney, and he had no reason to expect anything out of the ordinary. If he had started several days earlier, he would in all likelihood never have left the smallest mark on history.

Upon crossing the Humber River into Lincolnshire on or about October 4, Aske found himself in the midst of something extraordinary. Just two or three days before, a spontaneous protest had erupted in the town of Louth and begun spreading across the county. The trouble was triggered by reports that a group of royal commissioners was approaching

and was not only shutting down monasteries but confiscating the treasures (chalices, processional crosses, and the like) of parish churches.
The situation was developing with startling speed: by the time Aske arrived on the scene, some of the commissioners had been taken prisoner
by the protesters and set free after being given a list of demands that
they were to deliver to the king. The people wanted an end to the suppression of monasteries, punishment of Thomas Cromwell's notorious
henchmen Legh and Layton, an end to the subsidy recently levied by
Parliament, and the removal from office of Cromwell, Thomas Audley,
Richard Rich, and a number of bishops including Cranmer. The demands made no mention of the king's claim to supremacy—to object to
that was to commit treason—but obviously they arose out of opposition
to the entire royal program of ecclesiastical reform. That the impulse
behind the uprising was essentially religious and deeply conservative
was underscored when the people of Horncastle near Louth raised a
banner that was soon adopted wherever the rebellion spread. It showed
the eucharistic host, a chalice, and a figure of Christ bearing the five
wounds of the crucifixion.

Aske, who would have been recognizably a member of the gentry,
was taken into custody by the protesters. This was in no way unusual: in
its origins the rising was an eruption of the pent-up fears and frustra-
tions of the common people—to the extent that the initial outburst at
Louth had a leader, that leader was a shoemaker named Nicholas
Melton—and from the start the participants displayed a desperate hope
of recruiting men educated enough to articulate their case and respectable enough to get a hearing from the authorities. Wherever such
men fell into the hands of the demonstrators, they were threatened with
hanging if they refused to swear "to be true to almighty god to christ's
catholic church to our sovereign lord the king and unto the commons of
this realm so help you god and holy dam and by this book." It was a
rough way of finding leaders but surprisingly effective. And the rebel
oath, innocuous enough when considered without context, would have
been heavy with significance for the people of Lincolnshire—and no
doubt for the king and his people, too, when they learned of it. It acknowledged not just the church but the *Catholic* Church, the king but
none of his lieutenants. When coupled with the demands that the
demonstrators had already sent south and would be repeating many

times in the months ahead, the words of the oath lost all ambiguity. They were a call for a full restoration of the old ways and the removal and punishment of those—the king alone excluded—who had undertaken the work of destruction. There is nothing surprising about the exemption of the king from criticism; anything else would have been astounding. In a society where the person of the king was quasi-sacred, at a time when the idea that the king derived his authority from God was winning wide acceptance, the humanly natural inclination to blame unpopular measures not on the sovereign himself but on his counselors and deputies was becoming more pronounced than ever.

The fact that a number of the individuals who were coerced into taking the oath quickly and voluntarily became prominent in the rising is one indication of the extent to which people at all levels of society, gentry and nobility included, were in sympathy with its aims. Aske made himself one of the most prominent of all, galloping about Lincolnshire to help spread word of the movement. Within days the rebels had tens of thousands of men in the field and took possession of the city of Lincoln. Divisions, however, soon appeared. The common folk were eager to push on toward the south, where they would have greatly outnumbered the few thousand troops that nobles loyal to the king were finding it possible to muster. But the gentry among them, perhaps mindful of how much they stood to lose in an unsuccessful contest with the Crown, insisted on waiting for Henry's response to their demands. That response, when it came, was chilling. The king denounced Lincolnshire as a "brute and beastly" place (he had never seen it, never in his life having visited the north), ridiculed the rebels for presuming to offer advice on how to rule, and ordered them to hand over their leaders and return to their homes. Failure to comply would result in "the utter destruction of them, their wives and children." Behind all this was the threat—to the rebels it would have appeared to be the imminent threat—of an attack by the forces of the king. The dukes of Norfolk and Suffolk and the Earl of Shrewsbury were all known to be assembling troops, and though they were experiencing severe difficulties—not least the unwillingness of many of their own liegemen to suppress a rebellion the aims of which they heartily supported—the rebels were probably unaware of any of this. Suffolk, who was closest to Lincoln, found himself unable to muster more than a thousand men. He would have been overwhelmed if the rebels, at least sixteen thousand of whom carried weapons of war, had advanced without delay. But the rebels had delayed and thereby lost their momentum, their leaders were quarreling confusedly among themselves, and for all they knew they stood on the brink of annihilation. Frightened and discouraged, they disbanded and began to head for home. Their rising had collapsed without encountering serious opposition.

Aske, meanwhile, had crossed back into Yorkshire, where the population was now aware of what was happening on the other side of the Humber and itself beginning to boil over. He threw himself into introducing some measure of order and organization where otherwise there would have been chaos, persuading the towns through which he passed to take no action until they received a signal from him—the agreed signal being the ringing of the church bells. When on October 10 the signal went out and the Yorkshire rising began, Aske issued a proclamation stating that its purpose was "the preservation of Christ's church . . . and to the intent to make petition to the King's highness for the reformation of that which is amiss in this his realm." He declared himself "chief captain" in his part of the county, and by October 16, the day on which ten thousand armed rebels entered the city of York, they were using the name that he had given their movement: the Pilgrimage of Grace.

As word of what was happening spread, people all across the north began to join in. The movement quickly became bigger than it had been before the collapse in Lincolnshire, with perhaps as many as thirty thousand rebels advancing southward toward the royal stronghold of Pontefract Castle. On October 20 the castle's garrison surrendered without a fight. The pilgrims had with them Edward Lee, the archbishop of York, though whether he had joined or was a prisoner is not clear. Most were mounted and armed, and as they moved on to Doncaster they encountered the Duke of Norfolk at the head of a force that they outnumbered by nearly four to one. Aske, by now established as the movement's spokesman and public face, found himself in an immensely strong position. There was every reason to think that if his men attacked they could roll over Norfolk's eight thousand troops and be on the outskirts of London within several days. Meanwhile King Henry, whose situation was far more dangerous than he understood, was cursing the pilgrims as "false traitors and rebels" and demanding that his nobles attack and destroy them without delay. From start to finish he regarded the Pilgrimage as an unforgivable insult to his dignity as monarch. He despised the participants and was interested in nothing but revenge.

But Norfolk, the man on the scene, had to deal with reality. The pilgrims sent him a new but not-much-changed version of the same demands originally presented in Lincolnshire: no more closing of monasteries, the removal of Cromwell and Cranmer and Rich, et cetera. Norfolk met with their representative on Doncaster Bridge and offered a deal: he himself would take the pilgrims' demands—which they were now calling "articles"—to the king along with two of their representatives, who would be allowed to explain themselves to Henry in person. Meanwhile the armies on both sides were to disband. Norfolk, aware of how weak his position was and that many of his own soldiers were not to be relied upon in this extraordinary situation, was stalling for time and hoping that somehow the rebels could be talked into withdrawing without a fight, perhaps even into disbanding as had happened in Lincolnshire. He had the king's grudging permission to agree to whatever the rebels asked, but only for the sake of delay. There was never any thought, certainly not on the king's part, of actually *keeping* whatever promises might have to be made. The pilgrims were appropriately skeptical. They agreed only to meet again with Norfolk early in December, after he had returned from conferring with the king, warning that they would not do even that unless their safety were guaranteed.

On December 2 Aske and other Pilgrimage leaders assembled at Pontefract to prepare for another round of negotiations. In the intervening weeks the rank and file had grown restless—just keeping so many thousands of men fed would have been impossible except for the willingness of farmers across the north to contribute livestock and other foodstuffs to the cause—and Aske had had his hands full holding them together. At Pontefract he was again the most conspicuous member of the leadership (some historians suggest that he was to some extent a front man for more important personages who preferred for their own safety to maintain a low profile), drawing up a new and more comprehensive set of articles for presentation to Norfolk and, through him, to the king. As before there was much emphasis on reversing the religious reforms of the past several years, strengthened now with an explicit call for an end to the separation from Rome, and a number of striking new items were added. The pilgrims wanted the legitimacy of Henry's daughter Mary restored, the statute that allowed the king to choose his successor repealed, and a new Parliament summoned to meet not at Westminster as usual but in the north—specifically at York or Nottingham. Their articles went into considerable detail where the proposed Parliament was concerned: they called for less royal involvement in the selection of the members of Commons, less control over the business of Commons by officers of the Crown, and more freedom of speech for members. Finally they demanded a full pardon for everyone involved in the rising.

It was a startling document. If implemented, it would have reversed virtually everything that Henry had accomplished since first deciding to divorce Catherine. By weakening his grip on Parliament, it would have moved England closer to democracy than it had ever been, or would be for centuries. It illuminates as nothing else does the depth of northern unhappiness with the innovations of the 1530s and popular awareness of just how completely the king and his men—Cromwell in particular— had not only the machinery of government but the law itself under their control. For Henry, of course, the articles were an abomination, an insult, a gross and unforgivable violation of his rights. To a man like Norfolk, too, a proud exemplar of the old warrior nobility, they were an affront, a despicable attempt by presumptuous commoners to overturn the natural order.

But even now, more than two months after the first explosion at Louth, Henry and Norfolk and the nobles allied with them had been unable to assemble nearly as many men as the pilgrims still had under arms at Doncaster. The king's position was not unlike that of Richard III in 1485, when he attempted to rally his kingdom for what should have been the easy task of crushing the invasion of the first Henry Tudor. Richard had issued his call, but not enough men had responded because not enough wanted to save him. Now it seemed possible that, if the pilgrims marched, much of the kingdom would not only do nothing to impede them but might join them in bringing the second Henry Tudor to heel. Thus the king, despite being toweringly indignant, had no choice but to accept Norfolk's insistence that there was no possibility of defeating the "traitors" by direct attack. It remained necessary to stall. And so on December 6, when a delegation of thirty Pilgrimage leaders (ten knights, ten esquires, and ten commoners) met with Norfolk as agreed, the duke accepted every demand. A new Parliament would be summoned, and once in session it would take up the pilgrims' articles. Meanwhile no more religious houses would be closed, and those that the Pilgrimage had restored would be allowed to continue. The pilgrims themselves would be pardoned in return for returning peaceably to their homes.

At first blush this was a tremendous victory, but among the pilgrims there was skepticism. Doubters pointed out that the promised pardon did not apply to those involved in the Lincolnshire rising, that Norfolk had said nothing about when or even where the promised Parliament would meet, and that nothing had been put in writing except the *promise* of a pardon rather than the pardon itself. Under such circumstances, some argued, it would be madness for them to lay down their arms. Aske saw things differently. For him it was inconceivable that the king would not be as good as his word, would not honor promises made to loyal subjects who wanted only to free him from evil subordinates. When the promise of pardon was read aloud, Aske, to show his comrades that this was good enough for him, tore from his tunic the badge of their movement (like the banner, it depicted Christ and his wounds) and declared that he was captain no more and henceforth would wear no insignia except his king's. It was effective theater: the other pilgrims removed their badges, the banners were furled, and within a few days a huge rebel army had melted away to nothing.

Then came the strangest episode of the entire affair. Aske received a letter from the king, inviting him to spend Christmas at court because "we have conceived a great desire to speak with you and to hear of your mouth the whole circumstance and beginning of that matter [the rising]." The letter repeated Norfolk's assurances of "our general and free pardon, already granted unto you." Aske accepted—such an invitation was an almost unimaginable honor—and found himself treated with stupefying friendliness all through his visit. At Henry's request he wrote an account of the Pilgrimage, receiving from the king's hands the gift of an expensive coat. When he returned to the north, he did so in the conviction that Henry was his ally, supporter, and friend. In the next few months he would repeatedly show himself to be the supporter and friend of a king who had concealed his hatred under a blanket of hospitality and was now waiting until it became safe to exact his revenge.

None of the other pilgrim leaders had been exposed to the king's charm, and few were able to share Aske's enthusiasm. What they saw, rather, was that a new year had begun and nothing was being done to put into effect any of the promises made at Doncaster. Cromwell and Cranmer and the other officials of whom the pilgrims had complained all remained at their posts, the Crown continued to collect its ten percent of every kind of church revenue (though this, too, was among the things the pilgrims wanted stopped), and government troops were being moved north to fortify strongholds. Aske wrote to warn his new friend the king that feelings were again running high, asking Henry "to pardon me in this my crude letter and plainness of the same, for I do utter my poor heart to your grace to the intent your highness may perceive the danger that may ensue; for on my faith I do greatly fear the end to be only by battle." When he learned that former pilgrims were planning to attack Hull and Beverley, which were under royal control, Aske vainly begged them not to proceed and urged others not to join them. When the attacks failed and their leaders had been captured, Henry sent him a letter of thanks. Scattered and uncoordinated outbreaks of violence continued, each one sapping whatever strength and cohesion the remaining fragments of the Pilgrimage still had, and when eight thousand Westmorland men tried to take the city of Carlisle and failed miserably, it became clear that the movement was exhausted. Norfolk was able to move his troops into pilgrim territory, impose martial law, and begin a program of summary executions that quickly took scores and then hundreds of lives. Those monks who had returned to their suppressed monasteries at the invitation of the pilgrims were singled out for especially harsh treatment.

So, inevitably, was Robert Aske. With the north subdued, Henry was free to remove the mask of conciliation. Aske and other Pilgrimage leaders, members of the nobility among them, were arrested and put on trial in York. Norfolk, in a nice touch of sadism that brings to mind his own prominent role in the trial and sentencing of his niece Anne Boleyn, arranged to have Aske's brother put on the jury. The defendants were found guilty on two counts of treason, first for conspiring to deny the king his "dignity, title, name, and royal state . . . of being on earth the supreme head of the English church," second for trying to force the king "to summon and hold a parliament and convocation." Aske pointed to the fact that he had been pardoned both by the king and by Cromwell and had done nothing to oppose either of them since his pardon, but that counted for nothing. The convicted men were transferred to London, where they were condemned to death. Most of them, along with two abbots and three priors caught up in Norfolk's dragnet, were hanged, drawn, and quartered at Tyburn. Aske alone was hauled back to York and hanged there, not by rope but in a tangle of chains around his body so as to make his death a slow agony of exposure and dehydration. His body was kept on public display until nothing remained but bones. The population was paralyzed with fear, the king more firmly in control than ever.

Henry's triumph was capped with glorious news: Queen Jane was pregnant. The joyful couple departed on a celebratory summer progress, keeping well clear of the north in spite of a pledge Henry had made to show himself to his subjects there. It was left to Norfolk to complete the subjugation of the northern counties, and to Cromwell to resume the destruction not only of the smaller monasteries but, more broadly, of anyone refusing to align himself with the new English church. In May, the month of Aske's death, the Crown's choice as new prior of the London Charterhouse formally recognized Henry as supreme head and signed the house over to him. Twenty of the house's monks and lay brothers, broken by the two years of harassment that had followed the execution of John Houghton, gave up their resistance. The ten who refused were chained up in Newgate Prison and left to starve in their own filth. By mid-June half of them were dead, and by September only one remained alive. The sole survivor was then moved to another place of confinement, where he clung to life so tenaciously that at last he had to be butchered. With that single exception, however, Henry and Cromwell were able to eliminate the last of the Carthusians by allowing them to perish slowly, horribly, and in deepest obscurity, avoiding the kind of anger that would have resulted from the public execution of such transparently innocent men.

One of the most striking aspects of King Henry's reign, his determination to make all of his subjects change their beliefs exactly as he changed his, became more painfully awkward with the passage of time. Complete uniformity would have been unachievable under any circumstances during the decades of Henry's rule; even if he had remained

Roman Catholic and wanted his subjects to do the same, the ideas of Luther and the other continental reformers would have attracted English adherents and made doctrinal strife unavoidable. But Henry had compounded the discord in breaking with Rome, accelerating the process by which his subjects came to be divided into a multitude of contending sects, and his subsequent insistence on conformity made the situation impossible. By the time of his third marriage three religious factions were numerous or influential or both. One—the only one acceptable to the king—was made up of those many people who welcomed or at least had no objection to the break with Rome but wanted to retain their traditional beliefs and practices (the sacraments, for example, and the idea of purgatory). Another, probably larger, stood by the entire conservative package including the leadership of the pope. Finally, definitely smallest in numbers but afire with the zeal of the continental Reformation, was the circle for whom the whole of the old religion was superstitious nonsense that had to be swept aside in order for a simpler, purer Christianity based on the inerrancy of the Bible to become possible. To arrive at a single set of doctrines acceptable to all three of these groups would have been impossible, and the king's inextinguishable hopes of imposing uniformity, after he himself had done so much to create division, were both ironic and doomed. His efforts in that direction would have been pathetic if they had not also been so tragically destructive. They were yet another reflection of Henry's infantile belief in himself as a flawlessly wise ruler.

Late in 1536, annoyed that the dissemination of his Ten Articles had failed almost completely to settle the many roiling questions about what England was now supposed to believe, Henry turned the problem over to the bishops, instructing them to produce a more comprehensive, less ambiguous set of answers. But the bishops themselves were divided. At one extreme were men like Stephen Gardiner of Winchester, John Stokesley of London, and Cuthbert Tunstal of Durham, conservatives who almost certainly regretted the break with Rome and hoped to retain as much of the old ways as possible. At the other end of the spectrum there stood, for example, Hugh Latimer of Worcester, who went so far in his rejection of tradition that even other militant reformers accused him of heresy. The debates in which the bishops tried to decide how to carry out the king's instructions were long and contentious and never came close to achieving agreement. The result of the bishops' labors, a document whose official title was *The Institution of a Christian Man,* was less a thought-through compromise or a coherent response to the many questions stirred up by the establishment of an autonomous national church than a semidesperate packing together of incompatible, sometimes conflicting positions.

But the king had demanded action, and the bishops had done as well as anyone should have expected considering the depth of their differences. Most of them wanted to satisfy the king, certainly; they were all too aware of what could befall any cleric who failed to do so. But on both sides of the doctrinal gulf were men prepared to fight if perhaps not to die in defense of their beliefs. In the absence of specific royal guidance, with nothing to fall back upon but their own divergent convictions and their impressions of what Henry was likely to find acceptable, ultimately they had little choice—unless they could find the courage to do nothing—but to give everyone some voice in what they finally produced. When they finished in mid-July, no one could be entirely comfortable with what had been accomplished. Though the *Institution* was in many respects conservative—upholding, for example, the validity of all seven sacraments, whereas the earlier Ten Articles had specifically recognized only three—the most conservative bishops were neither satisfied that it was conservative enough nor confident of how the king would react to it. The evangelicals hated much of it; Latimer wrote to the king to protest that the *Institution* should not be printed until cleansed of Catholic "old leaven." It was offered to the king and Cromwell as a working draft, and accompanied by a timorous request that they review it and decide whether the bishops could tell the world that it had royal approval. They got no answer. When it appeared in print in September, it contained a most peculiar preface in which the bishops abjectly "confess that we have none authority either to assemble ourselves together for any pretence or purpose or to publish any thing that might be by us agreed on and compiled." This preface asked the king to approve or amend what the bishops had done as he saw fit. Printed with it was a curious message from the king himself, declaring that he had not found time to read the book but had merely "taken as it were a taste of it." From that day to this *The Institution of a Christian Man* has been better known as the Bishops' Book, an unofficial title that makes clear that it should not be taken as a guide to the beliefs of the supreme head of the Church of England because, according to the head himself, he had little idea of what it contained. How anyone could have regarded such a work as worth printing, how anyone could have expected it to be of the slightest value even to subjects eager to be scrupulously faithful to the royal theology, surpasses understanding. Perhaps Cromwell or Henry assumed it must be close enough to the king's truth to be of some use for the time being.

When he did read it at last, some three months after publication, the king was not at all happy with what he found. Much of it was obviously calculated to please and surely must have done so. The bishops had explicitly denied the supremacy of the pope and asserted that of the king, declared the king to be accountable to God only, and warned that nothing could justify rebellion against him (a reflection of the fact that they completed their work shortly after the failure of the Pilgrimage of Grace). The only legitimate way of seeking relief from political oppression, their book said, was to ask God to change the monarch's heart. Henry entered more than 250 comments in the margins of his copy. Many of these were challenges and objections that led him into a debate with Archbishop Cranmer, who had used his influence as primate to inject his own increasingly evangelical views into the text. In the end, of course, Henry's opinion was the only one that mattered. No doubt to Cranmer's intense disappointment, a new edition was prepared with all passages that referred favorably to justification by faith expunged. The new version also affirmed belief in the real presence of Christ in the Eucharist. Such changes were inevitable considering the king's conservative approach to almost all questions of doctrine, but in 1537 he was also affected by what the Pilgrimage of Grace had revealed about popular attachment to the old religion. He had been given reason to proceed carefully in separating the mass of his subjects from the faith in which they had been raised.

Some of Henry's changes rose out of that contempt for almost everyone except himself that had become an integral part of his character. The Bishops' Book as first published had asserted that God sees all men as equal; the king inserted a clarification to the effect that equality must be seen as "touching the soul only," whatever exactly he might have meant by that. A passage about the duty of Christians to attend to the needs of the poor was amended to exclude from charity those "many folk which had liever live by the graft of begging slothfully"—easy words for a man who since adolescence had been able to regard the wealth of all England and Wales as his to do with as he wished and had rarely in his adult life been obliged to do anything he didn't want to do. Because Henry kept a court astrologer, he deleted astrology from the bishops' list of superstitions to be shunned. He also deleted a passage stating that rulers have a duty to "provide and care" for their subjects, and changed a warning that rulers in forcing their subjects to obey must act "by and according to the just order of their laws" so that it applied only to those acting in the ruler's name, not to the ruler himself. Some of Henry's changes were difficult even for Cranmer to swallow. What the archbishop found particularly irksome was the king's rewriting of the First Commandment (where, in an absurd anachronism, he inserted the name "Jesu Christ") and the closing words of the Lord's Prayer. That Henry felt no hesitation in changing such ancient and supposedly divine texts is perhaps the most striking evidence we have of the heights to which his arrogance could rise, his exalted view of his own place in the hierarchy of the living and the dead.

Between the first appearance of the Bishops' Book and the point where Henry found time to undertake its improvement, there occurred an event that he himself would have considered among the greatest of his life and reign. At two in the morning on October 12, after a labor of more than two days, Queen Jane gave birth to a healthy son. Henry was not present for the birth, having fled days before to his residence at Esher to escape an outbreak of plague. Upon receiving the news he rushed back to Hampton Court, ordering celebrations that soon had bells ringing from every church tower in England and the guards at the Tower firing two thousand rounds of artillery. Henry was said to have wept when he held his son for the first time. Almost exactly ten years had passed since he first undertook to rid himself of Catherine of Aragon, and at last, at forty-six, he had his heir. Amid great precautions aimed at keeping the plague out of the palace, the boy was baptized on October 15. He was given the name Edward, less in honor of his grandfather Edward IV than because he had been born on the eve of St. Edward's Day. His godfathers were Thomas Cranmer and the dukes of Norfolk and Suffolk. His godmother was his half-sister, the recently humbled and rehabilitated Mary. The baptismal oil was carried by the four-year-old Elizabeth. She in turn was carried in procession by Queen Jane's brother Edward Seymour, who, being now the uncle of a future king, was shortly made the Earl of Hertford.

The celebrations continued, but two days after her son's christening Jane was taken ill and soon was in gravely serious condition. Henry departed on a long-planned hunting trip—it was, after all, the start of the season—but returned to court on the evening of October 24 after receiving word that his wife had hemorrhaged and was not expected to live. She died that midnight of causes that can never be known with certainty. It has often been stated that a cesarean section had been performed to save her child after two days and three nights of fruitless labor, but this cannot be the case; a cesarean meant certain death in the sixteenth century, and though it is hardly inconceivable that the court physicians would have sacrificed Jane to save their master's heir, in the days following Prince Edward's birth Jane was expected to recover and appeared to be doing so. A more plausible explanation is that she died because part of the placenta had been left inside her womb after she gave birth. By a sad irony, midwives of the kind who assisted at almost all deliveries in Tudor times, and who were well schooled in such practicalities as removal of the placenta, had been excluded from the royal birthing chamber. Only physicians of the loftiest reputation had been permitted to attend the queen. The state of academic medicine being what it was in the sixteenth century, such worthies probably knew less about the realities of childbirth than any experienced midwife. Henry left Hampton Court and went to Windsor Castle. Three weeks later, when the queen's embalmed body arrived at Windsor for interment, he moved again, this time to Whitehall. It would be ungenerous to doubt that his grief over the death of his wife was as great as his joy over the birth of a son, but his recovery appears to have been swift. In rather short order he was reported to be in good spirits—"in good health and merry as a widower may be"—and to be scheming with Cromwell about where to find his next wife.

One would have thought that Henry might be a satisfied man by this point. He was definitely the most feared, and arguably the most powerful, king in the history of England. Not only the government but the church were his to command. His word was law, almost literally, and his word was religious doctrine as well; no noble or bishop would have dared to contradict him. And now at last, on the threshold of what in his time was old age, with a lifetime of self-indulgence taking its toll on his mighty physique, there was a male heir to the throne. Suddenly it was at least possible that the Tudor dynasty, which just recently had passed its fiftieth anniversary, might have a future. A lesser man than Henry might have decided that, having done as much as any of his predecessors and far more than most, he had done enough. A better man might have decided that he had shed enough of his subjects' blood.

But Henry was Henry, nothing better and nothing less, and he was far from satisfied. The Pilgrimage of Grace, in bringing to a halt the closing of monasteries in many parts of the north and making it possible for some of the expelled monks and nuns to return to their houses, had given rise to rumors that members of the various religious orders had encouraged and even helped to lead the rebellion. (The possible truth of such stories remains beyond reach. Nothing in the way of conclusive evidence exists one way or the other.) That had given the king and Cromwell an excuse to resume and broaden their attack on monastic establishments generally. The closing of the smaller houses was soon completed, and the attention of the agents of the Crown was turned to the larger, richer houses. Parliament having passed no law that permitted confiscation of establishments whose income exceeded £200 per annum, the royal commissioners reverted to using fear and greed to extract "voluntary" surrenders. This proved to be difficult in places, but usually not impossible. Over all the houses there hung the memory of those the Crown had already killed. Such memories were freshened by the execution, between March and May 1537, of the uncooperative abbots of Kirkstead, Barlings, Fountains, and Jervaulx, the prior of Bridlington, and an unknown number of the members of their communities. It is hardly surprising that, learning of these killings and finding themselves exposed to the questions, accusations, insinuations, threats, and promises of Cromwell's commissioners, most of the houses gave up the struggle. No decision could have been more rational: those who signed most speedily received promises of pensions—very handsome pensions in the case of the senior officers of the largest houses, along with new positions and sometimes even grants of land—while the only possible result of refusal was a death that could do nothing to stop the suppression process. The surrendered lands and buildings became the property of the Crown. So did everything inside the buildings—the accumulated treasure of the centuries. All the money flowed into the Court of Augmentations, from which Richard Rich parceled it out under Cromwell's direction.

In March 1538 the leg ulcers that by now were making Henry's life an intermittent agony began to block the flow of his blood. There may have been a clot in his lungs as well; he became unable to speak, barely able to breathe. For a week and a half he lay near death. But then, with a speed that surprised his physicians, it all passed, and he was up and active again. He had eight years and eight months more to live. They would be memorable years—as eventful as those that had come before. They would be extravagantly wasteful, they would be bathed in blood, and they would bring military and financial disaster.

THE SPORT OF KINGS

THE FATHER AT LAST OF A HEALTHY AND LEGITIMATE BABY boy, father also of a new national church that (if somewhat confused doctrinally) was free of any connection to Rome, Henry VIII found himself free to turn to fields still unconquered. It was almost inevitable that he would look exactly where he had looked when seeking to demonstrate his greatness at the start of his reign nearly three decades before: across the English Channel. The old dream of winning glory on the fields of France had never stopped burning in his breast.

But that dream had been a foolish one even in 1509, and it made no sense at all three decades later. Henry had succeeded his father at a time when it was all too easy for English kings to look down on the ruling house of France. Louis XII, product of the dynasty that had ruled France for some six hundred years, was entering his second decade as king then, and though not yet fifty he had already, much like Henry VII of England, slipped into a premature old age. After two marriages he remained sonless, and because France's Salic law prohibited daughters from inheriting the throne, he seemed destined to be the last of his branch of the Valois line. When younger he had conquered much of Italy, but his successes there gradually came to nothing as his armies were driven out of both Milan in the north and Naples in the south.

The whole dynasty seemed to be in the last stages of entropy. Louis had come to the throne only because his predecessor, the Charles VIII who as a boy-king in the 1480s had been an admiring supporter of the first Henry Tudor's invasion of England, died at twenty-eight (killed by striking his head against the stone lintel of a castle doorway) without sons, brothers, male cousins, or uncles. The family tree was so bare that the royal genealogists, in their search for an heir, had to explore branch after barren branch before finally declaring that the only grandson of a younger brother of Charles's great-grandfather should be crowned as

Louis XII. Louis as it happened was himself not only sonless but without brothers or uncles, so that his heir was a second cousin once removed, the boy Francis of Angoulême.

It must have seemed almost a joke, therefore, when in 1515 the Holy Roman emperor renounced the betrothal of his young grandson Charles of Hapsburg to Henry VIII's sister Mary, and Cardinal Wolsey retaliated by arranging the princess's marriage to King Louis. Mary was eighteen, an elegant and accomplished young woman of exceptional beauty. Her bridegroom, though a good man much loved by his subjects, was in his fifties and seriously decrepit, toothless and crippled with gout. If the courts of both kingdoms recycled tired witticisms about the dangers for old men of taking desirable young wives, in this case they were vindicated. Louis was dead within weeks of the wedding. It was said that he had been danced to death. "Danced," perhaps, was a euphemism.

At the time of his death Louis was actually the youngest of the continent's leading royal figures. Old Ferdinand of Aragon, embittered by the failure of his dynastic ambitions, still occupied the crown of Spain at sixty-three, and the fifty-six-year-old Maximilian of Hapsburg was in his third decade as Holy Roman emperor. Henry of England, after six years on the throne, continued to stand alone as the one youthful, conspicuously virile crowned head. All that changed abruptly, however, when Louis XII's successor stepped onto the world stage. In Francis I, France had a monarch even younger than Henry (he was only twenty) and in every way his equal: tall and powerfully built, brimming with intelligence and vitality, ambitious to expand French power and to make his court a magnet for the leading intellectual and artistic figures of the day. (He would entice even Leonardo da Vinci to leave Italy for France.) Francis opened his reign by making himself the kind of authentic military hero that Henry had hoped but failed to become with his earlier invasion of France, attacking Milan and achieving an astonishing victory over a supposedly invulnerable force of Swiss mercenaries. Almost overnight he supplanted Henry as the most glamorous figure in Europe, and there flared up between the two kings a rivalry that would not be extinguished until the pair of them died only weeks apart. It was a contest of massive egos, fueled by resentment, jealousy, and pride. Ruthless in the pursuit of their own aggrandizement and indifferent to what that pursuit cost

others, they would make war on each other so often, entering and breaking alliances so easily, that the military and diplomatic history of their
reigns is a confused blur, far too complicated for brief description.

Henry and Francis met for the first time in northern France at what
came to be known as the Field of the Cloth of Gold. This happened in
1520, a year after the death of Maximilian vacated the office of Holy
Roman emperor. Both regarded themselves as uniquely well suited to
wear the most venerable crown in Europe, and so both had put themselves forward as candidates in opposition to Maximilian's grandson
Charles. But Charles, who by this time had inherited Spain and its vast
dominions from his maternal grandfather Ferdinand, and Burgundy and
the Low Countries from his father Philip the Handsome, had the advantage of being German like the secular and ecclesiastical princes who
elected emperors. He increased this advantage by borrowing heavily
enough to distribute even richer bribes than Francis. (Henry, though in
earnest, was never seriously in the running financially or otherwise.) The
1520 meeting was supposed to be a kind of summit conference—Francis, anticipating war with Charles, was hoping for an English alliance—
but it turned into something both more remarkable and less productive.
Throughout most of June the two kings put on a competitive display of
wealth and splendor on a scale never seen in Europe before or since. In
Henry's entourage were most of England's nobility, most of the hierarchy
of the church, more than five thousand men and women in all, along
with nearly three thousand horses. Cardinal Wolsey's party included
twelve chaplains, fifty gentlemen, and 237 servants, Catherine of Aragon's nearly twelve hundred people in total. Huge, ornate temporary
palaces were constructed for the occasion by both sides, man-made
fountains flowed with wine, and the days and nights were filled with
jousts, tournaments, musical and theatrical entertainments, and feasting.
Henry, sadly for himself, precipitated the best-remembered event of the
whole gathering by jovially challenging Francis to a wrestling match and
promptly getting himself thrown; it was a humiliation from which he
never quite recovered. When the festivities were finished, nothing had
been accomplished except an agreement under which Henry's little
daughter Mary was pledged to one day marry Francis's equally little eldest son. Francis hoped that this would lead to the alliance that he

craved, but it did nothing of the kind. In short order Mary's parents promised her to her cousin Charles, and he rather than Francis became England's ally.

A fourth young dynamo entered the picture in the same year as the
Field of the Cloth of Gold when Suleiman the Magnificent became sultan of the Islamic Ottoman Empire, which had already conquered a substantial part of southeastern Europe and was threatening to take more.
From his capital at Constantinople he would cause much trouble over
the following decades, but almost exclusively for the unfortunate
Charles. Among the Christian monarchs it was Francis who proved the
greatest cause of instability, largely because Italy was for him what
France never ceased to be for Henry: a field of dreams, the setting for
conquests endlessly envisioned but rarely achieved. French and Hapsburg armies fought in Italy from 1521 to 1525, with England providing
Charles with substantial financial support up to the point where his
forces achieved their great victory at Pavia and Francis was hauled off to
Madrid as his prisoner. Henry saw Pavia as a gateway to the fulfillment
of his dreams, an opportunity to eliminate France as a major power.
Charles, he proposed, should help himself to great expanses of southern
and eastern France while he, Henry, became king of what remained. The
emperor, however, was a sensible fellow with little interest in conquest
and less in glory, seeking only to hold on to what he had inherited. In
any case he was virtually bankrupt by this time. He therefore declined to
cooperate, which so disgusted Henry that he soon broke with Charles altogether and allied himself instead with France and the Papal States.

Reversals of this kind went on year after year. In the aftermath of
Pavia, England, France, and the pope remained at war with Charles until
the emperor's aunt and Francis's mother negotiated a separate peace that
left England suddenly and frighteningly isolated. In 1530 the widowed
Francis went so far as to marry Charles's sister Eleanor, though not even
that could slake his thirst for conquests in Italy. By 1536 he and Charles
were again at war over Milan, but two years after that they agreed to a
truce so alarming to Thomas Cromwell that, in his desperation to find
Protestant allies, he arranged King Henry's marriage to Anne, the sister of
the Duke of Cleves. Nothing was ever really settled, and there continued
to be no basis on which a lasting peace could be constructed. Francis remained as fixed as ever on the dream of driving the Hapsburgs out of

Italy, and to accomplish that he showed himself willing to become the ally not only of Germany's Protestant states but of the sultan Suleiman. Charles for his part remained determined to surrender not a yard of his patrimony.

All this was of incalculable value to Henry as he broke with Rome and embarked upon the destruction of England's monasteries. If a real peace had been possible between Francis and Charles, a crusade by the continent's Catholic powers to return England to the old faith might have become feasible as well. Certainly that was what Pope Paul III hoped for once he understood that Henry was never going to be coaxed back into the fold.

Henry should have been thankful to be left alone. He should have been content to leave the continent alone. But even now, with so much accomplished, it was not in his nature to be satisfied, and the very existence of Francis of France seems to have caused him torment. Though their two kingdoms were no longer even remotely equal in size, wealth, or strength—after the absorption of Brittany and Burgundy and other provinces, France's population was six times England's—for Henry the thought of being inferior in anything was unendurable. Early in his reign, in the Loire valley, Francis had started construction of the Château de Chambord. Twenty years later, in the late thirties, it was still under construction, on the way to its eventual total of 440 rooms, 365 fireplaces, eighty-four staircases, and more than a dozen different *kinds* of towers. Six months after the birth of his son, Henry decided that such a flagrant display could not go unanswered. He undertook a project specifically intended to surpass Chambord. The result was the stupendous Nonsuch Palace, the largest building ever seen in England up to that time, utterly unnecessary because not far distant from Hampton Court or Richmond or Greenwich or Whitehall or others of Henry's many residences, so ornate with its hundreds of feet of high-relief sculptures of gods and goddesses and emperors and kings all surmounted by huge representations of Henry himself and the child Edward that after £24,000 had been spent it would still not be nearly finished.

Nor was that enough. Henry could never be satisfied, probably, so long as Francis remained alive and securely in possession of his throne. He would continue to wait, to watch for the opportunity to show himself the greater man.

16

The Last of Henry

It was January 27, 1547, and the ulcers on King Henry's thighs were once again alarmingly inflamed. Clogged veins had swollen his legs until the skin seemed about to split, old open sores filled his bedchamber with an atrocious stench, and the royal body was jolted at unpredictable intervals by electric stabs of pain. This was the third such episode in less than a year; with a single brief remission it had been going on for more than a month, and this time Henry really *was* dying. At age fifty-five he was an old man at the end of his strength, bald, wrinkled, and gray-bearded, unable to read without spectacles, so grotesquely fat that he could no longer climb stairs and even on level ground had to be rolled about on chairs fitted with wheels. His physicians were cauterizing the ulcers with red-hot irons, adding to his agony. His many other afflictions—the headaches, the itching, the hemorrhoids—now seemed trivial by comparison.

He was, essentially, alone. Even his wife Catherine Parr, who had been twice widowed before becoming the king's sixth bride and was an experienced and solicitous nurse, had been sent away before Christmas and not summoned back to court since. His children—Mary, in her late twenties now and still unmarried, Elizabeth, who was just entering adolescence, and the child Edward—also were kept away. No one had access to the king except his physicians and the gentlemen of his privy chamber, who were busy fending off questions about his condition and denying that he was seriously ill or even, as some believed, already dead. On January 16, during a temporary resurgence of some of his old vitality, Henry had been strong enough to meet with the ambassadors of his old friends and enemies Francis of France and the emperor Charles, and that had put the rumors to rest for a while. The world, however, had seen nothing of him since then.

Though Henry's physicians didn't know *why* he was dying, exactly, it was obvious to all of them that he could not last long. The breakdowns had been coming with increasing frequency in recent years, the periods of recovery progressively shorter and less complete. His once-powerful constitution was so overburdened with problems (thrombosed varicose veins, possibly infected bones, possibly, too, a condition called Cushing's syndrome that would explain both his distended torso and face and his savagely irrational behavior) as to be in a state of general collapse. Whatever the facts of his condition—a condition far beyond the reach of sixteenth-century medical science—no one who could get close enough to the king to tell him that his life was at an end, to suggest that perhaps he might want to prepare himself for death, was willing to do so. Even now Henry was too dangerous to be trusted. Just eight days earlier he had had put to death, on a flimsy charge of treason, young Henry Howard, Earl of Surrey and son and heir of the Duke of Norfolk. In addition to being a poet of considerable brilliance, the originator of what would come to be known as the Shakespearean sonnet, Surrey had been arrogant and reckless. But he was not a traitor by any reasonable definition of the term. Even less was his father the duke a traitor, but now he, too, after an often hard life of service to the Crown, was in the Tower awaiting execution. Small wonder that none of the men huddled in the king's bedchamber dared to tell him the one thing that might, in his extremity, have been of some use to him. Long before, Henry had made it a crime to foretell the king's death. People had been punished severely on charges of having done so. And so Henry lay in solitude among the deep pillows of his great bed, while his retainers hung back and left him alone with his thoughts.

He had no shortage of things to think about. If he suspected that he was dying—and he surely did, having spent the last of his strength making arrangements for the management of the kingdom after he was gone—his thoughts would have turned inevitably to the old question of the succession. Prince Edward, the heir whose birth had been made possible by so many deaths, was still only nine years old. He was a bright child, perhaps exceptionally so, and like his half-sisters he gave every evidence of worshipping his mighty father. But he was a frail reed on which to hang the future of the dynasty—years before, when the boy was sick with fever, the court physicians had warned that he was not likely to live long—and far too young to take a role in governing or even protecting his own interests. Henry would have wished that the boy were older and more robust, or that he had a brother or two. His thoughts might have turned to the efforts he had made to produce more sons even as his potency ebbed away. To the three marriages he had contracted after the death of Jane Seymour—marriages that had cemented his reputation as England's bluebeard while at the same time making him the laughingstock of Europe.

There was sweet, dull Anne of Cleves, "the mare of Flanders," to whom he had betrothed himself sight unseen in 1538 when France and Charles were allied against him, an invasion of England seemed not only possible but likely, and a marital connection with the Protestant princes of Europe (of whom the Duke of Cleves was one) seemed the only safe haven. The marriage was a fiasco from the start; Henry found his bride so unappealing, her big, slack body so repellent, that though for a while he shared her bed he never attempted consummation. A pretext was found for having the marriage annulled, and Anne, who had no wish to return to the continent, was contentedly pensioned off with two handsome houses, a staff appropriate to her new station as the king's "sister," and an annual stipend of £500.

There had followed the far greater catastrophe, the profound public humiliation, of Catherine Howard. The nineteen-year-old niece of the Duke of Norfolk and first cousin of Anne Boleyn, petite and vivacious if rather mindless, Catherine had been dangled before the king like a juicy morsel by courtiers who thought that if they could draw him into marrying her the consequences would be good for the whole sprawling Howard clan, good for the religious conservatives, and bad for the brothers of Jane Seymour, evangelicals who had been prospering mightily since the birth of their nephew Prince Edward. Henry rose to the bait with a speed that must have astonished the anglers. His infatuation with Catherine became obvious well before the end of his marriage to Anne of Cleves, and he made her his wife eighteen days after the Cleves marriage was annulled. He was enchanted with the girl, lavished gifts on her, proudly put her on display during his annual summer progress. But there was much, sadly, that Henry did not know. Catherine, whose ne'er-do-well father had been absent through much of her childhood and died before she was brought to court, had had an undisciplined upbringing in the crowded household of her stepgrandmother the Dowager Duchess of Norfolk. She brought to her position as maid of honor to Anne of Cleves a good deal more sexual experience than the king would have found acceptable had he been aware of it. Trouble probably was inevitable from the day she was married, through no choice of her own, to an obese and diseased man some thirty years her senior, and when it came it came in squadrons. Soon after becoming queen, in an act of astounding recklessness, Catherine appointed her lover Francis Dereham to be her private secretary, later transferring her favors to a young gentleman of the king's privy chamber named Thomas Culpeper. In due course she was found out and reported, and the end of her story was similar to that of Anne Boleyn except that this time the queen was guilty. Dereham and Culpeper both were executed in December 1541, the latter receiving the mercy of a simple beheading but Dereham subjected to the protracted horrors reserved for traitors. The foolish and unfortunate Catherine was beheaded the following February. With her died her friend and accomplice in deceit Lady Jane Rochford, who on an earlier occasion had saved her own neck by providing damning testimony against her husband, George Boleyn. The king showed far more grief, for far longer, than he had after the death of Jane Seymour. Probably it was not grief so much as chagrin at having been cuckolded before the eyes of all Europe.

Why Henry would choose to marry yet again must remain a mystery. There could have been little chance of his becoming a father at this point, but hope may have sprung eternal in a man so proud. And Henry, in his increasingly brutal and self-defeating way, had always been hungry for affection. In any case marry he did, and wisely this time. Catherine Parr, who made little secret of being motivated by duty rather than love in accepting the king's proposal, was an attractive thirty-one-year-old widow of great dignity and self-possession. She proved skillful at adapting herself to her husband's moods and maintaining a pleasant household not only for him but for all three of his children—the first and only time that Henry's offspring were ever together even intermittently in something resembling a normal family home. But Henry proved a dangerous partner even in her case, at one point not only professing outrage at her evangelical beliefs but issuing a warrant for her arrest and dispatching guards to search her quarters and take her to the Tower. He soon changed his mind, however—if the whole episode was a kind of malicious practical joke, it was not the first time he had toyed cruelly with people close to him in this way—and as the queen learned to keep her theological opinions to herself domestic tranquillity was restored. The fact that she was kept at a distance throughout the painful final weeks of Henry's life, however, suggests that there must have been rather severe limits to whatever intimacy the two had achieved. In any event there was little about his marital history that Henry could have considered with satisfaction as he approached his final hour on earth. He could sentimentalize only about Jane, who had done him the supreme favor of bearing a son and then dying before he could lose interest.

Nor is he likely to have wanted to give much thought to the subject of money. No ruler in the history of England had reaped a bounty of gold to compare with Henry's, and yet somehow it had all ended with the economy of the kingdom in a parlous state and its government virtually bankrupt. And there had been absolutely no reason why things *had* to end up this way: it had all been Henry's doing, and he had done it for no better reason than the satisfaction of his own appetites and the demands of his swollen ego. The floodgates had opened wide in the aftermath of the Pilgrimage of Grace, when the campaign began to bully and bribe the inhabitants of the larger religious houses into surrendering their lands and possessions (and to kill them when neither bullying nor bribery would suffice). The climax of that campaign came in May 1539 with Parliament's passage of the Second Act of Dissolution, which declared all the church property confiscated since 1536 (when the smaller houses were condemned) and all the church property to be confiscated in the future to be lawfully the property of the Crown. This statute remedied an awkward legal flaw in the surrenders signed by the leaders of the larger houses: those leaders were not the owners of the monasteries they headed and had no right to give them away. It speeded the completion of the greatest redistribution of English land and wealth since the Norman Conquest in 1066. The whole suppression worked to the direct and immediate advantage of the king, who rather abruptly became richer than any other monarch in Christendom. By the spring of 1540 not a single monastic establishment remained in existence in England or Wales. Hundreds if not thousands of the monks and nuns expelled from them had become itinerant beggars, wandering from village to village in search of work or charity. The number of England's schools, hospitals, and institutions for the care of the aged and indigent had undergone an abrupt collapse from which it would not recover for centuries.

At the same time that all this was happening, Henry ordered the destruction of the shrines that had long been objects of veneration and destinations for pilgrims not only from England but the whole Christian world. The most famous of these was the fabulous tomb of Thomas Becket at Canterbury Cathedral, where for many generations wealthy visitors had been leaving offerings of jewels, gold, and silver. It was targeted for liquidation not only because of the immense treasure it contained (a treasure that had itself become a kind of tourist attraction, visible behind iron bars) but also because the man it honored had been murdered for defending the liberties of the church in defiance of an earlier King Henry. A farce was played out in which an order was issued for Becket, who had been dead for 370 years, to appear in court and face charges of rebellion and treason. When after thirty days he had not appeared, a trial was held at which the saint was represented by counsel appointed by the king and, upon being found guilty, was sentenced to have his bones burned and scattered. Not coincidentally, the court ordered also that the treasures of Becket's tomb should go to the Crown. The valuables hauled away from the tomb filled twenty-four wagons—this in addition to two chests so laden with precious gems that "six or eight strong men could do no more than convey one of them." Similar if less awesome troves were gathered up elsewhere. Particularly disgraceful was what happened at Winchester, where, in the course of looting the ancient shrine of St. Cuthbert, the king's agents broke open the coffin and scattered the bones of the most heroic figure in all of English history, the only English king ever to be called "the Great," the ninth century's genuinely courageous, good, and wise Alfred, King of Wessex. The loot from all these tombs went of course into the royal treasury.

Quite apart from the colossal sums that flowed into the king's coffers from the shrines, and ultimately dwarfing them, was the £140,000 in rent generated annually by the monastic lands that now came into the king's possession. Parliament, in being asked ("instructed" would be a better word) to approve Henry's appropriation of possibly as much as five percent of all the rental income in the kingdom, was told that this would make wondrous things possible. The king would be able to rule—even to wage war—without ever having to levy taxes. He would be able to expand the ranks of the nobility (an exciting thought for wealthy and ambitious families), increase spending on education, and advance religion by creating and endowing eighteen new bishoprics. This was Cromwell's great plan: to make the Crown financially independent and Parliament very nearly irrelevant. If carried out, it could have changed English history by giving future kings an endowment sufficient to support all the operations of their governments for any number of generations.

Nothing of the kind came to pass. Instead Henry ran through his windfall with a speed that defies belief. Almost as soon as the church lands fell into his hands he began selling them, in some cases even giving them away to a fortunate few. In the last eight or nine years of his life he divested himself, and his heirs, of land with a value of approximately £750,000. There were political advantages in this: by giving the most powerful families a share of the monastic spoils, and by allowing other families to become powerful from feasting on the pillage, he created a potent constituency with the strongest possible reason for supporting what he had done. Most of the sold lands went for prices approaching fair market value, rather than being deeply discounted or given away. If Henry had husbanded his receipts, they could have not only given him unprecedented and potentially permanent autonomy but also funded at least some of the good things promised to Parliament. But instead he squandered it, almost literally threw it away, creating a legacy of financial neediness that would cripple his successors for a hundred years and finally contribute to the collapse of the monarchy under his great-great-grandnephew King Charles I.

He squandered his riches at home first, spending half a million pounds on building in the 1540s, much of it on coastal fortifications but as much as £170,000 on the construction, expansion, and unending improvement of his many palaces. (Even Hampton Court, which grew to more than a thousand rooms with luxurious sleeping accommodations for three hundred guests, was dwarfed by Nonsuch Palace, which was still a work in progress when Henry died, would never become an important royal residence, and in the space of a few generations would disappear from the landscape almost without leaving a trace.)

But what ruined the Crown financially was Henry's resumed pursuit, as the 1530s ended and his mastery of church and state seemed complete, of military glory. As in the first years of his reign and again in the 1520s, he made war on both France and Scotland, and as before, there was no real point in attacking either. As before, he accomplished nothing of consequence, did nothing to enhance his reputation at home or abroad, and aggravated problems that would torment his successors. Even in their most farcical aspects, Henry's last international adventures were painfully like his first. They began in 1543, when Francis of France and the emperor Charles—who five years earlier had signed a meaningless ten-year truce and then, with equal lack of seriousness, pledged that neither would enter into additional alliances without the other's consent—once again went to war with each other and began to court England. Henry, who had no good reason to involve himself in this sterile old quarrel and many good reasons to stay out, nevertheless entered into a treaty with Charles by which both promised to invade France in the following year. Henry did in fact lead an army into France in July 1544—his deplorable physical condition made him less the army's leader than a cumbersome part of its baggage—but predictably he and Charles neither cooperated nor even attempted to coordinate their operations.

Within two months Charles was making a separate peace with Francis, ending whatever chance Henry might ever have had of accomplishing anything. The conflict with Scotland was equally confused, confusing, and intermittently ridiculous. In 1542 Henry insisted on making a major issue of the kinds of skirmishes that had long been routine in the borderlands that separated the two kingdoms, demanding that the Scots acknowledge him as overlord of their king. The death of his

his nephew King James V after the English victory at Solway Moss in that year (Henry did not participate) opened up the possibility not only of peace but of union between the two countries. In 1543 Scotland's infant queen was betrothed to little Edward, Prince of Wales, as part of the Treaty of Greenwich, but the Scots were soon repelled by England's "rough wooing." In each of the following two years an angry Henry sent armies under the late Queen Jane's brother Edward Seymour not only to invade Scotland but—these were Seymour's specific instructions—to cause as much mayhem as possible. One result was an outlandish amount of death and destruction. Another was the raising of Scottish hatred of the English to a pitch rarely seen before. The Scots turned to France for support, and the stage was set for the marriage of their queen into the French royal family. In the end the only result of Henry's aggressive policy was the cementing of a French-Scottish alliance.

The French and Scottish campaigns cost England, in the five years leading up to Henry's death, the stupendous total of more than £2.2 million—this at a time when the Crown's customary revenues (those exclusive of the money from the monastic suppression) were in the neighborhood of £200,000. Just the three-month incursion into France in 1544 cost £586,000, and the subsequent defense of that campaign's one trophy (the city of Boulogne, which had little real value to England, and which in any case the English had no chance of holding on to permanently) cost another £426,000. The war against Scotland, conducted at Henry's insistence with gratuitous and self-defeating savagery, consumed £350,000, and the building up of an English navy took another £265,000. England had never seen spending on this scale. In almost any previous reign the burden imposed on the king's subjects would have sparked resistance, even revolt. So cowed were the people by the 1540s, however, that Henry had little difficulty in matching his unprecedented spending with unprecedented taxation. Almost literally, he pulled out all the financial stops.

Students of the subject have calculated that as early as 1535, with Wolsey and Cromwell showing the way, Henry had accomplished the amazing feat of taking in (and just as quickly spending) more tax revenues than all his predecessors combined. But in the following dozen years the Crown would take in more than twice as much again—and again we are speaking of taxes only, the riches taken from the monasteries not included. From 1540 to 1547 Parliament approved six of the traditional payments known as "fifteenths and tenths," a percentage of the value of movable property. Each of these grants yielded approximately £29,000. During these same years Parliament also approved three "subsidies," each requiring the clergy to give the Crown 20 percent of their income for three successive years and the laity to pay an annually increasing percentage of the value of their real and personal property. Nor was this all, or even nearly all. In 1542 Henry borrowed £112,000 from his wealthier subjects (everyone known to have an income of at least £50 received a letter informing him of how much he was expected to "lend"), and two years later Parliament declared the king free of any obligation to repay any such debts incurred since the start of 1540. Next Henry demanded and got something that Richard III had abolished because of its unpopularity and even Wolsey had been unable to revive because of parliamentary opposition: a so-called "benevolence," a gift to the Crown that in this instance totaled £270,000. Two London aldermen dared to object. One was required not only to join the war against Scotland but to take with him a troop of soldiers raised at his own expense; soon captured, he had to pay a hefty ransom to secure his freedom. The other was simply sent to prison, where he remained for three months until being allowed to purchase his release. Throughout all this Henry was also borrowing from continental moneylenders. Foreign loans totaled some £272,000 in all, at interest rates of up to 14 percent. Much of this debt remained unpaid at the time of Henry's death.

Even this was not enough to keep the Crown solvent. Something more was needed, and it was found in the most underhanded device available to the governments of the time: a systematic debasement of the coinage. As early as the reign of Henry VII, England had, in a legitimate response to a lowering of the value of continental currencies, occasionally and by modest amounts decreased the amount of silver or gold in its coins. In 1544, however, the royal mint began mixing more and more base metal into the coinage, not to keep in step with the Europeans but as a way of skimming off wealth. Soon its coins were only half gold or silver, and not long after that they were two-thirds base metal. Henry reaped £373,000 by this expedient, which caused his cash-strapped last chancellor, Thomas Wriothesley, to gratefully describe the royal mint as the regime's "holy anchor." Few outside the government had reason to celebrate. Prices rose some 25 percent in the last two years of the reign, and the increasingly dubious value of the coinage became an embarrassment to Englishmen trying to trade abroad.

The cumulative effects of Henry's changes were profound. If the old vision of a society in which wealth brought obligations had never come close to fulfillment, now even the ideal was dying. Stability was replaced by plunder, the institutions of government became the tools of the plunderers, and their aim, when it was not to pull in still more plunder, was to make sure that no one threatened the bounty that Henry's revolution had funneled to them. There is no better measure of the kind of England that Henry had created than a statute passed by his Parliament at the instigation of his ministers just months after his death. Under this law, anyone who "lived idly and loiteringly for the space of three days" could have the letter V (for vagabond) branded on his chest and could be required to spend two years serving whoever had reported him (or, presumably, her). Those impressed into bondage in this way were entitled to nothing more than bread and water, could be made to wear iron rings around their necks, and were legally obliged to do whatever work their masters ordered "however vile it might be, by beating, chaining or otherwise." Any who made themselves unavailable to their masters for two weeks or more were to have an S (for slave) burned into their faces and their two years of bondage extended into a life sentence. Further offenses could result in execution. No such law would have been conceivable in England between the coming of Christianity and the last years of Henry VIII's reign. It was a classic case of punishing the victim, singling out for final humiliation the very people left most helpless by the pillaging of institutions that for centuries had attended to the needs of the weak and the destitute. It was too outrageous to be tolerated even by the new oligarchy for more than a few years, but it expressed in extreme form something of the spirit of the age. In a sense it was the zenith of Henry's achievement, the highest expression of the new values that were growing out of the ruins of the old order.

In the years between the failure of the Pilgrimage of Grace and Henry's death, the ancient understanding that there were and must be limits on royal power even in the secular sphere, slowly hammered out during centuries of conflict, was crushed underfoot and left behind. The possibility that anyone other than the king might possess rights or powers not deriving from the king became something that no one dared mention. The king's word literally became law as early as 1539, when a Proclamations Act gave royal pronouncements the same force under the law as statutes passed by Parliament, prescribed imprisonment and fines for anyone failing to obey them, and made it high treason to flee England to escape punishment. This was such an extreme expansion of the power of the Crown that even the craven Parliament that Cromwell had put in place balked, but passage was secured by amendments which forbade the use of proclamations to override statutes already on the books, confiscate private property, or deprive subjects of life or liberty. There followed, within weeks, a fresh delineation of exactly which religious beliefs were now acceptable through an Act for Abolishing Diversity of Opinion. This law, better known as the Six Articles, prescribed the death penalty and confiscation of all possessions for anyone denying transubstantiation, the real presence of the body of Jesus in the Eucharist. It also, remarkably, forbade the extending of mercy to anyone willing to withdraw his denial. It was somewhat less harsh in meting out punishments for the denial of other things that the king was determined to make everyone believe (that it is not necessary to receive communion under the two forms of bread and wine, that priests must not marry and vows of chastity are irrevocable, that private masses are acceptable and confession to a priest necessary for forgiveness). The penalty in connection with these doctrines was merely imprisonment and loss of property for first offenders; a second conviction was necessary for the death penalty to be imposed. Archbishop Cranmer, who almost certainly did not himself believe in the Six Articles at this point in the evolution of his theology, responded by quietly shipping back to Germany the wife whose existence he was at this point still keeping secret from the king.

Despite the increasing severity of the penalties for dissent—sanctions more far-reaching and inflexible than anything previously seen in England—uniformity remained unattainable. One wag compared Henry, with his insistence on rejecting Rome while preserving nearly every Roman Catholic practice and dogma, with someone who has thrown a man off a high tower and then commanded him to stop halfway down. The middle ground that Henry wanted all of England to occupy really was, in practical terms, as impossible as that. On the continent, in

Switzerland especially, reform had already moved far beyond anything that Henry was prepared to tolerate, and increasing numbers of England's reformers wanted to follow the Swiss model. There was no way, in a society where the old consensus had been shattered but faith was still taken so seriously that Parliament engaged in lengthy and passionate debates on transubstantiation, to get everyone to believe what the king told them to believe and to conduct themselves accordingly.

Henry's insistence on making his truth the universal truth led him deeper and deeper into futility and frustration. Even one of the centerpieces of the English Reformation, the delivery to the people of a Bible written in their own language, is a case in point. Such a Bible had been one of the supreme objectives of English reformers long before Henry was born, and nothing was more important to Luther and those who followed him than their conviction that true Christianity was to be found not in the rules and teachings of the church but in Scripture, especially the New Testament writings of the evangelists Matthew, Mark, Luke, and John. (Hence the name "evangelicals" for those reformers who went furthest in rejecting church tradition.) The early radicals had regarded as an outrage the banning of the translation of the New Testament produced by William Tyndale in the 1520s, scornfully brushing aside the hierarchy's contention that it objected not to translation as such but to Tyndale's ideologically motivated distortions (his use of "congregation" rather than "church," for example, and of "senior" rather than "priest"). Brushed aside, too, were the warnings of orthodox theologians that the Bible is an elusive work, easily misinterpreted by readers with little understanding of its linguistic and historical roots. In England as on the continent, the Reformation arrived on a wave of enthusiasm for Scripture as the one doorway to enlightenment and salvation. In 1538, as part of the enforcement of his second set of injunctions for the clergy, Cromwell ordered every parish church in England to obtain a copy of his so-called Great Bible (which was mainly Tyndale's translation and long afterward would provide more than 80 percent of the text of the King James Version). It became government policy to make the Bible directly accessible to every literate man and woman in England.

But Henry soon found the translated Bible an obstacle to uniformity. Readers found the interpretation of many passages open to debate;

many of them naturally began interpreting such passages in whatever way they themselves thought best, and inevitably their conclusions did not always agree with the truth according to Henry or Cranmer or anyone else in a position of authority. Translation launched the English church into diverging assertions of what Scripture does and does not say and hence into a bewildering array of sects. Henry, witnessing the start of this process, was offended by it and undertook to stop it in his usual way: by ordering it to stop or else. Thus in 1543 he drew out of Parliament an Act for Advancement of True Religion, the operative word being "true." True religion was to be preserved by removal of the Tyndale translation, condemned now as what the more conservative of Henry's bishops had persuaded him that it was: "crafty, false and untrue." Henceforth only clergymen were to read the Bible aloud in public, only nobles and gentlemen were to read it to their families, and only male heads of households, gentlewomen, and ladies of noble birth were to read it even in solitude. It was not to be opened by "prentices, journeymen, serving men of the degrees of yeomen or under, husbandmen nor laborers," and any caught doing so were to be jailed for a month. By such means the king sought to separate people "of the lower sort" from their "diverser naughty and erroneous opinions" and save them from "great division and dissension among themselves." The impact of this act on the lower orders is, at a remove of nearly five centuries, impossible to judge. Evangelicals, for the most part, maintained a prudent but resentful silence and bided their time. They took comfort in Henry's marriage to Catherine Parr, who saw to it that reformers of decidedly Protestant inclination were appointed as tutors to Prince Edward and Princess Elizabeth or otherwise provided with employment or patronage.

The king meanwhile soldiered on with the thankless and unending task of showing his people the way to salvation, to all appearances unaware that he could have spent his time more productively by trying to herd cats. Almost simultaneously with the Act for Advancement of True Religion he approved the issuance of what came to be known as the King's Book (its official title was *The Necessary Doctrine and Erudition of Any Christian Man*), an attempt to correct the flaws of the Bishops' Book and lay out yet again a system of beliefs that in most respects was Roman Catholicism purged of what even many conservative reformers often saw as superstition. The conservatives were generally pleased, the evangelicals unimpressed, and nothing really changed. The results were the same on Christmas Eve 1545, when Henry surprised Parliament by addressing it for what would prove to be the last time. Angrily, even tearfully, he complained of the divisions within the clergy, where "some be too stiff in their old Mumpsimus, others be too busy and curious in their new Sumpsimus." Somewhat oddly, considering that he was demanding an end to discord, he urged his listeners to report preachers of "perverse doctrine" to him and his council, saying that he was "very sorry to know and hear how irreverently that precious jewel, the word of God, is disputed, rhymed, sung and jingled in every alehouse and tavern." He found much to complain of that day, and he complained at length, but any who were moved by his sincerity could do little in response and nothing happened as a result. The man who had done more than anyone to make the religion of England a changeable and changing thing, to create and magnify confusion and division, was now very nearly begging his subjects to somehow come together as a united and happy fellowship of faith. If his lament was touching, it was also a bit ridiculous.

Not that the old man was to be scoffed at. To the contrary, at the time of his Mumpsimus speech, with only a little more than a year to live, he remained as murderous as ever, a hardened killer ruling by terror. There was no sure safety for anyone except of course his son and heir—not for his own relatives, not for strangers or those who had served him longest and best, not for reformers or conservatives. The whole last decade of his life was studded with the slaughter of men and women of every stripe, often in the most terrible ways that the technology of the time could make possible.

A representative sampling of Henry's reign of terror might well begin with the story of John Forest, who in the happier days of the 1520s had been a prominent member of the Observant Franciscans, Catherine of Aragon's confessor, and therefore connected to the royal family. He was among the first of the friars to speak out against the king's plan to divorce Catherine and marry Anne Boleyn, and he may already have been in prison by the time Fathers Peto and Elston challenged Henry in the Franciscan church at Greenwich. Later, however, he took the oath of succession, thereby escaping the grisly fate of his compeers, and was allowed to withdraw to the north of England. Still later it was reported that he was claiming to have sworn the oath "with his outward man, but his inward man never consented thereunto." This is plausible in light of the fact that in 1538, for reasons unknown, he was again taken into custody and returned to London for execution as a heretic. What makes Forest's killing noteworthy is the way it was turned into a kind of horrible joke. His death sentence came at the time when Cromwell was shutting down religious shrines and pilgrimage destinations all across England. It happened that at one of these shrines, Llandderfel in Wales, a wooden statue called Darvel Gadarn, an object of veneration from time immemorial, had recently been seized and was slated for destruction. There was a legend about Darvel Gadarn: one day, it was said, the statue would set a forest on fire. This gave someone a bright idea of the kind that no doubt appealed powerfully to officials with a broad enough sense of humor. Darvel Gadarn was hauled from North Wales to London for the burning not of *a* forest but of *John* Forest. On the day of his execution the friar, bound in chains, was suspended above a pyre on which lay the statue. Hugh Latimer, probably the most radical of Henry's bishops, preached a sermon at the end of which he offered to release Forest if he would acknowledge the royal supremacy. When Forest refused, the fire was lit, and for two hours he was slowly broiled until dead. He would remain the only papist executed for heresy rather than treason, and therefore burned rather than hanged. The less theatrical executions at about the same time of the abbot of Woburn and the prior of Lenton, both of whom had refused to sign over their houses, could pass almost unnoticed.

If fidelity to Rome could bring on a terrible death, so too could the rejection of things Roman. In the same year that Forest perished, John Lambert, a Cambridge-educated priest who had long been associated with the radical evangelicals and had been in trouble with the authorities even before Henry's break with Rome, was accused of having heretical opinions concerning, among other things, "the sacrament of the altar," the Eucharist. He appealed to the king, with consequences that must have gone far beyond anything he could have hoped for or feared. Henry decided to turn the case into another of his show trials, a demonstration of his mastery of theology. The great hall at York Place was transformed into a theater for the occasion, with scaffolds erected for onlookers and the walls hung with tapestries. When the trial opened on the morning of November 16, Henry presided from a high throne surrounded by phalanxes of nobles, bishops, judges, and scholars. He was resplendent in a costume of white silk, a kind of corpulent angelic vision. One can only imagine what poor Lambert must have thought, escorted into the center of this display of power and subjected to interrogation by such luminaries as Archbishop Cranmer (who, there can be no doubt, shared many of the beliefs that had brought Lambert to this pass), half a dozen bishops, and finally, most terrifyingly, the king himself, who as the day wore on took an increasingly prominent part in the proceedings.

Lambert was afforded no counsel, but he defended himself and his opinions heroically through hours of hard questioning. The climax came late in the day when, asked yet again to declare whether he believed that the bread and wine of the altar really were transformed during the mass into the body and blood of Christ in spite of undergoing no change in appearance, texture, or taste, Lambert replied that he believed it in the same way that Augustine of Hippo, one of the fathers of the church, appeared in his writings to have done. The king jumped on this.

"Answer neither out of St. Augustine, nor by the authority of any other," he demanded, "but tell me plainly whether thou sayest it is the body of Christ or nay."

"Then I deny it to be the body of Christ."

"Mark well!" said Henry. "For now thou shalt be condemned even by Christ's own words. *Hoc est corpus meum* [here is my body]."

And condemned meant condemned. When in the end Lambert simply abandoned the fight and threw himself on the king's mercy, Henry responded with contempt. He ordered Cromwell to declare the verdict, and the verdict was guilty. Six days later Lambert was dragged—literally dragged, shackled to the traditional hurdle—through the streets of London. Then he too was burned to death. Every sycophant at court praised and thanked the king for the brilliance of his performance.

The year ended with a final outburst of savagery that had only a tangential connection to religion but rose more directly out of the old questions about whether Henry, and his father before him, were rightfully kings of England. At the time of the Pilgrimage of Grace, the pope, having already made the king's cousin Reginald Pole a cardinal though he was not yet an ordained priest, had sent him north to see if the revolt might have inclined Henry to return to the Roman fold or, failing that, if Francis of France and the emperor Charles might be disposed to join forces for an invasion of England. Pole's mission came to nothing—by temperament he was a professional student, sometimes ineffectual in practical matters and sufficiently aware of his limitations to avoid politics—but news of it finished whatever affection Henry had retained for his troublesome young kinsman. It also inflamed his long-smoldering distrust of the entire Pole family. He saw an opportunity to accomplish something that he probably had long desired: the extermination of his remaining Yorkist cousins.

Reginald Pole's elder brother Sir Geoffrey was arrested and interrogated. He must have been a weak man; terrified, he tried to save himself by telling his captors whatever he could about ways in which members of his family had shown themselves to be unfriendly to the new church and therefore disloyal to their king. The evidence he provided was thin stuff, a secondhand account of vague idle talk about unhappiness with the current state of affairs and a longing for the old ways, but in the hands of Cromwell and the king it became sufficient for the arrest of Geoffrey and Reginald's eldest brother Henry, Lord Montague, who as the senior male member of the family and grandson of a brother of Edward IV and Richard III had a claim to the crown that he had never been foolish enough to pursue. Arrested with him were Henry Courtenay, Marquess of Exeter, who like Henry VIII was a son of one of Edward IV's daughters, and his twelve-year-old son Edward, Earl of Devon. Into the Tower they all went. The charges against them were worse than dubious—the Poles and the Courtenays alike had remained loyal to Henry through the various disturbances of the mid-1530s—but their royal blood doomed them all the same. On December 6 Montague and Exeter were beheaded, and the executions of others accused of involvement in the supposed Pole conspiracy went on until in the end sixteen people were dead. Montague's little son, who had been sent to the Tower with his father, was never seen again and is assumed to have died in confinement. Margaret Pole, Countess of Salisbury, the Pole brothers' mother and onetime governess of the king's daughter Mary, was arrested soon after Montague's execution and, after long days of questioning in which nothing could be found to suggest that she might be guilty of anything, attainted of high treason. Exeter's widow, too, was imprisoned and attainted.

It went on in this way year after year, killing following gratuitous killing and every death ugly in its own new way. In the months following the attack on the Poles, as the last and largest of England's religious houses were pulled down and their valuables carted off to London, the abbots of the three great Benedictine monasteries at Colchester, Glastonbury, and Reading became the last to refuse to submit. No one could have been surprised, after what had already transpired, to see them arrested on charges of treason and condemned without trial. But their ends were shocking all the same. The eighty-year-old Abbot Richard Whiting of Glastonbury, a man so far above reproach that even Cromwell's commissioners had praised him and his house at the end of their first visit, was not merely executed. After a debilitating period of imprisonment in London he was returned to his monastery, dragged prostrate to the top of Glastonbury Tor, a conelike geological freak that is the highest promontory in its region, and there put to death along with two of his brother monks. His body was quartered, with the four parts put on public display in the towns of Wells, Bath, Ilchester, and Bridgwater. His head was mounted atop the entrance to the abbey. Henry, keeping his scales balanced, was at this same time having evangelicals imprisoned and burned for failing to conform to the Six Articles.

The year after that, as if in confirmation that what goes around comes around, even Thomas Cromwell was abruptly stripped of his offices and put to death. Contrary to what has often been asserted, he did not die because he had used a deceptive painting by Hans Holbein to trick the king into marrying a miserably homely Anne of Cleves. He died, rather, because he had become too closely identified with the evangelical party in England and the Protestant cause in Europe, and because the collapse of the latest alliance between Francis of France and the emperor Charles gave Henry a choice of Catholic allies and made Cromwell not only expendable but a diplomatic liability. Henry dispensed with him because he thought he no longer needed him, and because he thought he would be better off without him. The endlessly useful Richard Rich (he was *Sir* Richard now, on his way to becoming Lord Rich) testified against his longtime master with effect as deadly as his earlier contributions to the destruction of Fisher and More. He quoted Cromwell as saying that he was prepared, if necessary, to fight for the evangelical cause even in defiance of the king. It is not easy to believe that the wily Cromwell would have said any such thing within Rich's hearing, but the standards of evidence were even lower in his case than in Fisher's or More's because he had no actual trial. Interestingly, at the moment of his arrest, Cromwell pulled off his hat and angrily flung it to the ground. It was the exasperated gesture of a gambler learning that he had made a bad bet, a trickster tricked. There would be no more opportunities to roll the dice.

In the days before his death Cromwell begged Henry for "mercy, mercy, mercy," and just before being executed he professed to having always been a good Catholic. (He could not have meant a good *Roman* Catholic.) It was not long before Henry realized that he *did* need Cromwell, and that in executing him he had deprived himself of as effective a chief minister as any monarch could ever have hoped for. Characteristically, he blamed the loss not on himself but on Cromwell's enemies at court—men and women who had in fact wanted to see the secretary ruined but would have been powerless to accomplish any such thing without the king's active cooperation. Throughout the 1540s Henry would pay and pay again for having extended that cooperation.

Two days after Cromwell's execution the prominent evangelicals Robert Barnes, William Jerome, and Thomas Garrett were all burned at the stake for heresy, and three distinguished Roman Catholics were hanged, drawn, and quartered for treason. All these deaths remain shrouded in mystery. As with the abbots and Cromwell, there had been no trial, no presentation of evidence, no defense; the king was now simply killing whomever he chose without taking the trouble to explain. The atrocities went on and on. Some, such as the 1541 execution of the seventy-year-old Margaret, Countess of Salisbury, the mother of the Poles, were small affairs barely deserving notice except for their brutality.

The countess, whose father, brother, and son had been murdered by Edward IV, Henry VII, and Henry VIII respectively, and whose small grandson had disappeared while in prison, was obviously guilty of nothing. All her life she had been a loyal if independent-minded member of the royal family, though her early support of Catherine of Aragon had caused her to be dismissed from court and the defection of her son Reginald to the old religion had brought trouble down on the entire family. When brought to the chopping block, Margaret refused to cooperate. "No," she said, "my head never committed treason. If you will have it,

you must take it as you can." Her death became a grotesquely protracted affair. The executioner had to chase her around the scaffold,
slashing at her awkwardly with his blade until at last he had "literally
hacked her head and shoulders to pieces in a most pitiful manner."

Some of the atrocities were on a vastly bigger scale. In late 1543, after
the Scots repudiated the Treaty of Greenwich and the betrothal of their
infant queen to Prince Edward, Henry sent Edward Seymour on an unnecessary and ultimately counterproductive invasion. Seymour's orders
were to annihilate every man, woman, and child wherever resistance
was encountered, which was likely to mean wherever English troops appeared. Every place of habitation was to be destroyed "so that the upper
stone may be the nether and not one stick stand by another." Seymour
questioned these instructions, sensibly thinking that an approach with
less resemblance to genocide might be more conducive to long-term
peace. When told to proceed as ordered, he did so with such diligence
that most of Edinburgh was reduced to rubble and the countryside
around was scoured clean. The following year, when Seymour again
crossed into Scotland, his orders were the same as before: to carry out a
program of wholesale and indiscriminate destruction. This time he demolished sixteen castles, seven major abbeys, five towns, and 243 villages, killing uncounted hundreds or thousands of Scots. Henry, still not
satisfied, ordered the execution of several Scottish hostages whom he
had been holding for more than two years and gave his support to a plot
(which succeeded) to assassinate the Cardinal Beaton who had long
been the leader of the most anti-English faction in Edinburgh. This last
he did secretly, however, "not misliking the offer" of the men who vol-
unteered to murder Beaton, thinking it "good they be exhorted to proceed," but regarding such a project as "not meet to be set forward
expressly by his majesty."

This was the Henry who, on January 27, 1547, having been told at last
by a brave gentleman of his privy chamber that he was dying and asked
if he wished to confess, replied that he was confident that his sins would
have been forgiven even if they were far greater than in fact they were.
Again he was asked if he wished to see a confessor. He said perhaps
Cranmer, safe old Cranmer, but not quite yet, not until he had slept
awhile. He drifted into a sleep that became a coma, so that later, when
his gentlemen tried to rouse him, they were unable to do so. Cranmer

was summoned and came in a hurry, taking the king's hand and trying to talk with him but getting no response. Finally he asked Henry to signify his faith in Jesus Christ by squeezing his hand. The king, Cranmer said later, squeezed hard and died.

Something very big had come to an end. It was time for the aftermath, whatever that might prove to be. As for Henry, perhaps his best hope was that he had been wrong all along and the evangelicals right, and all that was needed to save his soul was the gift of faith. No doubt he himself would have been willing to be judged by his works, but it might not have been a good bet.

Sources and Notes

Nothing could be easier, in connection with the Tudors, than the assembly of an impressively weighty bibliography. The available literature, even the fairly *recent* literature, is so vast as to bring the concept of infinity to mind. And few exercises could be of less real value to the general reader for whom this book is intended. What may have some value—at least in a book that is an attempt at synthesis, without any claim to plowing new ground in original source materials—is an indication of which works the author has found to be particularly useful.

As to source notes, to the extent that the facts of the Tudor story are knowable (many are not, and after more than four centuries it is unlikely that they ever will be) they have by now been sifted and settled by something like fifteen generations of scholars and writers. Many of the facts, often the most significant or just plain interesting, recur so frequently in the literature of the Tudor era that to give sources for them would (while requiring dozens of pages) be no less pointless than a comprehensive bibliography. The author of the current work has elected, therefore, to provide sources in particular cases only: for quotations that do not appear to have become widely familiar as a result of frequent previous use, and—what seems especially necessary—for those facts and opinions that are most likely to challenge the reader's preconceptions because they are most at variance with popular views of the Tudors. The resulting source notes appear below, along with citations of those books to which the author feels particularly indebted. Both things are arranged under headings corresponding to the four parts of this book.

In assembling and verifying the facts out of which his narrative has been constructed—dates and biographical details, for example—the author has relied heavily on one of the world's most awesomely comprehensive and authoritative resources: the sixty-volume 2004 edition of the *Oxford Dictionary of National Biography* (*DNB* in the notes below). Use has also been made of *The*

Encyclopaedia Britannica, and for the same reasons. Readers seeking to confirm statements of fact for which sources have not been provided, or to sue additional information, are encouraged to begin by consulting those two works.

The Subject Overall

Studies dealing in depth with the reigns of all five Tudor monarchs have always been rare, at least in comparison to biographies of individual figures, and some of those that were once well known are now discredited and largely forgotten. Examples are the works of Macaulay and Froude, who survive as masters of style and of storytelling, but not of scholarship. An exception is the relevant part (volumes 4, 5, and 6) of John Lingard's *History of England* (New York: Publication Society of America, 1912). Though inevitably superseded in many details since it first appeared early in the nineteenth century, this remarkable work (pioneering in its use and sophisticated evaluation of original source material) remains a fruitful and broadly reliable guide to sixteenth-century England, rich both in facts and insights. Lingard is obscure today mainly because he has *always* been obscure. He was too far ahead of his time, replacing fable with fact more than a century before England was ready for so much objectivity.

Noteworthy among much more recent treatments of the whole dynasty are works by G. R. Elton, especially *England Under the Tudors* (Methuen, 1955) and *The Tudor Constitution* (Cambridge University Press, 1960); John Guy's *Tudor England* (Oxford, 1988); and Penry Williams's *The Tudor Regime* (Oxford, 1979). These are scholarly achievements of a very high order and immensely useful, though not well suited—or indeed intended—for a general audience.

PART ONE
An Excess of Good Fortune

In tracing the careers of the first two Tudor kings, the author has taken as his guide two biographies generally still regarded as the best on their subjects: S. B. Chrimes, *Henry VII* (University of California Press, 1972), and J. J. Scarisbrick, *Henry VIII* (University of California Press, 1968). G. W. Bernard's *The King's Reformation: Henry VIII and the Remaking of the English Church* (Yale University Press, 2005) provides a massive and magisterial overview of the first of the Tudor reformations.

Other notably good sources of the information and ideas presented in this section (and in several cases later parts of the book as well) include:

Duffy, Eamon. *The Stripping of the Altars: Traditional Religion in England, 1400–1580*, 2nd ed. Yale University Press, 2005.

Fraser, Antonia. *The Wives of Henry VIII*. Vintage, 1994.

Griffiths, R. A., and R. S. Thomas. *The Making of the Tudor Dynasty*. Alan Sutton, 1985.

Loades, David, ed. *Chronicles of the Tudor Kings*. Bramley, 1996.

———. *Henry VIII: Church, Court and Conflict*. National Archives, 2007.

Mackie, J. D. *The Earlier Tudors, 1485–1558*. Oxford, 1952.

Marius, Richard. *Thomas More*. Vintage, 1985.

Mattingly, Garret. *Catherine of Aragon*. Little, Brown, 1941.

Smith, Lacey Baldwin. *Henry VIII: The Mask of Power*. Houghton Mifflin, 1972.

Starkey, David. *Six Wives: The Queens of Henry VIII*. HarperCollins, 2003.

Williams, Neville. *Henry VII*. Weidenfeld & Nicolson, 1973.

Notes for Part One

PAGE

5 *But because we have no eyewitness accounts . . .* : Good if conventional introductions to the Battle of Bosworth appear in Griffiths and Thomas, *Tudor Dynasty*, and Michael Bennett, *The Battle of Bosworth* (Sutton, 2000).

11 *The detailed descriptions in countless books . . .* : The conventional understanding of Bosworth is seriously and responsibly challenged by Michael K. Jones in *Bosworth 1485: Psychology of a Battle* (Tempus, 2002).

31 *On top of all his other blessings . . .* : As Lawrence Stone observes in *The Causes of the English Revolution, 1529–1642* (Harper & Row, 1972), p. 88, the concept of the divine right of kings figured importantly in the thinking of radical (anti-Roman) religious reformers from William Tyndale onward. Henry VIII's exposure to and embrace of such thinking, and Anne Boleyn's role, is shown in Fraser, *Wives*, p. 145, among other sources.

33 *When the seemingly endless demands for new taxes . . .* : Popular resistance to the tax levies of the mid-1520s, and the shift of blame to Wolsey, is in Carolly Erickson's *Great Harry* (Simon & Schuster, 1980), p. 173.

46 *One of the mentors of Henry's youth . . .* : John Fisher's upholding of Henry's marriage to Catherine of Aragon is in Fraser, *Wives*, p. 139.

47 *Henry, clutching at straws, suggested . . .* : The question of how Leviticus should have been translated is an insuperable one for anyone lacking knowledge of Hebrew. Bernard, *King's Reformation*, p. 17, and others take the position that Henry's interpretation lacks merit. By contrast, Richard Rex in *The Tudors* (Tempus, 2002), p. 56, is more supportive.

47 *About this, too, he was proved wrong . . .* : Bernard, *King's Reformation*, p. 18.

50 *"No one would ever have taken her . . ."* : This quote, and the one on the following page about Henry being "struck by the dart of love," appear in the *DNB* entry for Anne Boleyn.

51 *In one of the many letters he sent her . . .* : *DNB* entry for Anne Boleyn.

51 *It is entirely possible* . . . : Bernard, *King's Reformation,* p. 7, provides reasons why Henry might have chosen to defer consummation of his relationship with Anne.

53 *"I close my eyes before such horror"* . . . : Scarisbrick, *Henry VIII,* p. 216.

55 *No easy solutions were open* . . . : The extent to which Clement VII had freedom of action in dealing with Henry's annulment suit is one of the unresolved and probably unresolvable questions of Tudor history. The ambiguities and contradictions of the pope's situation are explained in ibid., p. 197.

57 *Instead of congratulating her* . . . : Erickson, *Great Harry,* p. 199.

57 *To this group he delivered an address* . . . : Fraser, *Wives,* p. 155.

58 *When it came back to him* . . . : Erickson, *Great Harry,* p. 223.

67 *That Wolsey himself felt any compelling* . . . : While Scarisbrick, *Henry VIII,* p. 47, argues persuasively that Wolsey would have pursued very different policies had he aspired to the papacy, Elton, *England Under,* p. 84, says without offering much evidence that the cardinal wanted to be pope throughout all his years in high office.

70 *"Sir," she began in the accent* . . . : Fraser, *Wives,* p. 160.

72 *"No, my lord, not so"* . . . : Bernard, *King's Reformation,* p. 105.

73 *He felt obliged to do this* . . . : Loades, *Henry VIII,* p. 83.

74 *A considerable exercise of the imagination* . . . : Among the many good introductions to England in the sixteenth century are Penry Williams, *Life in Tudor England* (Batsford, 1964) and John Morrill, ed., *The Oxford Illustrated History of Tudor and Stuart Britain* (Oxford University Press, 1996).

74 *The great humanist scholar Erasmus* . . . : Penry Williams, *Life,* p. 104.

76 *The population, which in the year 1300* . . . : Loades, *Henry VIII,* p. 9.

76 *By 1485 the population was again growing* . . . : Guy, *Tudor England,* p. 10.

79 *"The people here are held in little more esteem* . . .": W. G. Hoskins, *The Age of Plunder* (Longmans, 1971), p. 105.

84 *"Inasmuch as ye, the fathers of the laws* . . .": Scarisbrick, *Henry VIII,* p. 238.

85 *"God forbid that he should die!"* . . . : Lingard, *History of England,* p. 4:537.

85 *On October 26, in conversing* . . . : Scarisbrick, *Henry VIII,* p. 246.

87 *As early as 1515 during a dispute* . . . : Elton, *England Under,* p. 107.

87 *"God hath made in every realm* . . .": Guy, *Tudor England,* p. 121.

88 *"This," he is supposed to have said* . . . : Mackie, *Earlier Tudors,* p. 352.

89 *Henry, whose opinion of himself* . . . : Smith, *Mask of Power,* p. 124.

90 *Genuine and legitimate power, More said* . . . : Marius, *Thomas More,* p. 365.

91 *The England of 1530 contained* . . . : Good introductions to the religious life of pre-Reformation England are Penry Williams, *Life;* Maurice Keen, *English Society in the Later Middle Ages* (Penguin, 1990); Francis Aidan Gasquet, *England Under the Old Religion and Other Essays* (G. Bell & Sons, 1912); and most important, Duffy, *Stripping of Altars.*

99 *Stern and unfamiliar penalties* . . . : Guy, *Tudor England,* p. 144.

101 *When he had heard Cranmer out* . . . : Scarisbrick, *Henry VIII,* p. 255.

103 *"Stop, sir," he said in French* . . . : Lingard, *History of England,* p. 4:545.

104   *Martin Luther himself, while insisting . . .* : Ibid., p. 4:549.

106   *According to one of his confidants . . .* : Ibid., p. 4:555.

106   *Henry, meanwhile, the bit in his teeth . . .* : Bernard, *King's Reformation*, p. 38.

111   *By the end of the reign this number . . .* : David M. Loades, *The Tudor Court* (Barnes & Noble, 1987), p. 185.

116   *At the same time he involved himself . . .* : The words about Wolsey being "persuaded from vainglory," and those on the following page about presumptuous sinister practices," are in Scarisbrick, *Henry VIII*, p. 239.

118   *"Father Abbot," he said upon arrival . . .* : Smith, *Mask of Power*, p. 107.

119   *Delay, long a source of frustration . . .* : Bernard, *King's Reformation*, p. 52, and Scarisbrick, *Henry VIII*, p. 291, explain Henry's gradually emerging desire for delay.

121   *In the message that conveyed their offer . . .* : Elton, *England Under*, p. 125.

121   *If they came from John Fisher . . .* : Marius, *Thomas More*, p. 379, says: "The saving words usually have been incorrectly ascribed to John Fisher. But their insertion seems to have been an effort by the government to soften the blow . . ."

122   *He blithely assured Tunstal . . .* : Bernard, *King's Reformation*, p. 180, and Scarisbrick, *Henry VIII*, p. 278.

123   *A letter signed by seventeen members . . .* : Scarisbrick, *Henry VIII*, p. 277.

124   *"This proposition cannot be counted as heretical" . . .* : Marius, *Thomas More*, p. 380.

125   *In a stroke of sheer good luck . . .* : Mackie, *Earlier Tudors*, p. 350.

127   *The comptroller of the king's household . . .* : Neville Williams, *Henry VIII and His Court* (Macmillan, 1972), p. 117.

135   *"God grant him a good conscience" . . .* : Bernard, *King's Reformation*, p. 75.

138   *"My lord," a surprisingly good-humored . . .* ": Lingard, *History of England*, p. 4:562.

139   *The supreme oddity, in any case . . .* : Elton, *England Under*, p. 131, suggests that the initiative lay with Cromwell rather than the king, while Bernard, *King's Reformation*, p. 60, takes the opposite position.

143   *Cromwell had pulled it off . . .* : The adherence of most of England to the old religion is accepted today by all of the most respected historians. See Elton, *England Under*, p. 109, and Scarisbrick, *Henry VIII*, pp. 241 and 328. Duffy, *Stripping of Altars*, provides an exhaustive demonstration of the vitality of the pre-Reformation English church.

144   *The churchmen were ordered to give . . .* : Mackie, *Earlier Tudors*, p. 355.

149   *In doing so he crushed whatever autonomy . . .* : Ibid., p. 749.

153   *Henry VIII on more than one occasion . . .* : Francis Aidan Gasquet, *Henry VIII and the English Monasteries* (John Hodges, 1889), p. 1:156.

153   *"I beseech your Grace to take good heed . . ."*: Derek Wilson, *In the Lion's Court* (St. Martin's Press, 2002), p. 339.

155   *From the start of the crisis . . .* : Bernard, *King's Reformation*, p. 173.

156   *"Well-beloved subjects," Henry told . . .* : Scarisbrick, *Henry VIII*, p. 299.

157   *Thus it was that May 15 became . . .* : Ibid., p. 300.

160   *It seems an exceedingly strange coincidence . . .* : Among fruitful one-volume

introductions to the Reformation both in England and on the continent are A. G. Dickens, *The English Reformation* (Schocken, 1968); James D. Tracy, *Europe's Reformations 1450–1650* (Rowman & Littlefield, 1999); John Bowker, ed., *The Cambridge Illustrated History of Religion* (Cambridge University Press, 2001); Geoffrey Woodward, *The Sixteenth Century Reformation* (Lion, 2001); and Gordon Mursell, gen. ed., *The Story of Christian Spirituality* (Hodder & Stoughton, 2001).

164 *Europe's leading humanist . . . :* Gasquet, *Henry and Monasteries,* p. 1:120.

167 *He had been drafting, presumably for delivery . . . :* Marius, *Thomas More,* p. 421.

173 *Knowing little of who Cranmer . . . :* Scarisbrick, *Henry VIII,* p. 310.

174 *Cromwell was ready with an answer . . . :* Elton, *England Under,* p. 132; Mackie, *Earlier Tudors,* p. 357; and Guy, *Tudor England,* p. 132.

174 *This happened on March 30 . . . :* A detailed account of the oddities of Cranmer's installation ceremony is in Lingard, *History of England,* p. 5:6.

175 *By all accounts the news . . . :* Scarisbrick, *Henry VIII,* p. 313.

175 *But when he wrote to the king . . . :* Fraser, *Wives,* p. 190.

PART TWO

Monster

W. G. Hoskins's *The Age of Plunder* (Longmans, 1971) delivers what its title promises: a trenchant study of the price paid by the population of England for the innovations of Henry VIII. David Starkey's *The Reign of Henry VIII: Personalities and Politics* (Vintage, 2002) is rich in insights about the last two decades of Henry's life. Much detail about the end of the reign is to be found in Jesse Childs, *Henry VIII's Last Victim* (Jonathan Cape, 2006), and Robert Hutchinson, *The Last Days of Henry VIII* (William Morrow, 2006).

Notes

PAGE

181 *The first victim . . . :* The story of Elizabeth Barton is told in Scarisbrick, *Henry VIII,* p. 321, and in much greater detail in Bernard, *King's Reformation,* p. 87.

182 *It is not certain that these reported confessions . . . :* Fraser, *Wives,* p. 211, writes that Barton *"was said"* (italics added) to have recanted, and Bernard, *King's Reformation,* p. 94, refers to her "scaffold speech" as having been *"put into her mouth"* by an unfriendly writer.

184 *There Barton, perhaps because she was . . . :* Bernard, *King's Reformation,* p. 94.

186 *The act's assertion that Henry was to be succeeded . . . :* The 1534 Succession Act appears in its entirely in Elton, *Tudor Constitution,* p. 6.

186 *Conveniently, Parliament neglected to specify . . . :* Marius, *Thomas More,* p. 459.

187 *Cromwell continued to take care* . . . : Guy, *Tudor England*, p. 135.

195 *A special version of the succession oath* . . . : Bernard, *King's Reformation*, p. 157.

196 *The results of the visits were* . . . : Ibid., p. 157.

197 *Several were clearly unhappy* . . . : Ibid., p. 178.

199 *To be guilty of high treason* . . . : Elton, *Tudor Constitution*, p. 61.

200 *This probably explains the insertion* . . . : The intent behind the inclusion of "maliciously," and the word's significance for the king, are in Guy, *Tudor England*, p. 139, and Marius, *Thomas More*, p. 480.

200 *It was called the Act of First Fruits* . . . : The act is explained in Elton, *Tudor Constitution*, p. 42, and it appears in full on page 53 of the same book. The resulting increase in Crown revenue is detailed in Guy, *Tudor England*, p. 136.

200 *He was given a traditional levy* . . . : Taxation on the basis of "fifteenths and tenths" is explained in Mackie, *Earlier Tudors*, p. 353.

201 *The king's gambling, his many luxuries* . . . : Fraser, *Wives*, p. 211, and Hoskins, *Age of Plunder*, p. 208, provide details on Henry's spending on palaces.

202 *Even the most reform-minded of the bishops* . . . : Lingard, *History of England*, p. 5:51.

203 *Background: Monks, Nuns, and Friars*: An excellent introduction to the religious orders of England is C. H. Lawrence, *Medieval Monasticism* (Longmans, 1993).

209 *Nothing of the kind can be said* . . . : The story of the Carthusians is in Lingard, *History of England*, p. 5:39, and in much greater detail in Bernard, *King's Reformation*, p. 160. An entire chapter on the subject, with many of the statements about Sir John Gage and John Houghton and others in the pages that follow, appears in Gasquet, *Henry and Monasteries*, pp. 1:202ff.

216 *It is possible that the king himself was present* . . . : This and Houghton's words *"I call almighty God to witness"* are attributed to Eustace Chapuys in Gasquet, *Henry and Monasteries*, p. 1:224.

217 *"Lo, dost thou not see, Meg* . . .*"*: Marius, *Thomas More*, p. 491.

219 *"Now I have in good faith discharged my mind* . . .*"*: Bernard, *King's Reformation*, p. 145.

219 *The new pope, Paul III, unwittingly* . . . : Scarisbrick, *Henry VIII*, p. 328.

219 *He warned that the pope could send* . . . : Lingard, *History of England*, p. 5:40.

220 *He told the court that when the king* . . . : Bernard, *King's Reformation*, p. 123.

221 *"What a monstrous matter is this!"* . . . : Ibid., p. 124.

222 *He asked the people to pray* . . . : Ibid., p. 125.

228 *What Rich had to say* . . . : Ibid., p. 146.

230 *"Can it therefore seem likely* . . .*"*: Marius, *Thomas More*, p. 506.

230 *Being a good lawyer, More* . . . : Bernard, *King's Reformation*, p. 149.

231 *"God preserve all my friends* . . .*"*: Lingard, *History of England*, p. 5:45.

231 *In January he had been given* . . . : Ibid., p. 5:51, and Bernard, *King's Reformation*, p. 245.

233 *What Cromwell and the king intended* . . . : Mackie, *Earlier Tudors*, p. 376.

235 *The men Cromwell chose* . . . : The character, motives, and conduct of the monastic visitors are subjected to critical scrutiny in Bernard, *King's Reformation*, p. 254; Elton, *England Under*, p. 144; Lingard, *History of England*, p. 5:54; and Geoffrey Moorhouse, *The Pilgrimage of Grace* (Weidenfeld & Nicolson, 2002), p. 27. However, Bernard, *King's Reformation*, p. 247, argues that the original intent of Cromwell's visitations was entirely honorable.

236 *Two of the most active* . . . : Citing the reports and correspondence of the visitors themselves, Gasquet, *Henry and Monasteries*, p. 1:286, details the astonishing number of monasteries examined by Layton, Legh, and others in only a few weeks.

237 *"Thanks for excusing my getting up* . . . " : Ibid., p. 1:278.

237 *When Chancellor Audley could find no basis* . . . : Ibid., pp. 1:278–80.

237 *There is no reason to think that Eustace Chapuys* . . . : Ibid., p. 1:265.

239 *Nor was there any acknowledgment* . . . : Bernard, *King's Reformation*, p. 258.

247 *"Lastly, I make this vow* . . .": Catherine's words and the autopsy results are in Fraser, *Wives*, pp. 228 and 229.

248 *Henry, remembering the restraint* . . . : That and "Much scratching and by-blows" are in Carolly Erickson, *Anne Boleyn* (Macmillan, 1984), p. 242.

248 *According to one story, she tried* . . . : Henry's jousting accident is in Scarisbrick, *Henry VIII*, p. 485, the story of Jane Seymour on the king's knee in Fraser, *Wives*, p. 233.

248 *All the larger and richer houses* . . . : Mackie, *Earlier Tudors*, p. 376.

250 *He began to complain that Anne* . . . : Fraser, *Wives*, p. 233; Mackie, *Earlier Tudors*, p. 379.

251 *On May 19, in the moment before* . . . : Fraser, *Wives*, p. 257.

252 *Two days after Anne was found guilty* . . . : Neville Williams, *Henry VIII*, p. 146.

253 *The information gathered by Cromwell's visitors* . . . : Mackie, *Earlier Tudors*, p. 378, put the number of smaller monasteries at 399—372 in England and 27 in Wales—and estimated that 220 of these were eliminated in the first round of suppressions. Writing half a century later, Bernard, *King's Reformation*, p. 271, put the total at 419 and said 243 were dissolved.

254 *Some of the confiscated land was sold* . . . : Mackie, *Earlier Tudors*, p. 378.

255 *"We beseech your favor* . . .": This letter, and the appeal for the Carmarthan house, are in Gasquet, *Henry and Monasteries*, p. 2:34, giving Chapuys's reports as source.

256 *The monks inside, informed that* . . . : Gasquet, *Henry and Monasteries*, p. 2:37.

257 *After comparing Henry not only to Richard III* . . . : Bernard, *King's Reformation*, p. 220.

258 *He wrote to Mary, calling her* . . . : Lingard, *History of England*, p. 5:80.

258 *Still later, sufficiently rehabilitated* . . . : Neville Williams, *Henry VIII*, p. 152.

259 *In a truly extraordinary step* . . . : Mackie, *Earlier Tudors*, p. 381.

260 *Even today scholars disagree* . . . : Bernard, *King's Reformation*, p. 281, says that the Articles expressed Henry's search for a "middle way." Elton, *England Under*, p. 153, says similarly that they were a "compromise" between the demands of conservatives and evangelicals. By contrast Guy, *Tudor England*, p. 179, emphasizes their "reformed" character, and Scarisbrick, *Henry VIII*, p. 399, their "Lutheran" content. But Mackie, *Earlier Tudors*, p. 382, notes that even Reginald Pole found little to object to in them.

260   *This is unmistakable in the preface* . . . : Bernard, *King's Reformation*, p. 277.

261   *The dedication offered to that king* . . . : Neville Williams, *Henry VIII*, p. 162; Penry Williams, *The Tudor Regime* (Oxford, 1979), p. 361.

262   *Sixteenth-century Europe was a world* . . . : See Alison Sim, *Food and Feast in Tudor England* (Sutton, 1997).

267   *The story of how* . . . : Succinct but detailed accounts of the Pilgrimage of Grace are in Bernard, *King's Reformation*, p. 293; Scarisbrick, *Henry VIII*, p. 339; and Lingard, *History of England*, p. 5:82. Moorhouse, *Pilgrimage of Grace*, is of course a much fuller account.

268   *This was in no way unusual* . . . : Mackie, *Earlier Tudors*, p. 387.

268   *Wherever such men fell into the hands* . . . : Bernard, *King's Reformation*, p. 306.

269   *The king denounced Lincolnshire* . . . : Scarisbrick, *Henry VIII*, p. 342.

269   *He would have been overwhelmed* . . . : Mackie, *Earlier Tudors*, p. 388.

270   *Meanwhile King Henry, whose situation* . . . : Scarisbrick, *Henry VIII*, p. 343.

273   *Aske received a letter from the king* . . . : Words from the letters exchanged by Henry and Aske are in Gasquet, *Henry and Monasteries*, p. 2:131.

277   *When they finished in mid-July* . . . : Extensive treatments of the Institution are in Scarisbrick, *Henry VIII*, p. 399, and Bernard, *King's Reformation*, p. 475.

277   *The evangelicals hated much of it* . . . : The bishops' groveling preface, and the message from the king, are in Scarisbrick, *Henry VIII*, p. 404.

278   *The Bishops' Book as first published* . . . : Henry's changes are in Scarisbrick, *Henry VIII*, p. 405.

280   *A more plausible explanation is* . . . : Chris Skidmore, *Edward VI: The Lost King of England* (Weidenfeld & Nicolson, 2007), p. 19.

280   *In rather short order he was reported* . . . : Erickson, *Great Harry*, p. 282.

281   *Such memories were freshened by* . . . : Mackie, *Earlier Tudors*, p. 397.

289   *His once-powerful constitution* . . . : Perspectives on Henry's health problems are in Smith, *Mask of Power*, pp. 15 and 264; Erickson, *Great Harry*, pp. 328 and 360; and Scarisbrick, *Henry VIII*, p. 485.

290   *But he was a frail reed* . . . : Smith, *Mask of Power*, p. 94.

292   *But Henry proved a dangerous partner* . . . : The story of the near-arrest of Catherine Parr is in Fraser, *Wives*, p. 388.

293   *A farce was played out* . . . : Lingard, *History of England*, p. 5:189.

293   *The valuables hauled away* . . . : Mackie, *Earlier Tudors*, p. 396.

294   *Quite apart from the colossal sums* . . . : Lingard, *History of England*, p. 5:97.

294   *He would be able to expand the ranks* . . . : Ibid., p. 5:99.

294   *In the last eight or nine years* . . . : Mackie, *Earlier Tudors*, p. 400.

294 *He squandered his riches at home first . . .* : Guy, *Tudor England*, p. 184.

296 *The French and Scottish campaigns . . .* : The financial figures in this paragraph are all from Guy, *Tudor England*, p. 192.

296 *Students of the subject have calculated . . .* : Lingard, *History of England*, p. 5:195.

297 *In 1542 Henry borrowed £112,000 . . .* : The forced loans of this period are in Mackie, *Earlier Tudors*, p. 411. The financial consequences of the campaigns in France are in Elton, *England Under*, p. 198, and Scarisbrick, *Henry VIII*, p. 453.

297 *Next Henry demanded and got . . .* : Smith, *Mask of Power*, p. 244.

297 *Two London aldermen dared to object . . .* : Lingard, *History of England*, p. 5:193, and Mackie, *Earlier Tudors*, p. 411.

297 *Foreign loans totaled some £272,000 . . .* : Mackie, *Earlier Tudors*, p. 413.

297 *Soon its coins were only half gold . . .* : Erickson, *Great Harry*, p. 352.

297 *Henry reaped £373,000 . . .* : Smith, *Mask of Power*, p. 172.

297 *Prices rose some 25 percent . . .* : The inflation rate and the "holy anchor" quote are in Erickson, *Great Harry*, p. 353.

298 *Under this law, anyone who "lived idly . . .".* : Hoskins, *Age of Plunder*, p. 106.

298 *Those impressed into bondage in this way . . .* : Lingard, *History of England*, p. 5:258.

298 *The king's word literally became law . . .* : Ibid., p. 5:129.

299 *The penalty in connection with these doctrines . . .* : Ibid.

301 *Thus in 1543 he drew out of Parliament . . .* : The Act for the Advancement of True Religion, with the condemnation of Tyndale's translation, is in Mackie, *Earlier Tudors*, p. 429, and Lingard, *History of England*, p. 5:159.

301 *It was not to be opened by "prentices . . ."*: Guy, *Tudor England*, p. 194.

301 *Almost simultaneously with the Act . . .* : Scarisbrick, *Henry VIII*, pp. 399 and 407.

302 *Angrily, even tearfully, he complained . . .* : Mackie, *Earlier Tudors*, p. 433, and Lingard, *History of England*, p. 5:202.

302 *Still later it was reported . . .* : Bernard, *King's Reformation*, pp. 157 and 489.

303 *In the same year that Forest perished . . .* : Erickson, *Great Harry*, p. 294.

304 *"Answer neither out of St. Augustine . . ."*: Smith, *Mask of Power*, p. 154.

305 *On December 6 Montague and Exeter . . .* : Erickson, *Great Harry*, p. 288.

306 *Contrary to what has often been asserted . . .* : Bernard, *King's Reformation*, p. 574; Guy, *Tudor England*, pp. 178 and 186; and Scarisbrick, *Henry VIII*, p. 376.

306 *The endlessly useful Richard Rich . . .* : Neville Williams, *Henry VIII*, p.195.

308 *"No," she said, "my head never . . ."*: Lingard, *History of England*, p. 5:126.

308 *The executioner had to chase her . . .* : Fraser, *Wives*, p. 342.

308 *Every place of habitation was to be destroyed . . .* : Erickson, *Great Harry*, p. 334.

308 *This time he demolished . . .* : Data about the destruction in Scotland and the quote about Henry's "not misliking" the plan to assassinate Beaton are in Lingard, *History of England*, p. 5:184.

List of Illustrations

1. Henry IV and Joan of Navarre from their tomb at Canterbury Cathedral. Henry IV's usurpation of the crown caused the turbulent Wars of the Roses. © Elizabeth Norton and the Amberley Archive.
2. King Henry VI depicted c.1500 as a saint on a screen at Ludham in Norfolk. He died in the Tower of London in May 1471 and was succeeded by Edward IV. © Jonathan Reeve JR1561folio6 14001450.
3. The marriage of Catherine of Valois to Henry V in the parish church of St John, Troyes, 2 June 1420. © Jonathan Reeve JR1729b90fp85 14001500.
4. Henry VIII and Henry VII, by Holbein, from the lost mural at Whitehall. © Elizabeth Norton and the Amberley Archive.
5. Elizabeth of York, queen consort of Henry VII and mother of henry VIII. By kind permission of Ripon Cathedral Chapter.
6. Margaret Tudor, daughter of Henry VII and Elizabeth of York, and Henry VIII's sister. © Jonathan Reeve JR982b20p837 15001600.
7. Perkin Warbeck, the false Plantagenet chosen by disaffected Yorkists to impersonate Edward VI's son Richard, Duke of York, the younger of the two 'Princes in the Tower'. © Jonathan Reeve JRCD3b20p795 14501500.
8. Matriach of the Tudor dynasty, Lady Margaret Beaufort, mother of Henry VII. She married Edmund Tudor, the first son of Catherine of Valois and Owen Tudor. Owen Tudor was Catherine's second husband, she had previously been Henry V's queen. © Elizabeth Norton and the Amberley Archive.
9. Henry VIII in about 1540 by Holbein. © Jonathan Reeve JR951b53p505 15001550.
10. Henry VIII processes to the opening of parliament in 1512. © Jonathan Reeve JR971b54p363 15001600.
11. Henry VIII, from a window in the chapel at Sudeley Castle. © Elizabeth Norton and the Amberley Archive.
12. Henry VIII portrayed in all his magnificence at King's College, Cambridge. © Elizabeth Norton and the Amberley Archive.
13. Title page of the first edition of 'The Great Bible', 1539. Enthroned as God's vicar, Henry symbolically hands out the Word of God to the spiritual and temporal hierarchies of his realm, headed respectively by Thomas Cranmer on his right and Thomas Cromwell on his left. © Jonathan Reeve JRCD2b20p929 15001550.
14 & 15. The Field of Cloth of Gold, 1520. Two bas reliefs from the 1520s. © Jonathan Reeve JR1177b2p167B 15001550 & © Jonathan Reeve JR1177b2p167T 15001550.
16. Act of Six Articles, 1539. © Jonathan Reeve JR1159b7p169 15001550.
17. Golden Bull of Pope Clement VII. This one was affixed to Clement VII's bull confirming Henry VIII's title as *Fidei Defensor*. © Jonathan Reeve JR1184b20p888 15001550.
18. Act of Succession, 1544. This section of the act spells out the oath that must be taken by all clergymen and royal officials, renouncing the 'Bisshopp of Rome' (the Pope). © Jonathan Reeve JR1185b20p920 15001550.
19. Declaration by the bishops, c.1536. © Jonathan Reeve JR1158b7p73 15001550.
20. Bessie Blount, one of Henry VIII's earliest mistresses who bore him a healthy son in 1519. © Elizabeth Norton and the Amberley Archive
21. The tomb of Henry Fitzroy, Duke of Richmond, Henry VIII's bastard son By Bessie Blount. © Elizabeth Norton and the Amberley Archive.
22. Mary Shelton, later Lady Heveningham, thought to have been one of Henry VIII's later mistresses. © Elizabeth Norton and the Amberley Archive.
23, 24, 25 & 26. English Ladies, by Holbein. © Elizabeth Norton and the Amberley Archive.
27. *Divorced*. Henry VIII Catherine of Aragon, Henry VIII's first wife. By kind permission of Ripon Cathedral Chapter.
28. Henry VIII riding at the tilts on 12-13 February 1511, with Catherine of Aragon looking on. From the Great Tournament Roll of Westminster. © Jonathan Reeve JR1098b2fp204 15001550.
29. The grave of Catherine of Aragon in Peterborough Abbey (which Henry converted into a cathedral in 1541). © Elizabeth Norton and the Amberley Archive.
30. A letter from Queen Catherine, acting as regent while Henry VIII was in France, to Thomas Wolsey, the King's Almoner. 2 September 1513, concerning the imprisonment of the Duke of Longueville, taken prisoner at the 'battle of the spurs' in the 17 August. © Jonathan Reeve JR962b20p895 15001600.
31. *Beheaded 1536*. Anne Boleyn. © Elizabeth Norton and the Amberley Archive.
32. Thomas Howard, Anne Boleyn's uncle. © Jonathan Reeve JR1175b2p110 15001550.
33. A letter from Cranmer at Dunstable, informing Henry VIII of the date when his 'grave grete matter' will be resolved. © Jonathan Reeve JR894b7p53 15001550.
34. One of a series of friendly letters which Anne Boleyn wrote to Cardinal Wolsey during the summer of 1528, when she was still looking to him as the man most likely to untangle the king's first marriage. She thanks him for the 'grete payne and trobell that yr grace doth take' about the matter (BL Cotton MS

Vespasian F.XIII, f. 73.). © Jonathan Reeve JR963b20p899 15001600.

35. Letter from Anne Boleyn to Stephen Gardiner, then in Italy pursuing the king's quest for an annulment of his marriage, 4 April 1529. © Jonathan Reeve JR964b20p900 15001600.

36. Queen Anne Boleyn was executed on 19 May 1536. © Jonathan Reeve JR965b20p921 15001600.

37. Hever Castle, the family seat of the Boleyns. © Elizabeth Norton and the Amberley Archive.

38. Design for a pageant tableau, by Holbein, staged on in honour of Anne Boleyn on the eve of her coronation, 31 May 1533. © Elizabeth Norton and the Amberley Archive.

39. Jane Seymour. © Jonathan Reeve.

40. Jane Seymour's badge of the phoenix, together with the Tudor Rose, from a stained glass window at the Seymour family home of Wolfhall, near Marlborough. It was moved to Great Bedwyn Church following the destruction of Wolfhall. © Elizabeth Norton and the Amberley Archive.

41. *Divorced 1540*. Anne of Cleves. © Amberley Archive.

42. Anne of Cleves, by Barthel Bruyn. © Elizabeth Norton and the Amberley Archive.

43. Anne of Cleves House. © Elizabeth Norton and the Amberley Archive.

44. *Beheaded 1542*. Catherine Howard, Henry's fifth wife. Detail from the window of King Solomon and the Queen of Sheba in King's College Chapel, Cambridge. It is believed that the image of the Queen of Sheba is modelled on Catherine Howard. This stained glass was created during Henry VIII's reign and paid for by Henry himself. © Elizabeth Norton and the Amberley Archive.

45. *Survived*. Catherine Parr. © Elizabeth Norton and the Amberley Archive.

46. Cardinal Thomas Wolsey (1471 or 1475-1530). © Jonathan Reeve JR1169b2p7 15001550.

47. A letter from Wolsey to the king, October 1529, written in the wake of his fall from favour. © Jonathan Reeve JR1093b20p902 15001550.

48. Archbishop Warham (1450-1532), by Holbein. © Elizabeth Norton and the Amberley Archive.

49. Thomas Cranmer (1489-1556). He was appointed Archbishop of Canterbury following the death of William Warham. © Elizabeth Norton and the Amberley Archive.

50. The Family of Thomas More, by Holbein. © Elizabeth Norton and the Amberley Archive.

51. Thomas More (1478-1535), by Holbein. © Elizabeth Norton and the Amberley Archive.

52. Henry VIII meets the Emperor Maximilian I. Henry's tent is marked with the royal arms, Maximilian's with the Habsburg double-headed eagle. © Jonathan Reeve JR1154b66p29 15001550.

53. Henry VII's chantry chapel in Westminster Abbey. This elaborate bronze structure houses the tombs of Henry VII and Elizabeth of York. © Jonathan Reeve JR1188b67plivB 16001650.

54, 55 & 56. Henry VIII's Great Seals. The Great Seal was the ultimate instrument of authentication for acts of royal power in Tudor England, and was affixed, for example, to treaties and charters. It depicted the king enthroned in majesty on the front, and riding into battle on the back, symbolising his power as fount of justice and leader in war. © Jonathan Reeve JR1170b2p11 15001550, © Jonathan Reeve JR1172b2p57T 15001550 & © Jonathan Reeve JR1173b2p57B 15001550.

57. Erasmus. This iconic woodcut by Dürer depicts the greatest scholar of the age, Desiderius Erasmus of Rotterdam, at work in his study. © Jonathan Reeve JR1160b4p600 15001550.

58. Holbein's design for a jeweled pendant for Princess Mary. © Elizabeth Norton and the Amberley Archive.

59. Thomas Boleyn, Earl of Wiltshire. Despite the executions of his son George and his daughter Anne in 1536, Thomas Boleyn himself died in his bed at Hever Castle in 1538. His funeral brass in St Peter's Church there, the only known likeness. © Jonathan Reeve JR1174b2p87 15001550.

60. Clement VII's judgment against Henry. After calling in vain upon the king to leave Anne and take back his first wife, Clement VII finally issued his 'definitive sentence' in favour of Catherine of Aragon on 23 March 1534. © Jonathan Reeve JR1171b2p45 15001550.

61. Henry VIII's will (30 December 1546). © Jonathan Reeve JRCD2b20p961 15501600.

62. The 'Lady Elizabeth' of Henry VIII's later years. © Jonathan Reeve JR998b66fp56 15001600.

63. Oatlands (Surrey), one of Henry VIII's many palaces, where he married Catherine Howard on 28 July 1540. © Jonathan Reeve JR1149pc 15001550.

64. Greenwich Palace. Massively and expensively rebuilt by Henry VII, Greenwich Palace was the birthplace of Henry VIII and a favoured residence of all the Tudors. © Jonathan Reeve JR735b46fp186 14501500.

65. Whitehall Palace. © Jonathan Reeve JR779b46fp192 15001550.

66. Hampton Court Palace, once the country home of the fallen Cardinal Wolsey. © Elizabeth Norton and the Amberley Archive.

67. Henry VIII's lock for his private apartments. Henry travelled from palace to palace with this lock and held the master key. © Jonathan Reeve JR976b61p709 15001600.

68. Richmond Palace as built by Henry VII. © Jonathan Reeve JR945b20p788 15001550.

69. Plan of the palaces of Westminster and Whitehall *c*. 1578. © Jonathan Reeve JRCD2b20p769 15501600.

70. Nonsuch Palace. Built by Henry VIII, Nonsuch was a far more intimate royal residence without the space for the entire court. From an old English engraving in the late Emperor of Austria's private library. © Stephen Porter and the Amberley Archive.

71 & 72. The keep of Windsor Castle and the St George's Chapel. A fortress rather than a favoured residence, but Henry VIII chose to be buried there alongside Jane Seymour. © Elizabeth Norton and the Amberley Archive.

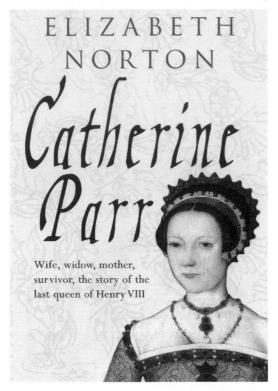

Also available from Amberley Publishing

JOSEPHINE WILKINSON

The Early Loves of

Anne Boleyn

The story of Anne Boleyn's early life, told in detail for the first time

But before Henry came into her life Anne Boleyn had already wandered down love's winding path.
She had learned its twists and turns during her youth spent at the courts of the Low Countries and France,
where she had been sent as a result of her scandalous behaviour with her father's butler and chaplain.

Returning to England she was courted by three different suitors in three very different circumstances.
This is the story of their three love affairs.

£20 Hardback
30 colour illustrations
288 pages
978-1-84868-430-0

Available from all good bookshops or to order direct
Please call **01285-760-030**
www.amberleybooks.com

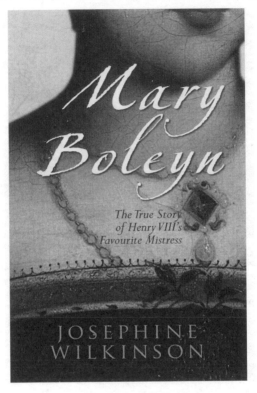

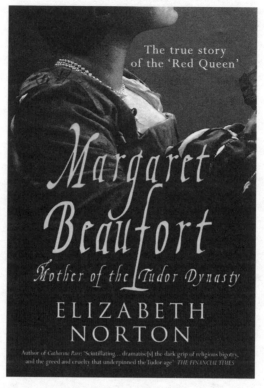

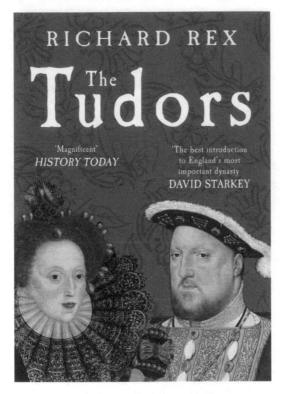

Available from March 2011 from Amberley Publishing

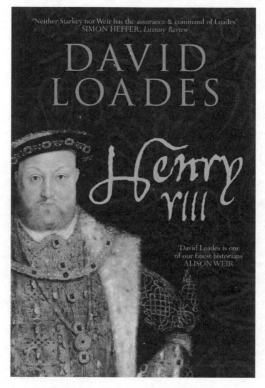

A major new biography of the most infamous king of England

'David Loades is one of our finest Tudor historians' ALISON WEIR

'David Loades Tudor biographies are both highly enjoyable and instructive, the perfect combination'
ANTONIA FRASER

Professor David Loades has spent most of his life investigating the remains, literary, archival and archaeological, of Henry VIII, and this monumental new biography book is the result. His portrait of Henry is distinctive, he was neither a genius nor a tyrant, but a man' like any other', except for the extraordinary circumstances in which he found himse. As a youth, he was a magnificent specimen of manhood, and in age a gargantuan wreck, but even in his prime he wa never the 'ladies man' which legend, and his own imagination, created. Sexual insecurity undermined him, and gave his will that irascible edge which proved fatal to Anne Boleyn and Thomas Cromwell alike.

£25 Hardback
113 illustrations (49 colour)
512 pages
978-1-84868-532-1

Available from March 2011 from all good bookshops or to order direct
Please call **01285-760-030**
www.amberleybooks.com

Index

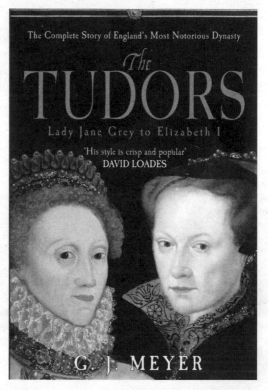